REGENTS' READING EXAMS

STRATEGIES FOR SUCCESS

LINDA L. ARTHUR, PH.D.

Kendall Hunt publishing company

Kendall Hunt
p u b l i s h i n g   c o m p a n y

www.kendallhunt.com
Send all inquiries to:
4050 Westmark Drive
Dubuque, IA 52004-1840

Copyright © 2010 by Linda L. Arthur

ISBN 978-0-7575-6442-0

Printed in the United States of America
10 9 8 7 6 5 4 3 2

CONTENTS

UNIT TWO

UNIT THREE

APPENDICES

PREFACE

I am delighted to be able to offer this textbook, *Regents' Reading Exams: Strategies for Success*, as a sequel to *Mastery of Regents' Reading Exams, third edition*. This text is designed for fellow educators and their students enrolled in Regents' Reading review courses at the college level. The explanatory sections of the text are informal, and the style of the book is aimed at maximizing student success. Special features of this edition are the following:

- Post Test
- Abundant Vocabulary exercises
- Vocabulary Journal
- Ten Timed Readings
- New strategies

Other features of the text include:

1) Test Anxiety Scale
2) general information about the reading portion of the Regents' Reading Exam
3) explanations of the reading skills required to master Regents' Reading Exams
4) exercises to practice the required reading skills
5) information on Reading Rate
6) Diagnostic Exam
7) Simulated Exams that provide more opportunities for practice in particular skills; exams are designed to be practical assessment tools with
   a. perforated pages for quick removal
   b. scantrons with diagnostic charts of skills for each test
8) practical test taking strategies for success on this type of exam
9) answer keys for chapters and for simulated exams
10) particular tests emphasize a particular skill (please refer to the end of each skills chapter)
11) the exams have been piloted in the Regents' Reading Review classroom

Of special interest is the *Graphics Answer Key* that maps answers in a visual format. Used in the classroom the Graphics Answer Key becomes versatile. Answers to questions in the Diagnostic Exam (Pre-Test), the Post Test, and Exams One through Three are graphically displayed and mapped.

   a. Instructors can make transparencies of the graphics and use them in the classroom as a teaching aid. Visual learners may be aided during classroom discussion through the use of such transparencies.

b. Simulated Exams Four through Nine are intentionally left unmapped so that the student may practice this strategy.

c. Because some students are anxious when they take tests, they sometimes read over an obvious answer or clues to an answer. These graphic illustrations will point students to the answers and give them a starting point for further discussion.

The format of the book encourages students to become successful and active readers. Most selections are 250 to 300 words. Passages are drawn from college textbooks and other college-level materials. Selections include narrative and expository materials—the latter representing topics from the social sciences, humanities, business, current events, sciences, pop culture, and health sciences.

DEDICATION

This textbook is dedicated to my daughter, Catherine Sermo Smith

Unit One

❧ Chapter One ❧

The Creation of the Regents' Reading Exam

The reasons for the creation of a regents' exam may vary from state to state. In the state of Georgia, for example, the Board of Regents of the University System of Georgia announced that system institutions must ensure that students receiving degrees possess minimum literacy competence. Literacy competence may be defined as "certain minimum skills of reading and writing." Students' scores on the exams are used to determine minimum levels of reading and writing competency for graduation. Since 1972 college students in Georgia have taken the Regents' Exam. However, in the academic year 2003-2004 the policy changed. The 2003 mandate states that

> Students with SAT-I Verbal scores of at least 510 or ACT Reading scores of at least 23 will be considered to have fulfilled the reading comprehension requirement of the Regents' Test and do not need to take the reading portion of the Regents' Test.

Upon entry to a college or university, students are informed of the Regents' skills requirement of taking and passing the Regents' Reading Exam. Effective Fall semester, 2008: "With few exceptions, all non-exempting students must take the Regents' Test every semester until they pass. . .non-appearance for a scheduled testing time—except for sound medical or other reasons deemed sufficient by the institution—will be treated administratively in the same way as a failure of the test." In addition, students who ignore the requirement and choose not to take the test when they are required to do so may be charged a fee. Students enrolled in Learning Support Reading must take the exam in the semester after they have exited the class. Please note that no differentiation is made for transfer students. Be aware that some institutions may have specific guidelines. Students are advised to check with the on-campus Testing Office to understand particular regulations and guidelines.

In Georgia the Regents' Skill Requirement Completion Rates for Sophomores Reaching 45 Hours are published. For the academic year 2004–2005, 87.9% of the students in a regional university completed the reading portion of the Regents' Test (University System of Georgia website). Obviously, this means that a college with a pass rate of 87.9% would have 12.1% of that same population designated as "repeaters"— some of whom may ultimately take a review course. It is true that many students enrolled in review courses are frustrated, but what if the university system offered no review classes? After taking the test several times, some repeaters may welcome the opportunity to have some academic assistance so that they have the optimal chance of achieving a passing score.

❧FORMAT AND SCORING OF THE READING PORTION OF THE REGENTS' EXAM

The description of the reading portion of the Regents' Exam from the Board of Regents is as follows:

> The Reading Test, which has an administration time of one hour, is a 54-item, multiple-choice test that consists of nine reading passages and five to eight questions about each passage. The passages usually range from 175 to 325 words in length, treat topics drawn from a variety of subject areas (social science, mathematics and natural science, and humanities), and entail various modes of discourse (exposition, narration, and argumentation). Students' responses to the items of the Reading Test are recorded on machine-readable answer sheets so that these responses can be read and scored by computer. A standard score is used to describe the Reading Test performance of each examinee. This score is derived by translating the student's total raw score (number-right) on the test to a Rasch scaled score with a range from 0-99. The minimum passing score on this scale is 61.
>
> (University System of Georgia, website)

The following raw scale score is found on the University System of Georgia's Regents' Testing Program website (http://www2.gsu.edu/~wwwrtp/conversion_table.htm).

Sample Number-Right to Scale Score Conversion Table: Regents' Reading Test

Number-Right	Scale Score		Number-Right	Scale Score
1	6		31	53
2	13		32	54
3	18		33	55
4	21		34	56
5	24		35	57
6	26		36	58
7	28		37	59
8	30		38	60
9	31		39*	*61
10	33		40	62
11	34		41	63
12	35		42	64
13	37		43	66
14	38		44	67
15	39		45	68
16	40		46	70
17	41		47	72
18	42		48	74
19	43		49	76
20	44		50	78
21	45		51	82
22	46		52	86
23	46		53	93
24	47		54	
25	48			
26	49			
27	50			
28	51			
29	52			
30	53			

*minimum passing score

From the table you can see that a passing score is 61 for this form of the Regents' Reading Test (this form, Form 23, has been "retired"). The number answered correctly is 39, which means that you can answer fifteen questions incorrectly and pass with a minimum score. Other forms of the test still require a student to achieve a score of 61, but for a passing score, the number correct might change; for example, on one form students may need to answer 40 correctly, while on another form they may need 38 correct answers to be successful.

In addition to the cut-off score for passing the exam, there are also designators of "Low-Failure" and "Above Low-Failure" for students performing at a very low level.

> **Low-Failure**: If the score on the Regents' Test on the first attempt is sufficiently low to be flagged at the low-failure level, the student will be required to participate in remediation in the next semester of enrollment.

> **Above Low-Failure**: If the score on the Regents' Test on the first attempt is flagged at the above low-failure level, informal advising/procedures may be used to determine whether the student should enroll in remediation or whether another attempt of the regents' Test without remediation is advisable. This is an institutional decision. (University System of Georgia, website)

Students are encouraged to visit the on-campus Testing Office or to access the Board of Regents' website for particular guidelines and policies.

OVERVIEW OF READING SKILLS

Reading is an active process that comprises many interrelated skills and abilities. Reading is not just a passive, laborious act. Instead, it is a process that requires quite a bit of energy on the part of the reader: it requires critical thinking. The ability to comprehend text material depends on several factors, such as 1) the background (prior knowledge) the reader brings to the printed page; 2) the reader's vocabulary base, including strategies for unlocking the meanings of unknown words; and 3) the reader's ability to interpret, evaluate, and synthesize the material in a meaningful way.

It is obvious that reading has not taken place unless you read with understanding. Merely knowing most of the words does not mean you are a successful reader. To be truly successful on the Regents' Reading Exam, you must understand the words within the sentences, the sentences within the paragraphs, the paragraphs within the passages. In addition to this, an understanding of the relationships between various components of the passage is necessary. The abilities required for the Regents' Reading Exam are referred to as higher-level reading skills—and these skills must be taught. If you have not previously been instructed in these skills areas, then it is unlikely that you have magically acquired them on your own. This may be the major reason why many students will benefit from taking the Regents' Reading review course—they will have the opportunity to perfect their higher-level reading skills.

There are four basic skills areas you will need to master for the reading portion of the Regents' Exam: vocabulary, literal comprehension, inferential comprehension, and analysis. In the chapters that follow, you will find a description of the skills and exercises designed to practice them.

REMEMBER: *There are four basic skills areas students need to understand to succeed on the Regents' Reading Exam:*

Vocabulary	*Literal Comprehension*
Inference	*Analysis*

❧GENERAL READING STRATEGIES FOR REGENTS' READINGS EXAMS

Consider these strategies for improving your score on the reading portion of the exam:

First, because there are nine passages on the test and 60 minutes is allowed, give yourself about six (6) minutes to spend on each passage. Practice limiting yourself to six minutes before you sit for the exam to get a sense of how long it takes you per selection.

Second, many literal comprehension questions ask for a name, a number, or a statement made in the passage, and it is only a matter of seconds before the student can point to the exact information in the passage. Students can use this information to their advantage by answering these types of questions first, passage-by-passage.

Third, as a corollary to the second strategy, students can answer many literal comprehension questions in the same time it takes to answer one main idea question. Within a passage, if there is a main idea question that is difficult to answer, skip it and come back to it *after* you have answered the literal comprehension questions. Answering the literal questions first may help you formulate an answer for the main idea. If you still cannot answer the main idea and are spending too much time on it, skip it and come back to it later if you have time. (*Note*: there should be no more than five to six main idea questions on the entire test, so this strategy will not defeat you; it should help you.)

Fourth, it is better not to read the questions before you read the passage. If you read the questions first the last time you took the test, then you already know that strategy did not work for you. Two negative consequences could occur from reading the questions before reading the selection: one, you could read the question wrong which will "color" how you read the passage; and two, you could obsess on one question and not absorb other critical information in the passage. Therefore, read the passage first as quickly as you can while concentrating, then look at the questions.

Fifth, although not crucial for mastering the Regents' Reading Exam, the ability to identify the type of question being asked will give students an advantage. Knowing how the test is constructed lessens the threatening nature of such a test. To practice this skill, students can mark the type of question on the exam itself and then check the scantron (types of questions are found at the bottom) to assess their responses.

Sixth, when you come across inference questions, do not skip them. There are too many of them to skip without penalizing yourself; rather, utilizing the strategy you have learned in this text, look for clues that will give you the answer.

Seventh, to answer Vocabulary and Analysis questions, rely on the signal words and indicators you learned in this textbook. In addition, try using the process of elimination.

Eighth, because material for the exam is chosen from a variety of disciplines across the curriculum, you already have some prior knowledge about various topics. The more you read your college textbooks before taking the exam, the more prior knowledge you will have—and the more vocabulary you will recognize. While taking the exam, depend on any background information you possess about a subject. The more you know about a topic, the faster you will be able to process the information presented on the Regents' Reading Exam.

Ninth, try using a process of elimination for all question types, but especially for vocabulary. There are ample opportunities to practice this strategy within the practice exams.

Tenth, during the review class, and particularly before you take a practice exam, ask yourself some prep questions relating to your physical condition. Make a note on your test before you begin, answering questions such as the following:

1. How many hours sleep did you get last night?
2. Are you tired or sleepy?
3. What have you eaten today?
4. Have you had any food with protein today?
   (Meat, eggs, cheese, peanut butter, tofu, beans)
5. Do you feel good physically today?

When you receive your score on the practice exam, look back to see how you felt before taking the exam. Monitoring your physical well-being is beneficial because before the day of the Regents' Reading Exam, you can make sure you have taken care of these physical considerations. They may make a difference in your performance on the test.

While taking a practice exam, it would be a good idea to circle the number of the question at which you became tired. After grading, find where you began to miss questions in groups (indicating a "tired point") on the test. Does this tired point correlate to the circle you made on the test? Discuss ways to keep alert with classmates.

Eleventh, during the review class, and particularly before you take a practice exam, ask yourself some prep questions relating to your emotional condition. Make notes on your test, answering questions such as the following:

1. Do you feel stressed today?
2. Did you talk to your significant other last night or today?
3. Are your relatives being supportive? Did you talk to them last night or today?
4. Has anyone upset you in the last 24 hours?
5. Do you feel "up" or "down" today? "Up"– happy, confident, sharp, having high self-esteem. "Down"--unhappy, worried, not focused, having low self-esteem.

When you receive your score on the practice exam, look back to see how you felt before taking the exam. Monitoring your emotional well-being is beneficial because before the day of the Regents' Reading Exam, you can make sure you have taken care of these emotional considerations. For example, if possible, do not speak to anyone who might upset you the day before or the day of the exam.

Twelfth, since the exam score is based on number right, do not leave any items blank. An educated guess is better than leaving a blank.

By analyzing your strengths and weaknesses and preparing yourself before the exam, you will be able to raise your score. And, by taking care of yourself before the exam—by taking care of physical and emotional considerations—you are preparing yourself for success on the Regents' Reading Exam.

A NOTE ABOUT TEST ANXIETY

The Board of Regents' in Georgia recognizes that some students may be test-anxious and that while taking a timed exam, test anxiety may interfere with test performance. Therefore, a student may be given extended time on the Regents' Reading Exam if she or he has been enrolled in the review class at least twice and there is evidence that the student has the skills required for passing. Because some students are affected by test anxiety, a test anxiety scale along with suggestions are provided in Appendix C.

❧ C h a p t e r   T w o ❧

Vocabulary (18% to 24%)

Each passage on the Regents' Reading Exam may include at least one underlined word that you must analyze. This means that a total of nine to thirteen questions of the test may entail vocabulary. To achieve mastery of the vocabulary items on the test, you must be prepared to identify the meanings of words as they are used in passages. Since a dictionary is not allowed into the testing situation, the student will rely heavily on his or her ability to use context clues.

It is not a good idea to answer a vocabulary question hurriedly—some of you may feel you already know the definition of a word. However, a word can have many different meanings depending on the way it is used in the sentence, so automatically choosing the first recognizable answer may not benefit you. In addition, students sometimes make a mistake by staring just at the underlined word, ignoring the words that surround the vocabulary word. If you isolate the word, you may miss a clue that actually gives you the meaning.

Context (the words, sometimes the sentences, around the underlined word) frequently clarifies the meaning of the unknown word. Often, especially on the reading portion of the Regents' Exam, a familiar word is used in an unfamiliar sense; therefore, you need to analyze the "situation" of the unknown word a little closer. Most of the time, if you add some context to the isolated underlined word, you will be able to formulate an approximate meaning because the added context will provide clues.

Context clues (the clues which help you determine the meaning of the word) may be found very close to the underlined word on the Regents' Reading Exam. They may be in the same sentence, the sentence before the underlined word, or the sentence after the underlined word.   Therefore, it is best not to view the word in isolation but to read *all the words and sentences surrounding the unknown word*, the context.

In addition to unlocking the meaning of the underlined word, you will also be required to recognize the words given as answer choices. When taking the Regents' Reading Exam, have you ever thought that you comprehended the underlined word only to look at the answer choices and recognize some of the words but not all of them?

For example, perhaps the underlined word in a vocabulary question you encounter on the exam is pretentious, and you know that it means "conceited." The choices you are given do not seem to fit—three of them, you are sure, do not mean "conceited." The fourth choice is the word, "ostentatious." You are completely unfamiliar with this word. In this case, probably your best strategy is to employ the process of elimination and choose "ostentatious" as your answer. In fact, "ostentatious" means "showy and conceited."

What may also help when confronted with answer choices listed in isolation is having a solid vocabulary base. In this chapter you will begin enhancing your vocabulary base, you will begin your vocabulary journal, you will learn a strategy to unlock the meaning of unknown words, and you will learn to decode individual words for meaning.

❧UNLOCKING THE MEANING OF WORDS: THE IMPORTANCE OF CONTEXT

Does context really work? Consider this: what if the Regents' Reading Exam just presented a list of words in isolation and made you choose a definition. This would be very difficult. But if you were given the word in a sentence, you would have a better chance of making an educated guess. For instance, do you know what the meaning of the word *geta*? Without looking up the word *geta*, can you make an educated guess as to its meaning? Unless you already knew this word from watching Japanese animation, you would be extremely lucky to guess the definition. However, you could probably define the word with some context. Remember, context means "with text" or "with other words." Adding context, consider the following sentence:

Japanese wear *geta*.

Because of the added context, you may now have an idea about the word *geta*. Obviously, the verb *wear* helps in determining what *geta* means. In the blanks below, list several things that people wear, and—if you can—things that Japanese people wear:

_____

_____

_____

As you can see, you are closer to a meaning, but there are still a great many things to which *geta* might refer. Adding more context aids in narrowing down the possible meanings for *geta*:

Japanese wear *geta* in the garden.

As used in the first sentence, the word geta most nearly means

1. skirts.
2. flower hair pins for Geisha.
3. kimonos.
4. wooden shoes.

Remember that on the Regents' Reading Exam you are asked for the word that "most nearly means" the same as the underlined word.

In this instance, you now have the information that whatever the word is, it is worn "in the garden."

Although Japanese are able to wear kimono and hair pins in the garden, do you think it would be a good idea to wear an ornamental hair pin or something silk in the garden? Since *in the garden* is a piece of specific information, maybe the question is asking about something that is specifically designed for wearing in gardens but not in other places. Can you eliminate some answers because they are too general? Do you have any prior knowledge about Japanese clothes and customs? If by now you have decided that *geta* probably means "wooden shoes," you are correct. Did you have a clue as to the meaning of *geta* before the context was added? Most people do not.

Context does help in many testing situations as well as in general college text reading, so use it to your best advantage.

Exercise 1. Consider for a moment these vocabulary words that are in isolation (they have no context). How many of them can you define? Write a definition for the words, tear out this page, then place this sheet under your desk; you will return to it later.

proliferation   _____

scrupulous   _____

ubiquitous   _____

meticulous   _____

parasitic   _____

advocate   _____

pessimistic   _____

skeptical   _____

culminated   _____

mentor   _____

~CONTEXT CLUES

How can the reader determine the meaning of an unknown word by using strategies that focus on context clues? Writers very often:

1. DIRECTLY DEFINE A WORD/DESCRIBE A WORD

The proliferation—more and more high-powered rifles, more and more grenades, bigger and more accurate missiles—has reached a point at which we humans are now armed deliberately.

Direct definition may be signaled by punctuation as in the example above. The dashes alert the reader that the definition "increase" is nearby.

REMEMBER: When you encounter an underlined word on the Regents' Reading Exam and do not know the meaning, look for these:

1. **commas, colons, dashes, parentheses, or brackets**
2. phrases/words that alert the reader that a definition of the unknown word is nearby:

  any form of the verb **to be**
  and (equating two things)
  the phrase, **that is**
  the word **since**

Example A. That law enforcement officer is known for being scrupulous *because* he has never been known to omit evidence in any case.

Notice that the word "because" signals that a definition/description is about to be given: "never been known to omit evidence in any case" would certainly imply that the officer has a sense of responsibility and of truth when it comes to crime. Therefore, the underlined word scrupulous must mean conscientious.

Authors might even

2. DIRECTLY EQUATE TWO OR MORE THINGS BY USING THE WORD "AND" OR BY LISTING

Example A. I can hardly enjoy watching my favorite television programs; advertising is ever-present *and* ubiquitous.

Since the word "and" equates things, ubiquitous must be similar in meaning to the word *ever-present.*

Example B. My cousin is an extremely <u>meticulous</u>, detailed, orderly, *and* careful individual.

In this example, what is the word "and" connecting?

Third, writers may

3. GIVE AN EXAMPLE OF THE WORD

Example A. <u>Parasitic</u> behavior is most evidenced by insects *such as* fleas, ticks, and leeches.

Although you may not be familiar with the adjectival form of "parasite" (i.e., "parasitic"), you have most likely encountered fleas and ticks. Since you know that these insects latch on to their host, you can deduce that parasitic means freeloading.

Example B. <u>Advocates</u> of Human Rights *like* Angelina Jolie who has supported efforts to end world hunger, *like* the late Princess Diana who fought to clear the world of landmines, and *like* Will Smith who campaigns for inner-city youth should be admired and respected.

Because you are given examples of celebrities fighting for a cause, you have an excellent idea of what an advocate is.

REMEMBER: *Definition by example may be signaled by these words and phrases*: **such as, like, as, the following, for example,** or **for instance.**

In addition, writers

4. CONTRAST THE WORD WITH ONE YOU ALREADY KNOW

Example A. *Whereas* Nicolas is very <u>pessimistic</u>, Steven is extremely hopeful.

Since you know the meaning of the word "hopeful," then by contrast you know the meaning of <u>pessimistic</u> (gloomy). Your signal word, of course, is "whereas," which tells you there is a contrast within the sentence.

Example B. Traditionally, scientists are <u>skeptical</u> of faith-based issues. *On the contrary*, religious believers are sure of their place in the afterlife.

You know the meaning of the word "sure," and you know that *on the contrary* is a contrast phrase; you also know that the opposite of "sure" is "uncertain." Therefore, what does skeptical mean?

> **REMEMBER:** *Contrast context clues are signaled by these words and phrases:*
> **whereas, or, but, however, although, though, on the contrary, unlike, conversely,** or **on the other hand**

Next, writers can

5. PRESENT A CAUSE-EFFECT SITUATION

Example A. In the 1820s, the Governor of Tasmania (an island of Australia) ordered the extermination of the aborigines. This order <u>culminated</u> in the almost complete genocide of the Tasmanian aboriginal population and resulted in The Black War.

In this instance the **CAUSE** is the order to exterminate the aborigines which resulted in the **EFFECT** which was the almost complete genocide. Culminated most likely means "ended" or "resulted."

> **REMEMBER:** *Definition by cause-effect may be signaled by these words and phrases:* **because, so, thus, consequently, therefore, since, if. . .then**

Sixth, writers may

6. HINT AT THE MEANING THROUGH LONG EXPLANATION

Example A. Catherine was my <u>mentor</u>. When I was confused, she would counsel me; when I was eager for knowledge, she taught me; in matters of faith, she guided me. How could I live without her comforting smile? However, to my surprise when she left that October day, even her silence laced with meaningful looks strengthened me.

How would you define <u>mentor</u>?

With Long Explanation, the reader is alerted to the meaning of an unknown word through explanation that is several sentences in length. The verb "counsel," for instance, implies that Catherine was kind. What are some other words that would describe Catherine? Once you determine other words to describe Catherine, give a definition for <u>mentor.</u>

REMEMBER: Definition by Long Explanation is signaled by an explanation that is often several sentences in length

---

NOTE: In addition to these five basic context clues, the student should always consider COMMON SENSE as well. If a sentence states: "The snake slithered through the high grass," with the underlined word being <u>slithered</u>, common sense tells us there are not that many things that a snake can do. As a result of using your common sense, you are indeed able to narrow down the options.

Exercise 2. Do you remember the list of words under your desk? Pick it up again and consider the words. Here, they are given to you in context, within a sentence. Now see if you can write a definition for those same words that were in isolation. Can you see how context really aids you in determining the meaning of an unknown word?

1. The <u>proliferation</u>—more and more high-powered rifles, more and more grenades, bigger and more accurate missiles— has reached a point at which we humans are now armed deliberately.

   proliferation   _____

2. That law enforcement officer is known for being <u>scrupulous</u> *because* he has never been known to omit evidence in any case.

   scrupulous   _____

3. I can hardly enjoy watching my favorite television programs; advertising is ever-present *and* <u>ubiquitous.</u>

   ubiquitous   _____

4. My cousin is an extremely <u>meticulous</u>, detailed, orderly, and careful individual.

   meticulous   _____

5. <u>Parasitic</u> behavior is most evidenced by insects such as fleas, ticks, and leeches.

   parasitic   _____

6. <u>Advocates</u> of Human Rights like Angelina Jolie who supports efforts to end world hunger, like the late Princess Diana who fought to clear the world of landmines, and like Will Smith who campaigns for inner-city youth should be admired and respected.

   advocates   _____

7. Whereas Nicolas is very <u>pessimistic</u>, Steven is extremely hopeful.

   pessimistic   _____

8. Traditionally, scientists are <u>skeptical</u> of faith-based issues. *On the contrary*, religious believers are sure of their place in the afterlife.

   skeptical   _____

9. In the 1820s, the Governor of Tasmania (an island of Australia) ordered the extermination of the aborigines. This order <u>culminated</u> in the almost complete genocide of the Tasmanian aboriginal population and resulted in The Black War.

   culminated   _____

10. Catherine was my <u>mentor</u>. When I was confused, she would counsel me; when I was eager for knowledge, she taught me; in matters of faith, she guided me. How could I live without her comforting smile? However, to my surprise when she left that October day even her silence laced with meaningful looks strengthened me.

    mentor   _____

Exercise 3. Now, go to Appendix B and work in your Vocabulary Journal. You have just added to ten words your vocabulary base.

Exercise 4. Are you ready to try more words in isolation? Take a stab at these; then, tear them out and place them under your desk.

1. perverse   _____

2. distorted   _____

3. flaunt   _____

4. prosperity   _____

5. susceptibility   _____

6. intricate   _____

7. digress   _____

8. eluding   _____

9. forlorn   _____

10. activists   _____

Exercise 5. Below are the same words you just tried to define in isolation, but this time you will try to define them with context added. In this exercise, there are three steps. First, you are to read the sentence and write a meaning for the underlined word. Second, you are to recognize the key word, phrase, and/or punctuation that alerted you to the meaning. Third, you are to write the context clue that aided you.

1. The young boy down the street has a <u>perverse</u> sense of humor—he heartlessly teases small animals and thinks it is funny.

meaning:

key words/phrases/punctuation:

context clue:

2. Unlike Kaley's photographs which always come out <u>distorted</u>, Mikya's are clearly in focus.

meaning:

key words/phrases/punctuation:

context clue:

3. Supermodels like Heidi Klum, Iman, and Cheryl Tiegs know how to <u>flaunt</u> their assets.

meaning:

key words/phrases/punctuation:

context clue:

4. Celebrity brings with it <u>prosperity</u> and riches. Celebrity has its downsides as well.

meaning:

key words/phrases/punctuation:

context clue:

5. Antonio has a weakness that his girlfriend is unable to help him with: he has a <u>susceptibility</u> to Internet sports gambling.

meaning:

key words/phrases/punctuation:

context clue:

6. I have always wanted to find that special person, but I am learning that human relationships can be complicated, complex, involved, and <u>intricate</u>.

meaning:

key words/phrases/punctuation:

context clue:

7. My International Studies professor is always getting off track. When we are discussing International Terrorism, he begins chatting about the time he spent in Thailand. From that rambling, he may wander into another conversation about the quarantine process for pets at the airport in Amsterdam. I have never seen anyone <u>digress</u> as much as he does, not even my great grandmother.

meaning:

key words/phrases/punctuation:

context clue:

8. The prisoner was incredible at <u>eluding</u>, evading, and all together avoiding law enforcement officers.

meaning:

key words/phrases/punctuation:

context clue:

9. Looking <u>forlorn,</u> the homeless were huddled by a barrel fire in an alley near Old Town in Atlanta.

meaning:

key words/phrases/punctuation:

context clue:

10.More than 23,000 elephants were killed by poachers in 2006 in Africa so animal rights <u>activists</u> exposed the tragedy.

meaning:

key words/phrases/punctuation:

context clue:

Exercise 6. Remember that list sitting under your desk? Take a look at it now. Grade it and grade Exercise 5. Which did you do better on? The one that had the added context?

Exercise 7. Now, go to Appendix B and work in your Vocabulary Journal for the ten words above.

Exercise 8. In this exercise, there are two steps.
>   *Step 1.* Read the sentence and choose the meaning of the underlined word by circling the best option.
>   *Step 2.* Recognize the key word, phrase, and/or punctuation that alerted you to the meaning and write it in the space provided.

Goldie was <u>defiant</u> when accused of stealing the candy, but Deidre yielded to the questioning and admitted she had taken some.

1. The word <u>defiant</u> most nearly means

a. rebellious.
b. irresistible.
c. shocked.

key words/phrases/punctuation:_____

2. Princess Diana was known throughout the world, so the manner of her death had a <u>profound</u> effect on citizens of virtually every country.

As used in the sentence, <u>profound</u> is best defined as

a. sharp and pointed.
b. intense and overwhelming.
c. shallow and superficial.

key words/phrases/punctuation:_____

3. After having a successful college career in sports, many college athletes <u>aspire</u> to play professional sports.

The word <u>aspire</u> most nearly means a

a. desire.
b. refuse.
c. snub.

key words/phrases/punctuation:_____

4. Monks are known for being <u>placid</u>, docile, mild-mannered, and calm.

As underlined in the sentence, the phrase <u>placid</u> can be defined as

a. quiet and peaceful.
b. arrogant and unfriendly.
c. natural and ordinary.

key words/phrases/punctuation:_____

5. <u>Noxious</u> materials lying around the house and garage like cleaning detergents, super-adhesive glues, antifreeze and so forth are harmful to pets.

<u>Noxious</u>, as underlined, signifies

a. abrasive.
b. critical.
c. poisonous.

key words/phrases/punctuation:_____

6. In contrast to the <u>affluent</u> society of New York City, the middle-class lives paycheck to paycheck.

As utilized in the sentence, <u>affluent</u> means

a. cozy.
b. wealthy.
c. relaxed.

key words/phrases/punctuation:_____

7. When Tootsie hit her thumb with the hammer she <u>suppressed</u> the urge to scream because the baby was sleeping, but tears streamed down her face.

The word <u>suppressed</u> most nearly means

a. succumbed to.
b. submitted to.
c. curbed.

key words/phrases/punctuation:_____

8. In Tokyo the young people in Harajuku Street are obvious with their Goth and Lolita styles; on the other hand, salarymen in the Shinjuku district are <u>inconspicuous</u>, always wearing the same, colorless, ill-fitting suits.

<u>Inconspicuous</u> can be defined as

a. important.
b. prominent.
c. unnoticed.

key words/phrases/punctuation:_____

9. The <u>predecessor</u> of the cell phone was the landline, home-based telephone.

The word <u>predecessor</u>, as underlined, most nearly means

a. forerunner.
b. successor.
c. competition.

key words/phrases/punctuation:_____

10. The International Space Station was <u>implemented</u> and put into operation to monitor deep space.

As used in the sentence, <u>implemented</u> signifies

a. decommissioned.
b. revised.
c. originated.

key words/phrases/punctuation:_____

Exercise 9 You have already added thirty new words to your vocabulary base. Go to Appendix B for more practice with your new words.

Exercise 10. Now try a few more. Read the sentences below and choose the correct answer for each. You will find several different types of clues in the context to help you determine the meanings of words. Circle the answer and then underline the key context clue which led you to the answer.

1. Although Steve was <u>ambivalent</u> about enlisting in the military, his sister, Mary, had no doubts or reservations about her decision to join.

   <u>ambivalent</u> most nearly means

      1. relaxed.
      2. unresolved.
      3. vigilant.
      4. jumpy.

2. Being new home buyers, we finally realized that purchasing a home in Buckhead or anywhere else was <u>contingent</u> upon our ability to obtain a loan. If we did not get the loan, we did not get the house.

   <u>contingent</u> most nearly means

      1. immaterial.
      2. extraneous.
      3. conditional.
      4. unfortunate.

3. The thunder and lightening alerted the Girl Scout troop that the storm was <u>imminent</u>.

<u>imminent</u> most nearly means

    1. impending.
    2. off in the distance.
    3. lingering.
    4. delayed.

4. The homeless children could not have know about the <u>insidious</u> landmines and menacing devices planted in the sand of the roadsides.

<u>insidious</u> most nearly means

    1. inoffensive.
    2. outdated.
    3. sinister.
    4. disabled.

5. In the field of <u>genetics</u>—that is, heredity—the future will most likely focus on the genetic engineering of the human body.

<u>genetics</u> most nearly means

    1. heredity.
    2. ancestry.
    3. origin.
    4. genealogy.

6. Mr. Smith continually <u>rationalized</u> his drinking and alcoholism by claiming that others drove him to it.

<u>rationalized</u> most nearly means

    1. praised.
    2. challenged.
    3. validated.
    4. ignored.

7. Amen, Sister-Friend, Inc. responded to the prosecutor's <u>allegation</u> that they had embezzled money from their parent company by stating that they earned the money

    <u>allegation</u> most nearly means

        1. scandal.
        2. propaganda.
        3. charge.
        4. falsehood.

8. The pre-recorded voice message of the corporation was <u>redundant</u>, repeating the same boring, unhelpful information.

    <u>redundant</u> most nearly means

        1. repetitious.
        2. irrelevant.
        3. novel.
        4. soothing.

9. Students at art institutes are eligible for scholarships if they employ <u>innovative</u> techniques to their work instead of traditional, hackneyed approaches.

    <u>innovative</u> most nearly means

        1. expensive.
        2. creative.
        3. profitable.
        4. conservative.

10. Sermo was <u>dubious</u> about securing employment at such a reputable architectural firm, but her mother was sure she would be hired.

    <u>dubious</u> most nearly means

        1. confident.
        2. enraged.
        3. dismayed.
        4. unconvinced.

Exercise 11. You have now accumulated 40 words to help you understand the passages on the Regents' Reading Exam. Go to Appendix B for more practice.

Exercise 12. Now, unlock the meaning of more unknown words by using context. Write a meaning for the word and the clue you used to decipher the meaning.

1. In some cultures, families live off of $1 per day and are destined to live in a state of penury the rest of their lives.

    penury probably means_____

    context clue: _____

2. My rock-star comrade has definitely had a tumultuous past, but my tree-hugger friend has always remained serene.

    tumultuous probably means_____

    context clue:_____

3. After returning from Japan, I never ingest—take—sugar in my tea.

    ingest probably means_____

    context clue:_____

4. Would you rather the women in developing countries be strong and autonomous or weak and dependent?

    autonomous probably means_____

    context clue:_____

5. According to some psychologists, many teens are narcissists, selfish to the extreme; but they grow out of it.

    narcissists probably means_____

    context clue:_____

6. With the onset of television shows like *Battlestar Galactica* and *Lost*, the sci-fi genre has turned out to be a <u>lucrative</u> business, generating billions of dollars.

      <u>lucrative</u> probably means_____

      context clue: _____

7. It would be interesting to study how many children's <u>aspirations</u> (e.g., to become a surgeon, an astronaut, a world leader) have come to fruition.

      <u>aspirations</u> probably means_____

      context clue:_____

8. Sensationalists base their astounding proclamations on unexplained <u>phenomena</u>, such as the Bermuda Triangle or the alien landing at Roswell.

      <u>phenomena</u> probably means_____

      context clues:_____

9. Women tend to scrutinize their features in the mirror and carefully check for any flaws.

      <u>scrutinize</u> probably means_____

      context clue:_____

10. Rather than his usual <u>sporadic</u> behavior, my dog, Mr. Bear, became a model of predictability.

      <u>sporadic</u> probably means_____

      context clue:_____

Exercise 13 Fifty new words! Go to Appendix B for more exercises focusing on vocabulary.

Exercise 14. Using context, your vocabulary base, and your knowledge of grammar and parts of speech, determine an appropriate "fit"; then fill in the blanks with the correct word. Choose from the list provided.

skinny	flinch	creature
forehead	souvenir	extraordinary
pleasant		

Harry walked across the dark room past Hedwig's large, empty cage, to the open window. He leaned on the sill, the cool night air (1)_____ on his face after a long time under the blankets. Hedwig had been absent for two nights now. Harry wasn't worried about her: she'd been gone this long before. But he hoped she'd be back soon—she was the only living (2)_____ in this house who didn't (3)_____ at the sight of him.

Harry, though still rather small and (4)_____ for his age, had grown a few inches over the last year. His jet-black hair, however, was just as it always had been—stubbornly untidy, whatever he did to it. The eyes behind his glasses were bright green, and on his (5)_____, clearly visible through his hair, was a thin scar, shaped like a bolt of lightning.

Of all the unusual things about Harry, this scar was the most (6)_____ of all. It was not, as the Dursleys had pretended for ten years, a (7)_____ of the car crash that had killed Harry's parents, because they had not died in a car crash. They had been murdered, murdered by the most feared Dark wizard for a hundred years, Lord Voldemort. Harry had escaped from the same attack with nothing more than a scar on his forehead. -Rowling, p. 6

Have all saints been "pure" before being named "saint?" Read the excerpt below to find out.

overcome	stepmother	intentions	repent
tirelessly	rivals	barefoot	debauchery

Margaret was so severely mistreated by her (8)_____ that she left home and became the mistress of a knight, living openly with him for nine years and bearing him a son. One day her little dog pulled at her skirts and led her to the body of her lover under a bush, murdered by his (9)_____ for Margaret. Rejected by her unsympathetic stepmother and (10)_____ with grief for her lover, Margaret blamed her beauty and vanity for the death and decided to (11)_____. Walking (12)_____, with a rope about her neck, she carried her son to the doors of a Franciscan convent in Cortona, Italy.

Margaret's beauty and charm were such that, combined with her reputation, the friars had to be convinced of her good (13)_____. To prove herself, she (14)_____ nursed the sick and poor and practiced extreme personal penitence: fasting, wearing hair shirts, depriving herself of sleep, and mutilating her body. She eventually earned her way into the convent and knew herself to be truly forgiven for her past (15)_____ when the figure of Christ on the crucifix supposedly leaned toward her while she knelt before him in prayer.

-Morgan, pp. 35-6

Exercise 15. Read the passage below from *The Lord of the Rings: The Two Towers* and answer the vocabulary questions that follow. As you answer each question, circle any context clues that aided you in responding.

Even as he gazed, Aragorn's <u>quick</u> ears caught sounds in the woodlands below, on the west side of the River. He froze. There were cries, and among them, to his horror, he could distinguish the <u>harsh</u> voices of Orcs. Then suddenly with a <u>deep-throated call</u>, a great horn blew, and the blasts filled the hills and echoed in the hollows, rising in a mighty shout above the roaring of the falls.

'The horn of Boromir!' he cried. 'Boromir is <u>in need</u>!' He sprang down the steps, leaping down the path.

As he ran, the cries came louder, but <u>fainter</u> now, and desperately the horn was blowing. Fierce and <u>shrill</u> rose the yells of the Orcs, and suddenly the horn-calls ceased. Aragorn raced down the last slope, but before he could reach the hill's foot, the sounds died away; and as he turned to the left and ran towards the Orcs, they <u>retreated</u>, until at last he could hear them no more. <u>Drawing</u> his bright sword he crashed through the trees.

Not far from the lake he found Boromir. He was sitting with his back to a great tree, as if he was resting. But Aragorn saw that he was <u>pierced</u> with many black-feathered arrows; his sword was still in his hand, but it was broken near the hilt. Many Orcs lay <u>slain</u>, piled all about him and at his feet.   -Tolkien, p. 3

1. The word, <u>quick</u>, as underlined in the passage, is best defined as

1. fast.
2. sharp.
3. lively.

2. The phrase <u>in need</u> connotes that Boromir

   1. is needy.
   2. was necessary.
   3. in trouble.

3. <u>Harsh</u>, as used in the passage, most nearly means

   1. brutal.
   2. gentle.
   3. unkind.

4. The phrase <u>deep-throated call</u> refers to

   1. Boromir.
   2. an Orc.
   3. the horn.

5. In the passage the underlined word, <u>fainter</u>, most nearly means

   1. dizzier.
   2. stronger.
   3. softer.

6. <u>Shrill</u>, as used in the passage, most nearly means

   1. firm.
   2. penetrating.
   3. precise.

7. In the passage the underlined word, <u>retreated</u>, most nearly means

   1. withdrew.
   2. advanced.
   3. turned.

8. The word, <u>Drawing</u>, as underlined, most nearly means

1. extracting.
2. sketching.
3. sheathing.

9. In the passage the underlined word, <u>pierced</u>, most nearly means

1. scratched.
2. punctured.
3. nicked.

10. The word, <u>slain</u>, as underlined in the passage, most nearly means

1. injured.
2. killed.
3. moaning.

Exercise 16 Try another one. Read the passage below from *The Lord of the Rings: The Fellowship of the Ring* and answer the vocabulary questions that follow. As you answer each question, circle any context clues that aided you in responding.

"Well, now, we're off at last," said Frodo, the ring tucked snugly into his secret pocket. They shouldered their packs and took up their sticks. When they had walked for about three hours they rested. They ate a very <u>frugal</u> supper of bread and water, and then went on again. Soon they struck out on a narrow road that went rolling up and down, fading grey into the darkness ahead.

"I can hear a horse coming along the road behind," said Sam. They looked back, but the turn of the road <u>obstructed</u> their view.

"I wonder if that is Gandalf the Wizard coming after us," said Frodo; but even as he said it, he had a feeling that it was not so, and a sudden desire to <u>camouflage</u> himself from the view of the rider came over him.

"It may not matter much," he said apologetically, "but I would rather not be seen on the road—by anyone. And if it is Gandalf," he added as an afterthought, "we can give him a little surprise, as <u>retaliation</u> for being so late. Let's get out of sight!"

Frodo hesitated for a second: curiosity or some other feeling was struggling with his desire to hide. The sound of hoofs drew nearer. Just in time he threw himself down in a patch of long grass behind a tree that overshadowed the road. Then he lifted his head and peered <u>warily</u> above one of the great roots. Round the corner came a black horse, no pony, but a full-sized horse; and on it sat a large man, who seemed to crouch in the saddle, wrapped in a great black cloak

and hood. Only his boots in the high stirrups showed below—his face was
shadowed and invisible.   -Tolkien, pp. 105-111

1. The word, <u>frugal</u>, as underlined in the passage, is best defined as

1. fast.
2. meager.
3. satisfying.

2. The word <u>obstructed</u> most likely means

1. hindered.
2. assisted.
3. contested.

3. <u>Camouflage</u>, as used in the passage, most nearly means

1. expose.
2. extricate.
3. conceal.

4. The word <u>retaliation</u> is defined as

1. reward.
2. payback.
3. the horn.

5. In the passage the underlined word, <u>warily</u>, most nearly means

1. in a careless manner.
2. with bravado.
3. in a guarded manner.

Exercise 17 Add any words you did not previously know from the paragraph work
(Exercise 14 through Exercise 16) to your Vocabulary Journal.

AN IMPORTANT NOTE

There are two major reasons students do not do as well as they want to on the vocabulary portions of the exam.

First, there may be too many technical or unknown words within the passage that slow the reader down, cutting into the time allotted for the exam. Notice how difficult the following passage is to read:

> The biosphere can be thought of as a discontinuous film over the surface of the earth, including the hydrosphere. It extends about the earth to elevations that may reach as high as 10,000 meters when microorganisms are carried aloft by updrafts. On land, the biosphere extends below ground to the chambers of subterranean caverns. Recent studies have shown that the biosphere extends much deeper than previously known, with the discovery of bacteria in crystalline rock aquifers over 1000m beneath the land surface of the Columbia River basin of Washington. In oceans, the biosphere extends to the deep-sea regions and even deep-ocean trenches, such as the Mariana Trench, provide habitat for heterotrophic organisms.
>
> -Southwick, p. 22

Look how many terms are not "common" to the English vocabulary! Though an ecologist may have not trouble comprehending this excerpt, I doubt too many individuals would be comfortable reading this selection. In fact, they may have to read it twice to get the gist of the passage. Why is this particular passage so difficult?

1. Most of the highlighted words and phrases are "technical"—that is, not words in common, everyday usage.
2. Ordinary words that you might know are not used in their "regular" way.
3. Because the unknown words force a reader to hesitate and break the flow of comprehension, a reader has to read the same sentence over again, thus wasting time and frustrating the reader.

Second, as mentioned previously, students sometimes complain that even though they can get a good sense of the meaning of the underlined word from context, they do not know some of the meanings of the answer choices (which appear, of course, in isolation). Consider another example of this predicament:

Example: As underlined in the third paragraph, the word <u>demolish</u> most nearly means

       1. to raze
       2. to conceptualize
       3. to conserve
       4. to construct

When considering the example, a reader may have an idea from the context (not provided here) that "demolish" means "destroy." So, number 4 as a choice can be eliminated. However, what happens if you do not know the meanings of #1, #2, or #3? There would not be a good probability that you would choose correctly.

As you can readily see, not understanding a good number of vocabulary words slows down the reader and devastates the time allotted for the test. What should a student do to overcome this dilemma? It is imperative to increase the number of words in your personal database so that while taking the exam you are not forced to hesitate and lose the flow of meaning.

The best strategy is to strengthen your general vocabulary *before the exam*. Context clues have already been discussed, and they will be a tremendous help to you. Other than knowledge of Context Clues, there are two effective ways you can enhance your vocabulary:

First, complete as much vocabulary buildup as possible months before the exam on your own. Make lists or stacks of index cards (of words you want to incorporate into your existing vocabulary base) when reading current articles in magazines, reading course textbooks, listening to words used in conversation, listening to words used in lectures, reading novels, or reading the newspaper. Keep the Vocabulary Journal found in Appendix A updated and handy for review before the test. Enter all the unknown words you encountered on the practice exams. You may be surprised how quickly your knowledge base expands.

Second, increase your knowledge of Word Structure (prefixes, suffixes, and roots). You probably came across lists of word parts when studying for the SAT or other standardized tests. The following section on Word Structure will arm you with knowledge of word parts and improve your chances of decoding and breaking down the actual words you encounter as choices on the Regents' Reading Exam. Had you already had a mastery of Word Structure, you could have answered the Example above correctly. That is, you would have been able to decode #2 and #3 and eliminate them as answers (using the Process of Elimination). You would have been left with #1, "raze" which is the correct answer. Along with Context Clues, Word Structure will allow you to have more knowledge to apply to unlocking the meaning of unknown words.

❧WORD STRUCTURE

Where did English words originate? Most words used in our language are not originally English; they derive from Greek or Latin.

English words can be made up of three parts:

1. a prefix that appears in front of the base element (root)
2. a root that is the base element of the word
3. a suffix attached at the end of the base element (root)

Consider the word, *monogamous*, in respect to where it originated and how it can be broken down into word parts:

	Prefix *mono*	Root *gam(y)*	Suffix *ous*
meaning: origin:	one (Greek)	*marriage* (Greek)	*having the quality of* (Greek)

Referring to the Affixes/Roots Chart 1 below, what would you think the following word means?

polygamous
poly   gam(y)   ous

Write a meaning here:

Chart 1. Useful Prefixes, Roots, Suffixes

a-	without
ab-	away from
ad-	toward
am-	love
anim	life
anthrop	mankind
annu	yearly
anti-	against
-ate	to cause
auto-	self
aud	hear
bene	good
biblio	book
bio	life
cide	killing
cogn	know
con-, com	together
contra-	against
cred	believe
de-	away
dic, dict	say
equ, equi	equal
ex-	out
extra-	over and above
gamy	marriage
gen	people, race
graph	write
habit	dwell
hom	man
in-, im-	not
in-, im-	into
inter-	between
-ic	pertaining to
-ist, -er, -or, -ant	one who
-less	without
-logy	study of
mal-	bad
matri, mater	mother
mort	death
multi-	many

Chart 1, continued

non-	not
omni-	all
-ous	full of
-pathe, pathy	feeling
per	through
poly-	many
port	carry
potent	power
post-	after
pre-	before
pseudo-	false
re-	back, again
sca	climb
somn	sleep
spect, spic	see
sub-	under
sui	self
super-	over and above
sym-, syn-	same
ten	hold
terre	earth
-(a)tion	act of, action
trans-	across
ven, ventu	come

Thus, by changing the prefix you can totally change the meaning of a word. *Mono*-gamous implies "staying faithful" to a spouse. *Poly*-gamous means having many spouses. To illustrate further, consider words with the root, *cide*. You know the meaning of *suicide*, but did you know that the prefix *sui*- means "self"? And *cide*, of course, means "killing." Therefore, the word is interpreted as "self-killing," or "killing of self."

If you changed the prefix, *sui*-, the meaning of the word would change. How many different words can be made with the root, *cide*? What would "genocide" mean? "Matricide"? "Pesticide"?

Exercise 18. Consulting Chart 1 or using your existing knowledge of vocabulary, give a meaning for these words that have *port* as their root.

1. transport _____

2. deport _____

3. import _____

4. export _____

5. portable _____

6. porter _____

7. support _____

8. transportation _____

9. report _____

10. portage _____

Perhaps you got all but the last one. Still, that means you understood and decoded nine out of ten (90%). Do you see the power of this strategy? You have already increased your knowledge of words related to the root, *port*, tenfold!

Are prefixes and suffixes just as powerful? Look at the list below and think of a definition or description for each word beginning with the prefix *pre-*. Use Chart 1 above, Chart 2 below, your existing knowledge of vocabulary, or a dictionary to find your answers.

11. pre-game _____

12. precognition _____

13. prerequisite _____

14. prehistoric _____

15. predict _____

16. preview _____

17. precede _____

18. preplanning _____

19. predate _____

20. prefix _____

Chart 2. Roots, Prefixes, Suffixes	
-able	ability
aqua	water
cede	go
circum	around
de-	away
dis-	not
gen	race, people
liber	free
loc(us)	place
mania	obsession
mim	copy
philo	love
sub, sup	underneath, below
theo	god

Exercise 19. Referring to Chart 1 and Chart 2, assign meaning to the "nonsense" words below and then try to choose the correct meaning from Column B.

Column A

_____1. philous

_____2. adpotent

_____3. acredo

_____4. pathous

_____5. dislibered

_____6. ammania

_____7. cideate

_____8. antidict

_____9. materless

_____10. nonven

Column B

a. gossip

b. atheistic

c. greedy

d. orphaned

e. murder

f. absent

g. emotional

h. infatuated

i. loving

j. imprisoned

Column A	**Column B**
_____11. aquagen	a. shack
_____12. suiless	b. writer
_____13. malhabit	c. owning
_____14. postgamy	d. saint
_____15. graphist	e. underground
_____16. benehom	f. divorced
_____17. abterre	g. blind
_____18. tenation	h. outerspace
_____19. nonspectable	i. the Navy
_____20. sublocus	j. unselfish

Exercise 20. Integrating knowledge of prefixes, roots, and suffixes as well as context clues, write a meaning of the affix and/or base element, and then give a meaning for the underlined word.

1. The termite <u>inspector</u> came to my house to look for damage.

in-:_____

spec:_____

-or:_____

meaning of word: _____

2. When put on the stand the accused tried to <u>circumvent</u> the truth to avoid getting caught.

circum-:_____

vent: _____

meaning of word: _____

3. Dictators like Idi Amin who was portrayed in the film *The Last King of Scotland* believed they were <u>omnipotent</u>.

omni-:_____

potent: _____

meaning of word: _____

4. The priest was <u>incredulous</u> when he realized that the twelve year old girl sitting across from him was addicted to heroin.

in-: _____

cred: _____

-ous:_____

meaning of word: _____

5. When I was in France, I asked my friend whether or not I should take the <u>intercontinental</u> railway to Germany.

inter-:_____

Meaning of word: _____

6. The proceeds from the Alicia Keys concert were to <u>benefit</u> orphans around the world.

bene: _____

meaning of word: _____

7. When Catie was in high school she was <u>cognizant</u> that other students only liked her for her good looks.

cogn:_____

meaning of word: _____

8. Grandmother Ethel's great-grandson was <u>disinherited</u> the day she passed away.

dis-: _____

meaning of word: _____

9. The <u>genocide</u> in Rwanda in 1994 was mostly ignored by the international community.

geno:_____

-cide: _____

meaning of word: _____

10. That puppy is <u>tenacious</u> when it comes to my old shoe.

ten-:_____

-ous: _____

meaning of word: _____

Exercise 21. In your Vocabulary Journal, complete the exercises on Word Structure.

➴IDENTIFYING VOCABULARY QUESTIONS

It is easy to recognize vocabulary questions on Regents' Reading Exams since the word itself is underlined in the question and in the passage. Use your scanning skills to quickly locate the underlined word in the passage. Question stems may be worded as follows:

-"(the underlined word), as used in the passage, most nearly means . . ."
-"As used in paragraph three, (the underlined word) is best defined as . . ."
- "(the underlined word) may be defined as . . ."

Internet Activity

A.   Access the Internet and find an article on a topic you are interested in within your major. Within the article find five words you do not know. Check Charts 1 and 2 and see if you can decode them through Word Structure. Once you have found their meanings, enter them into your Vocabulary Journal.

B.   Google "lists of roots and prefixes" which will lead you to some excellent web sites that give you a list of prefixes, roots, and suffixes as well as example words. Add at least five of each to your charts above.

For practice in determining the meaning of words on a simulated Regents' Reading Exam, go to Exam Eight.

☙Chapter Three☙

Literal Comprehension (18% to 24%)

Literal comprehension questions require you to recognize specific details. There will be about ten to thirteen literal comprehension questions on the Regents' Reading Exam. With literal questions, a reader can find the answer to the question by merely looking back at the passage. Many literal comprehension questions ask for a name, a number, or a statement made in the passage, and it is only a matter of seconds before the student can point to the exact information in the passage. In fact, Wassman and Rinsky say that an average reader scans approximately 1,000 words per minute. Perhaps this is the reason most students answer literal comprehension questions faster than any other type of question: their eyes will pick up numbers and capital letters very quickly, providing them with "literal" answers.

Once you have read the passage, you may come upon a literal comprehension question. The most efficient way to find the specific information is to put your index finger at the top of the passage (in the middle of the passage) and move it straight down the middle to the end of the passage. As your index finger moves down the page, your eyes will glimpse capital letters (which will answer *who, where,* and *what)*, numbers (which will answer *when, how many,* and *how much*), and underlined words (which designate vocabulary questions) in a matter of seconds. (*Note*: According to some reading experts, scanning the traditional way of moving your eyes from left to right may slow you down when reading columned material.)

You should have confidence when answering the literal comprehension questions on the Regents' Reading Exam; after all, you have been answering these kinds of questions for many of your school years.

☙IDENTIFYING LITERAL COMPREHENSION QUESTIONS

Literal comprehension questions themselves may be recognized by the following words and phrases which appear in the question stem:

who	*what*	*where*	*how much*	*how many*
when	*according to the passage, what....*		*which of the following....*	

Exercise 1. Read the brief paragraphs about astronomy and answer the literal comprehension questions that follow. Notice how quickly you are able to find the answers.

When you turn a typical amateur telescope to Jupiter, the mighty planet's ocean of clouds exhibits belts and zones in yellow, gray, white and brown. Jupiter's 4 large moons circle the giant. Brilliant Venus, so dazzling to the eye, offers phases like the Moon's. When viewing the Moon through a top-quality 6- or 8-inch telescope, one can detect features the width of a large football stadium—views corresponding to those visible out the window of a spacecraft orbiting a few hundred kilometers above the Moon's surface.

-Dickinson, p. 11

1. How many inches wide is the lens of a top-quality telescope?

2. What colors do the clouds of Jupiter exhibit?

3. How many moons does Jupiter have?

4. Other than Jupiter, what is the name of the planet (not a moon) mentioned in the passage?

5. Which two cosmic bodies have phases?

The region between planets is essentially empty space, except for a few thousand renegade asteroids—chunks of rocky material left over from the formation of the planets—that have drifted in from the asteroid belt beyond Mars. The largest of these are flying mountains that pose the threat of mass destruction if one were to hit Earth. Fortunately, such collisions are exceedingly rare. The last big impact occurred 65 million years ago, around the time of the extinction of the dinosaurs.

-Dickinson, p. 14

6. In regard to size, to what was a large asteroid compared?

7. How many years ago did the extinction of the dinosaurs occur?

8. True or False? According to the passage, an asteroid hitting the Earth is a rare phenomenon.

9. If you were travelling through space, what would you most likely find between planets?

In the 1990s, astronomers detected Jupiter-sized planets orbiting around more than 12 other Suns, revealing the existence of other solar systems. Our Sun now assumes its place as one star among many. Our nearest neighbor, Alpha Centauri, is a triple-star system 8,000 times farther from Earth than frigid Pluto. Distances between star systems are awesome.

10. What star system is our nearest neighbor?

11. How far is Alpha Centauri from Earth?

12. When did astronomers find other solar systems?

13. How many other solar systems did they find?

14. True or False? The other solar systems that astronomers discovered had planets.

       An incident that emphasizes just how far some city dwellers are removed from real stars occurred in the hours following a major Los Angeles-area earthquake in 1994. The 4:00 a.m. quake, centered in Northridge, California, had prompted almost everybody who felt it to rush outdoors for safety and to inspect the damage. But the trembling landscape had also knocked out power over a wide area.

       Standing outside in total darkness for the first time in memory, hundreds of thousands of people saw a sky untarnished by city lights. That night and over the next few weeks, emergency organizations as well as observatories and radio stations in the L.A. area received hundreds of calls from people wondering whether the sudden brightening of the stars and the appearance of a silver cloud (which was really the Milky Way) had caused the earthquake.

       Such a reaction—blaming the earthquake on the brightening of the night sky—emerged because people were not used to seeing the night sky during a power outage.
-Dickinson, p. 47

15. In what year did the Los Angeles earthquake occur?

16. Where did the earthquake occur?

17. At what time were people woken up by the trembling landscape?

What three places did people telephone to give their opinions about what caused the earthquake?

18.

19.

20.

NASA Solar System Collection

Jupiter Flyby

Although the main mission of the New Horizons spacecraft is to explore the Pluto system and the Kuiper Belt of icy objects, it first flew by the solar system's largest planet, Jupiter, in 2007 - a little over a year after the planned launch date. In this artist's rendering, New Horizons is just past its closest approach to the planet. Near the Sun are Earth, Venus and Mercury. The dim crescent shape at the upper right of the Sun is Callisto, the outermost of Jupiter's four largest moons. Just left of Jupiter is Europa. *Image Credit*: Southwest Research Institute (Dan Durda)/Johns Hopkins University Applied Physics Laboratory (Ken Moscati)

http://www.nasaimages.org/luna/servlet/detail/nasaNAS~20~20~120869~227571:Jupiter-Flyby

Exercise 2. Tear this page from your textbook. Read the passage and make ten literal comprehension questions for it (*who, what, when, where, how much, how many, which of the following . . .*, or true-false). Next, hand your questions to a classmate and have them answer the questions. (The following excerpt is from a case study completed by *Gendercide Watch*):

Honor killings can be defined as acts of murder in which a woman is killed for her actual or perceived immoral behavior. Such "immoral behavior" may take the form of marital infidelity, refusing to submit to an arranged marriage, demanding a divorce, flirting with or receiving phone calls from men, failing to serve a meal on time, or "allowing herself" to be raped.

Most honor killings occur in Muslim countries, but it is worth noting that no sanction for these murders is granted in Islamic religion or law. And the phenomenon is a global one (e.g., have taken place in Bangladesh, Britain, Brazil, Egypt, India, Israel, Jordan, Sweden, Turkey and Uganda). Pakistan is probably the country where such atrocities are most pervasive. A human-rights report (1999) stated that honor killings took the lives of 888 women in the single province of Punjab.

One of the most notorious honor killings of recent years occurred in April 1999, when Samia Imran arrived at her lawyer's office. She had engaged the lawyer a few days earlier because she wanted a divorce from her violent husband. Samia settled on a chair across the desk from the lawyer. Sultana, Samia's mother, entered five minutes later with a male companion. Samia half-rose in greeting. The man grabbed Samia and put a pistol to her head. The first bullet entered near Samia's eye and she fell. There was no scream. "I don't even think she knew what was happening," the lawyer said. The killer stood over Samia's body and fired again. The lawyer reached for the alarm button as the gunman and the mother left. "The mother never even bothered to look back at her daughter."

-Gendercide Watch

1._____

Classmate's answer:

2._____

Classmate's answer:

3._____

Classmate's answer:

4._____

Classmate's answer:

5._____

Classmate's answer:

6._____

Classmate's answer:

7._____

Classmate's answer:

8._____

Classmate's answer:

9._____

Classmate's answer:

10._____

Classmate's answer:

Exercise 3. Read these brief paragraphs. Then, read the sentences and circle whether or not the literal information is true or false

(c) Tiggy Ridley/IRIN

There are more than 250,000 child soldiers fighting around the world. Some children are kidnapped from their schools or their beds, and some are "recruited" after seeing their parents slaughtered. The children's very vulnerability makes them attractive to the warlords. The children, some as young as 8, become fighters, sex slaves, spies and even human shields. Once recruited, many are brainwashed, trained, given drugs and then sent into battle with orders to kill. In 2002 the International Criminal Court was established, and recruiting child soldiers was declared a war crime.   -O'Neill, 2007

1. True/False: According to the paragraph, child soldiers can be as young as 8 years old.

2. True/False: There are about 250,000 child soldiers fighting in the Middle East alone.

3. True/False: The children's very vulnerability makes them attractive to the warlords.

4. True/False: Although considered immoral, the recruiting of child soldiers is not a war crime.

Dara Torres has competed in four Olympics spanning three decades. She has never failed to bring home a medal. Now she's seizing the chance to become the oldest swimming medalist in history, at 41.

In 1984 Dara was a Beverly Hills teenager who helped the U.S. win gold in the freestyle relay in her Olympic debut. In 1988 Torres had just finished her junior year of college at the University of Florida, and her mission was to win medals in Seoul. Little did the public know, she had been battling bulimia since her freshman year of college.

By 2000 Torres had four Olympic medals, all from relays. At the 2004 Athens Olympics, Torres worked as a swimming commentator for NBC. In 2008? Dara is smiling after qualifying for her fifth Olympic team.   -Berg, 2008

5. True/False: Dara Torres is the oldest swimming medalist in history.

6. True/False: Dara Torres has won five Olympic medals.

7. True/False: In 1988 Torres was attending the University of Florida.

8. True/False: Torres competed in the Athens Olympics.

9. True/False: In 2008 Torres once again qualified to be on a U.S. Olympic team.

10. True/False: Dara Torres battled bulimia during her college years.

Exercise 4. Read the two passages below and answer the literal comprehension questions that follow.

Maggie Rizer's fresh-faced appeal made her a $30,000-per-day supermodel. Then her small-town stepfather got hooked on a lottery game called Quick Draw, and, *click*, all her money was gone.

Modeling, all great supermodels will tell you, is hard work. Some take to it as if they'd never known anything else. Others, however, are reluctant to let go of their old selves. Maggie Rizer, an oval-faced 27-year old from Watertown, New York, was one of the latter. She'd starred in campaigns for Prada, Versace, and Calvin Klein and been on the cover of *Vogue* and *Elle*, to name a few.

Rizer's small-town humility was far from a pose. She'd never outgrown her roots in Watertown. Along with her $1.6 million condo in Tribeca, she built herself a cottage on Lake Ontario, where she'd spent her summers growing up, and bought her family one of the nicest houses in Watertown. In New York City, she lived a fairly modest life by supermodel standards. In her first five years of modeling, she built up a nest egg of over $7 million, managed by her stepfather, John Breen, a jovial Watertown insurance man.

The first sign of trouble came in the summer of 2002, when Maggie went home and her stepfather gave her a gentle lecture. He told her she had no money. He said she needed to follow a real budget, work more, and needed to skimp on Christmas presents. Actually, her stepfather had become fascinated with a state-run lottery game called Quick Draw. (A state senator called it "video crack," which is what it became for John.) After John was sent to an in-patient rehab facility, it took several weeks to figure out that the $7 million fortune Maggie had amassed was almost completely gone.   -Pickert, 2005

1. How much did Maggie earn in one day as a supermodel?

a. $3,000
b. $30,000
c. $300,000

2. In regard to modeling as a career, Maggie

a. was reluctant to let go of her old self.
b. took to it as if she had done it her entire life.
c. regarded it as unimportant.

3. Of the following, which was not mentioned as a brand name designer for whom Maggie worked?

a. Versace
b. Prada
c. Gloria Vanderbilt

4. Where had Maggie spent her summers growing up?

a. Lake Ontario
b. Tribeca
c. Watertown

5. In her first five years of modeling, Maggie

a. lost her edge as a top model.
b. became addicted to gambling.
c. built up a nest egg of over $7 million.

6. According to the passage, when Maggie first began modeling, her relationship with her family was

a. a power struggle.
b. strained.
c. pleasant.

7. Who is John Breen?

a. Maggie's agent
b. Maggie's money manager
c. Maggie's biological father

8. One senator called the game Quick Draw

a. "video crack."
b. "lottery heaven."
c. "state-run lottery."

9. When telling Maggie she had no money, her stepfather also told her

a. that he was not responsible for her losses.
b. to work more.
c. that the family would still have a good Christmas.

10. John Breen's greatest mistake/flaw was that he

a. did not love his family more than himself.
b. was too strict and stern and demanded too much from Maggie.
c. he became addicted to gambling and lost all of Maggie's money.

❧IDENTIFYING A REFERENT

In addition to detailed questions you may be asked to identify referents. (You may encounter only a few of these.)   A referent is a word that refers to another word in the passage. That is, referents are used to point the reader back to their origins within the passage. On the Regents' Reading Exam pronouns are used quite often as referents. You will also find words like *first* and *second* or *former* and *latter* used as referents. Consider an example from the passage you just read:

> Modeling, all great supermodels will tell you, is hard work. Some take to it as if they'd never known anything else. Others, however, are reluctant to let go of their old selves. Maggie Rizer, an oval-faced 27-year old from Watertown, New York, was one of the <u>latter</u>.

On the Regents' Reading exam the word *latter* would be underlined. The question would most likely be formed like this:

The underlined word, <u>latter</u>, as used in the passage, refers to

1. modeling.
2. others reluctant to let go of their old selves.
3. all great supermodels.
4. some take to it as if they'd never known anything else.

To what is the word *second* referring? Option 2.

Exercise 5. Recognizing referents: Write to whom or to what the underlined word is referring.

1. *The Atlanta Journal*, (Sunday edition sports section) publishes scores for professional sports events. The *Macon Daily News* Sunday edition sports section focuses on local college and high school sports summaries. The first focuses on teams like the Atlanta Braves while the <u>second</u> focuses on teams like the Georgia Southern Eagles.

<u>Second</u>, as underlined refers to:_____

2. Setting up a computer can be tedious if you are not used to it. All of the following must be considered: the tower, the monitor, the keyboard, the mouse, the printer, and the speakers. You must determine which components need to be connected to the tower as well as which components need to be plugged into an outlet. In addition, an understanding of the relationships among <u>these "building blocks"</u> is essential in case you are faced with having to troubleshoot.

<u>these "building blocks"</u> refers to:_____

3. The Science Fiction genre in television has garnered much attention in the last few years. The *Star Trek* series, beginning in 1966 has spawned many pop culture references and, according to Wikipedia, is one of the biggest cult phenomena of modern times. *Star Trek: The Next Generation* won 18 Emmy Awards and was actually the first syndicated TV show nominated for the Emmy for *Best Dramatic Series* in its seventh season. Another example of the science fiction genre on television is *The X-Files* which aired from 1993-2002. It also became entrenched in pop culture and earned a Peabody, Golden Globe and Emmy. There is a major difference between these two shows, however. In the former, the audience

actually meets and becomes involved with other alien cultures; whereas, in the latter, the audience never really encounters "aliens" in a public sense. In fact, one of the central slogans of the show is "I Want to Believe."

the latter refers to:_____

Practice in Scanning

Exercise 6. Tear out this page. On the next page there is a page from a Publication List. You will have 90 seconds to scan for and write down the answers to the questions below so work quickly. Your instructor will tell you when to begin.

1. Who wrote *A Brief Survey of the Sociological Imagination*?_____

2. Which textbook is in its 9th edition?_____

3. Is there a textbook highlighting Islam?_____

4. How many books have a publication date of 2007?_____

5. When was *Introduction to Global Studies: Politics and Economics* published?_____

6. What is the name of the book that Diaz wrote?_____

7. How many books are over $60.00?_____

8. What is the ISBN# (found at top of each entry) for Maloney's book?_____

9. True or False? There are six 1st editions. _____

10. How many ISBN#s end in the number 5?_____

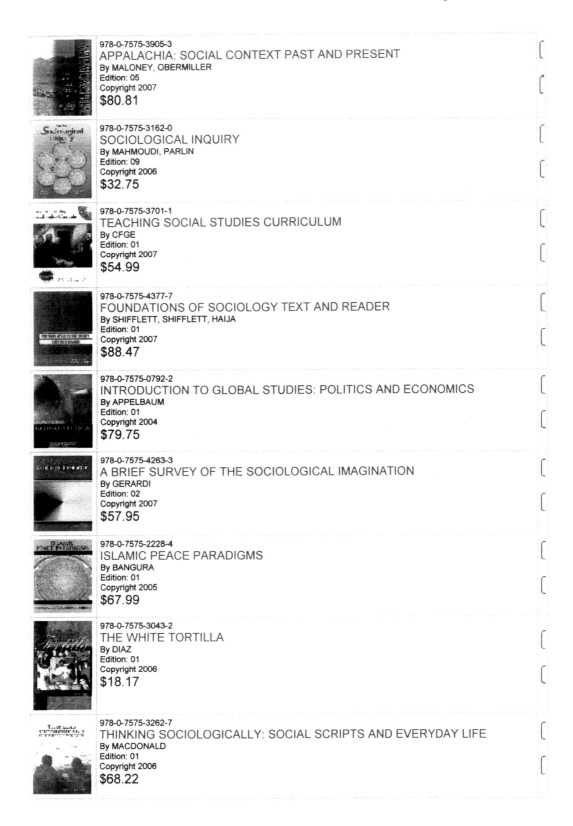

978-0-7575-3905-3
APPALACHIA: SOCIAL CONTEXT PAST AND PRESENT
By MALONEY, OBERMILLER
Edition: 05
Copyright 2007
$80.81

978-0-7575-3162-0
SOCIOLOGICAL INQUIRY
By MAHMOUDI, PARLIN
Edition: 09
Copyright 2006
$32.75

978-0-7575-3701-1
TEACHING SOCIAL STUDIES CURRICULUM
By CFGE
Edition: 01
Copyright 2007
$54.99

978-0-7575-4377-7
FOUNDATIONS OF SOCIOLOGY TEXT AND READER
By SHIFFLETT, SHIFFLETT, HAIJA
Edition: 01
Copyright 2007
$88.47

978-0-7575-0792-2
INTRODUCTION TO GLOBAL STUDIES: POLITICS AND ECONOMICS
By APPELBAUM
Edition: 01
Copyright 2004
$79.75

978-0-7575-4263-3
A BRIEF SURVEY OF THE SOCIOLOGICAL IMAGINATION
By GERARDI
Edition: 02
Copyright 2007
$57.95

978-0-7575-2228-4
ISLAMIC PEACE PARADIGMS
By BANGURA
Edition: 01
Copyright 2005
$67.99

978-0-7575-3043-2
THE WHITE TORTILLA
By DIAZ
Edition: 01
Copyright 2006
$18.17

978-0-7575-3262-7
THINKING SOCIOLOGICALLY: SOCIAL SCRIPTS AND EVERYDAY LIFE
By MACDONALD
Edition: 01
Copyright 2006
$68.22

Exercise 7. Georgia, like other states, has its famous, historical landmarks, but what about the quirky places that are not well-known? The content on the next two pages is an outlandish but fun list of the OFFBEAT LANDMARKS OF GEORGIA. See how quickly you can find the answers to the questions. Tear out this page of questions and the next page which lists the quirky places (it has a front and a back). You will have 2 minutes. Your instructor will tell you when to begin.

1. What is Claxton, Georgia known as?_____

2. What group first proclaimed that Hartwell, Georgia is the Center of the World?_____

3. Where is the Statue of Liberty replica located?_____

4. When can you visit the Tick Museum?_____

5. In what city is the Tick Museum located?_____

6. Is the World's Smallest Church still an active church?_____

7. What is the address for the Varsity in Atlanta?_____

8. If you were confirming times to visit the Babyland (Cabbage Patch Doll) Hospital, what number would you call?_____

   What two films (movies) are mentioned in the list?

9._____

10. _____

OFFBEAT LANDMARKS OF GEORGIA (from ROADSIDEAMERICA.COM)

Athens, Georgia
Address: Dearing St.

Tree that Owns Itself
Directions: Corner of Dearing and Finley St
Hours: 24 hours
A historic oak tree that legally owns itself and the land it stands upon

Atlanta, Georgia
Address: 61 N Ave NW

The Varsity
Directions: across from Georgia Tech
Hours: open 24 hours
Started in 1928 by Frank Gordy after he flunked out of Georgia Tech.

Cleveland, Georgia
Address: 73 W Underwood St

Babyland General Hospital: Birthplace of Cabbage Patch Dolls
Hours: M-Sa 9-5, Su 10-5
Call to verify: 706-865-2171
Birthplace of the Cabbage Patch Kids" in 1979. And, they're still being born.

Claxton, Georgia
Address:203 Main Street

Fruitcake Capital of the World
Hours: closed to public
Used to offer free tours, but insurance concerns ended that. You can still look in the front windows of the production area at seven huge fruitcake ovens in action.

Columbus, Georgia
Address: Linwood Cemetery

Coca Cola Inventor's Grave
Hours: M-F 10-4
Dr. John S. Pemberton, a pharmacist who concocted the original (and still secret) formula for Coca-Cola syrup died in 1888

Pemberton House & Apothecary Shop
Address: 11 7th Street
A recreated pharmacy scene and a Pemberton-like mannequin. Pemberton was allegedly a morphine addict. Sold the secret formula for $1,750.

Cornelia, Georgia
271 Foreacre Street

The Loudermilk Boarding House Museum
Directions: One block from City Hall
Hours: F-Su 10-5 (Apr-Nov) or by appointment
Call to verify: 706-778-2001
One of the 30,000 Elvis items in Joni Mabe's Panoramic Encyclopedia of Everything Elvis on display is a wart removed from his right wrist in 1958. She keeps it in a jar of formaldehyde

Hartwell, Georgia
Address: U.S. Hwy 29

Center of the World
Directions: 3 miles south of town
-historical marker proclaiming that this spot is the "Center of the World." At least to the Cherokee: Trails radiated in all directions from this hub, so the designation made

sense, at least, before people arrived from places that the trails didn't go (like Europe).

Juliette, Georgia

Address of cafe:

Fried Green Tomatoes Filming Site

443 McCrackin St, Juliette, GA
Phone: 478-992-8886
Juliette is the site for the filming of the movie "Fried Green Tomatoes"

McRae, Georgia

Address:

Statue of Liberty Replica
Hours: 24 hours
In 1986 the Lions Club built a Statue of Liberty of their own "as a reminder to citizens what America really means."

Plains, Georgia

Address: in front of Davis E-Z
  Shop, Hwy 45 N

Jimmy Carter Peanut

Directions: 1/2 mile north of town center on Hwy 45
(Buena Vista Rd)
Hours: Daylight hours. (Call to verify)
Phone: 229-824-7701
-Thirteen feet tall peanut with a wide grin
-world's second largest peanut
-made for a 1976 political visit to Illinois by
  Jimmy Carter

Statesboro, Georgia

Address:Georgia Southern
University, Technology Building

Tick Museum
Hours: W 1:30-2:30 or by appointment
Call to Verify: 912-681-5564
World's largest tick collection

Savannah, Georgia

Address: 14 E 73rd St

World Globe Gas Storage Tank
Hours: 24 hours
-Originally a storage tank for the local gas co.
-1956, cable mogul Ted Turner's father talked
  company into painting the round tank like a
  globe

Address: E. Hull & Bull Street

Forrest Gump Bench Site
-In Chippewa City Park, bench no longer there
-Was situated behind short wall next to One-Way sign

South Newport, Georgia

Address: Coastal Hwy 17

World's Smallest Church
Directions: Just south of I-95, on hwy. 17, 10 minutes
from Shellman Bluff
Hours: 24 hours
-Still active as a church
-Left unlocked
-Approximately 10' x 20'

Courtesy of Wally T. Orrel

-Has a tiny pulpit, pews and a stained
  glass window
-Note: There are 14 other US churches
  that claim to be the world's smallest
                    -Roadsideamerica, 2008

Exercise 8.   Now it is your turn. Make up 10 questions based on the Offbeat Landmarks of Georgia. Write the answers on a separate piece of paper. Tear out this page with your questions and exchange them with a classmate. Be sure to time each other. See how quickly you can find the answers. Then, let your classmate grade his/her paper.

1. _____

2. _____

3. _____

4. _____

5. _____

6. _____

7. _____

8. _____

9. _____

10. _____

Exercise 9. Read the passage about Hollywood icon Will Smith and answer the literal comprehension questions.

The history of pop icons attempting to make it in Hollywood is a long and often arduous one; however, the world of rap has a far better record. LL Cool J's star is rising, as is Queen Latifah's. And then there is the biggest of them all—Will Smith, surely the most successful crossover star of the modern era.

Born Willard Christopher Smith, Jr. in 1968, in Philadelphia, Smith grew up middle-class, his mother serving on the school board and his father owning a refrigeration company. The Smiths were a Baptist family, yet Will attended a Catholic school.

Influenced by Eddie Murphy, Will began rapping at the age of 12, quickly developing his own semi-comic style. His music was squeaky clean, a far cry from the new Gangsta Rap that was beginning to rear it bloodied head. His first single and his debut album made Will a millionaire at the age of 18. He would not stay rich for long, though. Forgetting to pay taxes, he was cleaned out by the IRS and forced to build his fortune again. In 1989 he won the first ever Grammy for Best Rap Performance. A further Grammy was won in 1991 for "Summertime."

But by this time, Will was already at the top of another profession. NBC cast Will as a sassy, street-smart kid coping comically with life in Los Angeles. The show, *The Fresh Prince of Bel-Air*, was a major success, ran for six years, and gave Will a foothold in Hollywood.

[Will Smith is a power to be reckoned with. He commanded a $20 million salary for the film, *Ali.*]   -Willis, 2008

1. According to the passage, as an actor, Queen Latifah

a. has already made it in Hollywood.
b. is up and coming in Hollywood.
c. was banished by the major players of Hollywood.

2. One actor who was mentioned as influencing Will in his early years was

a. Eddie Murphy.
b. LL Cool J.
c. Queen Latifah.

3. In 1991, Will won a Grammy for which of the following?

a. *Fresh Prince of Bel-Air*
b. Gangsta rap
c. "Summertime"

4. Will became a millionaire at the age of 18. He soon lost all his money because

a. his manager embezzled his money.
b. he forgot to pay his taxes.
c. he became addicted to drugs.

5. According to the passage, Will Smith is a Catholic.

a. True
b. False

6. The passage states that Will's rap career gave him a foothold in Hollywood.

a. True
b. False

7. Will began rapping as a pre-teen.

a. True
b. False

8. According to the passage, Will Smith was born and raised in Los Angeles.

a. True
b. False

9. For the film, *Ali*, Smith garnered $2,000,000 as salary.

a. True
b. False

10. Will was the first artist to win a Grammy for the genre of Rap.

a. True
b. False

SOME TIPS FOR ANSWERING LITERAL COMPREHENSION QUESTIONS

First, answering literal comprehension questions will work to your advantage. it is better not to spend too much time on one question. Consider this situation:

> You are being timed—you having a bit of trouble answering question #1 which is an inference question, and it has already taken up three minutes of your time. What if you have 5 questions that take up your time like #1? That adds up to15 minutes taken up for only 5 questions! How many literal comprehension questions could you have answered in the same amount of time? Many. So go to literal comprehension questions for the passage and answer them first. It will give you a sense of accomplishment. Go back to the harder question and see if you can answer it now. If not, circle it and come back to it later if you have time.

Second, as stated previously, it is probably better not to read the questions before you read the passage. If you read the questions first the last time you took the test, then you already know that strategy did not work for you. Two negative consequences could occur from reading the questions before reading the selection: one, you could read the question wrong which will "color" how you read the passage; and two, you could obsess on one question and not absorb other critical information in the passage. Therefore, read the passage first as quickly as you can while concentrating, then look at the questions.

Third, you may find that some literal comprehension question options are stated a little differently than the passage. Do not let these **restatements** fool you. They are just stating the same idea in a different way. For example, in the passage about Will Smith you just read above, one of the questions is:

1. According to the passage, as an actor, Queen Latifah

a. has already made it in Hollywood.
b. is up and coming in Hollywood.
c. was banished by the major players of Hollywood.

In the passage, it states that "LL Cool J's star is rising, as is Queen Latifah's." This means the same thing as Queen Latifah "is up and coming in Hollywood." Therefore, (b) is the answer.

Internet Activity

*Searching the web, print out a brief article concerning a topic that interests you. Read the article and then create 5 questions that answer **Who, Where, What, How much/many, Which of the following**, and/or **When** questions. Write the answers on another sheet of paper. Hand the article and questions to a class mate. After your class mate has finished the "quiz," hand her/him the answers for grading. (Build your confidence by recognizing how quickly you are able to answer this type of question.)*

Now, go to your Vocabulary Journal and add any words from your article that were unfamiliar to you.

For practice in determining answers for Literal Comprehension questions on a simulated Regents' Reading Exam, go to Exam Three.

Use the Internet to build your vocabulary base.

ལ Chapter Four ಉ

Inferential Comprehension (33% to 41%)

Different from answering Literal Comprehension questions, answering inference questions on the Regents' Reading Exam requires that you *interpret* material that is presented in a passage because the answer is not directly stated. That is, an inference is an educated guess based on available clues. Because the Regents' Reading Exam includes many questions that require you to infer (in fact, 18 to 22 may be this type), it is beneficial to master this skill. Since interpretive reading takes more time, you will not be able to answer the questions as quickly as Literal Comprehension questions. When reading for Inferential Comprehension (assuming your rate is 300+ wpm), your reading rate will decrease to a range of 150–300 words per minute (Wassman & Rinsky), much slower than the rate to read for specific details. Skimming or scanning is not useful in this instance because the answer is not something you can simply pick out. Therefore, you need to practice the skill of inferential reading until it becomes second nature to you.

Inferential Comprehension is best understood if you contrast it to Literal Comprehension. As mentioned, identifying specific or literal information is a relatively easy task. You, as a student, have been locating information in stories and passages since you began your school years. In the previous section you learned that *who, what, where, how much/many* and *when* are classified as indicators of Literal Comprehension question: Who is the main character? What was she asked to hide? Where did she hide the top-secret disk? How many secret service officers were searching for her? When did they catch her? The answers to Literal Comprehension questions are easily found in a passage; you can actually go back and pinpoint the answer because the answer is directly stated. But what if you are asked, "*Why* was this particular woman entrusted with the disk?" or "*How* did the woman end up with the disk?" Unless you are given the answer directly in the passage, you will have to make an educated guess—and you need to base your estimation on clues you find in the selection. You cannot wildly guess or let your imagination take over. The better you are at picking out clues, the better chance you have of making the correct inference. On the Regents' Reading Exam, *why* and *how* questions often indicate you are being asked to prove your ability to infer.

> **REMEMBER**: The more actual evidence you can gather, the more accurate your inference will be.

People use inference skills not only in reading material but also in their daily dealings. From each situation you find yourself in, you are inferring. In fact, it is inferring incorrectly that usually leads to breakdowns in communication and in relationships. Consider this example:

> Shepherd had turned off his cell phone because he didn't want to be bothered. He hadn't had any time to himself for days. Shepherd was excited because he was about to enter his favorite arcade at the mall. As he reached the door, he glanced left. He was startled because standing there window shopping was his girlfriend—and she was not alone. Next to her, leaning on crutches was his best friend, Jackson.

What can you infer from the clues you are given in this scenario?

Write your first reaction here:_____

Some of you may have written that Shepherd's girlfriend was cheating on him. In this instance, it is very tempting to quickly deduce this, but (with any degree of confidence) can you really infer that she is cheating? After all, you are only given information that he was standing next to her. By becoming emotional, did you infer correctly? Are there any neutral inferences you could deduce?

The girlfriend could have been there for other reasons:
  a) the girlfriend bumped into Jackson at the mall; or
  b) Jackson couldn't reach Shepherd by cell, so he called Shepherd's girlfriend for a ride to the mall (where his doctor's office was located).

Given the information and clues, the above are two inferences that are more reasonable.

REMEMBER: *If you are having trouble detecting clues, authors provide hints through words, phrases, sentences, and information they offer. Words have negative and positive connotations which convey an author's meaning and intent.*

When confronting inference questions there are several strategies to utilize:

  1. Try not to get emotional about your responses.
  2. Try not to allow your imagination and vivid thoughts to work overtime.
  3. Go back to the passage and mentally highlight or circle the clues.
  4. Make sure you have strong evidence for your answer so that you respond with a high degree of confidence.

> **REMEMBER:** *You will be asked 18 to 22 inference questions on the exam. That is, this type of question is asked most frequently. Be sure you understand the strategies for answering inferential comprehension questions.*

ஃIDENTIFYING INFERENCE QUESTIONS

You can identify inference questions by looking at the stem of the question. Recognizing this type of question is possible by using the following words and phrases as indicators:

probably   possible   maybe   most likely   conclude   imply   suggest   infer

On the Regents' Reading Exam inferential questions will most likely read as follows:

The reader might conclude that . . .
We can deduce that . . .
The passage implies that . . .
The selection suggests . . .
The author most likely believes . . .
It can be inferred that . . .
The writer would probably agree that . . .
With which of the following statements would the author most likely agree?

As mentioned, inference questions take longer to answer than Literal Comprehension questions do, but practicing Inferential Comprehension questions now will train you to look for clues, and it will become second nature to you before you sit for the exam.

Exercise 1. Tear out this page. Test your inference skills by reading the sentence, considering the clues, deciding upon a reasonable inference, and writing it in the blank provided. Be sure to write a statement about which you feel confident. Next, exchange your worksheet with your classmate and ask him to write his inference in the space provided. Are both inferences similar?

1. Erika has decorated her office walls with Japanese woodblock prints. In a small curio Japanese carved, ivory items were displayed. In addition, Erika carried an indigo purse with an image of a Geisha on it.

Inference: _____

Classmate's inference:

2. My dorm mate, Justin, is always talking about Australia. According to him, Australians love diversity, Australians are the best surfers, and Aussies are friendlier than Americans. Supposedly, his Australian parents are more understanding than any on the planet. Even the stars are prettier at night in the Outback.

Inference: _____

Classmate's inference:

3. When we received our papers back from the professor, I saw the beginning of a smile on Natika's face; then, I saw her mouth the word "Yes!"

Inference: _____

Classmate's inference:

4. First, there was a barely detectable tremor. Then the walls began to shake and portions of the ceiling began caving in. People began screaming and scattering in all directions.

Inference: _____

Classmate's inference:

5. My Grandmama Lillie Mae used to say that if you didn't have anything good to say about someone, it is better not to speak.

Inference: _____

Classmate's Inference:

6. After going to the ATM, I realized that money was missing from my checking account. Also, I found out that three credit card applications had been submitted—and not by me. I then frantically raced to the bank to inquire about my savings account.

Inference:_____

Classmate's inference:

7. One small town in Georgia has five Mexican restaurants and a Taco stand, too.

Inference:_____

Classmate's inference:

8. Iola planted several plum trees in her yard. She checked every spring for budding fruit and after three years, the trees started producing fruit. One day, after a few months, she checked the trees and the plums had turned purple. They looked delicious. She went to bed that night content that she would be reaping baskets of luscious plums the next day. In the morning she raced out to the trees and stopped in her tracks. There was not one plum on her trees!

Inference:_____

Classmate's inference:

9. My older sister, Monica, had her twenty-first birthday last night and came home at midnight. She wasn't able to walk in a straight line and kept bumping into furniture. When I asked her what was wrong, she slurred her words and mumbled something. I told her to sit on the couch and I would fix her some ice cream. When I came back into the room carrying the ice cream, there she was, lying on the couch—snoring.

Inference:_____

Classmate's Inference:

10. As we were eating dinner, we noticed a child running around in circles. Then the child was screaming at the top of her lungs while underneath the table. Next, the child was wrapped in the drapes at the windows. After about 10 minutes of these antics, the child ended up at the piano banging away.

Inference:_____

Classmate's inference:

Exercise 2. Below is an extraordinary article. It was published in the *Woman's Home Companion* in 1943. It was written by the first woman pilot to die in American history while on war duty. Shortly after submitting the article, Cornelia Fort was killed when the bomber she was piloting crashed in Texas.

©Bettman/Corbis

I knew I was going to join the Women's Auxiliary Ferry Squadron before the organization was anything but a radical idea in the minds of a few men who believed that women could fly airplanes. But I never knew it so surely as I did in Honolulu on December 7, 1941.

At dawn that morning I drove from Waikiki to the civilian airport right next to Pearl Harbor, where I was a civilian pilot instructor. Coming in just before the last landing, I saw a military plane coming directly toward me, passing so close that my celluloid windows rattled violently. I looked down to see what kind of plane it was. The painted red circles on the tops of the wings shone brightly in the sun. Honolulu was familiar with the emblem of the Rising Sun on passenger ships but not on airplanes.

I looked quickly at Pearl Harbor and my spine tingled when I saw billowing black smoke. Then I looked way up and saw the formation of silver bombers riding in. The rest of December seventh has been described by too many for me to reiterate.

I returned to the mainland. None of the female civilian pilots wanted to leave, but there was no civilian flying in the islands after the attack. Then, out of the blue came a telegram from the War Department announcing the organization of the WAFS (Women's Auxiliary Ferrying Squadron) and the order to report within twenty-four hours if interested. I left at once.

We have no hopes of replacing men pilots. But we can release a man to combat, to overseas work. Delivering a trainer to Texas may be as important as delivering a bomber to Africa if you take the long view. We are beginning to prove that women can be trusted to deliver airplanes safely and in the doing serve the country which is our country too.

-Cornelia Fort, July 1943

Answer the inference questions below by circling the correct answer, and then write the clues from the passage that led you to your answer.

1. The reader can infer that during the early 1940s it was generally accepted that women

a. flew airplanes better than men.
b. should not fly airplanes.
c. should be drafted the same as men.

Clues:_____

_____

2. We can conclude that the country that was bombing Pearl Harbor was

a. Russia.
b. England.
c. Japan.

Clues:_____

_____

3. It is suggested in the passage that Cornelia didn't explain the details of December 7, 1941 because

a. the details were well known by the general public.
b. everything about that day was classified top-secret.
c. it was too emotional an experience to re-live by speaking about it over and over.

Clues:_____

_____

4. The reader can conclude that during the conflict, pilots such as Cornelia wanted to do something for their country.

a. True
b. False

Clues:_____

_____

5. It is implied in the last paragraph that the jobs that female pilots were doing during WWII were

a. just as important as those the men were doing.
b. not as important as those the men were doing.
c. regarded as nonessential by the government.

Now write 5 factual pieces of information you gleaned from the passage.

6. _____

7. _____

8. _____

9. _____

10. _____

Exercise 3. After reading the passage about the Black Church Movement below, write two inferences along with the clues that led to your inferences.

Discrimination in white churches and the need for a separate spiritual community led to the establishment of Black churches in the South. The Baptists had congregational independence which helped free Blacks establish their own churches unhampered by church polity and structure. Consequently, the first African Baptist churches emerged in the late 1770s in South Carolina, Virginia and Georgia led by Black ministers such as Georgia Liele and Andrew Bryan.

The Methodists predominated in the upper South's cities. In one Norfolk Methodist church men sat on the left and women on the right. Free Blacks were seated apart from slaves. Class divisions appeared more frequently in the cities of the Lower South where light-skinned elites purchased pews in the white churches rather than worship in their own. Furthermore, along the Gulf, free Black Protestants often worshiped with Catholic free persons of color to gain the advantages of certificates of marriage and baptism needed to prove freedom.

During the 1820s legislators created laws to restrict the power of the Black churches. Immediately, Richmond free Blacks sought permission to establish a separate Black meeting house. Ignored, they took their petition to the local Baptist church. Still, with no support, they met in homes and alleys to organize and worship. The Black church movement could not be stopped.   -Salem, pp. 136-137

1. Inference:_____

Clues:_____

2. Inference:_____

Clues:_____

After reading the passage below, write two inferences along with the clues that led to your inferences.

> Having a pet in the family can make you feel like a kid again. You get to run around, throw balls, get chased and just plain act ridiculous. And since most pets love taking a good romp—vets recommend getting out for at least 20 minutes twice a day—you both get some vigorous exercise in the bargain.
>
> This is true not only for dogs, but in some cases for cats as well. In fact, walking a cat has some advantages over strolling with a canine counterpart. Cats don't lift their legs at every stop, constantly sniff the ground, or tug on the leash. Cats love getting out of the house and going for walks, particularly if you get them used to it when they're young.
>
> Cats wriggle out of collars easily; so many vets recommend using a harness instead of the usual choke collar. To get your cat used to the idea, first put on the harness without the leash. Once she's used to the harness, snap on the leash and take some practice walks around the house. When you both feel comfortable, head outdoors for an enjoyable jaunt; but don't expect your cat to heel like a dog. Basically, she's going to be walking you!   -Hoffman, p. 13

1. Inference:_____

Clues:_____

2. Inference:_____

Clues:_____

After reading the passage from *Katherine*, write three inferences along with the clues that led to your inferences.

The messenger met her gaze, then stared down pointedly at the Red Rose embroidered on his coat.

"His Grace, the Duke, wants you to come to him, my lady," said Raulin.

"Why does he send for me in secret?" Katherine pressed her hands tight against her chest to still the jumping of her heart, but she stood quietly, leaning against the table.

"Since his wife's funeral he has seen nobody but me, nor does he wish to, my lady, except now—you."

Katherine and Raulin rode back to the Savoy Palace in silence. He led her to a small wooden door which he unlocked. Katherine swallowed, and mounted the steps. They ended on the next floor where there was another door, concealed by a large painting. Raulin pushed it aside and knocked on the carved oak door. A voice said, "Enter!"

Raulin held the door, then shut it after Katherine, and went away. Katherine walked in quietly, her head lifted high, her cloak clutched around her. The Duke was sitting on a gold-cushioned window seat gazing out over the river. Katherine knelt and taking his hand, kissed it.

While she knelt, her cloak loosened and her hood fell back. He touched her curling rain-dampened hair.

"It is the color of carnelians," he said "the gem that heals anger. If only it could heal sorrow." He spoke as though to himself, in a low, faltering voice.

-Seton, pp. 201-202

1. Inference:_____

Clues:_____

2. Inference:_____

Clues:_____

3. Inference:_____

Clues:_____

After reading the passage about girls and boys, write three inferences along with the clues that led to your inferences.

> In life girls, it is said, have it much worse than boys, but in-depth research shows that girls and boys each have their own equally painful sufferings. To say girls have it worse than boys is to put on blinders. Consider these facts: parents talk to, cuddle, and breast-feed their boy infants significantly less than their girl infants. Male infants also suffer a 25 percent higher mortality than female infants; boys are twice as likely as girls to suffer from autism and more likely to suffer birth defects. The majority of schizophrenics are boys. Emotionally disturbed boys outnumber girls 4 to 1, and boys are twice as likely as girls to be the victims of physical abuse. Lastly, boys are four times as likely as girls to commit suicide.
>
> As kids get older, girls seem to have more opportunity and more encouragement than boys to get advanced education. In recent years, females out matriculated males in both college and graduate school.
>
> For the last few decades, our cultural microscope has focused on the oppression of girls and women. That focus has led us to many gains in public consciousness, national policy, and private life. Now the lens must focus on boys. Boys are in pain. For every boy who feels powerful at home or in his neighborhood there is another boy who feels lost. For every football star, there are far more male drug addicts, teenage alcoholics, high school dropouts, and juvenile delinquents.
>
> -Gurian, pp. xvii-xviii

1. Inference:_____

Clues:_____

2. Inference:_____

Clues:_____

3. Inference:_____

Clues:_____

Exercise 4 After reading the selection, answer the questions that follow, providing the clues that helped you arrive at your answer.

> Despite the best efforts of parents to treat their children the same with

regard to issues of discipline and fairness, children within the family, nonetheless, differ greatly from each other. The assumption that growing up in the same family will make people similar is a fallacy. One interesting phenomenon that influences this outcome is birth order.

According to Sulloway, there are siblings who are from the same family, but the order of their birth acts to create differences in their personalities—not similarities. Siblings are placed in competition with each other for survival (maybe in modern times, it's not so much to survive but to thrive). To do so, they need the support and attention of their parents. Firstborns use different strategies than laterborns to capture their parents' approval and interest. In some respects, firstborns have a ready-made advantage in this regard. Parents are naturally engaged with the first child; not only are they proud of their achievement and fascinated with the future prospects of this child (e.g., seeing a future astronaut or professional athlete), but they are unsure of the parenting process and thus focus more attention to it to ensure the baby's survival. Therefore, firstborns seek to maintain close ties to the parents by conforming to parental wishes, identifying with parental values and interests, and in general, not jeopardizing their relationship by rocking the boat or creating problems.

Laterborns, on the other hand, need to create a new niche that sets them apart from their older sibling and allows them to shine in their own right. They may often choose pursuits in which the older sibling has not already established a dominant superiority. In an effort to establish an area of accomplishment that separates them from the older sibling, the later child may not follow the example of the parents so closely. Instead, laterborns may seek unique ways to draw attention to themselves.

-Ellyson, et al., p406

1. The reader can infer that in the past researchers believed that the family environment was

1. an important factor in similarity among siblings.
2. not a factor in similarity among siblings.
3. detrimental when determining similarity among siblings.

Clue that helped you arrive at the answer:

2. We can conclude that

1. firstborns may get into more trouble than other siblings.
2. laterborns may get into more trouble than other siblings.
3. overall, because they are always seeking parental approval, siblings do not get into trouble.

Clue that helped you arrive at the answer:

3. The passage suggests that

1. laterborns receive more attention from parents because they are the "babies."
2. firstborns are most likely the favored children.
3. in the main, in the interest of fairness, parents do not favor one child over another.

Clue that helped you arrive at the answer:

4. The selection implies that

1. because they know they are special, firstborns have no need to seek parental attention.
2. parents try to encourage the laterborns to follow in the firstborn's footsteps.
3. laterborns may become tired of living in the firstborn's shadow.

5. The reader can conclude that firstborns

1. feel that the best way to their parents' approval is through conformity.
2. usually seek unique ways to draw attention to themselves.
3. know they are special because they were born first and do not care about parental approval.

⮞ FINDING THE MAIN IDEA

On the Regents' Reading Exam you will be required to find the main idea of a passage or a paragraph—in most cases when it is not directly stated. If the main idea is stated, you might find it stated as a sentence. Look for it in the first sentence of the first paragraph or the first sentence in the last paragraph. If, however, the main idea is not directly stated, you will need to rely on your inference skills to determine a main idea.

Perhaps the most effective way to find the main idea is to compile all the details in the passage first. (*Note*: on the Georgia Regents' Reading Test you are allowed to jot down notes on the test.) Follow these suggested steps:

Step 1. Look at all your details and try to either group them or identify what they have in common.

Step 2. Before looking at the question options, analyze the commonality of the details.

Step 3. Write one sentence describing what the main idea is.

Step 4.   Check the options to determine which one is closest to your written main idea. Practice this strategy as many times as you can before the actual test. You will become more at ease with finding the main idea the more you practice this method.

Exercise 5. Using Steps 1 through 3 in the four-step method above, write a main idea for the following paragraphs taken from *The Other Boleyn Girl* by Phillipa Gregory, p. 9.

A.   By stepping to one side a little and craning my neck, I could see the condemned man, accompanied by his priest, walk slowly toward the green where the wooden platform was waiting, the block of wood placed center stage, the executioner dressed all ready for work in his shirtsleeves with a black hood over his head. It looked more like a masquerade than a real event, and I watched it as if it were a court entertainment.

Step One. List details: _____

_____

_____

Step Two. Commonality of details:

_____

Step Three. Write one sentence describing the main idea of the paragraph.

_____

B.   The king, seated on his throne, looked distracted, as if he was running through his speech of forgiveness in his head. Behind him stood my husband, my brother, and my father, all looking grave. I wriggled my toes inside my silk slippers and wished the king would hurry up and grant clemency so that we could all go to breakfast. I was only thirteen years old, and I was always hungry.

Step One. List details: _____

_____

_____

Step Two. Commonality of details:

_____

Step Three. Write one sentence describing the main idea of the paragraph.

_____

      C.   The Duke, far away on the scaffold, pulled off his coat. He was close enough kin for me to call him uncle. He had come to my wedding and given me a gold bracelet. My father told me that the Duke had offended the king a dozen ways. The Duke had royal blood and he kept too large an army for the comfort of the king, not yet secure on the throne. Worst of all, the Duke was supposed to have said that the king had no son, could get no son, and that he would likely die without a son to succeed him to the throne.

Step One. List details:_____

_____

_____

Step Two. Commonality of details:

_____

Step Three. Write one sentence describing the main idea of the paragraph.

_____

Exercise 6. For this exercise you will add Step Four. Choose a main idea for the following paragraphs based on the main idea sentence you write.

      A.   China's history in the 20th century has been marked by occupation and civil war. This experience has fueled its strong desire for Great Power status and at the same time put it decades behind the West in technological development. Under the leadership of Deng Xiaoping, China has undergone a transformation, which has produced a tremendous economic turnaround. China is now a major trading nation which has built up an impressive foreign currency holding and is predicted to be the world's largest economy by 2010. Despite not facing any threat to its security, China has embarked on a path of radical change to both its military strategy and capabilities. The realization in the 1980s that the Soviet Union was no longer a threat for major conflict and scrutiny of the Gulf War have had a profound effect on Chinese military thinking. The strategic focus has now shifted to the offensive. The main theme is power projection and the ability to fight a modern war with advanced technology.   -Hynes, 1998

Step One. List details:_____

_____

_____

Step Two. Commonality of details:

_____

Step Three. Write one sentence describing the main idea of the paragraph.

_____

Step Four. Which one of the options below matches your main idea statement in Step Three above? Choose the correct answer.

The central focus of the paragraph is that

a. China built an impressive Army after feeling concern over the Gulf War and the "weakening" of the Soviet Union.
b. under the leadership of Deng Xiaoping, China has undergone a transformation.
c. China is now a major trading nation which has embarked on a path to change both its military strategy and capabilities.

B.   Those from the western world do not usually cherish the foot as a symbol of beauty. The practice of foot binding as a requisite for marriage or for the sake of beauty usually elicits a gasp from the typical person from the West. The idea of soaking the feet in hot water, massaging them, breaking all the toes except the big one, then folding the toes under and binding them tightly with bandages is hardly appealing. However, in China during the Sung dynasty, the painful art of foot binding took hold and the three-inch lotus foot was an ideal to be cherished. Over the centuries, approximately four and a half billion Chinese women endured the revered practice in order to gain status and identity.
       Although girls between the ages of three to eleven years old were the typical

groups subjected to the ritual, they were not the only ones. Prostitutes as well as male dancers also underwent the procedure to enhance their allure. The maintenance and binding of the feet usually took two years—each time the feet were unbound, they were bound tighter with new bandaging. From all accounts it is apparent that those who had their feet bound lived in excruciating pain. The dangers of foot binding have been well documented. According to an article by the BBC, foot binding 1) impeded blood circulation, resulting in the loss of toes; 2) toenails that were not trimmed would cut into the instep of the foot and cause infection and gangrene; and 3) the animal blood-and-herbs used for soaking the feet caused flesh to fall off.

Why, then would anyone undergo such a procedure? Culturally, bound feet were a status symbol and a requirement for an advantageous marriage. "It was believed that without husbands or children to tend to their graves, these women were condemned to spend their afterlife as hungry ghosts, roaming the Earth for all eternity." (BBC, 2003)

Note: In 1911 the new Republic of China banned foot binding. In 1998, the last factory to manufacture shoes for bound feet for women in Harbin, China, ended production.

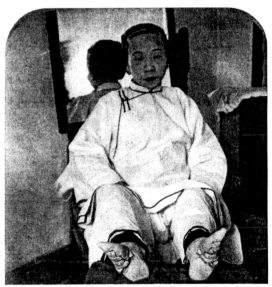

Photography by Underwood & Underwood, London & New York, from *Women of All Nations* (1911)

Step One. List details:_____

_____

Step Two. Commonality of details:

_____

Step Three. Write one sentence describing the main idea of the paragraph.

Step Four. Which one of the options below matches your main idea statement in Step Three above? Choose the correct answer.

The main idea of this paragraph is that

  a. girls typically begin having their feet bound when they are three years old but discontinued the practice when they reached age eleven.
  b. the dangers of bound feet are many, including the chance of contracting gangrene.
  c. foot binding was the only way for a woman to marry into money, securing her status and a place in the afterlife.

REMEMBER: *To find a main idea that is not directly stated, find what the details have in common; then, write one sentence to describe that commonality.*

✏ IDENTIFYING MAIN IDEA QUESTIONS

You can identify main idea questions by recognizing certain key words in the stem of the question:

What is the *central theme* of the selection?
What is the *focus* of paragraph two?
Which of these statements best expresses the *central idea* of the excerpt?
The *best statement of the main idea* is . . .
This passage *primarily* deals with . . .
The author's *main point is that*. . .
The *best title* for this selection is . . .
What is the *main idea* of the *passage*?
What is the *main idea* of *paragraph* five?

Internet Activity

  A. *Practice finding inferences by gathering three photos, three pictures, or three single-panel cartoon drawings on the internet. Print out your selections and then write inferences for them. Exchange your selections (without your written answers) with a classmate and have them write inferences for your photos/pictures/cartoons. Now, compare your answers with those of your classmate's. Did you draw the same inferences?*

B. Practice finding the main idea by gathering three photos, three pictures, or three single-panel cartoon drawings on the internet. Print out your selections and then write captions/main ideas for them. Exchange your selections (without your written answers) with a classmate and have them write captions for your photos/pictures/cartoons. Now, compare your main ideas with those of your classmate's.

Now, go to your Vocabulary Journal and add any words from this chapter that were unfamiliar to you.

For more practice determining Inferences on a simulated Regents' Reading Exam, go to Exam Two.

❧ Chapter Five ❧

Analysis (18% to 24%)

Most analysis questions do not ask about the content of the passage. Instead, analysis questions focus on the technique and organizational patterns the author uses to get his or her point across. Analysis questions are concerned with *how the passage is written* (tone, style, patterns of organization) or *why the selection was written* (author's purpose). When reading for analytical information, you will probably read at the same rate as reading for inferential questions: 150 to 300 words per minute.

❧ IDENTIFYING ANALYSIS QUESTIONS

You will notice that analysis questions are very straightforward:

> What is the tone of the passage?
> The author's attitude is one of . . .
> What is the author's style?
> What is the author's purpose in writing the selection?
> The purpose of the passage is . . .
> The author gets his point across through the use of. . .

> **REMEMBER:** *Analysis questions emphasize how and why the author wrote the passage.*

Below, you will find a description of each type of analysis question and lists of options for answering each type.

❧ TONE, ATTITUDE, AND STYLE

As we all know, an individual's mood can be shown through facial expressions, gestures, and body language. But how is mood, tone, or attitude portrayed through the written word? In passages, the most efficient way a writer can relate the tone is through his or her word choice.

By using a tone of voice, an individual is able to alert the listener to the way s/he is feeling, but how does a writer indicate tone? Authors carefully choose words and phrases to give impressions, express feelings, and plant images in readers' minds. What are the images conjured when reading the following:

1. The alarm sounded and alerted the audience.
2. The alarm sounded and the audience panicked.

We, the readers, know that in the latter, the feeling is a lot stronger. What would the difference in meaning be if the author chose to use the word "terrorized" instead of "alerted?" What about "scare," "worried," or "horrified?" As you can see, word choice makes a difference in tone and gives different nuances in meaning. In fact, you could even make a scale and rank each word from mild to extreme in terms of meaning.

On Regents' Reading Exams you can detect tone and attitude by noticing the words and phrases the author has chosen as well as noticing the way in which the subject matter is approached. Also, the situation will call for utilizing one word over another word. For instance, when writing an essay about someone you admire, say, Hillary Clinton, would you use the word "love" (i.e., "I love Hillary Clinton because . . .") or the word "respect" ("I respect Hillary Clinton because . . .")? Because writing an essay is usually a formal activity, the word "respect" is more appropriate. Writers of the passages on the Regents' Reading Exam do the same—they choose certain words that show their attitude toward the subject matter, and they choose words appropriate to the topic.

Exercise 1. Try ranking/rating these words in order from mildest to strongest. Use a dictionary if you need to.

dislike	hate	like	abhor	love

1.
2.
3.
4.
5.

Try ranking/rating these words in order from nicest to meanest. Use a dictionary if you need to.

syrupy	unpleasant	amenable	callous	sweet

6.
7.
8.
9.
10.

Exercise 2. Choose a more informal or formal word or phrase that corresponds to the word given.

	More Informal	More Formal
1. police officer		
2. money		
3. automobile		
4. child		
5. woman		
6. tired		
7. hungry		
8. killed		
9. geek		
10. awesome		

It is up to the author to choose words, sentence structure, and paragraph arrangement to convey his or her message as strongly and effectively as possible. The author chooses words carefully to ensure the writing is cohesive, vivid, and specific enough to bring life to it. For example, if the author of your history text wrote that Martin Luther King, Jr. was the *dude* who was shot and killed in the name of equal rights, as the reader you would think it strange. The terms *leader, pastor or activist* would have been more appropriate. *Dude* is the wrong choice—it is too informal, and is, in fact, disrespectful within the context.

Be aware that questions of this type are very straightforward and not meant to trick you: "What is the author's tone? What is the tone of the passage? What is the writer's attitude toward . . . ?"

Below you will find a list of words to describe tone and/or attitude that may appear as options on Regents' Reading Exams:

TONE AND ATTITUDE OPTIONS

angry	*hopeful*
apathetic	*hopeless*
argumentative	*hostile*
bitter	*humorous*
compassionate	*impartial*
complaining	*indifferent*
complimentary	*informal*
critical	*informative*

cynical	*neutral*
defensive	*nostalgic*
despairing	*objective*
disdainful	*optimistic*
distrustful	*pessimistic*
doubtful	*resentful*
dramatic	*sarcastic*
empathetic	*sentimental*
enthusiastic	*sincere*
formal	*skeptical*
hateful	*somber*
ironic	*subjective*
mocking	*suspenseful*
	tragic

Exercise 3. In each sentence you will detect a tone or attitude. Choose the best answer by circling it.

1. "I cannot believe you lost my briefcase!" screamed the American Ambassador. "I thought I had impressed upon you how valuable it was!"

a. sentimental
b. angry
c. pessimistic

2. Miranda is a really good writer; her use of descriptive adjectives is amazing.

a. neutral
b. serious
c. complimentary

3. It doesn't really matter whether he buys a tux for the prom or not.

a. indifferent
b. suspenseful
c. sarcastic

4. Every time Mildred thinks of her mother's last years and the pain her mother endured, tears flood her eyes.

a. distrustful
b. defensive
c. despairing

5. Though the judge did not like the choreography nor the costumes, she still gave the young performers ten points for musicality and dancing.

a. subjective
b. impartial
c. sincere

6. Heath always has something good to say about everyone in the office.

a. empathetic
b. optimistic
c. nostalgic

7. I feel like I'm going crazy—there's too much to do and no time to do it! Will this stress ever end?

a. dramatic
b. critical
c. informal

8. The greatest of all the women warriors among the tribes of Missouri lived among the Crows in the 1850s.

a. enthusiastic
b. hopeless
c. informative

9. I decided to take eighteeen hours this semester and I am unable to keep up. One teacher thinks his class is the most important and consequently gives homework every night. Does he think I'm just taking his course? I have five other courses, including one that requires the completion of two major projects.

a. doubtful
b. complaining
c. argumentative

10. The diet plans advertised on "paid television" make all kinds of claims: lose thirty pounds in two weeks, lose eight inches off your waist, and so forth. My roommate has signed up for one of them, but I am waiting to see how well she does on the plan she chose.

a. ironic
b. mocking
c. skeptical

Exercise 4. Decide on the tone in these short paragraphs. Then write the words (or phrases) that led you to the correct option.

1.   After a writer has completed the body paragraphs for the essay, the last step is to bring the essay to a close. In the body paragraphs several instances or explanations that showed the thesis to be valid were discussed and illuminated. The conclusion is the last paragraph of the essay where final opinions about the topic are given. At the end, readers are brought full circle, drawing them back by revisiting the original opinion.

The tone of the paragraph is

a. argumentative.
b. academic.
c. somber.

Words chosen by author to convey tone:_____

_____

2.   Like American women during World War II, Japanese women experienced the double-edge sword of being encouraged to work in industry, while cultural constraints went against the very idea of women working for wages. Japanese women were paid much less than their male counterparts. Food was scarce and Japanese women were haunted by continual hunger. In addition, the industrial work was hard, noisy, and dirty and many young women were kept in restrictive barracks near the factories.   -IEEEVM, 2008

Photo below: Courtesy of Library of Congress

Photo: Courtesy of National Archives and
Records Administration

The attitude of the author toward Japanese women during WWII is

a. optimistic.
b. objective.
c. sympathetic.

Words chosen by the author to convey attitude:_____

_____

3.   After drug dealing, trafficking-of-humans is tied with arms dealing as the second
largest criminal industry in the world—and is the fastest growing. Approximately 800,000
victims annually are trafficked across international borders. Human trafficking is a
form of modern-day slavery. Many victims of human trafficking are forced to work in
prostitution, but trafficking also occurs as labor exploitation (domestic servitude, restaurant
work, sweatshop factory work and migrant agricultural work). Traffickers use various
techniques to instill fear in victims. Some keep their victims under lock and key; however,
the more frequent practice is to use less obvious techniques such "confiscation of passport,"
"debt bondage," "isolation from the community," and/or "threat of violence toward victim's
family."   -U.S. Dept of Health & Human Services, 2008

What is the tone of the paragraph?

a. hopeless
b. nostalgic
c. resentful

Words chosen by author to convey tone:_____

_____

4.   Sven stood on the sidewalk, head hanging down. Other students leaving the school campus late either had cars or bicycles or would be picked up by their mothers. A teacher, Mrs. Wells, was leaving the faculty parking lot and saw Sven, and the forlorn expression on his unguarded face touched her heart. She drew up beside him. "Do you want a ride, Sven?"

The tone of the paragraph is

a. sarcastic.
b. apathetic.
c. compassionate.

Words chosen by author to convey tone:_____

_____

5.   They were jumping out of the water as they swam, like children playing in the sun. I felt happy watching them, and it seemed to me that they were happy, too. It was very exciting for me to see the dolphins so close but I had come to listen for something else. I put my head back into the water and held my breath again. A low-pitched sound, like a melody from the moon filled in the spaces between the sounds of the gentle waves breaking on the beach. Then, other, higher-pitched melodies and more low-pitched voices joined in. It was like listening to a symphony from space. The humpback whales were singing!
                                                                              -Zukav, p. 30

What is the tone of the passage?

a. tragic
b. uplifting
c. suspenseful

Words chosen by author to convey tone:_____

_____

Exercise 5. Choose five words from the list of Tone and Attitude Options above and create a sentence or scenario from your personal experience that describes that tone or attitude.

1._____

_____

2. _____

_____

3. _____

_____

4. _____

_____

5. _____

_____

A writer's style will vary according to his or her purposes. If s/he wants to entertain, then the style might be informal. If the author wants to inform and educate, then the style may be academic and formal. If the author wants to reach an elite audience, say a group of physicists, then the style best suited would be scientific. You may not see very many questions on an author's style on the Regents' Reading exam, but just in case you come across one, here are some terms to consider:

academic	factual	informal	indifferent	romantic
argumentative	formal	impersonal	humorous	riveting
biased	unbiased	chatty		

❧ AUTHOR'S PURPOSE

Obviously, this type of question asks the reader to determine why the author wrote the passage. The question stem will read: "The author's purpose is to . . ." or, more directly, "What is the author's purpose in writing the selection?" You will notice that Author's Purpose options are closely related to the options for Patterns of Organization discussed in the next section. That is because the author uses the optimal writing pattern to make his or her point.

OPTIONS FOR AUTHOR'S PURPOSE				
to amuse	to contrast	to educate	to illustrate	to report
to argue	to criticize	to entertain	to inform	to ridicule
to condemn	to define	to explain	to narrate	to shock
to compare	to describe	to expose	to persuade	to summarize

Exercise 6. Determine the author's purpose in the short paragraphs. Circle the correct answer.

1.   Boys do better with visual problems and interpreting visual information when it is presented to their left eye—the one that feeds the right hemisphere that specializes in spatial relationships. Girls do equally well with visual information no matter which eye it's presented to. Even in infancy, boys gaze at their mothers one half the amount of time girls do. Often mothers feel they are doing something wrong with their boys, or feel unloved because the boy doesn't seem to attend to their face for as prolonged a period of time. The real reason for his quick visual fix lies in his brain's need to move quickly from object to object in space.   -Gurian, p. 17

The author's purpose in writing the selection is to

a. contrast.
b. illustrate.
c. ridicule.

What clues did you use to arrive at your answer?_____

2.   It was late afternoon on a July day in the fourth year of the Great Rebellion. The sun was hot; the grass banks were brown; and the petals of the pansies were peppered with fine dust. A small party—two men and two women—trudged slowly along the road, their eyes fixed on the ground. One of the women was a hunchback, and it was this deformed one who carried a sleeping child. Sweat ran down her face; she wiped the sweat from her face and sat. She was silent, listening to the sound of footsteps on the road. A man and a woman came into sight, and the hunchback's eyes went to the sleeping child beside her; her right hand moved out and rested on its ragged clothes.   -Plaidy, pp. 11-12

The author's purpose in writing this excerpt is to

a. amuse.
b. explain.
c. describe.

What clues did you use to arrive at your answer?_____

3.   Anger is something we feel. It exists for a reason and always deserves our attention. We all have a right to everything we feel—and certainly our anger is no exception. There is, however, another side of the coin: If *feeling* angry signals a problem, *venting* anger does not solve it. Venting anger may serve to maintain the old rules and patterns in a relationship, thus ensuring that change does not occur. When emotional intensity is high, many of us engage in nonproductive efforts to change the other person, and in so doing, fail to exercise our power to change our own selves. Low self-esteem is inevitable when:

      -we fight but continue to submit to unfair circumstances;

      -we complain but live in a way that betrays our hopes; or

      -we find ourselves fulfilling society's stereotype of the bitter or destructive

        man or woman.   -Lerner, p. 4-5

The author's purpose is to

a. explain and inform.
b. narrate and describe.
c. shock and ridicule.

What clues did you use to arrive at your answer?_____

4.   Thirty-seven million Americans live in poverty. Through AmeriCorps, you can make a tangible difference. And, you'll find fulfillment using your knowledge and skills to help those in disadvantaged circumstances turn their dream into reality. AmeriCorps is the national service program designed specifically to fight poverty. Americorps volunteers commit to serve at a nonprofit organization or local government agency, working to fight illiteracy and strengthen community groups, and so forth. By serving through AmeriCorps, you'll gain new skills, friends, and experiences—plus you'll have the satisfaction that comes from helping others. Upon completing your service, you can choose to receive an education award worth $4,725 to pay for college, or $1,200 in cash. Learn more about AmeriCorps on-line.   -AmeriCorps, 2008

What is the author's purpose in writing the selection?

a. to report
b. to persuade
c. to summarize

What clues did you use to arrive at your answer?_____

❧ AUTHOR'S PATTERNS OF ORGANIZATION

To communicate their ideas, their stances on issues, and/or their general beliefs, writers produce written material which is related to and appropriate for their purpose. As stated, the Author's Purpose is closely related to the Author's Patterns of Organization. Patterns of Organization refer to the types of passages (or paragraphs) the author chooses to write to get his or her point across. It is a good idea to familiarize yourself with the types of passages you will encounter on the Regents' Reading Exam. Some of these types may seem familiar to you; that is because they, in some ways, parallel the context clues we previously discussed. Basically, there are ten kinds of patterns of organization you will find on the exam.

DESCRIPTION

Usually this type of paragraph presents information (in graphic detail) about an object, person, scene, scenario, or situation by infusing the paragraph with adjectives. Choice of words and phrases impact how well the author portrays the subject. For example, think of the difference between the words, *mad* and *ballistic* in describing someone who just found out that his new car was dented.

A more graphic, detailed description can always be generated just by using more imaginative words or phrases: *enraged, livid, furious, up in arms, beside himself, fuming, infuriated, exasperated.* The writer may also evoke a few of the five senses (touch, taste, smell, hearing, sight). Sounds, colors, tastes, textures, or aromas will enhance the feeling or atmosphere the writer is trying to relate. The author's ultimate goal is to reproduce an image that will elicit a response in the reader.

Example: Had he been a poisonous snake, I would have stepped on him. He stood so quietly among the trees as almost to have been one of them, and I did not see him until a grimy hand shot out and gripped me by the arm. Its companion clapped over my mouth as I was dragged backward into the oak grove, thrashing wildly in panic. My silent captor, whoever he was, seemed not much taller than I, but rather noticeably strong in the forearms. I smelled a faint scent, as of lavender, and something spicier. As the leaves whipped back into place in the path of our passage, I noticed something familiar about the hand and forearm clasped about my waist.

"Frank!" I burst out. "What in heaven's name are you playing at?"

-Gabaldon, pp. 36-37

Can you point out the adjectives used in this paragraph?
Can you determine the senses evoked and point to the words or phrases which evoke them?

PERSUASION

The purpose of a persuasive passage is to move the reader toward the author's opinion about an issue. To convince the reader, however, the author must present solid arguments and evidence in his or her favor. Because of the necessity to impress the reader, writers will draw on strong language and will most likely offer only one opinion considered to be "right" (the author's). The author will "stack the cards" in his or her favor and will probably not refer to any arguments which would be contrary to the stated position.

> *Example*: Polar bears main habitat is sea ice. They need that ice as a platform for hunting, for travel to denning areas to give birth, and for mating. As their sea ice melts and their food sources decline, polar bears are forced to swim further and further to ever-distant ice floes. During these extremely arduous swims, polar bears are increasingly drowning. And scientists predict that as the movement of sea ice increases, some bears will lose contact with a main body of ice and drift into unsuitable habitat, making it impossible to return. After a three-year legal battle waged by NRDC, the Center for Biological Diversity, and Greenpeace, new protection marks a step forward; however, the new plan is full of loopholes for oil companies and other global warming polluters that will leave the bear vulnerable to extinction. You can help by urging the current administration to give the polar bear full-fledged protection as an endangered species. -NRDC, 2008

How does the author persuade the reader to consider his opinion (i.e., what are his arguments)? What are some of the "strong" words that he uses in this excerpt?

COMPARISON-CONTRAST

Comparative/contrastive writing involves at least two subjects. While comparative writing focuses on the *similarities* of persons, places, issues, situations, and so forth, contrastive writing emphasizes the *differences*. Passages of these types are easily recognizable because several key indicators (signal words/phrases) will more than likely be present:

INDICATORS OF COMPARISON

like   likewise   both   in addition   similar   same   in the same way   analogous

---

Example: Like a few celebrities of the past, some of today's celebrities have become involved in politics by supporting specific candidates for the presidency. In the 1940s, actor Humphrey Bogart stumped for President Franklin D. Roosevelt. Abcnews.go.com reports that in 1972 superstar Warren Beatty organized celebrities for Democratic presidential candidate George McGovern. Likewise, according to the CNN Political Ticker, in 2007, actors Tom Hanks, Tobey McGuire, and Ben Stiller gave to Hillary Clinton's campaign for the Democratic nomination for president, and her opponent Barack Obama received monies from actors such as Jamie Foxx, Jodie Foster, and Will Smith.   -based on ABC &CNN

What/Who is being compared? _____

What are the signal words that let you know that the paragraph is one of comparison?

_____

INDICATORS OF CONTRAST

although	*differ*	*on the other hand*
but	*different*	*opposite*
in contrast	*however*	*parallel*
comparable	*more than*	*though*
conversely	*on the contrary*	*unlike*

more, better, worse, worst   words with the suffix *–er, -est*

Example: The lowest temperature ever recorded in the United States was -80° F on January 23, 1971 at Prospect Creek Camp located along the Alaska pipeline. In contrast, North America's highest temperature ever recorded was 134° F which occurred in Death valley, California on July 10, 1913.   -Osborn, 2008

What is being contrasted? _____

NARRATION

One distinguishing feature of a narrative passage is that the reader has a distinct feeling a story is being told—that quite a bit of action (or a significant event) is taking place. The writer's purpose is to tell a story, hopefully engaging readers so that they want to know "what happens next" to the characters. Another way to identify a narrative selection is to look for dialogue (designated, of course, by quotation marks).

Example: "Rumon cleared his throat, and Merewyn turned around. She got up and looked at him quietly, startled by the changes in him.

"Good day, Merewyn," he said smiling and with constraint. "I am distressed to hear of the reason for your journey—the death of the Abbess—may she rest in heavenly peace."

"Thank you," said the girl in a small voice. She noticed the constraint, and that after the first moment Rumon looked beyond her. So he was *not* glad to see her; there was still the barrier he always kept up. Nothing had changed.

But it had, and Merewyn's interpretations were wrong. Rumon, suddenly, and to his dismay, found the girl appealing, and realized that he had never forgotten her, despite the years of silence. For he had dreamed of her several times—dreams of tenderness and companionship. Preposterous!

"You wanted to see me?" he asked abruptly. Come, we can sit on the bench near the kitchen; it's not forbidden to women. How long do you intend staying in Glaston?" He asked.

She stiffened. "I believe I shall leave tomorrow."

"So *soon*?" he cried involuntarily, dismayed to find that he did not want her to go. He added quickly, "I mean you won't have time to see the place properly—and you really should climb the Tor. The moon's nearly full tonight. I'll guide you up The Tor after dinner if you like. The place has a particular feeling at night—one can see the Isle of Avalon as it used to be."

"It is not here anymore, is it? Avalon?" said Merewyn, puzzled by Rumon's sudden offer—uncertain what to say.   -Seton, pp. 217-218

How do you know this paragraph is narrative text?_____

What is the most obvious clue?_____

Why would the reader be interested in these two characters?_____

_____

DEFINITION

Within a definition paragraph or passage, the reader will encounter straightforward information and a repetition of the word or concept being defined. In addition, verb forms of *to be, to include, to comprise*, etc., are used. Also, examples may be incorporated in the selection to clarify the definition, and the style of writing is more objective than in other types of passages. Here are some signal words and indicators to look for when reading:

SIGNAL WORDS AND INDICATORS OF DEFINITION

comprise   include   contain   consist of   encompass   have
forms of the verb *to be* repetition of the topic word or pronoun

[Note: In the following example the repetition of the concepts being defined are in bold lettering. Notice how many times the defined words or their referent pronouns are repeated.]

Example: **Booby traps and IEDs** (Improvised Explosive Devices) are similar to landmines in that **they** are designed to kill or incapacitate soldiers. **They** are placed to avoid detection. The use of **booby traps and IEDs** is limited only by the imagination of the adversary. The enemy will watch reactions and procedures of soldiers when they move through an area. In Vietnam, the enemy noticed that American soldiers liked to kick empty soda cans that were lying on the ground. It was not long before the U.S. troops found that the enemy was leaving explosive devices in empty cans that were activated when the cans were kicked. Though many **booby traps and IEDs** are victim-activated devices, **some** may involve remote detonators. **They** are intended to create terror and may or may not encompass areas of tactical significance.   -globalsecurity.org

What is being defined?_____

What are the signal words and indicators?_____

What is the example (that helps the reader understand what an IED is) incorporated into the paragraph?

_____

EXAMPLE

In the section on context clues, you were instructed that the definition of an unknown word may be deduced by examples given as clues. In a passage, one example or a few examples may be given to illustrate the author's idea. The author will usually state a main idea, then use examples as support for his or her argument. To recognize a passage or paragraph that has Example as its overriding pattern of organization, look for these words:

SIGNAL WORDS OF EXAMPLE		
another	*example*	*illustration*
as	*for example*	*including*
depict	*for instance*	*like*
elaborate	*illustrate*	*represent*
such as		

Example: College athletes who are reprimanded and sometimes expelled from the university for receiving money to play sports is not a recent phenomenon. For example, in 1915 the University of Michigan barred Sheehy and Maltby from further participation on the Wolverine baseball team: "the two men were found guilty of having played baseball for money and under assumed names, with independent teams." (*NY Times*, June 18, 1915). Another instance was in 1992 when Eric Ramsey, defensive back for Auburn, paid-for-play which cost Coach Pat Dye his job. Further, in 1999 Peter Warrick of Florida State University was arrested at Dillard's department store after purchasing $412.38 of clothing for only $21.40. Warrick was Florida State's "star receiver."   -based on Lichtig & *NY Times*

What signal words alert you to the fact that this is an Example paragraph? Can you name the examples given?

CAUSE AND EFFECT

Cause and effect passages follow a rationale/consequence paradigm. "Why something happened" (the causes, the reasons) and "what happened as a result" (the consequences) are the focus of this type of passage.

SIGNAL WORDS AND PHRASES OF CAUSE AND EFFECT		
as a result	*for this reason*	*since*
because	*hence*	*so*
consequently	*resulting*	*therefore*
if . . . then	*first . . .subsequently*	*when . . .then*

Example: On two nights in 1980, just after Christmas, strange lights were seen in Rendlesham Forest, England, adjacent to the Royal Air Force Bentwaters and Woodbridge airbases. The twin-base complex was operated by the American military as part of NATO's front-line defenses. On both occasions, American personnel left the base to investigate the mysterious lights in the belief that an aircraft might have crashed. Disoriented and puzzled, they gave their testimony sometime afterwards. As a result, their testimony contributed to a widespread belief that the airmen had a close encounter with a UFO.

-Easton, 2001

Can you name the cause that led to the result? _____

What is the result? _____

What is the signal word/phrase?_____

CHRONOLOGY

All through your school years, you have read material that is organized through chronology. The material in history textbooks is a good example of how reading material is organized chronologically. You can easily remember that a passage is chronological if you think in terms of a timeline. Dates and times will be apparent throughout the selection. Or, the selection might be arranged by years, ages, or eras. Biographies are good examples of chronological writing because they usually start with the person's birth and end at their death. When a selection is organized through chronology, in addition to dates and times, you will find time words such as *first, last,* or *on, after, until,* and so forth. The following is a list of time words to look for while reading the exam:

first	*last*	*next*	*following*	*when*
as soon as	*once*	*before*	*after*	*by the time*
by	*at*	*on*	*in*	*throughout*
until	*by*	*as late as*	*as early as*	
any dates, times, eras, years, epochs, centuries, decades				

See if you can circle time words in the following example of a chronological passage:

By the turn of the century (1900) two-thirds of the nation's factory workers were immigrants (mostly European), welcomed by the efficiency-minded business men who were hostile to the labor unions. There was a growing momentum among organized labor for policies favoring immigration restriction. As early as 1902 the AFL membership voted for a literacy test for incoming foreigners, but it did not pass. Samuel Gompers expressed the prevailing view that "cheap labor, immigrant labor takes our jobs and cuts our wages." In 1907 the Dillingham Commission was appointed by Congress to investigate the impact of immigration on American society. The result was a 47-volume report that suggested foreigners brought with them social contamination. After many presidential vetoes, this spiteful campaign against immigrant culminated in the congressional enactment of the literacy test in 1917.

-Solberg, p. 230

Immigrants at Ellis Island in the early 1900s wait to have a physical examination. Doctors and inspectors decided who was healthy enough to be allowed to stay in the United States. Photo courtesy of Library of Congress

STATISTICS AND FACTS

Knowledge and information based on real occurrences are facts. Also, information based on repeated experiments that result in the same finding is factual. That is, a fact is not only something believed to be true or real but it is something that can be proved if tested. In our language we have many words and phrases that indicate that we consider facts important: *as a matter of fact, a fact of life, in point of fact, fact-based statement.* Once again, as with chronological writing, you have been exposed to fact-based writing throughout your lives, especially since being introduced to science while in elementary school—you already have a familiarity with facts and statistics. Also, your history text books present facts: "John F. Kennedy was assassinated November 22, 1963 in Dallas" is a fact that can be proved because so many people witnessed it and it is recorded on tape.

If you encounter a passage that is full of factual information, numbers, and names, then the writer is attempting to get his/her point across through the organizational pattern of Statistics and Facts. Below is a sample of such a passage:

A flash flood occurred on August 17, 1954 in northern Iran where total annual precipitation varies a great deal but hardly ever exceeds about 8 inches. A severe thunderstorm near the town of Farahzad soaked the south-facing slopes of the Elburz Mountains. A deluge of water rushed into the valley and converged on the Moslem shrine of Imamzadeh Davoud. A wall of water, estimated at 90 feet in height, overwhelmed a large number of pilgrims killing about 1,000 people.

-Ebert, p. 83

1. Underline the facts in the selection above: names, dates, and numbers.

2. How many facts are in this brief paragraph?_____

CLASSIFICATION

Classifying is a way of grouping or arranging people or things into categories—an orderly and systematic grouping according to established criteria. For example, you can classify departments at universities into groups/types: *the sciences, liberal arts, business, education, recreation.* These general classifications could then be broken down even further: *sciences* into biology, chemistry, astronomy; *liberal arts* into art, music, theater; *business* into management, accounting, international business; *education* into early childhood education, secondary education, higher education; *recreation* into sport management, leisure, and so forth. So, in a Regents' Reading passage that focuses on classification, you will be given a broad subject (such as university departments); then, subcategories of the broad subject will follow. Classification is a pattern often applied to scientific writing and you probably encountered it in your high school textbooks. Consider the following sample paragraph:

Based on linguistic and genetic information research, it has been proposed that the peopling of the Americas was the result of two or three migrations from Siberia. Linguists have classified the Native American languages into three groupings:

-*Amerind.* The language spoken by the native populations of North and South America

-*Na-Dene.* The language spoken by people who lived on the northwest coast of Canada and the United States

-*Eskimo/Aleut.* Includes languages spoken by the Eskimos and Aleutian Islanders living in Alaska, Greenland, and parts of Siberia.

-Frisancho, p. 188

What is being classified? _____

What are the classifications?_____

REMEMBER: *Since many of these patterns of organization seem to overlap, you may think that two options are correct (for example, description and narration). In almost all cases on the Regents' Reading Test, the choice should be clear. If not, always choose the option which is the **overriding pattern of organization***

Exercise 7. You are to decide what pattern of organization the author is using to get her/his point across. Read the selection, then write the correct pattern. Then, write the key words/ phrases and clues that led you to your answer. The ten patterns of organization are repeated here for you. There are nine paragraphs. Circle the pattern that remains after you have finished your work.

DESCRIPTION	**STATISTICS AND FACTS**	**DEFINITION**
PERSUASION	**EXAMPLE**	**CAUSE-EFFECT**
CHRONOLOGY	**NARRATION**	**CONTRAST**
CLASSIFICATION		

1.   One image of the American family is that it offers a safe haven in a dangerous world. This romantic image is countered by the amount of family violence that occurs in the United States each year. This violence is often called domestic violence. Domestic violence occurs between members of a family. There are basically three types.

Spousal abuse involves husbands and wives. A husband or lover beats his wife or girlfriend every 15 seconds, and 30 percent involves severe beatings.

Child abuse involves parents and their children. A majority of parents use some type of physical violence on their children. The younger the child, the more likely he or she is going to get hit or spanked.

Recently there has been a chilling addition to this list. It involves *elderly abuse*. Abuse toward the elderly by family members or those entrusted with their care is more prevalent than previously thought. Trying to take care of a spouse with a disease such as Alzheimer's can be exceptionally frustrating, especially for those who are not properly prepared, and that anger can result in elderly abuse.

-MacDonald, p. 243

What pattern of organization does the author use to get his point across?_____

_____

Key words/phrases/clues:_____

2.   The best evidence shows that as early as the year 1000AD the Norsemen in their finely crafted Viking ships successfully crossed the Atlantic Ocean and became the first white inhabitants of the Western Hemisphere. Their settlement, called Vinland, located on the northern tip of Newfoundland, lasted for at least three years. The gradual failure of this early experiment in New World living was caused by a number of factors, including the climate, hostiles, and the lack of gunpowder.

-Solberg, p. 2-3

What pattern of organization does the author use to get his point across?_____

_____

Key words/phrases/clues:_____

3.   Because of his youthful looks, many people are surprised to find out that Senator Barack Obama is 45 years old. Laying aside for the moment the fact that John F. Kennedy was younger than that when he was sworn in, by what standard is 45 "too young"? In the business world, that is an age when junior executives become senior management. In the athletic world, by the time you are 45 you are either preparing for your graceful retirement or you are totally washed up.

-Mobtown Blues, 2007

What pattern of organization does the author use to get his point across?

_____

Key words/phrases/clues:_____

4.   A hurricane is a tropical low-pressure storm. Hurricanes may have a
       diameter of 400 miles, a calm center (the eye), and they must have wind velocities
       higher than 75 mph. Some hurricanes attain wind velocities of 200 mph. –Ebert, p. 337

What pattern of organization does the author use to get his point across?

_____

Key words/phrases/clues:_____

5.   Inverlochy Castle is an imposing grey stone mansion built in the 1860s and
       embellished with towers. Inside it displays the grandeur and elegance of a small
       palace. The Great Hall has immensely high painted ceilings, the dining room glitters
       with silver, and the pool room is hung with an impressive collection of trophies of
       the hunt.   -Arnold, p. 33

What pattern of organization does the author use to get her point across?

_____

Key words/phrases/clues:_____

6.   For her birthday, Amanda's father gave her a performing bear. The bear
       understood only Russian while Amanda spoke only English. There could be no
       performance. What to do?
             Amanda made friends with the bear. She baked delicious meat loaves
       for him. She scratched his ears and fed him oranges, Oreo cream sandwiches
       and Dr. Pepper. Gradually, the bear began to do tricks on his own. He danced
       when Amanda played her concertina, he rode her silver bicycle, he balanced balls
       on his nose and smoked fine cigars.   -Robbins, p. 5

What pattern of organization does the author use to get his point across?

_____

Key words/phrases/clues:_____

7.   As president, Harding was not even master of his own administration.
Three of his cabinet members were convicted in the Teapot Dome Scandal of
1923 for taking bribes from oilmen who wanted access to federal oil reserves.
Attracted to dishonest friends, poker, bootleg whiskey, and a mistress, Harding
contributed to the decline of the power and prestige of the presidency, although
his warmth and good looks kept him popular.
          When President Harding died unexpectedly, his vice president Calvin
Coolidge took the oath of office. Unlike Harding "Quiet Cal" cleaned up the
administration. Coolidge sought and succeeded in making his administration
respectable and stable.   -Solberg, p. 195

What pattern of organization does the author use to get his point across?

_____

Key words/phrases/clues:_____

8.   Comparable pay asserts that persons should be paid based upon their relative
worth, but comparable pay is not always implemented. The simplest example is
when men and women hold the same job with the same amount of seniority but are
not paid equally.
          Other indicators illustrate this well. In the United States, the earnings of
women are still less than 80 cents for every dollar that is earned by men. Some of
this inequality exists because of past discrimination that prevented women from
entering and advancing in many careers.
          This preference for men means that even today, after some changes have been
made, more men still have better paying jobs and are in senior positions that pay the
most money in corporations.
          Problems get even worse when one looks at how opportunity differences steer
men and women into different jobs. Consider the case in point that some academic
disciplines within universities, such as engineering, medicine, and science, are top-
heavy with men. Others such as English give greater access to women. Guess which
faculty gets paid the most?   -MacDonald, p. 221

What pattern of organization does the author use to get his point across?

_____

Key words/phrases/clues:_____

9.   Although Columbus's encounter with America had been preceded by that of other voyagers (he had Arab maps prior to his voyage of 1492), the excitement generated by his discovery led to a much broader interest in transAtlantic exploration. Until the sixteenth century, the Mediterranean Sea had been the hub of western civilization, the nerve center that connected its various peoples. After Columbus returned to the courts of Spain with the news of the New World's wealth, control of the Atlantic and what lay beyond became a prerequisite for global power for future endeavors.   -Solberg, pp. 4-5

What pattern of organization does the author use to get his point across?

_____

Key words/phrases/clues:_____

Internet Activity

Go to the Internet and select a brief article of your choice. Determine the following about the article:

1. Author's tone and attitude
2. Author's purpose
3. Author's pattern of organization overall
4. Author's pattern of organization for particular paragraphs

Now, go to your Vocabulary Journal and add any words from this chapter in addition to any words from your article that were unfamiliar to you.

To practice Analysis questions on a simulated Regents' Reading Exam, go to Exam Four.

❧ Chapter Six ❧

Reading Rate

Although no studies have been completed on reading rates for this exam or what the reading rate should be to finish the exam, instructors familiar with this test can give you good information about timing yourselves. If you did not finish the exam or felt rushed during the exam, it could have been because: 1) you read too slowly; 2) you did not keep track of time; 3) you skipped around and did not allow enough time to go back to unanswered items; 4) you spent too much time on one passage or on one question; 5) you read the questions before reading the passage, tried to skim for the answers, but you could not find them easily and had to go back and read the passage.

Consider the following to see if any of these ideas will help you:

1. It is a good idea for students to know how fast they are reading. Remember, you have been reading for many years now and probably at the same rate. It may be time for a change. Use the timed readings in this chapter to determine your rate. According to what has been stated about different reading rates for particular skills, it is reasonable to state that students should be reading about 200–250 words per minute. This rate should facilitate comprehension as well as insure that the student finishes the test. (*Note*: reading at 150 words per minute will probably not allow enough time to finish the test.) If you still feel that you need to improve your rate after completing this textbook, consider buying a book of timed readings or ask your reading instructor if s/he has any you could borrow.
2. If you are vocalizing while reading silently, you need to know that this habit will slow you down. "Vocalization" can be described as that little voice in your head that "says" the words as you read. To counter this habit, try "chunking," (i.e., reading words in groups instead of word-for-word). There are natural breaks in language; you are familiar with them because you use them when speaking. When reading, punctuation marks and word groupings (e.g., prepositional phrases) will determine some of the chunks, while your eye fixations and mental acuity will determine others.

For example, **instead of reading this way,**

On   April   19   2005   the   Department   of   Homeland

Security   Office   issued   a   report   that   indicated   no

improvement   in   effectiveness   in   screening   passengers   or

baggage.

Try reading in chunks,

On April 19, 2005   the Department of Homeland Security Office   issued a

report   that indicated   no improvement in effectiveness   in screening

passengers or baggage.

Looking at these two methods of reading, you can see how the second one is more efficient. Any time you can save (without sacrificing good comprehension) is especially helpful on a test like the Regents' Reading Exam.

3. Though we practiced scanning exercises in a previous chapter, it must be repeated that scanning is *not* the first strategy to use when encountering a passage. When reading a selection for the first time, you should read at your regular rate. Your scanning skills will aid you tremendously after you have read the passage and are going back to scan for specific answers to questions. Remember what was discussed in the Overview in Chapter One. It is better not to read the questions before you read the passage. If you read the questions first the last time you took the test, then you already know that strategy did not work for you. Two negative consequences could occur from reading the questions before reading the selection: one, you could read the question wrong which will "color" how you read the passage; and two, you could obsess on one question and not absorb other critical information in the passage. Therefore, read the passage first as quickly as you can while concentrating, then look at the questions.

4. Since losing your place and having to re-read material takes up precious time, practice using a pencil as a "pacer." You can practice pacing yourself by beginning with a 3 x 5 index card. Slide the index card down the page as you read. This will keep you on track and help you concentrate. Soon you will notice that the index card is slowing you down, and you can switch to your pencil. You will also improve your ability to read smoothly.

5. As your rate increases and you are able to maintain 70% or higher on the comprehension questions, you are preparing yourself for success on the Regents' Reading Exam. Find and add other timed readings to your progress chart (found at the end of the chapter) and use the chart not only for recording your timed readings but also as a motivational tool.

Directions for Timed Readings

Do not worry about reading to memorize every word of the passage. Just read at your regular pace and get the main points of the selection, retaining as much as you can.

Step 1. Tear out only the page with the passage you will be reading and place it face-down on your desk. Put your textbook under your desk. Wait for the instructor to begin the timed reading.

Step 2. Your teacher will time you and record times (in 10-second increments) on the blackboard. You may want to circle or underline information as you read. When you finish reading, look up at the blackboard and write the last time you see in the space at the bottom of your page. This is the number of minutes and seconds it took you to read the passage.

Step 3. Put your passage under your desk. *Because this is a traditional timed reading test, you may not look back at the passage while answering the comprehension questions.*

Step 4. Now look in your text and tear out the page that has the appropriate comprehension questions for the passage. Answer them to the best of your ability.

Step 5. Grade your test. Write your comprehension score on the passage page.

Step 6. Go to the Conversion Table at the end of the chapter and convert the time you recorded to Words Per Minute. Write down the Words Per Minute at the bottom of your passage page.

General Guidelines for Timed Readings

If you read:

A. *over 250 WPM*
   score: 80+

   Tip: you may read at a *slower* rate.

B. *over 250 WPM*
   score: below 70

   Tip: *slow down.*

C. *under 200 WPM*
   score: 80+

   Tip: read at a *faster rate*.

D. *under 200 WPM*
   score: below 70

> **Tip**: concentrate on the skills covered in the chapters of this book while gradually pushing yourself to read faster

TIMED READING TESTS

TIMED READINGS: PASSAGE ONE

Nearly a century after his execution, John Brown remains one of the most fiercely debated figures in American history. Was he a bloodthirsty vigilante and terrorist? Or was he one of the great heroes of American history, a freedom fighter for the cause of human liberty?

Born in rural Connecticut in 1800 to a deeply religious family, Brown grew up in Ohio's staunchly antislavery Western Reserve. He had little formal education and his personal life was filled with misfortune. He lost his mother when he was eight and his first wife died in childbirth. Of his twenty offspring, only eleven survived childhood. His business life was marked by failure. Still, at a time when white supremacy was the norm, Brown was one of a handful of white Americans who could interact with blacks on a level of equality.

Among the key issues raised by Brown's life is why he alone among leading Northern abolitionists chose violence as the way to end slavery: in 1856 John Brown, with four of his sons and three others, dragged five unarmed, pro-slavery men and boys from their homes along Kansas's Pottawatomie Creek, and hacked and dismembered their bodies as if they were cattle being butchered in a stockyard. Perhaps the answer lies in Brown's intense religiosity, which was rooted in the "New Divinity" of rural New England, a religion harshly critical of the pursuit of profit. To many proponents of the New Divinity, slavery represented society's obsession with materialism.

On the one hand, there are those who argue that Brown was little more than a murderer; but on the other hand, there are those who view Brown as an idealist and a genuine revolutionary who envisioned an America free of racial prejudice.

-Mintz, 2005

MY TIME: _____

WORDS PER MINUTE_____

COMPREHENSION SCORE_____

TIMED READINGS: PASSAGE ONE

TIMED READINGS: PASSAGE TWO

I'm the last of our crew to walk through Alex's front door. There is very little in this neighborhood that I haven't seen, but I'm completely unprepared for the large strip of duct tape running down the middle of the front hall.

According to New York State law, if one spouse moves out the other can claim abandonment and will most likely get the apartment. Some of these places go for fifteen to twenty million, forcing years of bitter cohabitation while each spouse tries to wear down the other by, for example, bringing in their exercise instructor to live.

"Okay, now you boys can play anywhere on *that* side, Murnel says, gesturing to the left side of the apartment.

"Nanny, why is there a stripe—" I fix Grayer with a quick Look of Death as I unbuckle his stroller and then wait until Alex is behind me to raise my finger to my lips and point to the tape.

"Alex's mommy and daddy are playing a game," I whisper. "We'll talk about it at home."

"My dad's not sharing," Alex announces.

"Now who wants grilled cheese?" Murnel says as the boys run off. She turns toward the kitchen. "Make yourself at home," she says, rolling her eyes at the tape. I wander into the living room and sit down on what I hope is the neutral territory of the couch. I become aware of a little nose resting on the arm of the couch. "Hey," I quietly acknowledge the nose.

"Hey," he replies, coming around the couch to slump face down onto the cushion next to me, his arms outstretched.

"What's the story?" I ask.
-Kraus & Mclaughlin, pp. 48-49

MY TIME: _____

WORDS PER MINUTE_____

COMPREHENSION SCORE_____

TIMED READINGS: PASSAGE TWO

TIMED READINGS: PASSAGE THREE

-New York Times MARCH 26, 1911. Nothing like it has been seen in New York since the burning of the General Slocum. The fire was practically over in half an hour. Three stories of a ten-floor building at the corner of Greene Street and Washington Place were burned yesterday. The building was fireproof; it now shows hardly any signs of the disaster that overtook it. But while the fire was going on, 141 young men and women (at least 125 of them mere girls) were burned to death or killed by jumping to the pavement below.

The victims now lying at the Morgue, were mostly girls from 16 to 23 years of age—mostly Italians, Russians, Hungarians, and Germans. They were employed making shirtwaist by the Triangle Waist Company. Most of them could barely speak English. Many of them came from Brooklyn, and almost all were the main support of their hard-working families.

A heap of corpses lay on the sidewalk for more than an hour. The firemen were too busy dealing with the fire to pay any attention to people whom they supposed beyond their aid. When the excitement had subsided to such an extent that some of the firemen and policemen could pay attention to this mass of the supposedly dead, they found about half way down in the pack a girl who was still breathing. She died two minutes after she was found.

The owners were in the building, but they escaped. They carried with them one of the owner's children and a governess, and they fled over the roofs. Their employees did not know the way, because they had been in the habit of using the two freight elevators, and one of these elevators was not in service when the fire broke out.

MY TIME: _____

WORDS PER MINUTE _____

COMPREHENSION SCORE _____

TIMED READINGS: PASSAGE THREE

TIMED READINGS: PASSAGE FOUR

Each tornado has its own characteristics; yet, most of them form behind the so-called *wall cloud*, that is, behind the usually heavy rain that pours out of the leading sector of the thundercloud. This veil of rain explains why most tornadoes are undetectable during their initial phase of development. They usually start as a short funnel-shape beneath the thunderstorm about 600 feet above the earth's surface. The early tornado may appear as a rotating whitish cloud. As it works itself downward, it may become temporarily invisible, and upon touching the earth's surface, the vortex sucks up dust and debris, and attains its well-known ominous black funnel appearance.

The two most fear-inspiring features of a tornado are its roaring noise, likened to hundreds of freight trains, and the threatening black, twisting funnel cloud, or vortex, extending from the parent cloud. Sometimes a series of two or more tornadoes form from the same cloud.

The total destruction often caused by tornadoes is the result of their extremely high winds, and the partial vacuum that exists within the vortex. The short life span, the unpredictable location within a storm system, and the violence within the tornado itself usually prevents the direct use of instruments to measure accurate wind speeds and pressure conditions. Estimates, based on engineering studies of tornado damage, indicate that horizontal wind speeds in the vortex may be higher than 300 mph.

The power of a tornado is illustrated by the fact that, according to U.S. Weather Service records, 2 x 4 wooden boards have been driven into and through brick walls. Another example of the power of a tornado is the 1975 Mississippi tornado that carried a home freezer for a distance of over a mile. In addition, a railroad car, weighing 83 tons, was lifted off its tracks.

-Ebert, pp. 107-109

MY TIME: _____

WORDS PER MINUTE_____

COMPREHENSION SCORE_____

TIMED READINGS: PASSAGE FOUR

TIMED READINGS: PASSAGE FIVE

Counting the number of cells in the human body is no easier than counting the number of people in the world, but the accepted estimate is 50 trillion. Placed under a microscope, the various kinds of cells—heart, liver, brain, kidney—look rather alike to the untrained eye. A cell is basically a bag, enclosed by an outer membrane, the cell wall, and filled with a mixture of water and swirling chemicals. At the center is a core, the nucleus, which safeguards the tightly twisted coils of DNA. If you hold a speck of liver tissue on your fingertip, it looks like calf's liver; you would be hard-pressed to discern that it is specifically human. Even a skilled geneticist would detect only a two percent difference between our DNA and a gorilla's.

As clouded as the mind-body issue has become, one thing is indisputable: somehow human cells have evolved to a state of intelligence. When a blood cell rushes to a wound site and begins to form a clot, it has not traveled there at random. It actually knows where to go and what to do when it gets there, as surely as a paramedic—in fact, more surely, since it acts completely spontaneously and without guesswork.

At any one time, the number of activities being coordinated in our bodies is quite literally infinite. Our physiology appears to operate in separate compartments that are invisibly connected: we eat, breath, talk, think, digest our food, fight off infections, purify our blood of toxins, renew our cells, discard wastes, vote for Republicans, and much more.

Our ecology is more planetlike than most people realize. Creatures roam our surface, as unmindful of our hugeness as we are of their tininess. Colonies of mites, for example, spend their entire life cycle in our eyelashes.

-Chopra, pp. 39-40

MY TIME: _____

WORDS PER MINUTE_____

COMPREHENSION SCORE_____

TIMED READINGS: PASSAGE FIVE

TIMED READINGS: PASSAGE SIX

Maybe the Surgeon General hasn't determined it yet, but staying in a bad relationship may be dangerous to your health. It can shake your self-esteem as surely as smoking can damage your lungs. When people say that their relationship with their partner is killing them, it may not be out of the realm of possibility. The chemical changes caused by stress can throw any of your organ systems out of kilter, can drain your energy, and lower your resistance to all manner of unfriendly bugs. And often it can drive one to the overuse of unhealthy escapes.

But even if there were no threat to your health, staying too long in a relationship that is deadening can cloud your life with frustration, anger, emptiness, and despair. You may have tried to improve it, but you have found that your efforts have been futile—nothing worked. You are certainly not alone. Many basically rational people find that they are unable to leave an unhealthy relationship. Their best judgment tells them to end it, but often, to their dismay, they hang on. Friends may have pointed out to them that in reality their "prison door" is wide open and that all they need do is step outside. Some approach the threshold, then hesitate. Some may make brief sallies outside, but quickly retreat to the safety of prison in relief and despair. People, in droves, choose to remain in their prisons, making no effort to change them—except, perhaps, to hang pretty curtains over the bars and paint the walls in decorator colors. This book is offered as a guide to those who are stuck in bad relationships and wish they were not. I will try to unravel the puzzle of what it is that makes people stay in such relationships. And, I will try to show them the way out.

-Halpern, pp. vii-2

MY TIME: _____

WORDS PER MINUTE_____

COMPREHENSION SCORE_____

TIMED READINGS: PASSAGE SIX

TIMED READINGS: PASSAGE SEVEN

For many people, the most exciting of all fossil finds are those of the remains of dinosaurs, the great reptiles that became extinct some 5 million years ago. Many species, both large and small, were often trapped in lowland swamps and quicksands. (Some, discovered in the Gobi desert, were apparently buried in sandstorms.) Great quantities of their bones, including entire skeletons, have been excavated on every continent except Antarctica.

But we know the dinosaurs by more than just their bones, for they left footprints behind as well. Tracks of all shapes and sizes have been found in the Connecticut River valley in New England. Much rarer than dinosaur tracks are the eggs. The most sensational discovery was made in 1922, when fossil eggs and dinosaur skeletons were found together in a large deposit in Mongolia. Many more eggs have since been unearthed, but, as with the tracks, it is usually difficult to say which species they belong to.

Near the end of the last ice age, mammoths, mastodons, and a host of other now extinct animals roamed the grasslands around what is now Los Angeles, California. And many suffered a common fate; they were mired in a series of tar pits at Rancho La Brea, located within the present-day city limits. These pools of viscous asphalt, formed by seepage from petroleum deposits, were natural death traps. Animals came to drink from pools of water that collected atop the asphalt, and many became hopelessly bogged down in the tar: coyotes and weasels, and more exotic ones as well, including saber-toothed cats, camels, and now extinct species of condors and storks. One of the richest fossil sites ever discovered, the tar pits have yielded more than a million fossil remains of an incredible array of vanished wildlife. -Sheffel, pp. 28-29

MY TIME: _____

WORDS PER MINUTE _____

COMPREHENSION SCORE _____

TIMED READINGS: PASSAGE SEVEN

TIMED READINGS: PASSAGE EIGHT

Decorating a home is a rewarding experience and not necessarily a costly one. However, few of us embark on a decorating project with total confidence. We may know in our mind's eye what we want our home (or a particular room) to look like, but turning this vision into a reality is often easier said than done. The difficulty, usually, is simply not knowing where or how to begin. Sometimes it's not being sure how to best express our tastes in a personal way. The best way to get over the initial hurdle is to spend some time making a realistic appraisal of your own living needs, your house and the space within it, and of course, your budget. Make this appraisal and you will be well on your way to creating a home that not only looks good, but is truly right for you.

The process of decorating a home begins long before the first piece of furniture is purchased. Actually, the process begins in childhood. Consciously or subconsciously, we take note of our own and other people's surroundings and form an image of what for us constitutes beauty and comfort. If our fondest memories include curling up with a good book in an overstuffed easy chair, it's likely we'll want to have a similar chair in our own home.

To expand our awareness of good design, it's necessary for most of us to study and observe. We can do this by making a concerted effort to expose ourselves to as many design influences as possible (books, magazines, museums, high-quality furniture stores, decorator showrooms), and by learning what we can about basic design principles, such as scale, balance, and contrast. One of the most important things to be learned from an increased awareness of good design is that good taste is not dependent on the size of one's bankbook.

-Knox, pp. 8-10

MY TIME: _____

WORDS PER MINUTE_____

COMPREHENSION SCORE_____

TIMED READINGS: PASSAGE EIGHT

TIMED READINGS: PASSAGE NINE

When Jeanne Louise Calment was born, Ulysses S. Grant was still president, and Vincent Van Gogh was buying colored pencils in her father's store in France. Calment, who lived to be 122, holds the record as the oldest person on Earth, having beaten the average life expectancy by 45 years. Most of us can expect to live about 75 years.

Every year, people are living just a little bit longer. This is because scientists are unlocking the secrets of aging itself. We're finding out why our bodies break down and how to put the brakes on our own destruction.

Researchers have finally identified one of the most important contributors to heart disease, wrinkles, cancer, arthritis, and many of the other problems of aging. "We rust," says William Regelson, professor of medicine at the Virginia Commonwealth University. Ironically, the same air that gives us life is what causes iron to rust, fruit to turn brown, and our bodies' cells to break down and age. Through a series of chemical changes, oxygen molecules in our bodies lose electrons, making them unstable. These unstable molecules are called free radicals.

In frantic attempts to stablilize themselves, free radicals pillage electrons from healthy cells throughout the body. To keep this destructive process under control, nature created an enormous arsenal of antioxidants, which are compounds in food that can stop free radical from doing harm. Even though the body naturally produces its own antioxidants, studies clearly show that the antioxidants in foods offer superior protection. Three of the strongest antioxidants are beta-carotene and vitamins C and E. The quickest way to get vitamin C is to have an orange. For beta-carotene, deep green vegetables or one sweet potato delivers more than the amount experts recommend. Nuts and seeds are good sources of vitamin E.   -Yeager, pp. 3-4

MY TIME: _____

WORDS PER MINUTE_____

COMPREHENSION SCORE_____

TIMED READINGS: PASSAGE NINE

TIMED READINGS: PASSAGE TEN

Rachel reached for the seedling. Bits of soil fell through her hands. She covered the roots, tamped down the soil, then sat back on her heels and admired the little tree. The other students had all finished more than twenty minutes ago. She sighed and got up to get a rake.

"Nice job." Gabriel's voice behind her sounded flat, far away, even if the words approved.

Rachel turned around. Gabriel stood an inch taller than Rachel, but wider and stronger, carefully dressed in brown pants that tied at the ankles, high boots, and a tight-fitting shirt that showed muscles. She wrinkled her nose at him and smiled. He didn't smile back. He looked upward, distracted, touching the bright metal and bead sculptures twisted into the long red-brown braid of his hair.

Rachel ran her fingers through her own short red hair, wondering if such a long braid was heavy. And what was he looking at? Harlequin. What so fascinated Gabriel about Harlequin and its ring high in the sky? She put the rake away and stood as near Gabriel as she dared, and looked up too. She said "Good night" out loud, alert for a response from Gabriel. None came.

In a few minutes she was home, ducking through a delicate blue fabric doorway. The inside of the tent was simple. Hangings divided it into four rooms—they shared bathroom facilities with four other families.

"The other kids have been back more than an hour," her father said, smiling at her.

"I wanted my trees to be perfect; the test is tomorrow."

"Did you get any information about when they plan to start the planting for this season?" her father asked.

"It'll be soon. It has to be. Gabe will be gone after the test, and I guess we'll stay and take care of things at the grove."

"Better call him Gabriel," her father said.

"Yes, Daddy."   -Niven & Cooper, pp. 17-21

MY TIME: _____

WORDS PER MINUTE_____

COMPREHENSION SCORE_____

TIMED READINGS: PASSAGE TEN

Questions for TIMED READING: PASSAGE ONE

1. It is implied in the passage, that people who discuss the main character in the passage portray him as

a. an American terrorist/murderer.
b. an American hero.
c. either a terrorist or a hero.

2. Where did John Brown grow up?

a. Ohio's Western Reserve
b. Connecticut
c. Pottawatomie Creek

3. According to the passage, the answer to why John Brown chose "violence as a means to end slavery" is

a. because his father had been rescued by a slave.
b. rooted in his religious beliefs.
c. because he was mentally unstable.

4. After his instigation of and participation in the slaughtering of pro-slavery forces, John Brown

a. escaped to Kansas.
b. repented and joined the New Divinity church.
c. was executed.

5. John Brown was against slavery mainly because

a. it represented society's obsession with materialism.
b. the African slaves were beaten on a daily basis.
c. his own life had been a miserable one, and he was empathetic.

True-False:
_____ 6. Some of Brown's relatives were involved in his antislavery violence.
_____ 7. John Brown had a satisfying personal life.
_____ 8. Only about half of Brown's children survived childhood.
_____ 9. The reader can infer that John Brown had African American relatives.
_____ 10. John Brown was a failure in business.

TIMED READINGS: PASSAGE ONE QUESTIONS

Questions for TIMED READING: PASSAGE TWO

True-False:

_____1. The narrator of the story is the nanny.

_____2. In New York the spouse who abandons the residence will obtain it in the divorce settlement.

_____3. The nanny was not familiar with Alex's neighborhood.

_____4. What surprised the nanny when she walked through Alex's front door was the strip of duct tape running down the middle of the front hall.

_____5. The reader can infer that Murnel is most probably a nanny.

_____6. The duct tape strip was running down the middle of the hall because the parents were playing a game.

_____7. Alex is unaware that his parents are having problems.

_____8. The pattern of organization for this selection is contrast.

_____9. The purpose of this selection is to entertain.

_____10. When the nanny sits on the couch she turns to find a puppy's nose resting on the arm of the couch.

TIMED READINGS: PASSAGE TWO QUESTIONS

Questions for TIMED READINGS: PASSAGE THREE

True-False:

_____1. The purpose of the news story is to inform.

_____2. By 1911 the Triangle Waist Company Fire had been the only major fire in New York.

_____3. Most of the girls and young women were Americans living in Brooklyn.

_____4. The females were 16 – 23 years of age.

_____5. The owners prided themselves on the fact that their workers were all fluent in English.

_____6. The owners were in the building when the fire broke out.

_____7. The owners showed the employees how to escape over the roof, thus saving most of the workers.

_____8. The first responders found a girl who had jumped to the pavement (and whom they assumed dead) alive.

_____9. Of the two elevators, one was not in service when the fire broke out.

_____10. The tone of the passage is shocking.

TIMED READINGS: PASSAGE THREE QUESTIONS

Questions for TIMED READINGS: PASSAGE FOUR

True-False:

_____1. The *wall cloud* is the heavy rain that pours out of the leading sector of the thundercloud.

_____2. The *wall cloud* explains why most tornadoes are undetectable during their initial phase of development.

_____3. The early tornado usually starts as a highly visible, short, round shape about 2,000 feet above the earth's surface.

_____4. The tornado becomes highly visible (the black funnel) after it touches the earth's surface.

_____5. The total destruction often caused by tornadoes is the result of the extremely high winds.

_____6. The two most fear-inspiring features of a tornado are its roaring noise and the lightening that comes with the thundercloud.

_____7. Wind speeds in the vortex of a tornado can be higher than 300 mph.

_____8. One example provided to show the power of a tornado is the one that touched down in Mississippi in 1975 and carried a home freezer for a distance of over a mile.

_____9. The purpose of this passage is to persuade.

_____10. It is difficult for the U.S. Weather Service personnel to accurately measure wind speeds and pressure conditions of a tornado.

TIMED READINGS: PASSAGE FOUR QUESTIONS

Questions for TIMED READINGS: PASSAGE FIVE

True-False:

_____1. There are approximately 50 trillion cells in the human body.

_____2. Cells of the heart, liver, brain, and kidney each have easily determinable differences (for example, the untrained eye can easily detect a heart cell vs. a liver cell).

_____3. Human DNA is completely different from the DNA of a gorilla.

_____4. Cells travel randomly to wound sites to heal the area.

_____5. The writer likens a cell to a bag with an outer membrane that holds a mixture of water and swirling chemicals within.

_____6. The number of activities being coordinated in our bodies at any one time is limited.

_____7. At the center of the cell are tightly twisted coils of DNA.

_____8. In the world of medicine, one thing is certain: human cells have evolved to a state of intelligence.

_____9. The pattern of organization for this excerpt is narration.

_____10. Colonies of mites may spend their entire life cycle in human eyelashes.

TIMED READINGS: PASSAGE FIVE QUESTIONS

Questions for TIMED READINGS: PASSAGE SIX

_____ 1. In this passage, an addiction to a bad relationship is figuratively compared to an addition to smoking.

_____ 2. According to the passage, chemical changes caused by stress can not impact the human organ system.

_____ 3. Within the context of the passage, "unfriendly bugs" refers to poisonous insects that leave toxins in the human body.

_____ 4. The reader can infer that finding oneself in a bad relationship is rare.

_____ 5. The writer of this selection is most likely a psychologist.

_____ 6. We can infer that the author of this book discusses bad relationships and why people engage in them, but he does not offer solutions.

_____ 7. According to the selection, people in bad relationships leave when they realize their self-esteem has been compromised.

_____ 8. This author likens bad relationships to prisons.

_____ 9. It is implied that some individuals make superficial changes to the relationship thinking it will make a difference.

_____ 10. According to the passage, when friends notice that a relationship is faltering and comment upon it, the unhappy partner finds the strength to leave.

TIMED READINGS: PASSAGE SIX QUESTIONS

Questions for TIMED READINGS: PASSAGE SEVEN

_____ 1. Dinosaur bones have been found on every continent of the world.

_____ 2. Dinosaur remains have even been found in the Gobi Desert and in Mongolia.

_____ 3. Though archaeologists have searched, no dinosaur fossils have been found in the United States.

_____ 4. According to the passage, no one has ever found a dinosaur egg.

_____ 5. According to the passage, dinosaurs roamed the grasslands of Los Angeles.

_____ 6. The La Brea tar pits are within the Los Angeles city limits.

_____ 7. Animals were trapped in the tar pits because they were searching for water.

_____ 8. The La Brea tar pits were formed from petroleum deposits.

_____ 9. The writer of this excerpt is probably a journalist interested in history.

_____ 10. The excerpt states that the Gobi Desert is one of the richest fossil sites ever discovered.

TIMED READINGS: PASSAGE SEVEN QUESTIONS

Questions for TIMED READINGS: PASSAGE EIGHT

_____1. The tone of the passage is hopeful.

_____2. The topic of the passage is that high-end decorating design should not be attempted by beginners.

_____3. According to the passage, the best way to begin a decorating project is to just dive in and begin painting.

_____4. The bottom line of designing and decorating is that it is a costly endeavor.

_____5. The purpose of the passage is to educate the reader by explaining what is involved in decorating a home or room.

_____6. According to the author, the process of decorating a home begins in childhood.

_____7. In order to expand our awareness of good design, it is suggested that people remember what they learned in school.

_____8. Examples of design influences are museums, high-quality furniture stores, and decorator showrooms.

_____9. The excerpt implies that most people already have a good foundation when it comes to basic design principles such as scale, balance, and contrast.

____10. The style of this selection is formal and academic.

TIMED READINGS: PASSAGE EIGHT QUESTIONS

Questions for TIMED READINGS: PASSAGE NINE

_____1. Most of us today can expect to live about 75 years.

_____2. Jeanne, who lived to be 122 years old was from France.

_____3. According to Dr. William Regelson, when humans age, they rust.

_____4. Dr. Regelson is a professor at the University of Virginia.

_____5. Free radicals were once healthy oxygen molecules in the human body.

_____6. Antioxidants help free radicals pillage electrons from healthy cells throughout the body.

_____7. Antioxidants produced in the human body are superior to antioxidants found in food.

_____8. Three of the strongest antioxidants are beta-carotene, and Vitamins A and C.

_____9. If you want to ingest beta-carotene, eat nuts and seeds.

_____10. The reader can infer that Vincent Van Gogh and Ulysses S. Grant lived during the same era.

TIMED READINGS: PASSAGE NINE QUESTIONS

Questions for TIMED READINGS: PASSAGE TEN

_____1. The reader can infer that Rachel is most likely an agricultural student.

_____2. Gabriel is behaving out of character and is preoccupied.

_____3. Rachel's status in society is that of the upper-class.

_____4. We can infer from the passage that Gabriel is Rachel's boyfriend.

_____5. Harlequin is probably a moon or another planet.

_____6. Rachel has long, red hair that she wears in a braid.

_____7. Rachel got home later than usual because she wanted her trees to be perfect.

_____8. Gabriel is scheduled to leave after the test has been given.

_____9. Rachel's father probably told her not to call Gabriel "Gabe" because it is disrespectful.

_____10. Rachel's father works for Gabriel.

TIMED READINGS: PASSAGE TEN QUESTIONS

CONVERSION AND PROGRESS CHARTS

TIME YOU RECORDED	WORDS PER MINUTE
1:00	300
1:10	256
1:20	225
1:30	200
1:40	176
1:50	167
2:00	150

*Note: Student needs to perform at 70% comprehension

%	#1	#2	#3	#4	#5	#6	#7	#8	#9	#10
100										
95										
90										
85										
80										
75										
70										
65										
60										
55										
50										
45										

TIMED READINGS: CONVERSION AND PROGRESS CHARTS

Unit Two

GENERAL DIRECTIONS FOR THE REGENTS' READING EXAM

DIAGNOSTIC PRE-TEST

NINE SIMULATED EXAMS

POST TEST

General Directions for the Exam*

This is a test of reading comprehension. It is designed to measure your understanding of the material that you read.

The test contains 9 passages. Following each passage is a set of questions about the passage. There are 54 questions on the test.

For each question following a passage, choose the *best* response on the basis of the content of the passage.

Do not spend too much time on any one question. If a question seems very difficult, make the most careful guess you can. *Your score is the number of correct answers* that you give; there is no added penalty for wrong answers.

You will have *60 minutes* to complete the test.

---

*(University System of Georgia website)

DIAGNOSTIC EXAM:

PRE-TEST

In Scottish history throughout the Highlands, the bagpipes succeeded the harp as a call to arms, especially when the call to arms involved several thousand half-frozen warriors, most of them out of earshot.

The courage of pipers in battle (who were inevitably a prime target for the enemy) is legendary throughout the centuries. At the Haughs of Cromdale, there's a stone onto which a badly wounded piper for the army climbed and continued to play until he died. The spot is still known as the "Piper's Stone." In the Battle of Philiphaugh far south in the border country of Scotland, another intrepid piper played until a bullet knocked him into the Ettrick River where he drowned.

Perhaps one of the most famous pipers of all is the clan Macdonald's piper who was sent to Duntrune Castle as a messenger during a feud during the seventeenth century. He was invited in, but then immediately overpowered and imprisoned. Luckily for the Macdonald clan, the captors neglected to confiscate their prisoner's pipes. Out over the water the sound of pipes could be heard, an unmistakable and undeniable and distinguishable note of warning.

Abruptly the piping stopped as the furious soldiers reached the dungeon and killed the piper as he played. Although no one knows the real fate of the piper, much later, under the floor of the castle hall, a skeleton was found with mutilated hands.
                                        -Wallace, pp. 44 ;75

1. The purpose of the last paragraph is to

    1. inform the reader.
    2. fascinate the reader.
    3. describe the piper for the reader.
    4. relate facts to the reader.

2. According to the passage, within the Scottish armies, who was the prime target of the enemy?

    1. the general.
    2. the clan leader.
    3. the piper.
    4. half-frozen warriors.

3. The word intrepid, as underlined in the passage, most nearly means

    1. fearless.
    2. cowardly.
    3. famous.
    4. eager.

4. The overall pattern of organization used in paragraph two is

    1. definition.
    2. contrast.
    3. cause-effect.
    4. examples.

GO ON TO NEXT PAGE

DIAGNOSTIC EXAM, PASSAGE ONE

5. The author of the selection would probably agree that

1. bagpipes were an important weapon of Scottish armies.
2. most pipers were used as messengers.
3. the "Piper's Stone" is an ill-conceived monument.
4. the piper of the MacDonald clan was a coward.

6. The underlined word <u>overpowered</u> is best defined as

1. killed.
2. gagged.
3. restrained.
4. greeted.

GO ON TO NEXT PAGE

DIAGNOSTIC EXAM, PASSAGE ONE

In the world of classical ancient Greece and Rome the making of art was generally viewed as a manual profession. Art was taught in workshops. Greek vase painting illustrates this workshop tradition. Apprentice vase painters, some of them female, worked side-by-side with the master of the shop. Women must have been given the lesser positions within the workshop, since no Greek vases signed by women are known.

The Middle Ages continued to identify art as a manual profession. Artists formed guilds: legal organizations rather like trade unions. These guilds not only assured professional standards but also reinforced the distinction between the mechanical arts and the liberal arts. During the Middle Ages, liberal arts encompassed arithmetic, geometry, astronomy, music theory, grammar, and logic.

This traditional classification of the visual arts as mechanical was transformed during the Renaissance. Both artists and writers began to emphasize the scientific and intellectual aspects of art. It was argued, for example, that arithmetic was needed by the artist for the study of proportion, and that geometry figured in the proper calculation of perspective. The artist was beginning to be seen as an educated professional knowledgeable of both the practice and theory of art. The new attitude that the artist was a skilled and educated individual was accompanied by a new social status. Artists became the companions of intellectuals, princes, and emperors.

-Wilkins, et. al., p, 31

DIAGNOSTIC EXAM, PASSAGE TWO

7. The author concludes that female apprentice vase painters of Greece were given lesser positions because

1. no Greek vases signed by women have been found.
2. women in ancient Greece were uneducated.
3. women were not considered equal to men.
4. only women from the lower classes were apprentices.

8. The word guild as underlined in the passage most nearly means

1. mechanical art.
2. profession.
3. artist.
4. legally organized group.

9. Overall, the main idea of the passage is that

1. visual arts were transformed into something more than a manual profession.
2. artists emphasized the scientific aspect of art.
3. artists were included in the courts of the emperors.
4. guilds of the Middle Ages assured professional standards.

GO ON TO NEXT PAGE

10. During which age was the classification
of mechanical arts changed?

1. the age of the emperors.
2. ancient times of Greece.
3. the Renaissance.
4. era of classical Rome.

11. In this context the word <u>encompassed</u>, as
underlined, most probably means

1. excluded.
2. surrounded.
3. exempted.
4. included.

12. The purpose of the passage is to

1. describe.
2. educate.
3. persuade.
4. compare.

13. From the selection, the reader can assume
that princes and emperors were

1. artistic.
2. arrogant.
3. skilled and educated.
4. only interested in Renaissance art.

GO ON TO NEXT PAGE

DIAGNOSTIC EXAM, PASSAGE TWO

If we do decide that humans should travel to another planetary system, how hard would that be? If we do go to the stars, we would probably be interested in visiting a system more like our own, such as Gliese 777A that has one known planet with about Jupiter's mass located in about Jupiter's location. This star is about 52 light years away. A one-way trip for light takes about 52 years. How long would such a journey take for humans?

NASA successfully tested an ion engine in 1998, a design suitable for interstellar travel at 1 percent the speed of light. With time added to gently accelerate and decelerate—human beings are fragile— it would take about 10,000 years to reach Gliese 777A. Obviously, the feasibility of such a feat is questionable: the astronomers would not live to see their goal. Solutions such as hibernation, deep-freeze, multi-generational ships, and so on, have been proposed, but none of them is yet technically possible. Boosting to speeds close to the speed of light would shorten the time of the trip in the time frame of the astronauts, but would require more energy than we now know how to produce at a reasonable cost. The vast distances between the stars is not the last frontier, but a chasm separating us from any neighboring civilizations. This is one of the reasons why astronomers have difficulty accepting that aliens have already visited Earth.

-Shawl, et al., pp. 664-665

DIAGNOSTIC EXAM, PASSAGE THREE

14. The purpose of the passage is to

1. persuade.
2. inform.
3. criticize.
4. enlighten.

15. From the information given in the passage, the reader can infer that

1. humans are afraid of planetary exploration.
2. the majority of humans do not believe there is life on other planets.
3. there is a definite interest in space exploration.
4. the government does not support interstellar travel.

16. The planet of Gliese 777A would probably be chosen as a destination because

1. it is more like planets in our own solar system.
2. it is the closest to Earth.
3. astronomers know more about it than any other planet in the universe.
4. it is the only planet in the last frontier.

17. The word feasibility, as used in the passage most nearly means

1. journey.
2. viability.
3. normality.
4. financing.

18. The passage implies that boosting an engine to the speed of light

1. was achieved with the ion engine.
2. has yet to be mastered within budget.
3. lengthens the travel time in space.
4. does not require a great amount of energy.

19. Astronomers, in general, do not accept that aliens have visited Earth because

1. other intelligent life does not exist in the universe.
2. aliens do not have the technology for interstellar travel.
3. the conditions of Earth's atmosphere can not support alien life forms.
4. there are vast distances, chasms, that separate aliens from Earth.

GO ON TO NEXT PAGE

DIAGNOSTIC EXAM, PASSAGE THREE

A Type A personality, either male or female, is characterized by intense drive, aggressiveness, ambition, competitiveness, and the habit of competing with the clock. He or she may give an impression of iron control, or wear <u>a mask of easy geniality</u>, but the strain glints through.

By contrast, Type B's manner is more genuinely easy, open. S/he is not glancing at his watch nor preoccupied with achievement. Type B is less competitive and even speaks in a more modulated style.

Most people are mixtures of Type A and Type B, of course, and Rosenman and Friedman have sharpened their interviewing techniques to the point where they recognize four distinct subdivisions of each group, ranging from A-1, the most <u>virulent</u>, down to B-4, the mildest. The ways the answers are spoken are as important as the responses to the interview question. An impatient subject, who shows his impatience, is probably an A, no matter what he says. Some questions even call for a pretense of stammering on the part of the interviewer. An A intrudes into the stammer, while B waits quietly.

The extreme Type A is the person who, while waiting to see the dentist, is on the telephone making business calls. He speaks in staccato, and rushes through a sentence. He frequently sighs faintly between words which is a sign of emotional exhaustion. He rarely goes to a doctor; indeed, many Type A's die of otherwise recoverable heart attacks simply because they wait too long to call for help.   –McQuade, pp. 26-27

DIAGNOSTIC EXAM, PASSAGE FOUR

20. The author has written this passage primarily to

1. contrast two types of personalities.
2. argue the point that Type B's have a better life than Type A's.
3. persuade the reader to aspire to Type A qualities.
4. narrate an incident that happened because a person was Type B.

21. How can Type A personalities be described?

1. unhappy
2. senseless
3. driven
4. undisturbed

22. As used in paragraph three, <u>virulent</u> most nearly means

1. kind.
2. hostile.
3. adaptable.
4. impatient.

23. The last sentence in paragraph one indicates that the person is, in truth, most likely to be

1. plain and simple.
2. fond of practical jokes.
3. friendly and relaxed.
4. intensely controlled.

GO ON TO NEXT PAGE

24. According to the passage Type A's

1. visit the doctor when they need to.
2. think doctors are useless.
3. wait too long to see a doctor.
4. never visit the doctor.

25. Which of the following is not mentioned as a characteristic of a Type B personality?

1. open
2. patient
3. less competitive
4. intrusive

GO ON TO NEXT PAGE

DIAGNOSTIC EXAM, PASSAGE FOUR

The model followed by the largest Japanese corporation draws on a long cultural tradition that emphasizes the importance of the group over the individual. When people join a major Japanese corporation, they are making a lifetime commitment which the corporation reciprocates: the corporation provides a whole range of services, including housing, recreation, health care, and continuing education. Unless the employee commits a crime, he or she will not be fired or laid off. All promotions are made from inside the organization; outsiders are not even considered. Most promotions are based on seniority, so people of the same age move more or less together through the organizational hierarchy, with little competition among them.

Workers are organized into small teams, and it is the teams—not the individual workers—whose performance is evaluated. Over the years, each individual may belong to many such teams, thereby gaining experiences throughout the corporation. Decision making is collective: rather than issue new policies, the top officials merely ratify them after they have been discussed and approved at every level of the organization (the Japanese word for this process literally means "bottom-up" decision making).

Unlike Western corporations, which usually limit the relationship between organization and employee to matters that are "strictly business," Japanese corporations take considerable responsibility for their workers' welfare.

The workers, in turn, show great loyalty to the company—perhaps by wearing company uniforms, singing the company song, working exceptionally long hours, or taking part in company-organized sporting activities. In short, the activities of the corporation and the lives of its members are closely intertwined. This <u>symbiotic</u> relationship between organization and worker reflects a deep difference between Japanese and western cultures: to the Japanese, it indicates a bond of commitment that ensures security and solidarity.　　　　-Robertson, p. 186

26. The author's style of writing is

1. informal.
2. subjective.
3. argumentative.
4. matter-of-fact.

27. In the second paragraph, which of the following does the author primarily use?

1. chronology
2. narrative
3. description
4. classification.

GO ON TO NEXT PAGE

DIAGNOSTIC EXAM, PASSAGE FIVE

28. As used in the passage, <u>symbiotic</u> means

1. estranged.
2. mutual.
3. complimentary.
4. strict.

29. It is suggested in the passage that the least attractive job applicant for a Japanese corporation is one who believes in

1. individualism.
2. commitment.
3. hierarchy of seniority.
4. group dynamics.

30. The reader can infer that someone from Japan working in Britain might experience

1. participating in company exercises every morning.
2. the stress of having to find housing.
3. team meetings every day.
4. being asked to sing the company song.

31. What is not mentioned as a characteristic of a Japanese company?

1. "strictly business" philosophy
2. the group dynamic
3. bottom-up decision-making
4. lifetime commitment from company

GO ON TO NEXT PAGE

DIAGNOSTIC EXAM, PASSAGE FIVE

Bulimia is the most common eating disorder in young women. It starts as a strategy to control weight, but it soon develops a life of its own. Life for bulimic young women becomes a relentless pre-occupation with eating, purging, and weight watching. Pleasure is replaced by despair, frenzy and guilt. Like all addictions, bulimia is a self destructive, compulsive, and progress-ive disorder. Binging and purging are the addictive behaviors; food is the narcotic.

Over time young women with bulimia are at risk for serious health problems; often they have dental problems, tears in the esophagus, gastrointestinal problems and some-times dangerous electrolyte imbalances that can trigger heart attacks.

Young women often experience personality changes as they grow to love binging more than anything else; they become obsessed and secretive. Driven for another binge and feeling guilty about their habit, they suffer loss of control that leads to depression. Often these women are irritable and withdrawn, especially in relations with family members.

While anorexia, another eating disorder, often begins in junior high, bulimia tends to develop in later adolescence. It is called the college girl's disease because so many young women develop it in sororities and dorms.

DIAGNOSTIC EXAM, PASSAGE SIX

Estimates of the incidence of bulimia run as high as one-fifth of all college-age women. Most are attractive women with good social skills. Often they are the cheerleaders and homecoming queens, the straight-A students, and the pride of their families. Bulimic young women, like their anorexic sisters are over-socialized to the feminine role. They are the ultimate people pleasers.
                                                    -Pipher, pp. 169-170

32. The overall pattern of organization utilized in the next to the last paragraph is

1. narration.
2. contrast.
3. cause-effect.
4. description.

33. According to the selection, women with bulimia

1. are basically very healthy.
2. can stop binging whenever they decide they want to quit.
3. are at risk for heart attack.
4. suffer physically but do not suffer emotionally.

34. As underlined in the selection, anorexia most nearly means

1. bulimia.
2. college girl's disease.
3. relations.
4. eating disorder.

35. The tone of the passage is

1. hopeless.
2. complaining.
3. defensive.
4. objective.

36. The central focus of the passage is that

1. college girls are at risk for bulimia.
2. bulimia is a common and dangerous disorder.
3. most female bulimics are over-socialized to the feminine role.
4. binging and purging are addictive behaviors.

37. The author would most likely agree with which of the following?

1. Bulimia very quickly overtakes a young woman's life if it is not controlled.
2. Bulimia affects a young woman physically but not emotionally.
3. Electrolite imabalances can be easily remedied and, consequently, do not pose a threat.
4. Young women who earn straight A's are not susceptible to bulimic tendencies.

GO ON TO NEXT PAGE

DIAGNOSTIC EXAM, PASSAGE SIX

The greatest of all the women warriors among the upper Missouri tribes lived among the Crows in the middle of the nineteenth century. Woman Chief was not a Crow Indian by birth. She was a Gros Ventre (a tribe closely tied with the Algonquin Indians) girl who, at the age of about ten, was captured by the Crows. The Crow family that adopted her soon found that she showed little interest in helping the women with their <u>domestic</u> tasks. She preferred to shoot birds with a bow and arrow, to guard the family horses, and ride horseback fast and fearlessly. Later she learned to shoot a gun accurately. She became the equal if not the superior of any of the young men in hunting on foot or on horseback.

She grew taller and stronger than most women. She could carry a deer home from the hunt on her back. She could kill four buffalo in a single chase, butcher them, and load them on pack horses without assistance. Yet, despite her prowess in men's activities, she always dressed like a woman. Although she was rather good-looking, she did not attract the fancy of young men. After her foster father died, she took charge of his lodge and family, and acted as both mother and father to his children.

She led her first war party against the Blackfeet; seventy horses were stolen. She succeeded in killing and scalping one Blackfoot and in capturing the gun of another. Her continued success as a war leader in a world dominated by males won her greater and greater honors among the Crows until she

gained a place in the Council of Chiefs of the tribe, ranking third in a band of 160 lodges.   -Dorenkamp, et al, pp. 84-85

DIAGNOSTIC EXAM, PASSAGE SEVEN

38. <u>Domestic</u>, as used in the first paragraph, means

1. local.
2. monthly.
3. home-based.
4. public.

39. In the context of this passage, Woman Chief was most unique because

1. she was not a Crow Indian by birth.
2. she was captured when very young.
3. she preferred to shoot birds than make clothes.
4. women were not usually invited to serve on the Council of Chiefs.

40. According to the passage, Woman Chief

1. was not feminine.
2. did not attract men.
3. was not good looking.
4. did not like children.

41. The reader can infer that male Crow warriors who resided in camp with Woman Chief considered her

1. too muscular and forward.
2. overbearing and arrogant.
3. a part of their warrior circle.
4. somewhat a threat but respected her.

42. The purpose of the second
paragraph is to

1. entertain the reader with stories of
    Woman Chief.
2. describe Woman Chief's stature and
    character.
3. criticize the choices Woman Chief
    made while on the Council.
4. define a female warrior chief.

GO ON TO NEXT PAGE

DIAGNOSTIC EXAM, PASSAGE SEVEN

Pyramids did not stand alone but were part of a group of buildings which included other tombs, temples, chapels, and massive walls. The scarcity of ancient records leaves us uncertain about the uses of all the buildings in the pyramid <u>complex</u> or the exact burial procedures. Remnants of boats that were used for burials have been excavated—the best preserved are at Giza, Egypt. From this evidence, it is thought that the king's body was brought by boat up the Nile to the pyramid site, having already been mummified in the Valley Temple.

On the walls of Fifth and Sixth Dynasty pyramids are inscriptions known as the Pyramid Texts: an important source of information about Egyptian religion. The funeral customs and beliefs of the ancient Egyptians called for the preservation of the body and ample provisions for the afterlife. An ancient Egyptian provided for life in the next World as best as he could.

Also, on the walls the Egyptians painted idealized scenes from daily life: scenes of agricultural work such as crop harvesting, cattle tending, and fishing. They illustrated scenes of artisans at their work, including gold workers and boat-builders. Detailed and colorful scenes on the walls provide information on a wide range of topics such as dress, architecture, crafts, and food production. These scenes represented the hoped-for afterlife and were thought to ensure an ideal existence in the next world. The goods included in the tombs along with the corpses add to this invaluable information resource.

For us today, a huge amount of information about daily life in ancient Egypt can be found in the Pyramid Texts.

-O'brien, 1999

43. The passage indicates that pyramid complexes were primarily built for

1. religious purposes.
2. the king.
3. artisans and craftsmen.
4. daily activities.

44. According the the passage, ancient Egyptians placed "goods" in the tombs with the corpse to

1. ward off evil spirits.
2. ease some of the guilt they felt about their relationship with the person.
3. to show the gods of the afterlife the wealth of the person.
4. ensure that the person would have ample provisions for the next world.

45. We can infer from the selection that through observing paintings of daily life, we can learn how the Egyptians viewed

1. the king.
2. the afterlife.
3. pyramids.
4. the Fifth and Sixth Dynasties.

DIAGNOSTIC EXAM, PASSAGE EIGHT

46. According to the passage, overall the Pyramid Texts give valuable information about

1. prevalent philosophies of ancient Egypt.
2. Egyptian religion and daily life.
3. building pyramids.
4. the lives of Egyptian kings.

47. complex, as used in the first paragraph, is best defined as

1. difficult.
2. intricate.
3. group of buildings.
4. phobia.

48. According to the passage, which was not mentioned as part of the daily life of an Egyptian?

1. fishing
2. boat building
3. gold working
4. military training

GO ON TO NEXT PAGE

DIAGNOSTIC EXAM, PASSAGE EIGHT

The current overall estimate of the number of wild polar bears world-wide is 20,000-25,000, and about 60% of these are in Canada. Polar bears are the top predator in the arctic and evolved from brown bears. They have adapted to life in the north where temperatures do not exceed 50°F in summer and typically fall to -22°F during winter. These bears have enormous paws that function like snowshoes, distributing their weight to keep them from breaking through ice and snow (male bears can weigh up to 1300 lbs.). Their thick white coat is made up of water repellent hairs that conserve heat. Under their dense fur is black skin, good for absorbing the rays of the arctic sun. A layer of fat up to 4.3 inches thick keeps the bears warm, especially while swimming.

Polar bears are usually <u>solitary</u> animals, but they gather together on land during the ice-free season to breed. There are usually 2 cubs, each weighing only 1.3 lbs., about the size of a guinea pig. Cubs are nursed until they weigh about 22 lbs. and are large enough to venture onto the sea ice. In most areas, they stay with their mother for about 2.5 years before striking out on their own.

Threats to the survival of polar bear include global warming which is melting the sea ice. Due to the extreme distances between ice floes, polar bears are forced to swim up to 60 miles to reach their destination and are drowning from exhaustion. Unbelievably, the main threat to polar bears remains over-hunting. Today, legal hunting of polar bears by non-native sport hunters is found in Canada. In addition, it has been documented that in areas such as East Greenland, both historically and currently, hunting takes place with no quota systems in place.   -WWF, 2008

49. The author makes his point mostly through the use of

1. dramatic narration.
2. facts and statistics.
3. descriptive events.
4. persuasive commentary.

50. The author's attitude toward hunters killing polar bears for sport is one of

1. apathy.
2. ridicule.
3. suspicion.
4. disbelief.

51. The word <u>solitary</u>, as underlined, most nearly means

1. social.
2. lazy.
3. lone.
4. distinct.

DIAGNOSTIC EXAM, PASSAGE NINE

GO ON TO NEXT PAGE

52. According to the selection, where do the majority of polar bears live?

1. Alaska
2. Greenland
3. Iceland
4. Canada

53. At this point in time, the main threat to polar bears is

1. global warming.
2. overhunting.
3. other large predators.
4. indigenous peoples of the Arctic.

54. Of the following, which keeps the polar bear warmest especially while swimming?

1. a layer of fat that is 4.3 inches thick
2. water repellent fur
3. their enormous paws that paddle rapidly in the icy water
4. their skin which is black

DIAGNOSTIC EXAM, PASSAGE NINE

EXAM ONE

King James awoke to the sunlight streaming through the window of his prison cell and laid for a long time reveling in the tranquility. Distant sounds underlined the peace rather than disturbing it, and he dozed again before stretching lazily and rising slowly from his bed. Still wrapped in the half-awareness of waking he went to the window, now without its winter shutters, and leaned out, resting his arms on the ledge.

Below him was a walled and secret garden closed in with sweet scented flowering trees. He let his eye linger on the blossoms. A robin fluttered into a branch with a flurry of wings. A small movement close under the window attracted his attention. He caught his breath in the surprise of the moment, for seated on a garden bench was a girl who glowed golden in the sun, the little hat she wore on her abundant hair shining as its beads caught the light. Bright feathers curled downwards over her cheek and shadowed the half-closed eyes, but James saw the outline of the cheek and the rounded chin.

How long he watched her he could not tell, but he feasted his eyes on her beauty, lost in the delight of her being. There seemed an aura of well-being and wholesome loveliness about her. Then, she was gone.

He turned away, trembling, and sat down on his ruffled bed. Here was his golden girl; here was the woman he had searched for down the years. Panic seized him when he realized she was no child and might well be claimed already.
-King, pp. 120-121

1. In the scenario, where is King James?

1. in his palace
2. in jail
3. in one of his noble's castles
4. in garden

2. The pattern of organization used by the author is

1. comparison.
2. example.
3. description.
4. persuasion.

3. As underlined in the first paragraph, reveling in, most nearly means

1. exposing.
2. shutting out.
3. denying.
4. soaking up.

4. The reader can infer that it is

1. Winter.
2. Fall.
3. Spring.
4. Christmas.

5. The tone of the last paragraph is

1. optimistic.
2. despairing.
3. apathetic.
4. objective.

GO ON TO NEXT PAGE

6. In the last paragraph, we can infer
that King James is panicked because

1. he will never get out of prison.
2. the girl may not love him back.
3. he may not have his true love.
4. the girl is too young to consider
   marriage.

GO ON TO NEXT PAGE

EXAM ONE, PASSAGE ONE

The *Sultana* docked at Vicksburg in the evening of April 22, 1865. The steamer had just arrived from New Orleans. While in New Orleans, the chief engineer had informed Captain Mason that one of the tube boilers was leaking. While docked at Vicksburg, the chief engineer told the captain that the boiler was not only leaking but was now "warped." With such alarming news, the captain <u>relented</u> and sent for a boiler repairman from Kleins Foundry who installed a patch on the boiler.

Meanwhile, the *Sultana* business agent had been busy arranging transport of Indiana soldiers who had been held prisoner in Andersonville, Georgia. All of the prisoners would be boarded on the *Sultana*—all 1,700. (The assigned limit for passengers on the *Sultana* was 376.) When they boarded, the happy, homeward-bound soldiers gladly accommodated to cramped conditions aboard the steamer. On April 24, 1865, at 3 p.m, the *Sultana* backed into the Mississippi and headed upriver, bearing happy, relieved, sick Union soldiers toward home.

The *Sultana* crossed the Mississippi and established upriver headway. The boat had steamed six miles upriver when a huge explosion occurred. Perhaps 200 souls were blown immediately into the flooded river. Panic ensued, and about 800 people jumped into the flooded river. The sudden mass of men in the water took down even the competent swimmers.

Rescue brigades of citizen boaters and canoeists were in the river and along the flooded banks looking for survivors. The grounded *Sultana* burned to water level and sank below the surface of the Mississippi within minutes of the removal of the last injured survivors.

The *Sultana* tragedy still remains America's worst inland marine disaster ever. More people were lost on the *Sultana* than in the sinking of the *Titanic* in 1912.   -Gray, 2008

7. The reader can infer that the *Sultana* exploded because

1. the steamer was sabotaged by Confederate terrorists.
2. a fire started in the kitchen.
3. the chief engineer was negligent.
4. the boiler exploded.

8. At what point was the captain first informed of the faulty boiler?

1. while docked in Vicksburg
2. when they reached Kleins Foundry
3. while docked in New Orleans
4. as the Union soldiers were boarding

9. How many released prisoners got aboard the *Sultana*?

1. 800
2. 1,700
3. 200
4. 376

EXAM ONE, PASSAGE TWO

10. What was the main reason most of the men drowned?

1. the sudden mass of men in the water
2. the men who could not swim, clung to the others, drowning them
3. there was no debris to cling to
4. they were too weak to swim

11. The word <u>relented,</u> as used in the passage, most nearly means

1. stood firm.
2. got angry.
3. gave in.
4. screamed.

12. The tone of paragraph three is

1. hopeful.
2. hostile.
3. indifferent.
4. suspenseful.

13. The *Sultana* incident is newsworthy because

1. the captain of the steamer was famous.
2. the released prisoners were being mistreated aboard the *Sultana*.
3. more people died in the *Sultana* incident than in the sinking of the *Titanic*.
4. citizens boaters and canoeists were the first responders.

GO ON TO NEXT PAGE

EXAM ONE, PASSAGE TWO

Arthur Ashe was one of the first African-Americans to become a great tennis champion. After a heart attack ended his career, he contracted AIDS through a <u>tainted</u> blood transfusion. For years, while he pursued many business interests and human rights projects, he kept his illness private. Then the possibility of a newspaper report forced him to reveal his condition to the public by way of a press conference held in April, 1992.

The day after the press conference Ashe was anxious to see how people would respond. He was thinking not only about the people he knew personally but also about waiters, and taxi drivers, bartenders and doormen. He knew all the myths and fears about AIDS. He also understood that if he hadn't contracted the disease and lived with it, he would probably share some of those myths and fears. He knew that he couldn't spread the disease by coughing, breathing, or using cups in a restaurant, but he knew that in some places his cups would receive some extra soap and hot water or be smashed and thrown away.

Ashe was glad that eventually he stopped concealing his condition from certain people. He had reminded himself from the outset that he had an obligation to tell anyone who might be materially or personally hurt by the news when it came out. Not one of the companies, not even HBO (for which he was a spokesperson), dropped him after he quietly revealed that he had AIDS. He waited for the phone calls and the signs that his services were no longer needed. None came.

Tennis champion Arthur Ashe died on February 6, 1993.

-Fawcett & Sandberg, pp. 506-508

EXAM ONE, PASSAGE THREE

14. What ended Arthur Ashe's career as a tennis player?

1. marriage
2. AIDS
3. shoulder injury
4. heart attack

15. Why did Arthur Ashe reveal his condition to the public?

1. his wife begged him to disclose it
2. the possibility of a forthcoming newspaper report
3. his associates pressured him
4. his appearance was deteriorating

16. The author's tone in regard to Arthur Ashe is

1. sympathetic and complimentary.
2. objective and neutral.
3. distrustful and critical.
4. bitter and defensive.

17. As used in the passage, <u>tainted</u> most nearly means

1. disgraced.
2. smeared.
3. contaminated.
4. unknown.

18. The fact that not one organization called Arthur Ashe after his announcement

1. surprised even Arthur Ashe.
2. proved that the public could not deal with people with AIDS.
3. meant that Ashe had lost respect.
4. was of no importance at all.

19. The purpose of the second paragraph is to

1. indicate that Ashe was being paranoid.
2. state that even the common man was concerned about Arthur Ashe.
3. illustrate the public fear associated with AIDS.
4. show that AIDS is a contagious disease.

GO ON TO NEXT PAGE

EXAM ONE, PASSAGE THREE

Basic to the Japanese tradition of Shinto are spirits or gods, called *kami*. Spirits are located in specific places in the world: in a temple, in a crib, or in a shrine. One of the Japanese estimates is that there are eight million *kami*. This term refers both to the sense of power felt in things of the world and to particular gods. A waterfall is a powerful spirit and recognizing it communicates the sense an observer has of its immense power.

Perhaps the most important spirits are those in the house. They occupy particular places and protect the members of the household when in those places: the god of the kitchen lives in the kitchen, the bathroom god in the bathroom, and so forth. There is also a guardian *kami* of the household. This spirit is made up of many ancestors who have merged to guard the house as a corporate unit that exists over time. The village has a guardian *kami*, often a fox god or an ancestor of a founding member. Villagers may ask the village god for help in their rice harvest or for success in schooling.

People create new *kami* as needed. In a less individuated way, all equipment (from computer chips to cameras to automobile production machinery) is thought to have a spiritual side. In 1990 engineers met at Tokyo's Chomeiji shrine to thank their used-up equipment for their service.　　-Bowen, pp. 29-30

EXAM ONE, PASSAGE FOUR

20. According to some estimates, how many Japanese gods are there?

1. 8
2. 80
3. 800
4. 8,000,000

21. The pattern of organization that the author uses in paragraph two is

1. definition.
2. example.
3. contrast.
4. narration.

22. corporate, as underlined, is best defined as

1. group.
2. business.
3. company.
4. unusual.

23. One aspect of Japanese spiritualism that may seem odd to non-Japanese is that

1. Japanese are religious.
2. villages have gods who protect them.
3. people are allowed to create new gods as needed.
4. Japanese gods are powerful.

24. According to the passage, the most important spirits are those found

1. in a temple or shrine.
2. at the rice harvest.
3. in the village.
4. in the house.

25. What may appear strange to westerners about the 1990 engineers meeting at Chomeiji shrine is that

1. scientists met at a religious location to show reverence for inanimate objects.
2. persons of science are also religious.
3. other scientists were not invited.
4. the meeting was not held in the office.

GO ON TO NEXT PAGE

EXAM ONE, PASSAGE FOUR

In Medieval Europe, most serfs were born, lived, and died on the same estate or manor, very traditional and limited in their outlook. Manors usually included a village, so serfs rarely needed to travel beyond the estate of their master. Serfdom represented a stage between slavery and freedom. Serfs were not sold individually; they could not be sold unless the land itself was sold. On the other hand, a serf did not rank as high as a freeman since he could not own his residence, nor marry outside the manor, nor give away his goods without the permission of his lord and master.

Serfs toiled on the land for the lord as well as for themselves. They also turned over one-tenth of their produce to the church. Each serf worked perhaps three days a week for the master and one day for the church, leaving him two days for himself and his family. It is interesting to note that if a runaway serf escaped to a town without being caught for a year and a day, he could gain his freedom.

Serfs' lives were miserable by our standards. Adults, children, and (in the winter) farm animals infested with bugs and fleas lived in a one-room, thatched hut. The hut often had a dirt floor and a hole in the roof for a chimney. In this crowded environment, accidents, disease, and malnutrition often took their toll, reducing the life expectancy of a serf to thirty or forty years. These workers had meat only a

few times a year, usually at Christmas and Easter time. Their everyday <u>fare</u> was the perpetual cabbage soup and grain bread (and if lucky, cheese and ale for dinner). Not aware of the germ theory of disease, medieval serfs rarely washed their utensils or their hands.

All in all, not much is known about the serfs of Medieval Europe. Written records are virtually empty of any notation of them—perhaps the nobility and clergy did not find any of them worthy of mention.

-based on Keboe, et. al., p. 319

EXAM ONE, PASSAGE FIVE

26. The purpose of paragraph one is to

1. show cause and effect of the actions of a master and serf.
2. narrate the restricted life of one serf.
3. describe the status of a serf.
4. persuade the reader to be compassionate toward serfs.

27. According to the passage, life expectancy for a serf was about

1. 20-30 years.
2. 30-40 years.
3. 30-50 years.
4. 50-60 years.

28. How could a serf gain his freedom?

1. by working for the master for twelve years
2. by appealing to the village church elders
3. by escaping and not getting caught for one year and one day.
4. by marrying into the nobility

29. The main idea of paragraph three is that

1. serfs led miserable lives.
2. the types of food a serf ate were malnutritious
3. farm animals infested with bugs and fleas lived in the house with the serf's family.
4. medieval serfs rarely washed their utensils or their hands.

30. As used in paragraph three, <u>fare</u>, most probably means

1. menu.
2. ticket.
3. habit.
4. list.

31.   The author of this passage uses a style which is

1. informal but informative.
2. scientific and analytical.
3. formal and informative.
4. argumentative and persuasive.

GO ON TO NEXT PAGE

EXAM ONE, PASSAGE FIVE

Television images haunt us—bony, stunted bodies. This is hunger in its acute form. But hunger comes in another form. It is the day-to-day hunger that over 700 million people suffer. Every year this hunger, largely invisible, kills as many as 20 million people. So we ask ourselves, what is hunger, really? Is it the physical <u>depletion</u> of those suffering chronic undernutrition? Yes, but it is more.

As long as we have a conception of hunger only in physical measures, we will never truly understand it, certainly not its roots. What would it mean to think of hunger in terms of universal human emotions? <u>Here's an idea of what we mean</u>.

Dr. Clements writes of a family in El Salvador he tried to help whose son and daughter had died. "Both had been lost having chosen to pay their mortgage rather than keep the money to feed their children. Thus, being hungry means *anguish,* the anguish of impossible choices.

In Nicaragua four years ago, we met Amanda Espinoza who never had enough to feed her family. She had endured six stillbirths and watched five of her children die before the age of one. To Amanda, hunger means *grief.*

Walking into a home in the rural Philippines, the first words the doctor heard were an apology for the poverty of the dwelling. Being hungry also means living in *humiliation.*

In Guatemala in 1978, we learned that one of two men we had met had been forced into hiding; the other had been killed. For the wealthy land owners who monopolized farming in the region, the men's crime was teaching their poor neighbors better farming techniques. Guatemala's wealthy feel threatened by any change that makes the poor less dependent on jobs on their rich plantations. So, the last dimension of hunger is *fear.*   Lappe & Collins, pp. 2-4

32. Underlined in the selection, the word <u>depletion</u> most nearly means

1. strengthening.
2. abuse.
3. weakening.
4. restoration.

33. How many emotional dimensions to hunger are there?

1. one
2. two
3. three
4. four

34. When reading the sentence, <u>Here's an idea of what we mean</u>, what would the reader expect to read in the next paragraph?

1. emotional dimensions of hunger
2. physicality of hunger
3. how Dr. Clements define physical hunger
4. statistics about hunger

EXAM ONE, PASSAGE SIX

35. The last four paragraphs of the selection utilize the patterns of organization of

1. description and use of adjectives.
2. narration and summation.
3. example and cause-effect.
4. comparison and contrast.

36. The central focus of the selection is that

1. advertising uses horrific ads to persuade us to support world hunger relief organizations.
2. Guatemala's wealthy mistreat the poor farmers.
3. Dr. Clements did excellent work working with the poor.
4. hunger is not just physical; it is emotional as well.

37. The scenario about Amanda Espinoza illustrated the emotional dimension of

1. fear.
2. anguish.
3. humiliation.
4. grief.

GO ON TO NEXT PAGE

EXAM ONE, PASSAGE SIX

The presidency is today the paramount institution in the national government of the United States. While the Founding Fathers had no intention that it be so, the office has become the central energizer of government policy and the symbol at home and abroad of the American political system. It is the focus of the hopes (and fears) of countless individuals and groups. For better or worse, we tend to think about American history in four-or-eight-year chunks corresponding to the term in office of a particular president.

We invariably turn to the president when the times are out of kilter, demanding remedial action from him and then either blaming him if improvements are not immediately forthcoming or praising him unduly if the burden of problems is eased. We depend on the president to set the agenda for Congress, to define national objectives in time of war, and to represent the United States before the world.

In these and in countless other ways, the presidency embodies the headship of the government, surely not a monarch, but just as surely more than "first among equals." I shall argue that the office has reached this position over the course of our history—not because of random events, but because of certain developments in American capitalism.

-Greenberg, p. 228

EXAM ONE, PASSAGE SEVEN

38. The writer of this excerpt is most likely

1. a history professor.
2. the editor of the *Journal of American Government*
3. a political scientist.
4. a student interning at the White House.

39. The word invariably as used in the second paragraph most nearly means

1. petulantly.
2. variously.
3. reluctantly.
4. unfailingly.

40. Which of the following is stated in the passage?

1. American people turn to the president when times are out of kilter.
2. Americans do not commit to their president.
3. American capitalism played no part in establishing the office of the presidency.
4. The presidency today is only second to the monarchy of England.

GO ON TO NEXT PAGE

41. The paragraph which follows this excerpt will discuss

1. how the presidency is like a monarchy.
2. the office of the presidency over the course of history.
3. presidential behavior that manifests the concept "first among equals."
4. the idea that capitalism, not random events, influenced the office of the presidency.

42. In the first paragraph, overall the author uses which pattern of organization?

1. persuasion and argument
2. definition and description
3. chronology and timeline
4. classification and categorization

GO ON TO NEXT PAGE

EXAM ONE, PASSAGE SEVEN

In 1781, a slave named "Mum Bett" sued for her freedom.

Born in 1742 to African slaves in Claverack, New York, Mum Bett was purchased by her new owner, Colonel Ashley of Sheffield, Massachusetts, when she was six months old. She served as his house servant through middle age. When the master's wife, in a fit of rage, went to strike Mum Bett's sister, Mum Bett received the blow instead. Injured, she left her master's house and refused to return. When her master appealed to the court for her recovery in 1781, she sought the help of a young lawyer, Theodore Sedgwick of nearby Stockbridge.

During the years of the Revolution, Mum Bett had heard discussions about the 1780 Declaration of Rights in the Massachusetts Constitution and told the young lawyer that those rights certainly must apply to her since she was not a "dumb beast." Sedgwick argued the case for her and another of Colonel Ashley's slaves, Brom. Both slaves won their freedom, and the colonel had to pay the cost for court. Mum Bett changed her name to Elizabeth Freeman.

Although Colonel Ashley offered her wages to return, Mum Bett went to work for the Sedgwicks as their housekeeper and even protected their house from vandals during Shay's Rebellion in late 1786. After she moved in with her daughter "Little Bett," she became a respected nurse and midwife. Mum Bett lived with

her daughter through the War of 1812 and until her death in 1829.   -Salem, p. 87

43. The reader can infer from the passage that Mum Bett was a unique woman in that

1. the slave owners all respected her.
2. she, being a slave, took a slave owner to court and sued him.
3. as a free woman, she became a midwife.
4. she forced Colonel Ashley to pay court costs.

44. A central theme of the passage is that

1. during the years of the Revolution, there were discussions about the Declaration of Rights found in the Massachusetts Constitution.
2. Colonel Ashley was the stereo-typical slave owner who abused Mum Bett.
3. Mum Bett was an extremely courageous woman who fought for her civil rights.
4. most laws of Massachusetts in the late 1700s dealt with slave owner-ship.

45. We can infer from the selection that Elizabeth

1. was well liked by the Sedgwicks.
2. was given respect by the Ashleys.
3. was buried in New York.
4. loved children.

EXAM ONE, PASSAGE EIGHT

46. Why do you think Mum Bett chose
the surname of Freeman?

1. that was her name at birth
2. she took Thomas Sedgwick's wife's
   last name
3. her daughter suggested it
4. to celebrate her freedom

47. After moving in with her daughter,
Elizabeth

1. continued her duties at the
   Sedgwick's.
2. became a nurse and midwife.
3. served as a house servant.
4. had to retire due to illness.

48. According to the passage, why did
Mum Bett leave Colonel Ashley's
estate?

1. Colonel Ashley freed her.
2. She was too old to handle the
   physical chores.
3. His wife tried to hit Mum Bett's
   sister.
4. She wanted to live with her daughter.

GO ON TO NEXT PAGE

EXAM ONE, PASSAGE EIGHT

We have found that different non-verbal signals and gestures are used in various cities. Understanding the fact that there are differences can keep one out of embarrassing situations.

Recently, while flying from Atlanta to New York, we encountered this phenomenon in a discussion with a very gracious lady who was from the South. She disliked going to New York City because of the supposed indifference that people displayed toward others. "Moreover," she said, "I especially don't enjoy not being looked at and made to feel that I don't exist. Why, in the South, we take the time to look at people and, as you know, to smile at them." Indeed, it has been observed that Peachtree St. in Atlanta is a location where one is smiled at often. We explained to our new acquaintance that individuals' nonverbal signals vary from city to city and region to region.

In densely populated areas such as New York City and Tokyo, people give the impression that they are disregarding one another. A new-comer might take their gestures to mean complete indifference. Yet studies conducted to determine how people in crowded cities react during a time of crisis—such as the 1965 New York power blackout—reveal that an overwhelming majority respond by helping others in need. These "good Samaritans" with hard-shell exteriors show their true colors at such times. In less densely populated areas where individuals depend on each other more and Southern hospitality prevails, signals such as smiles, winks, and a warm "hey" are commonplace. A New Yorker, however, would probably be taken aback if greeted in this manner by a stranger.

-Nierenberg & Calero, pp. 140-141

49. The authors of this article are most probably

1. tour guides.
2. public relations agents.
3. geographers.
4. sociologists.

50. The author's tone is

1. mostly nostalgic.
2. a bit ironic.
3. chatty and informal.
4. somewhat persuasive.

51. The phrase, taken aback, found in the last sentence, is best defined as

1. stunned.
2. insulted.
3. angry.
4. contented.

52. The authors of this passage would most likely agree that

1. Southerners are too friendly.
2. recognizing and understanding gestures is a valuable tool in communication.
3. people from densely populated cities are worthless during a crisis.
4. due to their hard-shell exteriors, New Yorkers are standoffish.

EXAM ONE, PASSAGE NINE

53. The woman whom the writers met on the airplane

1. was on her way to Tokyo.
2. had just spent a month in New York City.
3. was going to New York City.
4. had just finished touring Peachtree Street area in Atlanta.

54. The phrase, <u>overwhelming majority</u>, as underlined in the passage, refers to

1. New Yorkers.
2. others in need.
3. Southerners.
4. people in a crowded city.

EXAM ONE, PASSAGE NINE

EXAM TWO

The reforms and foreign policy of King Mongut of Thailand were carried out by his son and successor. King Rama V came to the throne as a frail youth of sixteen and died one of Thailand's most loved and <u>revered</u> kings. He had a remarkable reign of 42 years. Indeed, modern Thailand may be said to be a product of the comprehensive and progressive reforms of his reign. For these touched almost every aspect of Thai life.

King Rama V faced the Western world with a positive and eager attitude: eager to learn about Western ideas and inventions, positively working towards Western-style "progress" while at the same time resisting Western rule. He was the first Thai king to travel abroad; he did not just travel as an observer or tourist but worked hard during his trips to further Thai interests.

The King also traveled within his own country. He was passionately interested in his subjects' welfare and was intent on the monarchy assuming a more visible role in society. He wanted to see how his subjects lived and went outside his palace often, sometimes <u>incognito</u>—and was never recognized. His progressive outlook led him to his first official act, forbidding prostration (the requirement to lie face down) in the royal presence. He gradually abolished the institution of slavery, a momentous and positive change for Thai society.

With so many achievements to his credit and a charisma that was enhanced by his longevity, it was no wonder that the Thai people grieved long and genuinely for King Rama V when he died. October 23, the date of his death, is still a national holiday, in honor of one of Thailand's greatest and most beloved kings.

-Office of the Prime Minister, pp. 23-27

1. <u>revered</u>, as used in the passage, is best defined as

1. honored.
2. tolerated.
3. unpopular.
4. aged.

2. The first official act by King Rama V was

1. traveling abroad.
2. visiting his subjects around the country.
3. making his birthday a national holiday.
4. forbidding prostration.

3. The author gets his point across through the use of

1. statistical and factual documentation.
2. persuasive language.
3. respectful and admiring language.
4. impartial narrative and dialogue.

4. <u>incognito</u>, as used in the passage, most nearly means

1. apparent.
2. disguised.
3. unaccompanied.
4. escorted.

EXAM TWO, PASSAGE ONE

5. The main idea of the passage is

1. Rama V was not as good a king as his father, King Mongut.
2. the king traveled abroad as well as within his own country of Thailand.
3. a national holiday is celebrated in honor of King Rama V.
4. Rama V was one of Thailand's most loved and revered kings.

6. According to the passage, what was Rama V's attitude toward the West?

1. admiring but cautious.
2. bitter and distrustful.
3. apathetic and indifferent.
4. mocking and sarcastic.

GO ON TO NEXT PAGE

EXAM TWO, PASSAGE ONE

After work one day I set out for the ballpark; I wanted to catch a Giants game. I marched out to the bleachers only to find them completely full. It was standing room only, six deep in fans. Discouraged, I turned back, hoping food would help. Passing up the hot dog kiosks, I bought a roasted squid on a stick.

The Yomiuri Giants were playing the Nippon Ham Fighters. The players bowed to each other—the game was about to begin. I glanced up at the electronic scoreboard that displayed (in Chinese characters) all the players' names and a vast array of information, including wind direction, speed, and team names. Actual team names were not taken from their geographic headquarters but rather from the companies that owned them, such as the Yomiuri news firm that owned the Giants, or the Hanshin railway company who were the owners of the Hanshin Tigers. But who in the world, I wondered, would want to be owned by the Nippon Ham Company?

The noise surged as the game began, with cheerleaders prancing atop the dugout roofs, exhorting their teams. They flailed the air with pompoms and banners in the teams' colors, and beat an ancient native drum. The noise level of the sections of "home" and "away" rooters reminded me more of American college football than baseball. Horns blared, people howled, toilet paper and confetti streamers arched through the night sky.

EXAM TWO, PASSAGE TWO

Several more differences from American baseball practices were glaring: every time a foul or a home run carried the ball into the riotous stands, it was politely returned to the field. Also, no matter how obvious, the official scorers virtually refused to charge fielders with errors. Propriety prevailed, even amidst hysteria.

-Katzenstein, pp. 28-30

7. We can assume from the passage that the writer

1. had never been to a Japanese baseball game.
2. had limited experience at sports events.
3. was agreeably impressed with the Japanese fans' enthusiasm.
4. thought that the Japanese protocols should be adopted by American baseball teams.

8. According to the passage, Japanese baseball teams are named after

1. their geographic headquarters.
2. famous Japanese samurai.
3. the manager's choice of names.
4. the companies that own them.

9. The purpose of the passage is to

1. describe.
2. entertain.
3. define.
4. explain.

10. According to the passage, when the writer marched out to the bleachers

1. they were empty.
2. only half of the seats were taken.
3. only fans rooting for the Nippon Ham Fighters were at the game.
4. they were crammed full.

11. When the author asks "But who in the world, I wondered, would want to be owned by the Nippon Ham Company?" he is

1. asking an academic question.
2. showing respect.
3. being sarcastic.
4. criticizing Japanese industry.

12. As used in the last sentence, propriety most likely means

1. good manners.
2. indecency.
3. hysteria.
4. corruption.

GO ON TO NEXT PAGE

EXAM TWO, PASSAGE TWO

Most school psychologists and counselors feel that the family is the most significant, single influence on the development of the child. The family is the primary <u>structure</u> that provides the developing human being with his or her attitudes, beliefs, values, and sense of self. Educational researchers have shown that persistence and academic performance are strongly related to family background and interactions.

The school system is probably the second most important structured environment that influences the developing human being. When a student is having difficulty adapting to the school system, the school system's intervention plans have, for the most part, tried to influence the individual student while ignoring the most significant influence in the student's life—the family.

From the family-systems perspective, many of these school intervention programs (such as punishments and individual or group counseling) are doomed to failure. This is especially true if the family's influence and value system are different from the school system's intended behavior change. For example, the school may try to stop a student from fighting at school, while the parent's message to the child is, "Don't let anyone push you around. Stand up for yourself." From the family-systems perspective, it is imperative that the family be involved if you wish to see more effective and enduring behavioral changes at school. -Valentine, pp. 15-16

EXAM TWO, PASSAGE THREE

13. According to the passage, the most significant influence on the development of a child is

1. a favorite teacher.
2. the school environment.
3. the family.
4. siblings.

14. In the context of this passage, if a child does well in school, it is most likely a result of

1. cramming.
2. the family environment.
3. the school atmosphere.
4. studying with a tutor.

15. The author would probably agree that if a child is having problems with school work

1. the child should go to after school classes.
2. the child should change to a private school.
3. after-school punishment should be required.
4. school teachers should speak with the child's primary caretaker at home.

16. It can be inferred from the passage that the writer

1. believes in punishment.
2. is in favor of group counseling.
3. has been a principal.
4. is an advocate of the family-systems perspective.

17. The word <u>structure</u> as used in the first paragraph most nearly means

1. group framework.
2. edifice.
3. arrangement.
4. construction.

18. Which of the following sentences from the passage best expresses the main idea?

1. The school system is probably the second most important structured environment that influences the developing human being.
2. It is imperative that the family be involved if it wishes to see more effective and enduring behavioral changes at school.
3. When a student is having difficulty adapting, the school's intervention plans have tried to influence the student while ignoring the family.
4. This is especially true if the family's value system is different from the school system's intended behavior change.

GO ON TO NEXT PAGE

EXAM TWO, PASSAGE THREE

Conrad Hilton, founder of Hilton hotels and father to Paris, started with only a dream—no money—just a big, big dream. But he did what most people are not willing to do. He added action, and turned his imagination into a plan. He gave the plan details, scheduled the details, and made alternate plans in case the first plan failed. Most importantly, he put his plan into action and made it come true. Hilton believed that if you don't dream big, you certainly won't achieve much. One of the basic laws that governs man is: unless you can visualize something, you cannot attain it.

Amazing as it sounds, the great majority of people in the U.S. don't spend even an hour a week, pencil in hand, planning a strategy for their financial future. Hilton once said, "Most people are so busy earning a living, they never make any money." And it's true!

As soon as the typical American has a small amount of money saved, he is tempted to spend it on depreciating assets such as cars, camping, boats, or trailers which devalue as you drive them off the lot. Most spend their entire lives saving just enough to buy something to keep up with their neighbors. They never have enough left over to make meaningful investments.

To belong to that exclusive group of millionaires, the one out of a thousand, you must begin by following the Rule of Ten Percent. Any increase in the Ten Percent Rule speeds you on the

way to making your fortune. The rule is a simple one, but a difficult one for some individuals to follow: you must save a minimum of 10% of your gross earnings. The second part of the rule is that you never, never spend that savings!
-Haroldsen, p. 16

19. One of the major points of the selection is

1. most people make enough money to live "the good life."
2. most Americans spend their money on boats or trailers.
3. most Americans have a plan, but they do not execute it.
4. if you don't dream big, you certainly won't achieve much.

20. According to the selection, the reason the typical American can not save is that

1. s/he is tempted to spend it on depreciating assets.
2. relatives are always borrowing from her/him.
3. s/he gives it to neighbors.
4. her/his attitude of "I made it, so I can spend it on whatever I want."

21. depreciating assets, as underlined in the passage, most nearly means

1. reductions.
2. run down vehicles.
3. items decreasing in value.
4. valued means of transportation.

EXAM TWO, PASSAGE FOUR

22. The style of writing employed by
the author is

1. formal and staid.
2. chatty and informal.
3. humorous and entertaining.
4. somber and depressing.

23. When Conrad Hilton initiated his
first plan of action, he

1. did not have much imagination,
    but did have a lot of capital to invest.
2. had no alternate Plan B because he
    was so sure Plan A would work.
3. was indifferent to the outcome.
4. had no money.

24. The last paragraph leaves the reader
with a sense of

1. glamor.
2. helplessness.
3. encouragement.
4. pride.

GO ON TO NEXT PAGE

EXAM TWO, PASSAGE FOUR

In the nineteenth century, children lived alongside adults in Illinois' poor houses, asylums, and jails. By 1899, several issues moved social reformers to institute a juvenile court in Chicago—the nation's first separate court for children:

1) Prosecutors attempted to hold youthful offenders (between the ages of seven and 14) responsible for their crimes as adults;

2) If convicted, such juveniles would be <u>incarcerated</u> with an adult prison population; and

3) as in ten cases before 1900, juveniles were executed.

Consequently, in 1899 Illinois legislation gave courts jurisdiction over juveniles who were charged with crimes as well as over children who were neglected. It also provided for confidentiality in regard to the youthful offender's records. In another protective step, the act required the separation of juveniles from adults when incarcerated and barred the detention of juveniles under 12 years old in jails altogether.

On the other hand, in addition to the usual run of adult crimes, children could be charged with offenses such as truancy, habitual delinquency, and sexual delinquency. The creation of a distinct process for minors presented only a small victory for the reformers. The court relied heavily upon institutionalization rather than the family preservation initially envisioned by reformers.

In 1965 the state legislature overhauled the Illinois Juvenile Court Act, giving significant legal protections to minors, including the provision of a public defender. During the next decade, however, public opinion demanded harsher treatment. A 1982 revision to the Illinois Habitual Juvenile Offender Act decreed that any juvenile aged 15 or older (charged with murder, armed robbery, or sexual assault) face prosecution as an adult in criminal court, and if convicted be committed to the Illinois Department of Corrections.

In 1997 in Cook County alone, between 1,500 and 2,000 cases were heard every day, representing 25,000 active delinquency and 50,000 active abuse and neglect cases.

-Couto & Stutts, p. 17 and Dodge, 2005

25. The word <u>incarcerated</u> most nearly means

1. acquitted.
2. involved.
3. imprisoned.
4. executed.

26. The authors convey their point by

1. defining the word "juvenile."
2. describing the Illinois state legislature.
3. giving a testimonial.
4. presenting facts and legal information.

EXAM TWO, PASSAGE FIVE

27. The reader can deduce from the information that the 1982 revision was a result of pressure from

1. state legislature.
2. the public.
3. federal judges.
4. reformers.

28. Which of the following was not given as a reason for changing the criminal court system in Chicago?

1. juveniles were being jailed with the adult population.
2. thousands of children had been executed.
3. children as young as seven were prosecuted as adults
4. there was no confidentiality for the youthful offenders' records.

29. The main focus of the last paragraph is

1. how difficult it is to charge parents with neglect.
2. how expensive it is to prosecute so many juvenile cases.
3. that there are not enough attorneys to handle all the juvenile cases.
4. that there is an overwhelming number of active delinquent and neglect cases.

30. Most probably the authors are

1. journalists.
2. criminologists.
3. state senators.
4. experts on prison systems.

GO ON TO NEXT PAGE

EXAM TWO, PASSAGE FIVE

"Open the shutters, will you?"

The bowed head next to her bed snapped erect, and she heard the sound of rosary beads clattering to the floor.

"My lady—?"

"The shutters. Open them, please." Through the small, high window, she could see a sliver of moon glinting hard and clear; the sky was drenched silver with stars. She blinked feebly, and when she looked again, they had retreated, playful and aloof, beyond her grasp once more.

How long had she lain there? Weeks? Perhaps only days. She did not know, nor did she care enough to ask. Earlier this evening after prayers, the nun who sat by her bed had suddenly gasped and run to fetch the board and stick. She heard her race through the cloister, furiously beating the death board.

Heloise laughed to herself. She was not ready; she would not be hurried. For so long she had hungered to embrace this moment, prayed for it, ached with anticipation, and now that the time had arrived, she felt no need to hurry. Somehow she had lived through sixty-three summers, playing her tedious roles in the convent, forever smiling, never allowing the world to glimpse the real woman.

Quickly, she corrected herself. To him she had sometimes revealed her true self—sometimes. But even he could not accept her. The letters, those shameless shreds, those offerings of truth delivered up to his aghast silence; her hands clutched the coverlet in stinging memory. Ah, my very sweet

EXAM TWO, PASSAGE SIX

friend, she thought, you didn't understand my love. In the end you learned to love God, and even, in your own way, to love me.　　　　-Meade, pp. 9; 11

31. The phrase, this moment, refers to the moment

1. Heloise turned sixty-three.
2. Heloise fell in love.
3. of death.
4. Heloise heard the sound of the death board.

32. We can infer from the passage that the setting is

1. day time.
2. before evening prayers.
3. night time.
4. weeks after Heloise became ill.

33. According to the passage, Heloise is

1. at a funeral home.
2. at a monastery.
3. in an infirmary.
4. in a convent.

34. The phrase death board, as underlined in the passage, refers back to

1. prayers.
2. board and stick.
3. the nun.
4. Heloise.

35. The reader can infer from the passage that "he"

1. answered all of Heloise's letters.
2. could not read.
3. did not receive Heloise's letters.
4. never answered Heloise's letters.

36. The main idea of the last paragraph is

1. the elderly nun's love for "him" was not returned in the way she had wanted.
2. due to her illness, the elderly nun was always having to correct herself.
3. every time the elderly nun remembered him, she felt a sense of peace.
4. the thought of the letters was the only thing that pulled the elderly nun through times of crisis.

GO ON TO NEXT PAGE

EXAM TWO, PASSAGE SIX

There are some very real differences between fathers and mothers in terms of their involvement with a child. In general, research shows that compared to mothers, fathers spend less time with the children. In 1983 Pleck reported that employed fathers with children less than five years old spend an average of 27 minutes once per day in care giving or other activities with their children. This may not be because fathers work outside of the home. Even when both parents are home, fathers generally spend less time with children than mothers. Even when a mother works outside of the home, fathers only spend about one-third the time that mothers spend in parenting activities.

Why the disparity? One reason for the lack of involvement by fathers may be due to resistance by the mothers! Only 23 per cent of employed mothers and 31 percent of unemployed mothers stated that they wanted more help from fathers. In the study, it was concluded that the mothers were reluctant to share their role with the fathers.

In regard to punishment of children—whoever is administering it—many psychologists believe physical punishment, such as spanking or hitting should not be used at all. Physical punishment modifies the behavior of the child in the short run, but its use is also associated with many negative outcomes.

The first and most serious outcome of punishment is an increase in aggression, especially among boys. For example, parents who used punishment and

threats had more aggressive sons than those who did not use such techniques. Second, parents who use physical punishment may serve as models of aggressiveness for their children. Third, children may learn that violence is an acceptable method for resolving conflicts rather than employing other methods. Last, children who are punished frequently avoid the person who does the punishing.

-Kestner, p. 298

37. The purpose of the first two paragraphs is to

1. compare employed mothers with unemployed mothers.
2. contrast mothers' and fathers' involvement in child-related activities.
3. persuade the reader that 27 minutes a day is enough time to spend with a child.
4. argue that fathers are better parents than mothers.

38. According to the passage, who spends the least amount of time with their children?

1. fathers
2. mothers
3. employed fathers
4. employed mothers

EXAM TWO, PASSAGE SEVEN

39. According to the passage, the reason spanking should not be used at all is because

1. it leaves physical scars and bruises.
2. it is illegal.
3. its use is associated with many negative outcomes.
4. the child will not love the father.

40. The overall purpose of the last two paragraphs is to

1. contrast.
2. show cause-effect.
3. illustrate.
4. describe.

41. The most serious outcome of using physical punishment is that

1. there is an increase in aggression in the child.
2. there is a dramatic risk of brain damage.
3. the child will learn that aggression is an acceptable method for resolving problems.
4. the parent may go to prison.

42. In the Pleck study, how many minutes a day does an employed father spend in activities focusing on his children?

1. 23
2. 31
3. 27
4. zero

GO ON TO NEXT PAGE

EXAM TWO, PASSAGE SEVEN

In the process of growing up, and in the process of living itself, it is all too easy for us to become isolated from (or never to form) a positive self-concept. In addition, we may never reach a joyful vision of ourselves because of the negative input from others. Further, we may never have positive self-esteem because we have defaulted on our own honesty, integrity, and/or responsibility. Our self-concepts may have been ruined because we did not stand up for what we believed was right. Last, we may have judged our own actions with inadequate understanding and compassion which resulted in a poor self-image.

Apart from problems that are biological in origin, I cannot think of a single psychological difficulty—from anxiety and depression to alcohol or drug abuse, to underachievement at school to suicide—that is not traceable to poor self-esteem. Of all the judgments we pass, none is as important as the one we pass on ourselves. Positive self-esteem is a requirement of a fulfilling life.

Let us understand what self-esteem is. It has two components, a feeling of personal competence and feeling of personal worth. In other words, self-esteem is the sum of self-confidence and self-respect. It reflects several aspects:

    1. your ability to cope with the challenges of your life

    2. your ability to understand your problems;

    3. your right to be happy; and

    4. your ability to respect and stand up for your needs

Genuine self-esteem is not expressed by self-glorification <u>at the expense of</u> others; it is not expressed by the quest to make oneself superior to others; and it is not expressed in order to diminish others so as to elevate oneself.

-Branden, pp. 5-10

EXAM TWO, PASSAGE EIGHT

43. The pattern of organization utilized in paragraph one is

1. comparison.
2. cause-effect.
3. example.
4. narration.

44. Positive self-esteem involves all of the following except

1. the sum of self-confidence and self-respect.
2. a sense of personal worth.
3. a feeling of personal competence.
4. self-glorification at the expense of others.

45. In the fourth paragraph, the phrase <u>at the expense of</u> most nearly means

1. paid for by.
2. by withdrawing from.
3. without regard for.
4. by sharing with.

46. The author of this piece is probably

1. a psychologist.
2. a nurse.
3. an educator.
4. a high school principal.

47. Some people never attain a positive self-concept because

1. the process of growing up is all too easy.
2. they treat themselves with compassion.
3. they ignore the opinions of others.
4. they do not stand up for what they know to be right behavior.

48. Which of the following affects an individual's self-esteem most?

1. school experiences
2. the way one sees oneself
3. the media
4. parental guidance

GO ON TO NEXT PAGE

EXAM TWO, PASSAGE EIGHT

They were hoping for a son. It was a daughter. The future Catherine II of Russia was born at Stettin on April 21, 1729. She was given the names Sophie Augusta Fredericka Catherine. The young mother, Johanna, was distressed that she had not been able to produce a boy and spent little time watching over the cradle.

The mother was convinced that with her beauty and worldly wisdom she could have achieved a higher destiny. Instead of the brilliant rise she had once dreamed of, she had to be content with a husband of <u>modest</u> position. It was her family who had arranged the match, without consulting her. At fifteen, she had married Prince Christian Augustus, a man twenty-seven years her senior. Truly a person of no great importance, he was one of those obscure princes in the fragmented Germany of the eighteenth century. Her husband was a major general in the Prussian army. This worthy man, devoted to order, thrift, and religion, surrounded Johanna with affection, but that was far from enough to satisfy her. Johanna had a passion for worldly intrigue and <u>chafed at</u> holding so poor a place in society.

Fortunately, shortly after Catherine was born, the family was able to move into the fortified castle of Stettin. It was a small promotion. The following year, there was another piece of good news—Johanna at last gave birth to a boy. God had heard her prayers! She lavished the affection and pride she had denied her daughter upon the infant.

Catherine, still very young, suffered bitterly from her mother's preference for the newcomer.   -Troyat, pp. 1-2

49. The word, <u>modest,</u> as used in the selection most nearly means

1. famed.
2. worldly.
3. ordinary.
4. shy.

50. The focus of this passage is

1. Johanna.
2. Catherine the Great.
3. the Prince.
4. Stettin.

51. Johanna's attitude toward the Prince was one of

1. adoration.
2. passion.
3. sincerity.
4. bitterness.

52. The reader can infer from the passage that Catherine's mother was

1. kind and sympathetic.
2. indifferent and impartial.
3. nostalgic and homesick.
4. self-centered and spoiled.

EXAM TWO, PASSAGE NINE

53. According to the passage, Johanna preferred

1. her husband to her children.
2. court life over her family.
3. her daughter to her husband.
4. her son to her daughter.

54. The phrase <u>chafed at</u> as underlined in the selection most likely means

1. raged at.
2. accepted.
3. ignored.
4. excelled at.

EXAM TWO, PASSAGE NINE

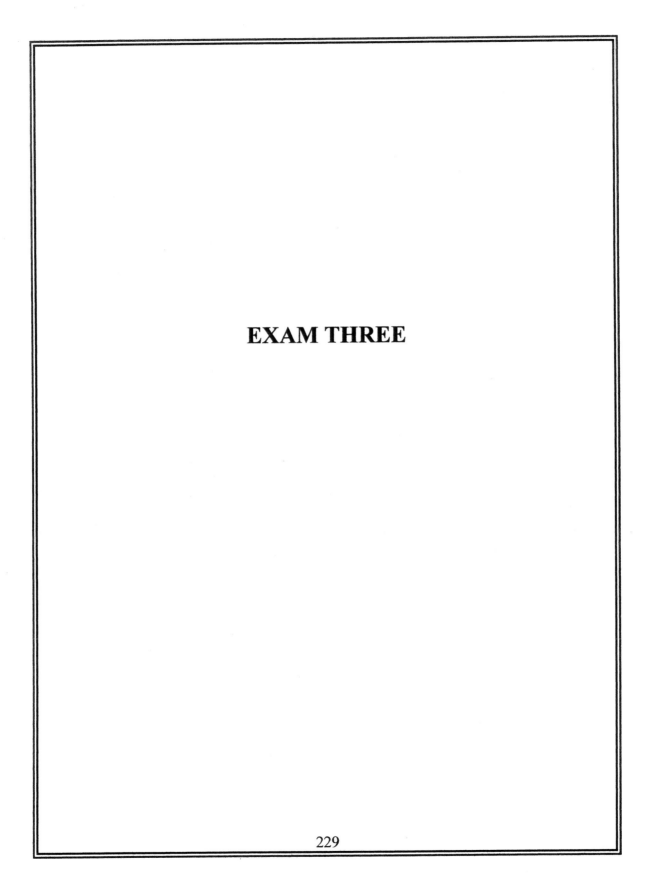

EXAM THREE

Throughout human history volcanoes have been viewed with an awe instilled by their spectacular eruptions. For a visitor such stupendous events can be a once-in-a-lifetime experience. Yet, for the population living in the immediate areas of volcanic hazards, the specter of pending destruction is a daily companion.

There are many examples that illustrate this situation:

1. Mt. Vesuvious buried Pompeii in 79A.D. and had erupted 83 times by 1944. Yet, villages and towns are thriving on and near its slopes, and the great city of Naples is located a few miles from the volcano

2. Taal, on the Philippine island of Luzon had erupted at least 33 times by 1977, and its companion, Mayon, 46 times by 1978. Again, agricultural communities dot the landscape around these volcanoes

The question arises as to why people are willing to live with such dangers. This question is not easy to answer because of many variables involving culture, economics, and the individual willingness to take risks. In most cases it is just a matter of finding fertile land. This is especially the case in wet tropical lands where volcanic soils are among the most productive and permit multiple cropping.

In other circumstances it is the attitude of the people. They tend to worry more about the loss of property than fear the loss of life. In a study of a hazard area around Puna, Hawaii, 41 percent of the respondents to an inquiry stated that they do not worry when they learn that an eruption of Kilauea is imminent. Ninety percent believed that there are greater advantages in living in that area than disadvantages. This view is held despite the history that Kilauea has erupted more than 70 times since 1750.   -Ebert, pp. 30-31

1. One purpose of the passage is to

1. inform the reader of reasons why populations may remain in the vicinity of volcanoes.
2. thrill the reader with stories of survival of volcanic eruptions.
3. argue that Puna, Hawaii is more dangerous than Naples.
4. persuade the public not to live near a volcano.

2. According to the passage, most people who reside near a volcano believe

1. they have no choice in the matter.
2. there are more advantages than disadvantages.
3. the volcano will never erupt.
4. it is a thrilling once-in-a-lifetime experience.

3. The reader can infer that Mt. Vesuvious is

1. on the island of Luzon.
2. in Hawaii.
3. in the Philippines.
4. in Italy.

GO ON TO NEXT PAGE

4. Which of the following was not mentioned as a rationale for living near a volcano?

1. economics.
2. willingness to take a risk.
3. family inheritance of land and property.
4. better soil

5. The word <u>imminent,</u> used in the fourth paragraph, most nearly means

1. spotted.
2. threatening.
3. prophesized.
4. called off.

6. Of the volcanoes mentioned, the most active has been

1. Mayon.
2. Taal.
3. Kilauea.
4. Mt. Vesuvious.

GO ON TO NEXT PAGE

EXAM THREE, PASSAGE ONE

Most everyone has heard of Stonehenge in England. More than 900 stone rings exist in the British Isles, and Stonehenge is the most Visited and well-known. Current theories regarding its function include both the idea that it was used for astronomical observation and the idea that it served for ritual functions. Not many individuals, however, have heard of the replicas of Stonehenge that exist in the United States. There are several, but the discussion below focuses on two of them: one in Maryhill, Washington, and one near Elberton, Georgia.

The first American replica of Stonehenge (and the one built to scale) was constructed on a lonely bluff overlooking the Columbia River in Maryhill, Washington. The creator was Sam Hill, a Quaker from Minnesota, who wished to memorialize soldiers and sailors who had lost their lives in World War I. It was the first WW I monument in America. Built out of reinforced concrete, the memorial was dedicated in 1918 but wasn't finished until twelve years later—right before Sam Hill's death in 1931. By then, Maryhill, an experimental Quaker community, had been abandoned. Hill is buried in a lone grave at the base of the bluff.

Almost fifty years later, a granite company near Elberton, Georgia was approached by "R.C. Christian," an enigmatic stranger. (He admitted that R.C. Christian was not his real name.) Mr. Christian wanted a Stonehenge built and actually had brought a model of it in a shoe box. He selected Nuberg (just north of Elberton) for two main reasons: first, because it was remote, and second, because it offered good granite. Mr. Christian reportedly left $50,000 in a local bank, told the locals that they would never see him again, and vanished forever.

The citizens of Nuberg built what are now known as The Georgia Guidestones, on top of a hill in the middle of a cow pasture—four granite monoliths, each nineteen feet tall. The main cluster was completed on March 22, 1980, using granite quarried from nearby Elberton.

7. Paragraph one of the selection is used to

1. present information on the 900 stone rings in the British Isles.
2. praise the construction of Stonehenge in England.
3. introduce the stonehenges that exist in the U.S.
4. describe Maryhill, Washington.

8. The word, enigmatic, as used in the selection, most nearly means

1. insane.
2. kind.
3. mysterious.
4. intelligent

EXAM THREE, PASSAGE TWO

9. According to the selection, one function of the Stonehenge in England was that it was

1. used as a place for human sacrifice.
2. constructed to boost tourism.
3. built to imitate the Stonehenge in Maryhill, Washington.
4. used for astronomical observation.

10.   The reader can deduce from the selection that Maryhill, Washington

1. is a site of World War I battles.
2. most likely never regained its place as a Quaker community.
3. was an industrialized area.
4. is a town founded on the fishing trade.

11.   What is the monument near Elberton, Georgia called?

1. The Georgia Guidestones
2. Nuberg
3. R. C. Christian Monument
4. The Georgia Stonehenge

12. The Maryhill Stonehenge was completed

1. right after Sam Hill's death.
2. right before Sam Hill's death.
3. during WWI.
4. in 1918.

EXAM THREE, PASSAGE TWO

13. One of the reasons Christian chose Nuberg was that it was remote; the second reason was that

1. Christian had grown up there.
2. Nuberg citizens requested the memorial.
3. more WWI veterans lived in Nuberg than any other U.S. town.
4. it offered good granite.

GO ON TO NEXT PAGE

Edward II was clearly a Plantagenet. He was as tall, strong, golden-haired and good-looking as his father; but, inside this magnificent shell there was no king. He made no effort to rule his subjects. Edward cared nothing for the duties of a king. His only desire was to use the advantages of his position to enrich his friends and amuse himself. In London he was joined by the best of his friends, Piers Gaveston, a handsome knight with an eye to fame. Piers had been Edward's close companion since childhood. Edward's demonstrations of affection toward Piers were extravagant.

In spite of his preference for Piers, Edward married Isabella of France. Many of the wedding presents, though, were given away to Piers, and at the crowning of Edward as king, Edward shocked the Court by demonstrating that he preferred the couch of Piers to that of the Queen.

Gaveston himself did nothing to quell the hatred and jealousy that the King's generosity aroused in the hearts of the nobles; he was playing a dangerous game. Though exiled many times, Piers appeared openly at the Christmas Court during the holiday season a year after the king's coronation. Enraged, his enemies hunted him down and murdered him.

Isabella, too, had her revenge. She was sent to France as a peacemaker in 1325; and, there, she joined Roger Mortimer who had barely escaped from Edward's anger a few years before. Together they returned to England,

took the throne, and sent King Edward II to the dungeon of Berkeley Castle. There his jailers, having failed to starve him to death, satisfied their order "to kill him but leave no mark on his body." They made sure his injuries were internal, and Edward II died a horrible death.

-Fraser, pp. 88-91; 96

14. According to the passage, Edward used his position to

1. go to war with France.
2. help his people who were in need.
3. arrange a favorable marriage.
4. enrich his friends and amuse himself.

15. In paragraph two, that refers to

1. the wedding.
2. the presents.
3. the couch.
4. Edward's preference.

16. It can be inferred that the main reason Piers Gaveston remained with King Edward was

1. because he cared about the king.
2. to make a name for himself.
3. to get revenge.
4. to prove he was better than the nobles.

GO ON TO NEXT PAGE

EXAM THREE, PASSAGE THREE

17. According to the passage, Edward

1. cared deeply for his people.
2. died in his sleep in Berkeley Castle.
3. was not as good looking as his father.
4. was a pathetic figure of a king.

18. We can infer that Piers Gaveston

1. was angry at Edward for exiling him.
2. was well-liked at Court.
3. was afraid of the nobles.
4. felt secure about his position at Court.

19. Quell, as used in the third
paragraph, most nearly means to

1. calm.
2. worsen.
3. aggravate.
4. enhance.

GO ON TO NEXT PAGE

EXAM THREE, PASSAGE THREE

Although Ludwig Mies van der Rohe was primarily an architect, he was also known for creating furniture which was reflective of his generation. Trained as a stone mason in his father's workshop and in traditional architectural offices in his home town in Germany, he designed furniture which was minimal and elegant. He openly rebelled against the previous generation's idea of beauty. His path was that of the modernists of his day—a trend toward professional simplicity rather than elaborate design. That is, instead of the heavy, ornately carved, tasseled, velvet pieces of the past, the modernists reinforced their technological society by producing pieces that reflected a more democratic lifestyle.

Mies van der Rohe was a visionary of his century. The simplicity of his designs, the pure geometry, and the use of readily available materials attracted the public of his day. He liked comfortable, spacious chairs, and enjoyed using metal, a material considered extremely <u>hygienic</u>, and one that everyone could afford.

Mies's most famous pieces were, amazingly, chairs. The *Barcelona* chair, designed in 1929 and deemed his most creative work, has never gone out of style.

Over his many years as designer and architect, Mies seldom admitted influences on his work, but a woman named Lilly Reich held great sway with this intriguing rebel. Lilly Reich was also a designer and Mies, who rarely solicited opinions from others, was always eager to hear hers. Not only did they work side by side in an association called the *Werk-bund*, but eventually they also had an intimate relationship. When Mies emigrated to the United States in 1937, Reich continued to tend to his affairs. No one knows for sure whether she ever joined him in America. What *is* known is that Reich died at the age of sixty-two, not in the United States but in Germany, shortly after the war.   -Smith, 2001

EXAM THREE, PASSAGE FOUR

20. It can be inferred from the passage that

1. Mies became a United States citizen.
2. Reich attended to Mies' affairs because she was his only friend.
3. Mies never married Reich.
4. Mies created the Barcelona chair while vacationing in Spain.

21. Lilly Reich was

1. Mies's wife.
2. an office manager.
3. American.
4. Mies's inspiration.

22. Modernist furniture can be equated with the idea of

1. German nationalism.
2. professional simplicity.
3. elaborate design.
4. ornate carving.

23. Ludwig Mies van der Rohe first trained as a

1. stone mason.
2. wood worker.
3. metal craftsman.
4. furniture designer.

24. The style of writing of this passage is

1. chatty and informal.
2. argumentative and critical.
3. academic and scholarly.
4. somber and depressing.

25. hygienic, as used in the second paragraph, most nearly means

1. sanitary.
2. large.
3. clean.
4. comfortable.

26. Mies's idea of beauty included all of the following except

1. principles of simplicity.
2. a hygienic look.
3. pure geometry.
4. tasseled, velvet pieces.

GO ON TO NEXT PAGE

EXAM THREE, PASSAGE FOUR

The pattern of drug use can be sorted into a number of useful categories.

Recreational drugs are often locally produced and consumed and generally available to all members of society— for instance, wine and beer all through Asia/Africa; mushrooms in Russia; and various herbal preparations worldwide.

Workplace drugs are cheap and available to all workers to ease stress of labor—coca for Andean silver miners; caffeine for French 19th century coal miners; and cannabis for Indian laborers and Mbuti elephant hunters.

Drugs for war are generally the property of the military field commander or individual warriors and are used to induce the "fighting spirit"—alcohol as a rage inducer and fear inhibitor in medieval battles; and mushroom cocktail for berserkers.

Historically, different drugs were con trolled and used by individuals within a culture or by special groups within a culture. Usage or non-usage was not determined by a culture-wide rule. In industrialized cultures the above-mentioned traditional roles for drugs remained, and a new one, *illicit drugs*, was added.

Illicit drugs are drugs made illegal by the state. Many of these banned drugs are derived from easily grown plants and are thus difficult to track.

As the U.S. acquired overseas colonies and interests, missionary fervor against illicit drugs increased. Drugs were perceived as relating to the "lesser races" and as the cause of unChristian immorality. Laws restricting the use of hallucinogens in Native American religions were passed. Passage of the Harrison Narcotic Act in 1914 and the Eighteenth Amendment in 1919 restricted the sale and use of narcotics and alcohol in the U.S. Following this legislation, crime related to drugs increased and the organized crime syndicates became prominent in U.S. society.   -Downhower, pp. 199-200

27. The main idea of the selection is that

1. illicit drugs are readily available to the public.
2. several laws have restricted the sale and use of narcotics and alcohol in the U.S.
3. there are diverse classifications and uses for drugs.
4. in industrialized cultures traditional roles for drugs remain.

28. According to the passage, drugs for war are

1. utilized to cauterize wounds.
2. distributed only by medics.
3. given to make warriors more aggressive.
4. provided to calm soldiers who are facing battle.

GO ON TO NEXT PAGE

EXAM THREE, PASSAGE FIVE

29. Of the following, which was not usually found in non-industrialized countries?

1. illicit drugs
2. workplace drugs
3. drugs for war
4. recreational drugs

30. It can be inferred from the passage that

1. Harrison was in favor of a policy of leniency in regard to restrictions on drug use.
2. U.S. crime syndicates flourish when laws prohibit the sale and use of narcotics and alcohol.
3. the consumption of mushrooms in Russia has recently been banned.
4. present-day military commanders support use of drugs for the battle-field.

31. Drugs that are produced locally are classified as

1. illicit drugs.
2. workplace drugs.
3. drugs for war.
4. recreational drugs.

32. According to the passage, illicit drugs are defined as

1. recreational drugs.
2. illegal drugs.
3. drugs of necessity.
4. society-sanctioned drugs.

EXAM THREE, PASSAGE FIVE

33. In the paragraph about recreational drugs, the author primarily uses which pattern of organization?

1. Chronology
2. Statistics
3. Contrast
4. Example

34. According to the selection, which drug was used as a rage inducer during Medieval battles?

1. coca
2. caffeine
3 alcohol
4. cannabis

GO ON TO NEXT PAGE

Feminist ideas about the status of women were presented systematically for the first time around 1690 and represented a fundamental challenge to the ways of traditional societies. Women writers began to suggest concrete proposals for changing their status.

The most systematic of these writers was the English writer Mary Astell (1666-1731), the daughter of a businessman and herself a conservative supporter of the Anglican religious establishment. In 1694 she published her book, *A Serious Proposal to the Ladies*, in which she proposed founding a private women's college to remedy women's lack of education. Addressing women, she asked, "How can you be content to be in the world like 'Tulips in a Garden,' to make a fine show and be good for nothing?"

Astell advocated intellectual training based on Descartes's principles, in which reason, debate, and careful consideration of the issues took priority over custom or tradition. Her book was an immediate success, and five printings appeared by 1701.

In later works, Astell criticized the relationship between the sexes within marriage: "If absolute rule is not necessary in state government, how is it so in a family?. . . .If all men are born free, how is it that all women are born slaves?"

Her critics accused her of promoting <u>radical</u> ideas and of contradicting the Scriptures.   -Hunt, et al., p. 641

EXAM THREE, PASSAGE SIX

35. In paragraph one the central focus is that around 1690, for the first time,

1. women writers, in a concrete way, discussed ideas about changing the status of women.
2. women challenged businessmen for discriminatory actions against women who were applying for jobs.
3. women were being published by major publishing houses.
4. women proposed to men.

36. The topic of paragraph two is

1. Mary Astell's birthplace and lineage.
2. Mary Astell's religious beliefs.
3. famous sayings of Mary Astell.
4. Mary Astell as a visionary.

37. Overall, the author uses which pattern of organization?

1. Comparison
2. Persuasion
3. Example
4. Description

38. The reader can infer that Mary Astell

1. was against marriage.
2. considered a vocation as a nun.
3. was a revolutionary of her times.
4. was restrained by her father as a child.

39. Astell followed the teachings of Descartes which celebrated

1. theory of chaos and blind faith.
2. reason and careful consideration of the issues.
3. conservative natures.
4. custom and tradition.

40. The word radical as used in the passage most nearly means

1. conservative.
2. obscene.
3. reverant.
4. extremist.

GO ON TO NEXT PAGE

EXAM THREE, PASSAGE SIX

In the late nineteenth century, professional baseball players and most other professional team sports prohibited interracial competition. White players played for the highest salaries, in the best stadiums, before the most spectators.

But on April 18, 1946, the sports world was focused on a baseball field in Jersey City. It was the opening day for the Jersey City Giants of the International League. Their opponents were the Montreal Royals (the Brooklyn Dodgers' leading farm team).

Playing second base for the Royals was Jackie Robinson, a pigeon-toed, highly competitive, and marvelously talented African-American athlete. The stadium was filled with curious spectators, and in the press box sports writers from New York, Philadelphia, Baltimore, and cities further west fidgeted with their typewriters. It was not just another season-opening game. Baseball, America's national game, was about to be integrated.

In the third inning, Robinson took his second turn at bat. With runners on first and second, he lashed out at the first pitch and hit it over the left field fence 300 feet away. In the field, he was tough, intense, and smart, and for the times in which he lived, a reverse image of the black athlete. It was a fine day for Robinson and his supporters.

-Martin, pp. 948-949

EXAM THREE, PASSAGE SEVEN

41. According to the passage, in the first game he played, what did Robinson do that secured his position on the team?

1. He hit a home run.
2. He made a triple-play.
3. He outsmarted the umpire.
4. He pitched a no-hitter.

42. The reader can infer that Robinson was most valuable to his team

1. because he was African-American.
2. as an infielder.
3. as a hitter.
4. because he satisfied the spectators' curiosity.

43. The overall purpose of the passage is to

1. relate and narrate.
2. inform and entertain.
3. describe the game of baseball.
4. persuade the reader to become interested in the history of baseball.

44. The main idea of the passage is that

1. the Jersey Giants were the best baseball team in the late nineteenth century.
2. Jackie Robinson changed the face of American baseball.
3. as a national sport, baseball has always been discriminatory.
4. Jackie Robinson was a talented athlete.

As he moved across Georgia, Sherman cut a path fifty to sixty miles wide; the totality of the destruction was awesome. A Georgia woman described the "Burnt Country" this way: "The fields were trampled down and the road was lined with carcasses of horses, hogs, and cattle that the invaders, unable either to consume or to carry with them, had shot down to starve our people. The stench in some places was unbearable." Such devastation diminished the South's material resources, and more importantly, it was bound to damage the faltering southern will to resist.

After reaching Savannah in December, Sherman turned north and marched his armies into the Carolinas. Wreaking great destruction as he moved through South Carolina into North Carolina, Sherman encountered little resistance. The opposing army of General Johnston was small, but Sherman's men should have been prime targets for southern guerrilla raids and harassing attacks by local defense units. The absence of both led South Carolina's James Chestnut, Jr., to write that his state "was shamefully and unnecessarily lost. We had time, opportunity and means to destroy him. But there was a lack of energy and ability required for the occasion." Southerners were reaching the limit of their endurance.   -Norton

45. According to the passage, Sherman's destruction diminished

1. the material resources of the South.
2. his own armed militia's resources.
3. the entire infrastructure of Georgia, South Carolina, and Florida.
4. the guerilla factions of the Southern resistance.

46. By December Sherman had reached

1. Georgia.
2. North Carolina.
3. Savannah.
4. Atlanta.

47. It is implied that many Southerners who were in the path of destruction

1. dug in and fought back succeeding in their efforts to thwart Sherman.
2. merely starved to death.
3. gathered their belongings and evacuated to the west.
4. rebuilt their homes in defiance as soon as Sherman left the area.

GO ON TO NEXT PAGE

EXAM THREE, PASSAGE EIGHT

48. Which of the following statements from the selection is an opinion and not a statement of fact?

1. After wreaking havoc in South Carolina, Sherman marched through North Carolina.
2. The Burnt Country was a path fifty to sixty miles wide.
3. Sherman was a military commander who carried out a destructive campaign throughout Georgia.
4. The South could have won the Civil War if their will had not been so devastated by Sherman's march.

49. The author implies that

1. James Chestnut was proud to be a South Carolinian during Sherman's march through the South.
2. General Johnston was a better general than Sherman in regard to military strategy.
3. The local defense units of South Carolina would have been successful if they had attacked.
4. Sherman was in South Carolina during the Fall months.

GO ON TO NEXT PAGE

EXAM THREE, PASSAGE EIGHT

Dependency in the male is equated with weakness, so much so that even normal amounts are often suppressed. There is little that makes a father more proud than to see his five or six-year-old son acting like a "little man." If the mother tolerates or encourages dependency, she stands to be accused of emasculating him. Father, ever mindful of the competitive struggles of his everyday life, overreacts and sees his son's dependency as a disadvantage.

From early childhood on the boy learns that masculinity means not depending on anybody and reacts negatively to those who lean on others. Dependency, in the typical male mind, spells disaster.

The male resistance to asking for help ties in closely with his resistance to dependency. As a boy, he may struggle for hours over a problem or task because he is too embarrassed to ask for help. As an adult, he may drive around lost for an half-hour, hoping to stumble on the right direction rather than to stop and ask for help He hides his business and other worldly problems because he is convinced that no one can help him anyway. Others might, he thinks, even use his helplessness against him.

This resistance tends to devastate his relationships with intimates, spouse, friends, and children. If they love him, he believes, they will know what he needs—and he quietly resents it when they don't.   —Goldberg, pp. 46-47

EXAM THREE, PASSAGE NINE

50. The author's purpose is to show that

1. boys are dependent.
2. dependency is an advantage in males.
3. men equate dependency with weakness.
4. others take advantage of weak, dependent men.

51. When a mother encourages dependency she is accused of

1. strengthening character.
2. emasculating the boy.
3. good parenting
4. instilling values.

52. Men do not like to ask for help because they

1. do not need other people.
2. believe women will become dominating.
3. really do not want help.
4. they view it as a sign of weakness.

53. The author implies that the fear of dependency in males

1. destroys relationships because there is no communication.
2. helps relationships because some fear is healthy.
3. encourages females to be maternal.
4. leads to suicidal behavior.

54. Which of the following is not specifically mentioned in the passage?

1. son
2. mother
3. father
4. daughter

EXAM THREE, PASSAGE NINE

EXAM FOUR

There is some evidence that an adolescent's emotional reactions to divorce are similar to the mourning reactions to the death of a person; however, the adolescent is mourning the death of the parents' marriage.

Briefly, the stages of emotional reaction to divorce include the following: first, because adolescents' initial reaction to divorce is one of emotional upheaval, a first response to this situation is to *deny* that it is really happening. The denial of the reality of divorce is more commonly found among early adolescents.

As the reality of the divorce sets in, adolescents experience feelings of *anger and guilt*. They experience anger that such a profound disjunction could be occurring in their lives and guilt that somehow they must be responsible for the divorce. This guilt appears to be the case for both younger and older adolescents. Many adolescents attempt to *bargain* with their parents in an effort to reunite them. When adolescents realize that nothing more can be done to save their parents' marriage, some level of *depression* is a common outcome which may lead to a reduced level of self-esteem.

In the final stage, the adolescent understands that the security and safety of his or her previous family life is gone. The emphasis is now on finding *positive ways of relating* to parents and others.

Acceptance of parental divorce and recognition of self-worth are difficult tasks to accomplish at the same time. However, most adolescents do accomplish these tasks.

-Schiamberg, pp. 614-615

EXAM FOUR, PASSAGE ONE

1. The purpose of the second paragraph is to

1. contrast the terms "reality" and "denial."
2. classify the term "adolescence."
3. describe the terms to be used in the rest of the passage.
4. introduce the reader to the first-stage reaction to divorce.

2. The word mourning as underlined most nearly means

1. odious.
2. dying.
3. grieving.
4. guilty.

3. The reader can infer from the passage that most adolescents

1. recover a sense of self esteem after their parents divorce.
2. are scarred for life by divorce.
3. never move past the stage of denial.
4. are not affected by divorce and bounce back quickly.

4. According to this passage, adolescents use the bargaining stage to

1. receive a better allowance.
2. demand to live with a particular parent.
3. reunite their parents.
4. ensure the divorce becomes a reality.

5. The author's tone in the last two paragraphs is

1. bitter.
2. complimentary.
3. despairing.
4. hopeful.

252 Regents' Reading Exams

Four factors are most important in determining whether most infectious diseases are mild or severe problems:

First is the "naivete" of the population—American Indians were terribly <u>vulnerable to</u> the diseases introduced by conquerors of North America: small pox brought over to the new land eliminated entire tribes.

Second is the nutritional status of any group beset by an infectious epidemic disease—well-fed people are better able to fend off the worst effects of disease.

Third is the age of the afflicted person—children have undeveloped immune systems and are more at risk for all types of infections; elderly people have immune systems that are deteriorating in efficiency.

Last is societal development—availability of antibiotics, immunizations, good medical care, and basic sanitation (clean water and food free from harmful infections).

In this century, the development of antibiotics has changed the pattern of <u>mortality</u>, but the change has been selective: death is still most often caused by infectious disease in poorer nations (countries without a strong infrastructure for sanitation or food distribution).

However, in developed nations, people die more often of degenerative diseases such as cancer, heart disease, strokes, and diabetes. Generally, health care, sanitation, food quality and shelter are of sufficient quality that people live long enough to die of body failure, not infectious disease.

–Downhower, pp. 221-222

6. Which of the following was not mentioned as a factor in determining the level of severity of infectious diseases?

1. nutritional status.
2. risk level for infection.
3. hereditary factors.
4. naiveté of the population.

7. As used in the passage, the word <u>mortality</u> most nearly means

1. death.
2. health.
3. poverty.
4. illness.

8. The author gets his point across by

1. blaming the Native Americans for being vulnerable to disease.
2. discussing the chronology of the journey of the conquerors of North America.
3. contrasting the immune systems of children and adults.
4. listing important factors in determining the mildness or severity of infectious disease.

GO ON TO NEXT PAGE

EXAM FOUR, PASSAGE TWO

9. The phrase <u>vulnerable to</u>, as underlined, most nearly means

1. resistant to.
2. at risk for.
3. untouched by.
4. inquisitive about.

10. Of the following, which group would have more susceptibility to infectious disease?

1. a kindergartener who is home-schooled
2. a fifty-year-old professor with asthma
3. a malnourished grandmother living in a nursing home
4. a teenager who plays organized sports

11. According to the passage, in this century, what has changed the pattern of mortality in developed nations?

1. the virtual elimination of infectious diseases
2. medical breakthroughs in developing nations
3. nutritional education
4. the availability of antibiotics

GO ON TO NEXT PAGE

EXAM FOUR, PASSAGE TWO

(In the Barnyard) Wilbur liked Charlotte the spider better and better each day. Her campaign against insects seemed sensible, and she made use of it. Wilbur admired the way Charlotte managed. He was particularly glad that she always put her victims to sleep before eating them.

As the days went by, Wilbur grew and grew. He ate three big meals a day. He spent long hours lying on his side, half asleep, dreaming pleasant dreams. He enjoyed good health, and he gained a lot of weight. One afternoon the oldest sheep walked into the barn and stopped to pay a call on Wilbur.

"Hello!" she said. "It seems to me you're putting on weight."

"Yes, I guess I am," replied Wilbur. "At my age it's a good idea to keep gaining."

"Just the same, I don't envy you. You know why they're fattening you up, don't you?"

"No," said Wilbur.

"Well, I don't like to spread bad news," said the sheep, "but they're fattening you up because they are going to kill you, that's why!"

"They're going to *what*?" screamed Wilbur.

"Almost all young pigs get murdered by the farmer as soon as the real cold weather sets in. There's a regular conspiracy around here to kill you at Christmastime. Everybody is in on the plot," explained the old sheep.

"Save me, somebody! Save me!" cried Wilbur frantically.

"Be quiet, Wilbur," said Charlotte who had been listening to this awful conversation.

"I can't be quiet! I don't want to be killed. Is it true what the old sheep says, Charlotte?" screamed Wilbur.

"The old sheep has been around this barn a long time. I'm sure it's true. It's also the dirtiest trick I ever heard of."

Wilbur burst into tears.

"You shall not die," said Charlotte, briskly.

"What? Really? Who is going to save me?"

"I am," said Charlotte.

-White, pp. 48-51

12. Wilbur's tone after hearing the old sheep's comments was one of

1. pity for all the piglets who had lived in the barnyard before him.
2. gratitude for finally hearing the truth.
3. incredible optimism.
4. sheer terror.

13. Who told Wilbur that he was going to be murdered?

1. Charlotte
2. the farmer
3. his other pig friends
4. the old sheep

14. Charlotte's response upon hearing of Wilbur's pending murder was that

1. she was glad she was not a pig.
2. the old sheep should be killed instead.
3. she would have to do something to save him.
4. it was a part of a pig's life.

EXAM FOUR, PASSAGE THREE

15. The phrase <u>dirtiest trick</u> refers to

1. humans killing baby spiders.
2. the sheep revealing Wilbur's fate.
3. Charlotte numbing her victims before
    she eats them.
4. Wilbur's pending murder.

16. The genre of this excerpt is a

1. narrative fantasy.
2. documented story.
3. descriptive saga.
4. factual account.

GO ON TO NEXT PAGE

EXAM FOUR, PASSAGE THREE

Mother's ambition, passed on to me like a disease, was that we both wanted to become writers. It was a defect that, as Southern women, we sought to overcome—she, by submission to appearances, I, through early marriage and motherhood.

We had observed that Carson McCullers, Flannery O'Connor, Margaret Mitchell, and her creation of Scarlett O'Hara had all been punished for their ambition by illness, death, or the loss of love.

My favorite story—a true one—was that of a woman in Washington, GA, during the nineteenth century who, accused of the murder of her husband, had been condemned to death by jurors whose jealous wives insisted upon it; she had gone to her hanging in the streets of the town (known for its antebellum beauty) wearing her prettiest silk gown.

After hearing and reading stories of what had happened to exceptional Southern women, I shivered: was this the fate that awaited every woman who <u>craved</u> more than the traditional feminine role?   —McCarter, pp. 114-115

17. The jurors condemned and hanged the woman from Washington, Georgia for

1. being beautiful.
2. murdering her husband.
3. being ambitious.
4. becoming a writer.

18. According to the passage, by becoming a mother, the author

1. fulfilled her aspiration of living a traditional role.
2. enhanced her chances to write by experiencing a different side of life.
3. was able to push her daughter to become a writer.
4. conquered her need to write.

19. Both the author and her mother wanted to be

1. famous writers.
2. accepted by Southern society.
3. like characters in a novel.
4. wives and mothers.

20. The reader can infer that in reality the woman from Washington, Georgia was hanged by

1. a jury of men.
2. the wives of the jurors.
3. the county judge.
4. the town citizens.

21. In the context of the last paragraph, the word, <u>craved</u>, most nearly means

1. ate.
2. required.
3. rejected.
4. yearned for.

EXAM FOUR, PASSAGE FOUR

GO ON TO NEXT PAGE

22. By using the phrase, "like a disease," the author implies that

1. she became ill through her efforts to become a writer.
2. her writing and fame spread quickly.
3. she was obsessed with thoughts of becoming a writer.
4. she was unable to control her anger at not succeeding as a writer.

23. The author makes her point in paragraph three by utilizing

1. persuasive argument.
2. a contrastive statement.
3. unfounded documentation.
4. an anecdote.

GO ON TO NEXT PAGE

EXAM FOUR, PASSAGE FOUR

The American economy has grown from its revolutionary beginnings almost 200 years ago to become the most productive in the world. The productive capacity created by this growth has allowed the people of the United States to enjoy a continually rising standard of living. In no small measure, the economic success of our country can be attributed to a people (who in their private lives and in their businesses) have acted freely and with a minimum of governmental control.

The free enterprise system in our country has provided a framework of political, economic, and financial stability for individuals, institutions, and businesses. Few other economies offer such varying degrees of risk and reward to meet different individual and institutional needs.

Continued growth and prosperity in the United States depend entirely on the continuation of our present economic system. Our economy may continue in the future in a modified form, but it must retain its inherent basis—the awareness of the moral responsibility of one man or woman to humankind. This implies that if our growth as a nation in a competitive world society is to continue, it must depend upon a people who are educated and knowledgeable about investments— who are willing to accept the risks of our economic system as well as the rewards.

-Amling, p. 1

24. In the first paragraph, the author makes his point through the use of

1. statistics and facts.
2. classification.
3. cause-effect.
4. chronology.

25. It can be inferred that in order to continue to thrive the economic system

1. needs to continue to meet only the needs of large corporations.
2. Americans need to educate themselves and become knowledgeable about investing.
3. Americans need to adopt the "every man for himself" philosophy.
4. Americans should invest their money in foreign markets.

26. The author would probably agree with which of the following statements?

1. The free enterprise system will eventually fail.
2. Free enterprise has not affected U.S. politics.
3. Without free enterprise U.S. prosperity will not continue to grow.
4. The reason the free enterprise system works is because it is geared only for group and collective needs.

GO ON TO NEXT PAGE

EXAM FOUR, PASSAGE FIVE

27. The author's purpose in the first paragraph is to

1. relate the idea that U.S. economic success is dependent on a system with minimum government control.
2. educate the reader to America's revolutionary beginnings.
3. argue that the American standard of living is in decline.
4. discuss the framework of private and business lives of the American people.

28. In the third paragraph the author is

1. threatening the American public.
2. denigrating the American public.
3. warning the American public.
4. praising the American public.

29. The word modified, as used in the last paragraph, most nearly means

1. violently altered.
2. slightly different.
3. unchanged.
4. distinctly shortened.

GO ON TO NEXT PAGE

EXAM FOUR, PASSAGE FIVE

Nazi oppression began quickly in the Netherlands. On May 18, Seyss-Inquart became Reich Commissar for Holland. A Viennese, he had aided in the Nazi takeover of Austria. Starting slowly, he ultimately forced the nation into submission, although a Dutch resistance movement soon grew and responded to the high-handed Nazi policies. When the Nazis began to ship out Jews to concentration camps, the Dutch people went on strike. Although this was <u>suppressed</u>, the Dutch actively aided Jews throughout the war. (It was in Amsterdam that teenager Ann Frank hid with her family for two years and wrote her famous diary before she was discovered and sent to a concentration camp where she died.)

German forces had also attacked Belgium on May 10. After mobilizing, the Belgian army comprised 900,000 men, but very little heavy artillery, no tanks, few anti-aircraft batteries, and only one squadron of fighter planes. The Belgian army put its faith in a series of ultra-modern fortresses which guarded the wide, level gateway into Belgium from Germany. The most formidable of these was Fort Eben Emael north of Liege. The fort had a garrison of 1500 men protected by thousands of tons of earth and concrete and was fortified with electrically operated artillery. It rose some 130 feet above the canal and had concrete defense works.

The Germans, however, landed gliders with about 300 soldiers on the west bank of the canal and moved so quickly that they captured two of the three bridges in tact. One group of gliders landed directly on the fort itself, and a force of 80 men was soon storming it. Using flame throwers and demolition charges, the German troops disabled the fortress within an hour.

-Layton, p. 22

30. According to the passage, Ann Frank was hiding in

1. Germany.
2. Vienna.
3. Belgium.
4. Amsterdam.

31. Which of the following was not mentioned as part of the fortifications for Fort Eben Emael?

1. concrete
2. 1500 men
3. resistance fighters
4. electrically operated artillery

32. The author makes his point through

1. personal opinion.
2. narrative.
3. public opinion.
4. historical timeline and facts.

EXAM FOUR, PASSAGE SIX

33. As underlined <u>suppressed</u> most nearly means

1. encouraged.
2. legalized.
3. stifled.
4. aided.

34. The reader can infer that the

1. Nazis were victorious at the Fort Eben Emael assault.
2. Belgian Army did not want to fight.
3. Belgian Army had superior air support.
4. Nazis were intimidated by the ultra-modern fortress of Fort Eben Emael.

35. Reich Comissar Seyss-Inquart was from

1. Germany.
2. Holland.
3. Belgium.
4. Vienna.

36. The Germans stormed the Belgian fort using

1. 900,000 troops.
2. gliders.
3. tanks.
4. fighter planes.

37. The author's attitude toward the Nazi strategy in the last paragraph is

1. scornful.
2. full of praise.
3. neutral.
4. hysterical.

GO ON TO NEXT PAGE

EXAM FOUR, PASSAGE SIX

The South is a land rich with historical continuity, a land of long days, bright in the sun and slow to cool in the evening shadows. On a summer's day the heat dances visibly along macadamized highways as well as on dusty country roads. Screen doors shut with loud report on hollow stillness. Soft Southern voices add to the muted effect.

Everywhere there is a sense of something old and stable. Go west in North Carolina through the great Smokies to Cherokee at twilight and watch Cherokee Indians from the nearby reservation act out the tragic story of their ancestors' trek, walking the "trail of tears" in the days of Andrew Jackson.

New Orleans is a special South within the South. The gems of architecture of the French quarter are perhaps unmatched in this country. Eighty miles upriver is Baton Rouge, where Huey Long built a skyscraper capitol.

The Gulf Coast makes a wide arc from Biloxi to the southern top of Florida's west coast, a coastal vacation land running down to the citrus groves and cattle farms and thriving tourist towns of Florida.

For all the changes from state to state, when the midday sun has softened: when afternoon shadows dapple tree-shaded streets; when children return to play after their naps, there is always Savannah or Charleston with red-brick sidewalks and colonial architecture and patio gardens to remind us of the unique beauty of the South.

-Runyan & Bergane, p. xvii

38. In paragraph two, the authors get their point across primarily through the use of

1. narration.
2. comparison.
3. example.
4. persuasion.

39. Trek, in paragraph two most nearly means

1. journey.
2. tale.
3. spirits.
4. revival.

40. It is suggested in the passage that the Southern states share a common bond because

1. each state has progressive urban areas.
2. each state offers historical continuity and unique characteristics.
3. they have not moved forward with time.
4. Native Americans live throughout the southern region.

GO ON TO NEXT PAGE

EXAM FOUR, PASSAGE SEVEN

41. The author's attitude toward the Cherokees can be described as

1. apathetic.
2. sinister.
3. compassionate.
4. dubious.

42. We can infer that Savannah

1. was established during the era of colonization.
2. has many master gardeners.
3. is on the Gulf coast.
4. is the only town considered to be truly Southern.

GO ON TO NEXT PAGE

EXAM FOUR, PASSAGE SEVEN

She was not known for her beauty, but she had dark, flashing eyes, and her long black hair was her crowning glory. As she rode in a carriage to her coronation, the folds of her heavy robes concealed her expanding figure. King Henry was confident that the new baby would be a son—astrologers had told him so. But again Henry was to experience bitter disappointment.

It was already obvious to royal observers that all was not well with the King's marriage. Shortly after her coronation, only months after their marriage, Henry had begun to lose interest in Anne Boleyn and was seen paying attention to other ladies of the court. When she complained, he told her crossly that she must put up with it— 'as one of her betters had done'. Anne, who had been critical, and often arrogant (even before her marriage) was growing more demanding every day.

In the months that followed Anne saw less and less of her husband as he left her alone at court. She loved affection and flattery and she had her admirers. Court gossip traveled fast, and there were spies to gather evidence to discredit her.

On May 15, at her trial in Westminster Hall, she was found guilty of adultery. On May 19, 1536 Anne Boleyn was beheaded on Tower Green. She wore a grey gown, her hair up in a net, and she met her death with dignity.

That evening the King called on Jane Seymour and the next day they were engaged.   -Wallace, pp. 71-73

[*The child that Anne was pregnant with and delivered before her execution later became Queen Elizabeth I.*]

43. Anne and Henry's child

1. was hiding behind Anne's heavy robes.
2. was a boy.
3. was a joy to them.
4. was a girl.

44. The word one in the phrase 'as one of her betters had done' probably means

1. a former wife.
2. another women of the court.
3. a former mistress.
4. Anne's lady-in-waiting.

45. The phrase, expanding figure, in the first paragraph, most likely refers to

1. Anne's insatiable appetite.
2. the fullness of the gowns worn at that time.
3. Anne's pregnancy.
4. her public image on coronation day.

GO ON TO NEXT PAGE

EXAM FOUR, PASSAGE EIGHT

46. In truth, Henry was bitterly disappointed because

1. Anne was in love with someone else.
2. Anne did not produce a son.
3. the Queen was caught gossiping about him.
4. Jane Seymour rejected his advances.

47. According to the passage, Ann Boleyn was

1. the third wife of Henry.
2. never accepted as the queen by the people.
3. elegant and dignified at all times.
4. becoming more demanding every passing day.

48. Which of the following is not true of Henry?

1. He was jealous of Anne's male friends.
2. He wanted a son.
3. He consulted astrologers.
4. He lost interest in Anne in less than a year.

49. In light of England's history, why was Anne and Henry's union significant?

1. Their daughter became the Queen of England.
2. Anne was the first Queen ever beheaded.
3. It illustrated how kings had absolute authority.
4. Corruption at Henry's court was finally exposed.

GO ON TO NEXT PAGE

EXAM FOUR, PASSAGE EIGHT

Born the illegitimate son of a Scottish merchant, Alexander Hamilton showed such promise that at 18 he was sent to King's College in New York for an education. A firm patriot, Hamilton wrote articles championing the American cause against Britain and caught the eye of George Washington. He became Washington's aide and led a bold charge against the British in the Battle of Yorktown.

After the war he married into New York's privileged society and began a law practice. Soon he became involved in politics and, as a strong patriot, was one of the first to call for a convention to write a new constitution. At the convention his ideas were so aristocratic that few would listen to him.

President George Washington made Hamilton the nation's first Secretary of the Treasury. The young genius used this position to strengthen the power of the federal government by tying the interests of the wealthy merchant class to it. His feud with Thomas Jefferson (who opposed more federal power) spilled over into the press and led to the start of political parties in America.

Hamilton had an enemy within his own party as well, Burr. In the election of 1800, when Hamilton's rival Jefferson was tied with his other enemy Burr, Hamilton threw his support to Jefferson. In Burr's bid for the governorship of New York, again Hamilton threw his

influence against Burr. This was a fateful decision.

The angry Burr challenged Hamilton to a duel and Hamilton accepted. In the early morning of July 11, 1804, the two met. Hamilton apparently fired into the air, but Burr's shot <u>mortally</u> wounded Hamilton; he died the following day.   -Solberg, p. 61

50. The reader can infer from the passage that although Hamilton was the son of a Scot, he

1. attended King's College in London.
2. fought against the Americans.
3. died at the hands of the British.
4. became an American citizen.

51. Why did people have a difficult time listening to Hamilton, even though he was considered a genius by some?

1. He was arrogant and self-centered.
2. His ideas were too aristocratic.
3. He was a war-monger.
4. He was constantly using legal terminology.

52. The word, <u>mortally</u>, as underlined in the passage most nearly means

1. mildly.
2. extremely.
3. fatally.
4. barely.

EXAM FOUR, PASSAGE NINE

53. Considering the times in which Hamilton lived and the fact that he was illegitimate, which of the following seems inconsistent?

1. He fought a duel.
2. He became an American patriot.
3. He married into the privileged society of New York.
4. He was highly intelligent.

54. According to the passage, political parties in America were established in part because

1. of the duel between Hamilton and Burr which attracted the press.
2. of the opposing views of Hamilton and Jefferson that attracted the attention of the media.
3. Washington ran against Jefferson in the election of 1800.
4. Alexander Hamilton made a fateful decision.

EXAM FOUR, PASSAGE NINE

EXAM FIVE

In the state of Georgia each county has one superior court, magistrate court, a probate court, and where needed, a state court and a juvenile court. Centuries of experience have shown that cases should be handled locally where the issues and persons are well known. Forum shopping for judges who favor a particular point of view is generally prohibited.

All criminal cases are tried where the crime was committed, except cases in the superior court where the judge is satisfied that an impartial jury cannot be obtained in that county. Every week in Georgia, around 400 people are sent to prison. They are convicted of serious felonies: murder, kidnapping, assault, robbery, and auto theft. A major reason for Governor's emphasis on increasing the number of prison beds is that with more than 23,385 inmates currently in the state prison system, there are more than 1,600 sitting in county jails waiting to be transferred.

Among the saddest types of criminal activity is the growing problem of child abuse. It is the duty of the legal system to hear cases involving a wide variety of deviant behavior: for example, cruelty to children, exhibitionism, and molestation.

It should be noted that "consent from the child" is usually no shield against punishment; with crimes like statutory rape there are *no* extenuating circumstances—not mistake, not consent, and not enticement by the child.

Because of the injury incurred by the community from these types of crime, public servants in Georgia have an enforceable legal obligation to report all such instances of child abuse to the proper authorities. Failure to inform legal officials of violations is itself a criminal offense, a misdemeanor. These laws apply to all public employees with a protective relationship with children, and to persons with licensed occupations. Physicians, dentists, nurses and psychiatrists are included, as are education personnel like teachers, child care workers and administrators. Social workers and law enforcement personnel are also included within the law.

-Allen & Saeger, pp. 47; 56-57

1. In Georgia, all criminal cases are tried where the crime was committed except

1. when the accused is a politician.
2. when twelve jurors can not be found.
3. in cases of child abuse.
4. where an impartial jury can not be obtained.

2. Every week, how many people are sent to prison in Georgia?

1. 1,600
2. 400
3. 23,385
4. only a few

3. The purpose of the passage is to

1. argue for stricter sentencing for child molesters in Georgia.
2. give statistics on murders and kidnappings in Georgia.
3. present an overview of some aspects of the criminal court system in Georgia.
4. illustrate that public servants in Georgia are failing to inform officials of violations against children.

EXAM FIVE, PASSAGE ONE

4. It can be inferred from the passage that currently county jails in Georgia

1. are used only to accommodate juveniles.
2. are at their full capacity and can not hold any more criminals.
3. are not as crowded as prisons.
4. do not employ enough deputies.

5. The author would probably agree that

1. under no circumstances should any child be molested or abused.
2. no more monies should be pumped into the Georgia prison system.
3. forum shopping for judges is an honorable strategy.
4. public servants very seldom engage in criminal activity.

GO ON TO NEXT PAGE

EXAM FIVE, PASSAGE ONE

[*Note: The Thirteenth Amendment outlawed slavery in 1865, but right on into the 20th century males of any ethnic origin were routinely drugged, beaten, and kidnapped to man America's mighty seafaring vessels.*]

William Davis, a cabinet-maker, left his home in the mid-1870s and headed for California where he hoped to earn up to six dollars a day by adapting his expertise to ship carpentry. He made the eight-hundred-mile trek with his wife, Isabelle, and three small children. Davis left his family in near by Vallejo while he made a brief trip into San Francisco in search of a job. Unfortunately, he chose to quench his thirst at a waterfront saloon. After passing out from a drug-laced drink, he awakened aboard a ship—chained and bound for Europe. William Davis had been "shanghaied" by crimps. After working all day, he was chained below every night. His family didn't see him again for nearly eight years.

The English word *crimp* arose in the eighteenth century to mean a person who lured and forced men into sea duty. New York and San Francisco were the predominant hunting grounds for crimps, and the practice thrived to a lesser degree in Portland, Boston, Norfolk, and Savannah. Since no seafaring knowledge was required for menial jobs aboard a clipper ship, any tourist, shoemaker, bricklayer, minister, or farmer would do. The means of entrapment ranged from opium-laced cigars to drugged liquor to trap doors in the floorboards of bars and boarding

houses. Much like today's high-level drug traffickers, crimps defied law enforcement, bribing city officials and threatening captains, who accepted the system partly from fear. The ship's captain had to pay the crimp a commission of five to seventy-five dollars per man.

Famous among San Francisco crimps was "Shanghai" Kelly, a red-bearded boarding master who led his profession in ruthlessness. Kelly's three-story building stretched out on pilings over a section of the bay at 33 Pacific Street and featured boardinghouse rooms, liquor, women—and trapdoors that could be reached by skiffs at high tide. Thousands of victims fell prey to crimps along the waterfronts of port cities during the last half of the nineteenth century.   -based on Keller, 1995

6. Why did William Davis travel 800 miles to California?

1. to try his hand at bartending
2. to fulfill his life-long dream by moving his family into the village of Vallejo
3. to become a crimp
4. he wanted a higher-paying job

7. In the first paragraph (do not count the *Note*) the author uses which pattern of organization?

1. persuasion
2. statistical data
3. cause-effect
4. narration

EXAM FIVE, PASSAGE TWO

8. The main purpose of the last paragraph is to

1. describe Shangai Kelly and his famous boarding house.
2. to show that crimpers were ordinary citizens of port towns.
3. illustrate that trapdoors were utilized by crimpers.
4. relate that port towns were more dangerous that inland towns.

9. From the information given, the reader can infer that *crimping* was

1. monopolized by female crimpers.
2. legally condoned by city officials.
3. welcomed by the sailors in port areas.
4. a type of slavery.

10. The pattern of organization employed in the second paragraph is

1. personal opinion and insight.
2. definition and description.
3. storytelling and narration.
4. chronology and timelines.

11. As underlined in the passage, shanghaied most nearly means

1. entertained, then drugged.
2. beaten and tortured.
3. kidnapped and enslaved.
4. unchained and liberated.

EXAM FIVE, PASSAGE TWO

GO ON TO NEXT PAGE

James I of Scotland set himself the task of restoring peace and order to the turbulent Highlands, and to this end he ordered all the Northern Chieftains, to assemble at Inverness for "peace talks." Not daring to disobey, they proceeded to Inverness. Immediately on entering Hall, no less than forty of them were arrested and cast into prison. Many of them were executed.

Angry about the severity and re-straint imposed upon them, the Chief-tans conspired against the King. Their smoldering spirit of treason culminated in a plot to murder him—the time chosen being during the Christmas festivities. The place chosen was a monastery where the King and Queen were staying. There, the rebellious Chieftains broke into the royal bed chamber. In the presence of the Queen and her ladies, they seized and murdered the King who was clad only in a night shirt. He had no weapon of defense, but he made a desperate attempt to resist. He was literally hacked to death by his kin, Sir Robert Graham and Sir Robert Stewart.

The Queen made a brave attempt to save her husband, during which she herself was wounded by the assassins. The next day she hunted them down and executed them with a terrible vengeance. Graham was dragged through the city and nailed alive to a tree. Afterwards he was tortured with hot pincers, while his son was killed before his dying eyes.

-Francis, pp. 12-13

EXAM FIVE, PASSAGE THREE

12. This passage primarily focuses on

1. the Chieftans of Scotland during King James I's reign.
2. the events surrounding the murder of James I.
3. James I's accomplishments.
4. Scotland during Medieval times.

13. The person who tried to save the King was

1. a relative of James.
2. one of the Queens' ladies.
3. Sir Robert Graham.
4. the Queen.

14. The phrase to this end as used in the first paragraph means

1. to the death.
2. in accordance with this goal.
3. completed.
4. when over.

15. As used in the second paragraph smoldering most nearly means

1. repressed anger.
2. open attitude.
3. deteriorating intentions.
3. smoke-filled atmosphere.

16. The passage implies that

1. kings usually carry weapons.
2. Scotland was normally quite serene.
3. the Queen was a smarter ruler than the King.
4. the King blamed the Chieftans for the country's unrest.

17. The reader can conclude that

1. The Queen took control after the King was murdered.
2. Graham became King.
3. the Chieftans overthrew the government.
4. Robert Stewart became Regent of Scotland.

18. The word clad, as underlined in the second paragraph, most nearly means

1. undressed.
2. wrapped.
3. attired.
4. enclosed.

GO ON TO NEXT PAGE

EXAM FIVE, PASSAGE THREE

The death of Sir Winston Churchill removes from the contemporary scene a statesman whose services to his country are unexampled in modern times—a man whose courage, clear-sightedness and gift for leadership the world owes many debts of gratitude. Yet if we must remember him for one thing above all, it is bound to be for the inspiration, the will to fight on, that he injected into his country and her allies in the dark days of 1940. He did not achieve this ability by accident. It was the logical culmination of a way of life and a way of thought.

To win wars, the qualities required are courage, foresight, and an absolute confidence in ultimate success. Combined with the aforementioned, an infinite patience, the power of judging in the heat of the fray, tireless energy and the ability to draw from others are necessary. All these qualities Churchill possessed in an exceptional degree.

From his youth onwards he had seen war as the ultimate test. No firebrand—though often labeled one— he had gravitated to wars like a scholar to books. As a subordinate he could be willful and scornful of those in authority, but nothing within his power was ever allowed to be ignored and his loyalty, once given, was absolute.

-Ferrier, p. 5.

19. The author states that Churchill had a gift for leadership

1. due to a culmination of a way of life and thought.
2. due to a childhood mentor.
3. because he was patient.
4. he was a firebrand.

20. The word, aforementioned, refers to

1. qualities.
2. courage, foresight, confidence.
3. wars.
4. patience, judgment, tireless energy, ability to draw from others.

21. The author describes Churchill as

1. eccentric.
2. volatile.
3. steadfast.
4. aloof.

22. The author's tone in the opening paragraph is

1. cynical.
2. impartial.
3. antagonistic.
4. reverent.

GO ON TO NEXT PAGE

EXAM FIVE, PASSAGE FOUR

23. The best meaning of the word
<u>subordinate</u> is

1. underdog.
2. overlord.
3. supervisor.
4. underling.

24. The author's style of writing is

1. obsequious.
2. fantastical.
3. unfavorable.
4. timid.

GO ON TO NEX T PAGE

EXAM FIVE, PASSAGE FOUR

Nearly 74 million Americans live in urban areas that do not meet federal clean air standards. Georgia's endangered species list has grown in the last 20 years by 400 percent. The 1989 Exxon Valdez oil spill in Alaska killed at least 350,000 birds, while a 45 mile stretch of the Sacramento River in California will take at least 40 years to recover from a 1991 pesticide spill.

Environmental problems have been an issue in the United States since the 1800s. The experience of watching 1400 buffalo massacred just for their tongues moved artist George Catlin to call for a "nation's park, containing man and beast, in all the wild freshness of their nature's beauty." The idea was entirely new. Thoreau had urged that some wild places be set aside, "if only to suggest that earth has higher uses than we put her to."

But it was among a relatively small group of well-to-do Easterners who lived in the city and escaped to the wilderness for relaxation that the idea of parks began to take tangible shape. Besides being impressed by the romantic idea that America's scenic resources were her greatest national asset and should be preserved, they had seen many of the endangered areas first hand. One of these areas, Yosemite Valley, was declared a California state park in 1864 largely because of the influence of these traveling easterners. Six years later, others visited the Yellowstone area in Wyoming. They returned determined to preserve the unique geysers, hot springs, and canyons they had seen. Supporters of a bill proposing the creation of a park there had to assure <u>skeptical</u> legislators that the area was too high and cold and would do "no harm to the material interests of the people." When Northern Pacific Railroad (foreseeing mounds of tourist dollars) lobbied for the bill, it helped the effort. Congress passed it in 1872, and the nation had its first national park.   -Solberg, pp. 345-347

25. The purpose of the first paragraph is to

1. contrast the Alaskan oil spill with the California pesticide spill.
2. prove that governments do not list environment problems as a high priority.
3. describe the Exxon Valdez oil spill.
4. introduce environmental problems through examples.

26. Who was responsible for promoting the idea of the first national park and making it a reality?

1. George Catlin
2. a small group of wealthy Easterners
3. Thoreau
4. U.S. Congress

GO ON TO NEXT PAGE

EXAM FIVE, PASSAGE FIVE

27. The word, skeptical, utilized in the
last paragraph most nearly means

1. prosperous.
2. convinced.
3. corrupt.
4. uncertain.

28. The author of this selection is
probably a

1. zoologist.
2. biologist.
3. conservationist.
4. science teacher.

29. The first national park was located
in

1. Wyoming.
2. Georgia.
3. California.
4. Alaska.

30. The author's attitude toward the idea
of parks and the preservation of
endangered species is

1. impartial.
2. cynical.
3. compassionate.
4. distrustful.

GO ON TO NEXT PAGE

EXAM FIVE, PASSAGE FIVE

[*Note: The Olympics as an international event has drawn enthusiasm from the world populace. Gold Medalists are applauded and celebrated. Sometimes overlooked, however, are the inspirational athletes. Read about two such examples below.*]

At the 2000 millennium games in Sydney, all eyes were on Cathy Freeman, an Australian of native Aboriginal descent who lit the Olympic torch in the opening ceremony. As the first Aboriginal-Australian athlete to compete in the Olympics, Freeman, a sprinter, was under intense pressure to perform big in the 400 meters in her home country. She had won the silver four years earlier in Atlanta, and she was now determined to prove her status as "Queen of the Track." And Freeman did not disappoint.

In taking her victory lap after <u>clinching</u> the gold, in a gesture of goodwill toward all Australians, Freeman draped the Aboriginal *and* Australian flags around her neck. Her commitment to her country, her heritage, and her sport has enabled fans to appreciate all that drives athletes.

Not many know the story of Lawrence Lemieux, a Canadian rower competing in the Finn dinghy class in the 1988 games in Korea. On that fateful day Lemieux performed an incredible act of bravery. The winds had picked up, and the water became exceedingly choppy. Lemieux was in second place during his race when he saw two sailors from the Singapore team in another race

fall into the water. Lemieux rowed over and rescued the sailors, hauling them into his small boat. Though winning was not a possibility, he finished his race after an official boat picked up the sailors. The Olympics committee awarded him an honorary second-place award. The IOC president said, "By your sportsmanship, self-sacrifice and courage, you embody all that is right with the Olympic ideal." Lemieux was not a big name, but his act of bravery brought honor to the Games.

-beliefnet, 2008

31. In regard to Lawrence Lemieux, the Olympics Committee

1. gave him the gold medal for his bravery.
2. disqualified him from the race.
3. disallowed his petition to compete in the race.
4. awarded him an honorary medal.

32. The main idea of the passage is that

1. the Aboriginals have been mistreated by the Australian government for centuries.
2. Lemieux performed an incredible act of bravery at the 1988 Olympic games in Seoul.
3. there are Olympic athletes whose unknown stories are inspiring.
4. Cathy Freeman won the silver medal in Atlanta in 1996, and she was determined to prove her status as "Queen of the Track."

EXAM FIVE, PASSAGE SIX

33. The word, <u>clinching</u>, as used in the last paragraph, most nearly means

1. winning.
2. grasping.
3. finalizing.
4. stealing.

34. It is implied in the passage that Freeman's "inspirational" act was

1. routing her global competitors completely in the 400 meter race.
2. a gesture of healing by symbolically draping both the Australian and Aboriginal flags around her neck.
3. being the first Aboriginal to compete in the Olympics thus creating an historical moment.
4. maintaining her status as "Queen of the Track."

35. The author's purpose in writing the passage is to

1. argue that if a person strives diligently, s/he too can win gold medals.
2. compare and contrast two Olympic athletes who overcame prejudice.
3. persuade the reader to look past the ordinary trappings of the Olympic games and to be inspired.
4. present an historical perspective of the Olympics from 1998 to 2008.

GO ON TO NEXT PAGE

EXAM FIVE, PASSAGE SIX

Triumph in the Persian Gulf in the early 1990s led to substantive Middle East peace talks. President H. W. Bush hailed these developments as the birth of a "New World Order." Taken from the Great Seal of the United States, this phrase was defined by the president as including "peaceful settlements of disputes, solidarity against aggression, reduced arsenals and just treatment of all peoples."

In a warning of things to come, however, the Bush effort to save Somalia from famine and restore civil order there came to grief in the "Black Hawk Down" incident. And, true to their historic pattern, the American people figured that with the Cold War finished and the Gulf War behind them, they could turn back to domestic concerns. Many more were concerned about the slumping economy and massive downsizing and layoffs by businesses across the country. President Bush, slow to grasp this mood shift, lost reelection in 1992 to Bill Clinton.

Clinton pledged to focus on the economy. But the world would not leave him alone. Saddam hung on in Baghdad, periodically causing alarms in Washington with one maneuver or another; North Korea was busy trying to develop nuclear weapons even as its people faced mass starvation; and a truck bomb possibly set up by Iranian agents killed 19 American servicemen based in Saudi Arabia.

The Clinton administration seemed to respond to these situations as they arose without any clear overall policy.

U.S relations with both Russia and China deteriorated as both countries resisted what they labeled as American dominance. The New World Order, widely anticipated at the end of the Cold War and hailed with the first Gulf War victory, never materialized.
-Solberg, pp. 294-298

36. The phrase New World Order can best be defined as

1. the Great Seal of the United States.
2. a time of chaos.
3. a world in which the U.S. is the only superpower.
4. a new world in which there is peace and prosperity.

37. In which country was there the first warning that the New World Order may not materialize?

1. China
2. Iraq
3. North Korea
4. Somalia

38. According to the passage, why was Clinton unable to focus on the economic problems of the U.S.?

1. Clinton was not as capable as H. W. Bush.
2. The world would not leave him alone.
3. He was preoccupied with several terrorist acts against Washington by Saddam Hussein.
4. China and Russia threatened war if Clinton attempted to establish a New World Order.

EXAM FIVE, PASSAGE SEVEN

39. The writer would probably agree that

1. Clinton was the worst president in modern American history.
2. Americans are cowardly in dealing with global turmoil.
3. Americans are not and never have been that interested in overseas problems.
4. H. W. Bush was a war monger.

40. What reason was given for Bush's failure to win re-election?

1. Bush was slow to grasp the mood shift of the American people.
2. Clinton was more knowledgeable in matters of foreign policy.
3. Bush lost the Gulf War by making unreasonable decisions.
4. He misled the American people concerning layoffs and downsizing in U.S. companies.

41. This passage was probably written by a

1. sociologist.
2. politician.
3. Somali ambassador.
4. political scientist.

42. The word, <u>domestic</u>, as used in paragraph two, most nearly means

1. within a marriage.
2. foreign.
3. within the United States.
4. household.

GO ON TO NEXT PAGE

EXAM FIVE, PASSAGE SEVEN

The term culture can be described as a <u>social script</u> that provides structure for customs and rituals in a society. Sociologists use the concept of culture to compare and contrast life in different societies. Suppose that you are visiting a country for the first time. It is natural to take for granted many customs based upon your own experiences. But your familiar ways of responding to others may not play well on your visit.

Let's look at some cultural script differences. Americans are often taught the importance of directly looking at someone when meeting them for the first time. But in some societies it is considered rude and offensive. In some Muslim communities women are not allowed in public without clothing that completely covers them. Women in some of these societies are not even allowed in public or to leave the house without a male family member present. Nor are they allowed to drive a car. These cultural differences have caused conflicts for American women serving in Iraq or stationed in countries like Saudi Arabia.

How different societies deal with time is another fascinating cultural difference. In some cultures, a concern with time is almost *nil* compared to how it is dealt with in the United States. The cultural custom of exhibiting <u>quietude</u> and taking it easy that is found in these societies stands in stark contrast to Americans who are impatient and always seem to be in a rush to get things done.

The nature of social bonds in different societies is another basis for different cultural scripts. Americans often have difficulty understanding the extent to which social bonds in more traditional societies such as Afghanistan and Iraq are based upon local factors such as blood, marriage, and community. It is often hard for people in these societies to think nationally when their everyday life reinforces thinking locally. The difficulty Afghanistan and Iraq are experiencing in developing a national government is due in no small part to this dynamic.   -MacDonald, pp. 7-8

43. The overall pattern of organization for this selection is

1. persuasion.
2. contrast.
3. comparison.
4. description.

44. The term <u>social script</u> most likely means

1. framework.
2. sociology.
3. overseas experience.
4. society.

GO ON TO NEXT PAGE

EXAM FIVE, PASSAGE EIGHT

45. According to the passage, what is one major reason why Afghanistan finds it difficult to establish a national government?

1. America often has difficulty understanding the blood bonds of Afghanis.
2. Foreign countries are putting obstacles in the way.
3. Afghanis have the cultural custom of taking it easy.
4. The people have a mindset that focuses on local thinking and living.

46. The passage suggests that American women stationed in Saudi Arabia

1. agree with the restrictions that curb their movement.
2. have been arrested for unintentionally breaking the law.
3. most likely do not drive off base when "on leave."
4. have protested the Saudi social scripts.

47. Which of the following was mentioned in the passage as an American behavior that may cause conflict when visiting other nations?

1. flashing money
2. behaving in an arrogant manner
3. drinking alcohol
4. being impatient.

48. The word <u>quietude</u> (paragraph three) probably means

1. chaos.
2. spontaneity.
3. stillness.
4. panic.

GO ON TO NEXT PAGE

EXAM FIVE, PASSAGE EIGHT

Two days without sunlight had re-arranged Michael Tolland's biological clock. Although his watch said it was late afternoon, Tolland's body insisted it was the middle of the night. Now, having put the finishing touches on his documentary, Tolland was making his way across the darkened dome. Arriving at the <u>illuminated</u> press area, he delivered the disk to the NASA media technician in charge of overseeing the presentation.

"Thanks, Mike," the technician said, winking.

Tolland gave a tired chuckle. "I hope the President likes it."

Tolland stood in the brightly lit press area and surveyed the convivial NASA personnel. Even though he wanted to celebrate, he felt exhausted, emotionally drained. He glanced around for Rachel Sexton, but apparently she was still talking to the President.

He wants to put her on-air, Tolland thought. Not that he blamed him. Rachel would be a perfect addition to the cast of spokespeople. In addition to her good looks, Rachel exuded an accessible poise and self-confidence that Tolland seldom saw in the women he met. Then again, most of the women Tolland met were in television—either ruthless power women or gorgeous on-air "personalities" who lacked exactly that.

Now, slipping quietly away from the crowd of bustling NASA employees, Tolland navigated the web of pathways across the dome, wondering where the other civilian scientists had disappeared. If they felt half as drained as he did, they should be in the bunking area grabbing a catnap before the big moment. The empty dome overhead seemed to echo with the hollow voices of distant memories. Tolland tried to block them out.

"Forget the ghosts," he willed himself. They often haunted him at times like these, when he was tired or alone—time of personal triumph or celebration. *She* should be with you right now, the voice whispered. Alone in the darkness, he felt himself reeling backward into oblivion.   –Brown, pp. 209-210

49. According to the passage, Michael Tolland is

1. in television.
2. a scientist.
3. an astronaut.
4. a media technician.

50. Overall, Tolland's attitude toward women in the media is

1. sentimental.
2. admiring.
3. bitter.
4. ridiculing.

51. The reader can infer that Tolland

1. admires Rachel Sexton.
2. believes Rachel Sexton is a high-ranking, undercover NASA official.
3. is involved romantically with Rachel Sexton.
4. distrusts Rachel Sexton.

EXAM FIVE, PASSAGE NINE

52. In the last paragraph, *she* probably
refers to

1. Rachel Sexton.
2. the ghost.
3. an absent love.
4. the gorgeous "on-air" personality.

53. Illuminated, as used in the passage,
most likely means

1. brightly lit.
2. dim.
3. darkened.
4. bustling.

54. The last sentence, "Alone in the
darkness, he felt himself reeling
backward into oblivion," most likely
indicates that Tolland

1. passed out from drinking too much.
2. fell into the darkened pit.
3. was abducted.
4. keeled over from exhaustion.

EXAM FIVE, PASSAGE NINE

EXAM SIX

Since the very first days of the European occupation of Australia, Aboriginal children were forcibly separated from their families. Then, in 1814 Governor Macquarie funded the first school for indigenous children: it attracted children from Aboriginal families, but within a few years it became evident that its purpose was to distance Aboriginal children from their families and communities.

The Australian government utilized various strategies to remove Aboriginal children from their families. When whites would raid the Aboriginal camps, the parents would hide their children. One woman recalls: "Often the white people—we didn't know who they were—would come into our camps. And if the aboriginal group was taken unaware, they would stuff us into flour bags and pretend we weren't there. We were told not to sneeze."

In 1957 Bruce Trevorrow (a thirteen-month-old Aboriginal infant) was stolen after being admitted to a hospital for stomach pains. His father had asked neighbors to take Bruce to the Adelaide Children's Hospital since he had neither telephone nor car. On admission, the hospital recorded that Bruce had no parents and that he was neglected and malnourished. Bruce never saw his father again.

While records are imprecise, the Australian Human Rights Commission Report indicates that from 1910 to 1970 Aboriginal children were forcibly taken from their families, transported across the vast continent, and placed in state or church run institutions, or with white foster or adoptive parents. Bringing Them Home, a landmark study of 1997,

EXAM SIX, PASSAGE ONE

found that at least 100,000 Aborigines had been taken from their parents and were part of a country wide assimilation program. That is, contact with their original families was forbidden, and they were often punished for speaking with their siblings in their mother tongue. Most were not even told that they were Aboriginal. These children, now grown, are known as The Stolen Generation.　　　-based on artistwd, BBC, & Council, 2008

[Note: In 2007 Bruce Trevorrow became the first of Australia's Stolen Generation to win in court.]

1. The main purpose of this passage is to

1. entertain.
2. inform.
3. describe.
4. argue.

2. In reality, the mission of the Governor's school was to

1. distance Aboriginal children from their families.
2. educate Aboriginal children in the same manner as white children.
3. provide housing and meals for orphaned children.
4. teach the children of indigenous customs and traditions.

3. The reader can infer that nothing of consequence was done about the children who were stolen until

1. 1960s.
2. 1970s.
3. 1980s.
4. 1990s.

4. <u>indigenous</u> is closest in meaning to

1. native.
2. poor.
3. homeless.
4. exceptional.

5. Used in the last paragraph, the phrase, <u>assimilation program</u>, most nearly means a program to

1. exclude.
2. house.
3. incorporate.
4. eliminate.

6. Bruce Treverrow was stolen

1. out of the classroom at school.
2. after being admitted to the hospital.
3. while sleeping in his bedroom at home.
4. out of his father's car.

GO ON TO NEXT PAGE

EXAM SIX, PASSAGE ONE

The boy's name was Santiago. Dusk was falling as the boy arrived with his herd at an abandoned church. The roof had fallen in long ago, and an enormous sycamore had grown on the spot where the chapel had once stood.

He decided to spend the night there. He saw to it that all the sheep entered through the ruined gate. He swept the floor with his jacket and lay down, using the book he had just finished reading as a pillow. He told himself that he would have to start reading thicker books: they lasted longer, and made more comfortable pillows.

It was still dark when he awoke, and looking up, he could see the stars through the half-destroyed roof. He had noticed that, as soon as he awoke, most of the animals also began to stir. It was as if some mysterious energy bound his life to that of the sheep with whom he had spent the past two years, leading them through the countryside in search of food and water.

The boy prodded them, one by one, with his crook, calling each by name. He had always believed that the sheep were able to understand what he said. So there were times when he read them parts of his books that had made an impression on him, or when he would tell them of the loneliness or the happiness of a shepherd in the fields. Sometimes he would comment to them on the things he had seen in the villages they passed.

But for the past few days he had spoken to them about only one thing: the girl, the daughter of a merchant who lived in the village they would reach in about four days. He had been to the village only once, the year before.

-Coelho, pp. 3-5

7. The reader can infer from the passage that Santiago

1. is lonely.
2. is in touch with the girl of the village.
3. will sell his sheep to the merchant.
4. is crazy.

8. Overall, the pattern of organization used in the selection is

1. example.
2. cause-effect.
3. comparison.
4. narration.

9. The tone of the last paragraph is one of

1. anticipation.
2. criticism.
3. depression.
4. enthusiasm.

10. When Santiago laid his head down on his pillow, it reminded him

1. how exhausted he was.
2. that he needed to water the sheep.
3. that he needed a thicker book to read.
4. of the happiness he had felt earlier in the day.

EXAM SIX, PASSAGE TWO

11. People may believe Santiago is unique because he

1. sleeps in abandoned churches.
2. wants to see the girl.
3. rises while it is still dark.
4. reads to sheep.

12. Santiago's attitude toward the herd was one of

1. optimism.
2. caring.
3. apathy.
4. resentment.

GO ON TO NEXT PAGE

EXAM SIX, PASSAGE TWO

Gossip is a familiar reality. Gossip is inconsiderate chatter about someone else who is known to those involved in the conversation exchange. The basis of gossip is rumors. Gossip can occur between friends, members of a social group, workers, or just about any place people congregate.

Malicious gossip is more than inconsiderate chatter about someone else. Malicious gossip degrades someone—the intent being to ruin the reputation of that person.

Gossips often use negative talk about someone else *to elevate their own self-esteem*. But the significance of gossip goes beyond that of the personality trait of someone who is insecure.

People who are confident may use gossip *to advance their own personal social position*. Gossip can discredit a work supervisor who imposes requirements that are excessive or offensive. "Did you know that he drinks heavily or did you know that she had an affair?"

Gossip can also be used *to deflect unfavorable attention*. The ploy is to switch negative attention from oneself to someone else. "Dad, I know you don't approve of what I did, but let me tell you what your favorite son did."

Gossip is also a way *to establish your personal boundaries*. By criticizing someone else, you announce your own personal preferences. Sometimes this is more effective than simply stating your preferences. By suggesting that you don't like what someone else did, you establish a personal boundary. It suggests that you would have a similar reaction if the person you are talking to engaged in that activity.

Gossip serves a different purpose when the goal is *to gain acceptance*. In this instance, gossip provides an opportunity to win someone's favor by appealing to what they value or what you think they want to hear.

Lastly, gossip serves as *a conversation filler* for those who can't think of anything else to say.

–MacDonald, pp. 37-38

13. According to the passage, malicious gossip is different from "regular" gossip in that malicious gossip

1. elevates the victim's status.
2. degrades the one who is gossiping.
3. intends to ruin another's reputation.
4. has no real effect.

14. The purpose of the selection is to

1. persuade the reader that gossip is a beneficial activity in some instances.
2. discuss why people gossip.
3. argue that gossip is based on truth.
4. illustrate how to establish personal boundaries.

15. Which of the following is not mentioned as a reason for gossip?

1. as a means of bestowing justice
2. to deflect unfavorable attention away from the gossip
3. to be malicious
4. to gain acceptance

EXAM SIX, PASSAGE THREE

16. With which of the following would the writer most likely not agree?

1. All gossips are inconsiderate.
2. Gossip may serve as a conversation filler.
3. Gossips may be attempting to elevate their own self-esteem.
4. All gossips are insecure.

17. According to the selection, the basis of gossip is

1. truth.
2. half-truths.
3. rumors.
4. chatter.

18. The main idea of paragraph six is that

1. you may be able to make people behave the way you want them to by gossiping about the bad behavior of others.
2. gossiping does not facilitate establishing personal boundaries.
3. everyone needs to state their personal preferences.
4. by criticizing someone else, you deny your own personal preferences.

GO ON TO NEXT PAGE

EXAM SIX, PASSAGE THREE

The United States is the only advanced industrial nation in the world that bases its medical system on a pay-for-service basis. Other industrial countries extend health protection to their entire populations. In the United States, health care is rationed on the ability to pay for services.

The only notable exceptions are Medicaid and Medicare. Medicaid provides some help for the poor. Medicare assists the elderly. Both programs typically pay for less than 50 percent of the health care costs of the poor and elderly who are eligible for their benefits. With Medicare the patient is responsible for paying what is not covered. Medicaid patients are not required to make up the difference, which is one reason why many medical providers to the United States refuse to treat them.

Americans continue to have the most expensive healthcare system in the world, despite the enormous gaps in coverage. Attempts to bring down the costs through the use of Health Maintenance Organizations (HMOs) had some initial success, but those gains have eroded. Physicians complain when cost containment lowers the fees they receive for their services.

Recent estimates about how many Americans go without health coverage is about 40 million plus. But even for people with some coverage from Medicaid or Medicare, the risk of financial ruin is one family health crisis away.

EXAM SIX, PASSAGE FOUR

The sad fact remains that in the United States healthcare remains rationed on the ability to pay. It is difficult to know with certainty whether or not the United States will develop new programs that make the healthcare system more accessible and affordable. Expect health care providers to resist these goals and to resist any changes that threaten their profits.   -MacDonald, p. 110

19. According to the passage, in the U.S., healthcare is rationed on the ability to pay. Therefore, it can be inferred from the passage that in other countries

1. health care is superior to that of the U.S.
2. the same system is utilized.
3. the health care is substandard.
4. minimal or no payment is required on the part of the patient.

20. Why do medical personnel refuse to treat Medicaid patients?

1. Medicaid patients only pay the amount not covered by insurance.
2. Medicaid patients are not required to pay anything.
3. Medicaid patients only pay a basic fee.
4. Medicaid patients are old and always ill.

GO ON TO NEXT PAGE

21. The reader can infer that the writer believes that

1. the U.S. health care system is acceptable.
2. since the U.S. has the best health care system in the world, citizens have no justification for criticizing it.
3. Americans are proud of the health care system.
4. the U.S. health care system needs to be revised.

22. The phrase is rationed, as used in the passage, most nearly means

1. is dispensed.
2. is withheld.
3. has a quota.
4. is helped.

23. The concept of cost containment in paragraph three most likely signifies that

1. HMOs do not make any money.
2. patients have undue pressure to pay unreasonable bills.
3. hospitals are allowed to charge outlandish fees.
4. doctors feel they are not being paid what they are due.

24. For most Americans, the most frightening aspect of the health care system is that

1. even with insurance, hospitals will not admit you.
2. because doctors are not paid well, they migrate to other countries to work.
3. financial ruin is one family health crisis away.
4. hospitals reject patients with certain injuries and diseases.

GO ON TO NEXT PAGE

EXAM SIX, PASSAGE FOUR

It had been by no means easy to flee into the mountains and to help set up what should have become a band affiliated with the Resistance movement. Contacts, arms, money and the experience needed to acquire them were all missing. We lacked capable men, and instead we were swamped by a deluge of outcasts, in good or bad faith, who came in search of a nonexistent organization: in search of arms, or merely of protection, a hiding place, a fire, a pair of shoes.

Three Fascist Militia companies, which had set out in the night to surprise a much more powerful and dangerous band than ours, broke into our camp one snowy dawn and took me as a suspect person.

During the interrogation that followed, I preferred to admit my status of 'Italian citizen of Jewish race'. As a Jew, I was sent to Fossoli where a vast detention camp collected all the people not approved of by the new-born Fascist Republic.

At the moment of my arrival, at the end of January 1944, there were about 150 Italian Jews in the camp, but within a few weeks their number rose to over 600. For the most part they consisted of entire families captured by the Fascists or Nazis through their naïveté or following secret accusations. A few had given themselves up spontaneously, reduced to desperation by the homeless life, or because they lacked the means to survive, or to avoid separation from a captured relation, or even—absurdly—'to be in conformity with the law'.

The arrival of a squad of German SS men should have made even the optimists within our camp doubtful; but we still managed to interpret the arrival in various ways without drawing the most obvious conclusions. Thus, the announcement of our deportation to the concentration camp in Germany caught us all unawares.   -Levi, pp. 13-14

25. "In conformity with the law" most nearly means

1. breaking the law.
2. ignoring the law.
3. altering the law.
4. being in line with the law.

26. The tone of the last sentence is one of

1. anger.
2. anticipation.
3. disbelief.
4. indifference.

27. The writer was a member of the

1. Nazi party.
2. struggling Italian Resistance.
3. Fascist Militia.
4. German SS squad.

GO ON TO NEXT PAGE

EXAM SIX, PASSAGE FIVE

28. Those who fled to the mountains perhaps were searching for all of the following except

1. money.
2. guns.
3. a warm place to sleep.
4. a safe haven.

29. The reader can infer that the Italian Resistance mentioned in the selection

1. was extremely effective.
2. helped most Italian Jews escape the Fascist regime.
3. was disbanded when the writer was caught.
4. was, in the main, ineffective.

30. The writer states that most Italian Jews were caught

1. and publicly denounced.
2. due to their own naiveté or following secret accusations.
3. because the German SS had known about them for years.
4. because they belonged to the Nazi Party and classified as traitors.

GO ON TO NEXT PAGE

EXAM SIX, PASSAGE FIVE

When management professionals write, they do it to get work done—to accomplish a task. They usually work in high-pressure, fast-paced environments, where there is never enough time to do everything, especially writing. Business writing requires a variety of tasks. So smart professionals complete three important steps every time they write:

First, business *communication happens between people*—every communication involves relationships. Readers' needs and writer's purposes are interdependent. Essentially, business writing is not just about you, the writer. Instead, it is primarily about what your readers need from you—having your readers in mind as a specific group with specific needs is very important to the ultimate success of a document or presentation.

Second before you write a business document, it is important *to clarify your purposes*—are you responding to a customer complaint, yet writing so that the reader will want to buy more products from your company? Suppose that you want to convince an organization to hold its training seminar at your hotel. Would the purpose of your first contact with the event planner be to get him or her to sign a contract right away? No, the purpose of your first letter would be to make the organization aware of your existence. That is, you would begin by building the foundation for a relationship.

Third, it is important to think about *what the writing situation requires*. The situation could be an historical moment such as a merger; or, it could be a dead-line, lack of money, or pressure from a boss. For instance, if the company is downsizing and resources are scarce, the situation presents a tough environment in which to make a monetary request. So, in this scenario, the solution might be to write a proposal to purchase used equipment. Conditions must be considered in any writing strategy; that is, they determine the limits that you will face as a business writer.

-Friedman, et al., pp. 1-3

31. When management professionals write, their ultimate goal is to

1. determine who will read their advertisements.
2. write proposals to obtain expensive business equipment.
3. express their aspirations of creating a successful business.
4. get work done and accomplish a task.

32. The overall purpose of this passage is to

1. persuade the reader to use the described strategies.
2. contrast business writing with scholarly writing.
3. explain the process of business writing.
4. compare business writing with personal written correspondence.

EXAM SIX, PASSAGE SIX

33.   The overall pattern of organization used in the last paragraph is

1. example.
2. narration.
3. description.
4. definition.

34. The author would agree that business writing

1. involves primarily the writer.
2. is not just about you, the writer.
3. must be proofread by a supervisor.
4. is more difficult than any other kind of writing.

35. The word, <u>scenario</u>, found in the last paragraph most likely means

1. play.
2. definition.
3. description.
4. situation.

36. The sentence that best describes the main idea of paragraph two is that

1. having your readers in mind as a specific group is unnecessary in business writing.
2. business writing is primarily about what you need from the readers.
3. in business writing, readers' needs and writer's purposes are inter-dependent.
4. business writing is insignificant compared to the goal of creating a successful business.

GO ON TO NEXT PAGE

EXAM SIX, PASSAGE SIX

[Note: *Hovering 250 miles above the Earth is the International Space Station. Costing 157 billion U.S. dollars to construct, it is our first city in space.*]

The International Space Station (ISS) plays a critical role in support of the vision for space exploration. It supports scientific research for the U. S. and international partners: to explore long-term human space travel, to develop technologies and engineering solutions for space exploration, and to provide ongoing practical experience living and working in space.

About the size of a football field, the ISS is our largest adventure into space to date. Weighing almost one million pounds, the ISS is the greatest construction project of humankind, rivaling the pyramids of Egypt or the Great Wall of China. Elements of the ISS include a Canadian-built, 55-foot-long robotic arm used for assembly and maintenance tasks on the space station, a pressurized European lab and transport vehicles; a Japanese lab with an attached exposed exterior platform for experiments; Russian life support systems and habitation modules. Boeing is the prime contractor for U.S. elements which include life support, thermal control, guidance, navigation, power systems and communications. The ISS is also scheduled to house a Crew Exploration Vehicle which can be used to take crews to and from the Moon!

A three-person expedition crew typically stays about four to six months aboard the ISS. If the crew needs to evacuate the station, it can return to Earth aboard a Russian Soyuz vehicle docked to the ISS. Crews aboard the ISS are assisted by mission control centers in Houston and Moscow. With an annual operating budget of about $2 billion, the station will go to a six-person crew in 2009.

NASA began the current plan to build a space station in 1984. Japan, Canada and nine European countries agreed to be partners in the program. Russia joined in 1993. NASA is committed to completing the ISS in 2010.

-NASA, 2008

EXAM SIX, PASSAGE SEVEN

37. The attitude of the writer toward the ISS is one of

1. criticism due to the internationalization of the project.
2. sarcasm since the project is viewed by the public as an impractical venture.
3. resentment due to the costs.
4. awe because of the superb abilities and potential of the station.

38. According to this passage, which country is not involved in the activities of the International Space Station?

1. Russia
2. Japan
3. China
4. the United States

39. Of the following, which is not a purpose of the International Space Station?

1. to explore long-term human space travel
2. to develop technologies and engineering solutions for space exploration
3. to provide ongoing practical experience living in space.
4. to house individuals with specific diseases to determine the affect of gravity on disease.

40. The construction of the ISS is compared to the construction of

1. the Egyptian Sphinx.
2. the pyramids.
3. a football field.
4. a Crew Exploration Vehicle capable of traveling to the Moon.

41. The style of writing employed in the passage is

1. informal and chatty.
2. critical and argumentative.
3. detached and objective.
4. informative and descriptive.

42. habitation modules as used in the passage most nearly means

1. environmental units.
2. living quarters.
3. research labs.
4. pressurized atmospheres.

GO ON TO NEXT PAGE

EXAM SIX, PASSAGE SEVEN

Trembling with fear, Ayla clung to the tall man beside her as she watched the strangers approach from the earth lodge. Jondalar put his arm around her protectively, but she still shook.

He's so big! Ayla thought, gaping at the man in the lead. He even made Jondalar seem small, though the man who held her towered over most men.

Ayla glanced at Jondalar and saw no fear in his face, but his smile was guarded. They were strangers, and in his long travels he had learned to be wary of strangers.

"I don't recall seeing you before," the big man said. Jondalar unclasped Ayla and took a step forward, holding out both hands, palms upward showing he was hiding nothing, in the greeting of friendliness. "I am Jondalar."

The hands were not accepted.

"Weren't there two foreign men staying with the river people that live to the west? It seems to me the name I heard was something like yours.

"Yes, my brother and I lived with them," Jondalar conceded.

The big man looked thoughtful for a while, then, unexpectedly, he lunged for Jondalar and grabbed the tall blond man in a bear hug.

"Then we are related!" he boomed, a broad smile warming his face. "Tholie is my relative!"

Jondalar's smile returned, a little shaken. "Tholie! She is my brother's mate! She taught me your language."

"I told you. We are related. I am Talut."

Everyone was smiling. Ayla noticed Talut beamed a grin at her, then eyed her appreciatively. "I see you are not traveling with a brother now," he said to Jondalar.

Jondalar put his arm around her again, and she noticed a fleeting look of pain wrinkle his brow before he spoke. "This is Ayla."

"It's an unusual name. Is she of the river people?"

Jondalar was taken aback by the abruptness of his questioning. He did not know what to say. Ayla was not going to be easy to explain.

-Auel, pp. 1-2

43. Overall, in paragraph two the author is

1. establishing the relationship between Ayla and Jondalar.
2. describing Ayla.
3. giving scenic background.
4. contrasting Jondalar and the big stranger.

44. wary, as used in the passage, most nearly means

1. hateful
2. open.
3. guarded.
4. fearful.

GO ON TO NEXT PAGE

EXAM SIX, PASSAGE EIGHT

45. It is most likely that Jondalar offered his hands "palms up" to

1. better grasp Talut's hands.
2. show he was holding no weapons.
3. be ready for a possible threat.
4. demonstrate his strength.

46. The reader can infer that Jondalar's brother most likely

1. stayed with his mate and the river people.
2. died a tragic death.
3. is going to meet up with Ayla and Jondalar in a few weeks.
4. had already met Talut.

47. The reader can infer that Ayla was trembling because

1. she was frightened.
2. she was excited.
3. Jondalar had a weapon at her back.
4. she was ill with a fever.

48. According to the passage, Tholie is

1. Jondalar's ex-partner.
2. Ayla's mother.
3. one of the earth lodge villagers.
4. Talut's kin.

GO ON TO NEXT PAGE

EXAM SIX, PASSAGE EIGHT

The ability to control fire represents one of the most important landmarks in the saga of human evolution. The emergence of early man and the full commitment to control fire and to manufacture tools represented a new way of dealing with the world.

First signs of human control of fire come from burned bones found at caves in Africa, dated at one million years ago. The climate of northern Europe and Asia was very cold, colder than it is at present. So cold were areas of Europe that one million years ago it became a <u>tundra</u>. For early humans to survive in such an environment would have required the use and control of fire. Thus, under these conditions, the success of humankind as a species depended a great deal on their ability to master the control of fire. Hence at the beginning, fire was probably used for keeping warm.

The application of heat to food, if for no other purpose than to thaw the frozen remainders of yesterday's kill, made an important contribution to subsistence at the cold edges of human occupation. Thus, because people could not have survived winters without being able to defrost meat from kills, cooking became obligatory for those occupying glacial zones 250,000 years ago.

Excavations in northern Israel also indicate that early man evolved the ability to control and use fire. The distribution of burned wood, plant seeds, and stone artifacts were in discrete clusters within layers of the site, indi-cating evidence of firesides in specific locations. These findings suggest that early humans might have used fire not only to keep warm and keep away predators but also for roasting plant and animal foods.

Since the sites show the remains of baboons and butchered elephants, the findings suggest that early man was able to hunt big game in an organized form, in which he may have employed fire as a tool to drive animals into a swamp or cave. Thus, the control of fire might have <u>catapulted</u> early man into the age of modern man.

-Frisancho, pp. 158-162

49. According to the selection, in the beginning fire was used

1. for keeping warm.
2. to keep away predators.
3. to drive large animals into swamps.
4. for cooking.

50. The selection states that which of the following most likely catapulted early man into modern man?

1. ability to capture large animals
2. the findings at the excavation sites
3. the control and use of fire
4. plants seeds and stone artifacts

GO ON TO NEXT PAGE

EXAM SIX, PASSAGE NINE

51. The word <u>catapulted</u> as used in the last paragraph most nearly means

1. withdrawn.
2. propelled.
3. originated.
4. taken back.

52. The word <u>tundra</u> as utilized in the second paragraph most likely means

1. area dominated by powdered snow.
2. iceberg.
3. blizzard.
4. frozen plain devoid of much vegetation.

53. Which of the following was not mentioned as an area that early man inhabited?

1. Asia
2. Africa
3. North America
4. Europe

54. The excavations in Israel were especially important because they illustrated

1. the utilization of firesides for rituals and ceremonies.
2. that early man was using fire for cooking.
3. that man was using fire to keep away predators.
4. that the first humans appeared 250,000 years ago.

EXAM SIX, PASSAGE NINE

EXAM SEVEN

The *Galileo* spacecraft arrived at Jupiter in December 1995 after a six-year trip. The main mission focused on detailed studies of Jupiter's moons. While Jupiter has a large complement of known moons, the four largest were first seen by Galileo: **Io, Europa, Ganymede, and Callisto**. [With the aid of the *Galileo* spacecraft and the Hubble Telescope, many interesting observations about two of these moons have been made; some are presented below.]

Io, the innermost, is multicolored, looking very much like a pizza! Its surface appears to be pitted, but it is not cratered, making it appear to be geologically young.

Jupiter's gravitational pull on Io is strong. Io is repeatedly stretched and squeezed and thus heavily stressed. Such stressing causes heating of the interior, just like the constantly changing stresses in a paper clip that is bent back and forth produces heat. From predictions of this tidal heating, planetary scientists predicted that Io might have active volcanoes. Imagine their pleasure when active volcanoes were observed on Io! This discovery makes Io the most geologically active body in the Solar System.

Europa, the smallest of the moons, has an orangish, off-white color and a high reflectivity indicative of an icy surface. The colors indicate contaminants in the ice. Its most distinguishing features are the lines 1,864 miles long and 62 miles wide running across the surface. Their depth is unknown. They may be extensive surface cracks in the 328-foot-thick surface ice. This moon has few craters and no tall mountains, indicating a surface that is not strong enough to hold a mountain's weight without sinking.

The spacecraft probe confirmed that Europa has an extremely thin, variable atmosphere that includes oxygen, and water ice has been observed on its surface. Does Europa have liquid water underneath the crust? If so, might it have conditions under which life might form? To help answer these and other questions, the *Galileo's* mission was extended an additional two years.

-Shawl, pp. 247; 257-261

1. The writer's attitude toward the discovery of volcanoes on Io is one of

1. apathy.
2. solemnity.
3. apprehension.
4. excitement.

2. Water ice has been observed on the surface of Europa. The most likely implication is that

1. humans can live on Europa.
2. the water ice will re-freeze to form an ice sheet.
3. there is a good possibility that liquid water exists on Europa.
4. life does not exist on Europa.

3. The fact that Io is not cratered illustrates that

1. Io is much like Jupiter.
2. Io is a young planet.
3. Jupiter's pull on Io is greater than it is on its other moons.
4. Io is an ice planet.

4. How long did it take the spacecraft *Galileo* to reach Jupiter?

1. 6 years
2. 4 years
3. 6 months
4. 2 months

5. To get his point across in paragraph three, the author uses which pattern of organization?

1. description
2. facts and statistics
3. cause-effect
4. contrast

6. Besides astronomers, it is implied that which type of scientist should be a forerunner in researching Jupiter's moon, Io?

1. geologists
2. geographers
3. astrologists
4. physicists

GO ON TO NEXT PAGE

EXAM SEVEN, PASSAGE ONE

The **hindbrain**, as the name implies, is the rear part of the brain. It begins where the spinal cord connects to the brain and is primarily concerned with quite basic, survival-oriented functions. The structures in the hindbrain and the functions they control are found across a wide range of organisms.

One of the structures is the **medulla**, which is located within the skull just beyond the spinal cord. The medulla controls a number of critical reflexes by way of the cranial nerves. These reflexes include breathing, heart rate, vomiting, and salivation. Damage to the medulla, or overdoses of drugs like cocaine or opiates, which affect the medulla, can be fatal.

The **pons** which is located between the medulla and the midbrain appears to play a role in sleep and dreaming. As early as 1949, Moruzzi and Magoun discovered that if this area of a sleeping cat was stimulated, the cat would awaken.

The final hindbrain structure is the **cerebellum**. It is a relatively large structure located behind the pons. It has two hemispheres and many folds like the cerebrum in the forebrain. The cerebellum has long been believed to be important in the control of movement and balance. It receives both sensory information and information about movement commands issued by the brain. The current view is that the cerebellum's main job is to coordinate information so that movements occur in a smooth, coordinated fashion. People whose cerebellums are

damaged are likely to be unable to engage in smooth, coordinated movements. If the damage is <u>extensive</u> enough, walking or standing may be affected. -Ellyson, pp. 85-86

7. The main idea of the passage is that

1. the medulla controls a number of critical reflexes by way of the cranial nerves.
2. the cerebellum is the most important part of the brain.
3. critical brain research began in 1949.
4. the hindbrain serves to facilitate important and critical physical functions.

8. The overall pattern of organization utilized in the passage is

1. contrast.
2. definition.
3. comparison.
4. example.

9. As a whole, the hindbrain's function is concerned with

1. sleep and dreaming.
2. salivation and vomiting.
3. movement and balance.
4. basic survival.

GO ON TO NEXT PAGE

EXAM SEVEN, PASSAGE TWO

10. <u>extensive</u> as used in the last paragraph most nearly means

1. widespread.
2. long.
3. minute.
4. additional.

11. Which part of the brain controls dreaming?

1. medulla
2. pons
3. cerebrum
4. cerebellum

12. In regard to brain functioning, why is it that cocaine use can be dangerous?

1. it affects the cerebellum which controls balance
2. it affects the pons which affects sleep
3. it affects the medulla which controls breathing
4. it affects each part of the hindbrain in equal measure

GO ON TO NEXT PAGE

EXAM SEVEN, PASSAGE TWO

You may think that if you read text material carefully and spend lots of time studying it, you shouldn't have to highlight, underline, or even take notes, but this is not the case.

Although you will be able to remember "learned" material longer than material you read or hear only once, you still won't remember enough of it by test time. If you *mark your text as you read it*, you will have a <u>vehicle</u> for reviewing the material before your exam.

One of the most common methods of reviewing for exams is to reread highlighted or underlined material. Unfortunately, most students do this in a rather passive manner. They quickly scan the lines of marked text, assuming that the information somehow will be absorbed into their memory.

In order to conduct an effective review, you need to remain actively involved in your reading. This means you should re-mark your textbook as you review to make decisions about the material that you marked before. If you used yellow highlighting when you first read the chapter, you could use a different color for re-marking. After having completed the chapter, worked through text questions, and listened to the professor's in-class lecture, and you want to continue studying, you may be able to reduce the amount of text even more.   van Blerkom, pp. 178-180

13. It is implied that students believe that once they have read and studied the assigned chapters for an upcoming test, they

1. need to take a break and eat a snack.
2. must re-read the chapters.
3. have studied sufficiently for a test.
4. should go back and highlight names and numbers.

14. According to the passage, one common mistake a student makes in studying is

1. passively re-reading the highlighted portions of the text.
2. reviewing homework.
3. creating test questions.
4. listening to the professor's lecture.

15. After following the techniques outlined in paragraph four, students will

1. earn an A on the test.
2. not have reduced the amount of text to be studied.
3. still need to highlight in two additional colors.
4. be able to say they conducted an effective review.

GO ON TO NEXT PAGE

EXAM SEVEN, PASSAGE THREE

16. The word <u>vehicle</u> as used in the
second paragraph most likely means

1. car.
2. way.
3. transportation.
4. means of expression.

17. An effective way to review for a test
is to

1. remain an active reader by re-reading
   all the assigned chapters.
2. be a passive reader and let your mind
   absorb the material on its own.
3. listen to tapes of your professor's
   lectures.
4. remain an active reader by remark-
   ing your text in a different color.

18. The author's style of writing for
this passage is

1. humorous.
2. informal.
3. dramatic.
4. riveting.

GO ON TO NEXT PAGE

EXAM SEVEN, PASSAGE THREE

The term *disaster* means, literally, "bad star" and, in a wider sense, implies a bad omen, a calamity, a misfortune, or a harmful impact. These words immediately raise fundamental questions: Is a volcanic eruption, or an earthquake, in an unpopulated and remote area a disaster? Must humans be hurt or killed, and their property destroyed, before a violent natural event can be called a disaster? There is no simple answer to this question. The definition of the word *disaster* varies with one's personal perception as well as with the purpose and application of the definition.

For example, on June 6, 1912, a violent eruption tore apart Mt. Katmai on the Alaskan Peninsula. The force of this explosion was estimated to be equivalent to 200,000 H-bombs; more than 7 cubic miles of lava ash overwhelmed the landscape. Rivers were blocked, thousands of acres of forest virtually disappeared, acids spilled into the coastal ocean, and all wildlife was killed within a vast area. There were no known human casualties, but surely, such a <u>devastating</u> event must be viewed as a true disaster.   -Ebert, p. 181

19. The main idea of the selection is that

1. in June a violent eruption destroyed Mt. Katmai.
2. people will describe or define a disaster in different ways.
3. to be named a disaster, the event must include loss of human life.
4. at Mt. Katmai thousands of acres of forests disappeared.

20. In paragraph two, to what was the explosion equated?

1. 7 cubic miles of lava ash.
2. acids spilled into the coastal ocean.
3. the destruction of Alaska itself.
4. 200,000 H-bombs.

21. The reader can infer that the Mt. Katmai incident should be called a disaster because

1. a portion of the face of our planet was destroyed.
2. the destruction involved loss of human life.
3. the Alaskan Peninsula sank.
4. rivers were blocked.

GO ON TO NEXT PAGE

EXAM SEVEN, PASSAGE FOUR

22. The author states that

1. there is no simple answer to the
    question of what constitutes a
    disaster.
2. an earthquake tore apart Mr. Katmai.
3. fortunately, wildlife in the region was
    not harmed by the Mt. Katmai
    incident.
4. the Mt. Katmai incident should not be
    classified as a true disaster.

23. In the second paragraph, overall
which pattern of organization is
employed?

1. definition
2. example
3. persuasion
4. narration

24. The word <u>devastating</u> as used in the
passage most nearly means

1. shocking.
2. disturbing.
3. surprising.
4. destructive.

GO ON TO NEXT PAGE

EXAM SEVEN, PASSAGE FOUR

One of the more obvious characteristics of human behavior is that it changes. The way you dress or talk very likely changes depending upon the situation you are in and the people who are present.

Your overall behavior has changed dramatically since you were born. A newborn has a very limited repertoire of behaviors; its motor behaviors are limited to primarily reflexive responses such as sucking and swallowing, and its vocalizations are pretty much restricted to crying.

By one year of age, most children have a much broader <u>repertoire</u> of motor skills from crawling and sitting to walking. Language behavior has also changed in the first year to include the repetition of sounds, syllables, and perhaps even a word or two. In everyday language we might say that the one-year-old has learned to sit up, to walk, and to talk. Therefore, one source of behavior change is the biological process of getting older called <u>maturation</u>.

Another source of behavior change is the effect of environment. When your behavior (how you dress and talk, for example) changes depending upon the situation you are in, we conclude that you have learned to act appropriately for the situation. In this case we are using environment to refer to any thing outside of the person, anything from weather conditions, to comments of other people, to an increase in salary. When behavior changes as the result of contact with the environment, we say learning has occurred.

Both biological maturation and con-

EXAM SEVEN, PASSAGE FIVE

tact with the environment are necessary for changes in behavior to take place.

-Kestner, p. 150

25. The main idea of this passage is that

1. the way you dress changes depending upon the situation you are in.
2. your overall behavior has changed dramatically since you were born.
3. change is a primary characteristic of behavior.
4. the only factor necessary for behavior change is biological maturation.

26. As used in context, <u>repertoire</u>, most likely indicates a

1. limitation.
2. catalogue.
3. collection.
4. range.

27. In the context of this passage, your environment may include all of the following except

1. your place of work.
2. internal decision-making processes.
3. gossip.
4. the weather.

28. According to the passage, which of the following is not described as a newborn's ability?

1. repeating syllables
2. swallowing
3. sucking
4. crying

29. Which would be an opinion and not a fact?

1. One source of behavior change is the effect of the environment.
2. People who rebel against society will not dress or talk appropriately in a given situation.
3. Most one-year-olds can crawl, sit up, and walk.
4. Maturation is a biological process.

30. maturation, as used in the passage, most nearly means

1. immaturity.
2. ripeness.
3. growing older.
4. life.

GO ON TO NEXT PAGE

EXAM SEVEN, PASSAGE FIVE

The question of dropping the atomic bomb on Japan had come up for the first time at a May 31, 1945 meeting of the committee created to advise President Truman about future use of the new weapon. One suggestion was for a non-military "demonstration explosion" in an isolated terrain that would so impress Japanese leaders that they would surrender. When no one could offer a satisfactory answer to the question of how to make such a demonstration convincing enough that the Japanese would end the war, the idea of a demonstration was ruled out.

Ultimately, the committee decided to recommend to President Truman that the bomb be dropped on Japan without any prior warning. The only mention of a target was that it be a military installation of some type.

Another committee, composed of scientists and military strategists, had been established to evaluate and determine potential targets. Initially, four cities were singled out. The first was the city of Kokura, the site of one of Japan's largest munitions plants. Hiroshima was selected because it was the site of some war plants and an assembly spot for Japanese naval convoys. Kyoto (once Japan's capital and the site not only of war plants but also of several universities and religious shrines) made the list as well.

Secretary of War Stimson quickly struck Kyoto from the list because of its historic and respected place in Japanese life and society. Nagasaki ultimately replaced Kyoto as a potential target. On July 23, 1945, President Truman approved the use of the atomic bomb against Japan.

Much debate has taken place over the years about the American decision to use the atomic bomb against Japan. Many still believe that a "demonstration explosion" of the weapon should have been staged instead.   -Layton, pp. 148-149

31. The term demonstration explosion means an explosion that

1. would have leveled Nagasaki.
2. could show the American public of 1945 the strength of its military.
3. involved military but not scientific personnel.
4. would have prevented loss of life.

32. Who gave the go-ahead for use of the atomic bomb against Japan?

1. the American public
2. President Truman
3. the committee of scientists and military strategists
4. the committee created to advise President Truman about future use of the new weapon

GO ON TO NEXT PAGE

EXAM SEVEN, PASSAGE SIX

33. It was stated in the passage that a demonstration explosion was ruled out because

1. the Japanese could never be convinced to end the war.
2. the American public rallied against it.
3. no one could figure out how to proceed with the idea.
4. President Truman vetoed the idea.

34. It can be deduced from the passage that the committees were more interested in destroying

1. Japanese military installations.
2. Kyoto, Japan.
3. civilian targets.
4. universities and religious shrines.

35. The reader can infer from the scenario given that the aggressors

1. were the American scientists interested in testing their new bomb.
2. bombed the military base, religious temples, and historic sites of Kyoto.
3. were non-military strategists who focused on making money off the war.
4. were victorious in their efforts to drop the atomic bomb over Japan.

36. The tone of this passage is

1. angry.
2. nostalgic.
3. academic.
4. sympathetic.

GO ON TO NEXT PAGE

EXAM SEVEN, PASSAGE SIX

And then there was the boarding school. I happened to go to a distant institution called the Pipestone Indian Training School. I'll never forget my first day there. We'd been riding on a school bus the better part of that day from Wisconsin to Minnesota, and we arrived at Pipestone around midnight. I thought for sure they would feed us— but they didn't do that. They marched us all, boys in one direction and girls in the other. The first stop was this little room that had four chairs in it. And there, everybody got their hair lopped off! I remember how I cried.

My mother used to take care of my braids and, I remember, when I left her earlier that day, she had tied an eagle feather in my hair. She said, "I want you to look nice when you get there." She also told me, "Always remember to take care of your hair. Braid it when you can but for sure keep it clean, comb it, tie it back. But always remember, when you go out to pray your hair must be in braids. And I want you to keep this eagle plume with you until we get back together." That same night they chopped off my hair. And I mean they cut it right down to the skin. And there on the floor lay my pretty eagle plume and the braids that my mother had so carefully fixed and tied.   -Wall & Arden, p. 55

37. The overall tone of the passage is

1. uplifting.
2. entertaining.
3. despairing.
4. chatty.

38. The author of this passage is probably a(n)

1. anthropologist interested in Native American culture.
2. sociologist who focuses on the behavior of indigenous peoples.
3. Native American who went through the experience.
4. journalist working for *National Geographic* magazine.

39. It is implied in the passage that long hair on an Indian is

1. valued.
2. embarrassing.
3. a drawback.
4. a matter of preference.

40. This passage focuses on

1. the abuses committed by staff at the Pipestone Indian Training School.
2. an Indian child's experiences at Pipestone Indian Training School.
3. the bus ride of an Indian child from Wisconsin to Minnestoa.
4. an Indian girl's first experience with discrimination.

EXAM SEVEN, PASSAGE SEVEN

41. The child's relationship with the mother was one of

1. arrogance and stubbornness.
2. respectful independence.
3. dependence and love.
4. indifference and apathy.

42. According to the passage, the first action the staff at Pipestone took was to

1. lop off all the children's hair.
2. take the children to the cafeteria.
3. complete a head count as the children got off the bus.
4. welcome the children.

GO ON TO NEXT PAGE

EXAM SEVEN, PASSAGE SEVEN

There was a time when the presence of women in business was largely limited to positions associated with business office routines. Even in the 1990s one sad note that needed consideration by leaders in business was the fact that women's 1995 median weekly earnings were only 75.5 per cent of men's.

In today's world we find more and more women serving as heads of state, as members of the U.S. Congress and as owners of businesses where they make tough decisions on a daily basis. Gone is the idea that women are too emotional to perform in some positions of leadership. Women have every right to expect equal opportunity in whatever endeavor they may choose to pursue.

One of the most exciting things I have seen happen in my lifetime is the manner in which America's women have moved into a greater leadership role in American Business. In the early seventies, women in America owned less than five percent of American businesses. According to data from the Census Bureau, in 1992 women owned over 6.4 million U.S. Businesses which employed more than thirteen million persons. These firms generated over $1.6 trillion in business revenues. A lot of decisions are being made by women managers. Those people who are a part of our world of business would be wise to give attention to this changing pattern of ownership.

–Lockwood, p. 5

43. As used in paragraph one, positions associated with business office routines most probably means

1. clerical positions.
2. top management positions.
3. middle management jobs.
4. mail service positions.

44. The author would probably agree that in today's world

1. men have all the top management positions.
2. women are paid the same wages as men for the same job.
3. women are just as qualified as men for most jobs.
4. though women deserve equal opportunities in the job market, they should not have ownership of American businesses.

45. The purpose of paragraph three is to

1. criticize males for taking twenty years to recognize the worth of women in business.
2. to shed light on the writer's leadership role in American business.
3. describe American business practices in the 1970s.
4. show the strides women have made in business.

GO ON TO NEXT PAGE

EXAM SEVEN, PASSAGE EIGHT

46. The author's attitude toward women in business in today's world is one of

1. resentment.
2. impartiality.
3. optimism.
4. skepticism.

47. In 1992, how many American businesses did women own?

1. thirteen million
2. 6.4 million
3. 1.6 trillion
4. 5 percent

48. The style of writing of this selection is

1. informal and persuasive.
2. cerebral and scholarly.
3. impersonal and uncongenial.
4. unbiased and detached.

GO ON TO NEXT PAGE

EXAM SEVEN, PASSAGE EIGHT

When I first laid eyes on her, Chablis was standing by the curb, watching me intently as I parked my car. She had just come out of Dr. Myra Bishop's office across the street from where I lived. Dr. Bishop was a family practitioner. Most of her patients were conservatively dressed black women. Those whose gaze happened to meet mine usually nodded solemnly and moved on. But not Chablis.

She was wearing a loose white cotton blouse, jeans, and white tennis sneakers. Her hair was short, and her skin was a smooth milk chocolate. Her eyes were large and expressive, all the more so because they were staring straight into mine. She had both hands on her hips and a sassy half-smile on her face as if she had been waiting for me. I drew up to the curb and rolled to a stop at her feet.

"Oooooo, child !" she said. "You are right on time, honey." Her voice crackled, her hoop earrings jangled. "I am serious. I cannot tell you." She began moving slowly toward me with an underlining walk. She trailed an index finger sensuously along the fender, "yayyiss!" . . .

We pulled away from the curb.

"I'm Chablis," she said.

"Chablis? That's pretty," I said. "What's your full name?"

"The *Lady* Chablis," she said. She turned sideways in the seat, pulling her knees up and leaning back against the door as if she were sinking into a luxurious sofa. "It's a stage name," she said. "I'm a showgirl."
-Berendt, pp. 96-98

49. Which paragraph would be considered a most descriptive paragraph of Chablis?

1. two
2. three
3. the last paragraph
4. the first paragraph

50. Chablis can be characterized as a(n)

1. conservative, staid actress.
2. flashy woman.
3. "loose" showgirl.
4. homeless, street person.

51. underlining, as underlined, most nearly means

1. restrained and controlled.
2. rocking and repetitive.
3. rippling and suggestive.
4. unsteady and shaky.

52. We can infer that "I"

1. left Chablis sitting in the car and went inside.
2. went with Chablis to her show.
3. asked Chablis to get out of his car.
4. gave Chablis a ride home.

EXAM SEVEN, PASSAGE NINE
GO ON TO NEXT PAGE

53. The main setting for this selection is

1. in Dr. Bishop's office.
2. on stage.
3. on the street.
4. on a luxurious sofa.

54. It is implied in the selection that the writer is

1. repulsed by Chablis.
2. angered by Chablis.
3. in love with Chablis.
4. intrigued by Chablis.

EXAM SEVEN, PASSAGE NINE

EXAM EIGHT

Did you know that Mahatma Gandhi and Martin Luther King were really very much alike? Although seemingly different in regard to ethnicity, culture, and upbringing, these two individuals had several very important things in common.

Mahatma Gandhi (1869-1948) was regarded as a great political and spiritual leader in India. After practicing law in South Africa, he worked for Indian independence from Great Britain. He gave up Western ways to lead a life of abstinence and spirituality. Gandhi led the fight to rid India of the caste system; he especially defended the rights of "untouchables." He asserted the unity of mankind under one God and preached Christian and Muslim ethics along with the Hindu.

Ghandi was a proponent of passive resistance. When violence broke out between Hindus and Muslims, he resorted to fasts and visits to the troubled areas in efforts to end the violence. While at a prayer vigil in New Delhi he was fatally shot by a Hindu fanatic who objected to Gandhi's tolerance for the Muslims.

Martin Luther King (1920-1968) was a black American clergyman and civil rights leader. He first gained national prominence much in the same manner as Gandhi—by advocating passive re-sistance (in King's case directed against segregation). He led a year-long boycott against the segregated bus line in Mont-gomery, Alabama. He then set up the Southern Christian Leadership Confer-ence as a base for nonviolent marches, protests, and demonstrations for black rights, such as the March on Washington and the voter-registration drive in Selma, Alabama. These nonviolent methods were comparable to those of Gandhi. King was awarded the 1964 Nobel Peace Prize, but his leadership was challenged as civil rights activists became more militant. King, like Gandhi, was assassinated. While planning a multiracial Poor People's March, he was shot and killed in Memphis, Tennessee.

–based on Levey & Greenhall, pp. 317-318; 452

1. The reader can infer that India had been colonized by

1. Muslims.
2. the West.
3. Great Britain.
4. South Africa.

2. In Ghandhi's case, passive resistance, as used in the passage, could mean

1. rebelling by fasting.
2. violently revolting.
3. resisting by eliminating Muslim leaders.
4. showing strength by carrying out assassinations.

3. The overall purpose of the passage is to

1. persuade the reader to become an adherent of passive resistance.
2. contrast two great leaders from different parts of the world.
3. compare Martin Luther King and Mahatma Ghandi.
4. praise Martin Luther King for receiving the Nobel Peace Prize.

EXAM EIGHT, PASSAGE ONE

4. Gandhi and King were alike in all of the following ways except

1. they both gained national prominence.
2. they both believed in passive resistance.
3. they were both assassinated.
4. they were both lawyers.

5. Of the following, with which would the author agree?

1. Gandhi was a more effective leader than King.
2. each leader had a desire to become a martyr for his cause.
3. both leaders were role models for millions of people.
4. each leader gave up Western ways to help his cause.

6. The main focus of the passage is that Gandhi and King were proponents of

1. peaceful solutions to conflict.
2. the Nobel Peace Prize.
3. Western ways.
4. violence under certain conditions.

GO ON TO NEXT PAGE

EXAM EIGHT, PASSAGE ONE

Should parents be the type who do not seem to notice when their child runs around a restaurant causing <u>havoc,</u> or should parents be strict, like drill sergeants, constantly barking out orders and demanding that the child listen without question?

These are important questions since the style a parent adopts is an important variable in influencing the child's later development. Researcher Baumrind identified four distinct patterns of parenting:

1. *Authoritarian* parents value strict obedience to their commands. They tend to be controlling, and use forceful techniques, such as threats or physical punishment. This style of parenting is associated with poor outcomes in children, such as unhappiness, aggressiveness in boys, and dependence in girls.

2. The *permissive* parenting style involves setting few limits and making few demands for appropriate behavior from children. Children are permitted to make their own decisions about many routine activities such as TV viewing, bedtime, and meal times. Permissive parents tend to be either moderately warm, or cool and uninvolved. Children of permissive parents tend to be low on self-control and self-reliance.

3. The *authoritative style* of parenting involves both control and warmth. These parents have high expectations of their children but also use rewards rather than punishments to achieve their ends. They communicate expectations clearly and listen to what their children have to say. This style of parenting is associated with the most favorable outcomes in children. The children tend to be high in self-control, friendly with peers, cooperative with adults, and independent and energetic; they strive for achievement.

4. The last style of parenting is called *uninvolved*. These parents seem to be uncommitted to parenting and emotionally detached from their children. It seems as if they place greater importance on their own needs and preferences than on their child's. Not surprisingly, uninvolved parenting is related to the worst outcomes in children, as they show lower self-esteem, increased levels of aggression, and greater impulsiveness.

-Kestner, p. 297

7. In paragraph two, the author gets her point across through

1. chronology
2. definition
3. narration
4. persuasion

8. We can infer from the passage that, in most cases, the best parent is the one who employs a(n)

1. uninvolved style
2. authoritarian style
3. permissive style
4. authoritative style

EXAM EIGHT, PASSAGE TWO

9. Children who have low self-control and low self-reliance were probably raised by

1. authoritarian parents.
2. uninvolved parents.
3. permissive parents.
4. authoritative parents.

10. The word <u>havoc</u>, as used in the first paragraph, most likely means

1. disarray.
2. order.
3. noise.
4. tidiness.

11. In the last paragraph, the author's commentary about parents who use an *uninvolved* style of parenting is one of

1. reluctant admiration.
2. total surprise.
3. sarcastic narrative.
4. critical analysis.

12. Of the styles of parenting, which two would most likely permit children to make decisions on their own?

1. authoritative and uninvolved
2. uninvolved and permissive
3. permissive and authoritative
4. authoritative and authoritarian

EXAM EIGHT, PASSAGE TWO

GO ON TO NEXT PAGE

Who runs for president of the United States? The field of potential candidates is limited by certain Constitutional standards of eligibility. Article II of the Constitution requires that the president be at least 35 years old and a natural-born citizen.

The Constitution imposes no religious, racial, sexual, or economic qualifications for holding office. Until well into this century, the party politicians who controlled the nominating process employed certain "unwritten laws" or norms in judging electability. For example, at the turn of the twentieth century, it was generally held that only white, protestant males—preferably of English stock—were electable. Democrats challenged the religious barrier in 1928 when they nominated a Catholic candidate, Al Smith. In 1960, Democrats nominated a Catholic for a second time, John F. Kennedy, who won a narrow victory over Richard Nixon. One remarkable result of Kennedy's election has been that since 1960 Catholicism has never been considered a disqualifying factor.

Today, there might still be resistance to the nomination of certain candidates because of their race, religion, or sex. But surveys indicate that such resistance is weakening among the voters. This trend has been illustrated in a number of ways. Democratic presidential nominee Walter Mondale chose a woman as his running mate in 1984.

In 1984 and 1988 the civil-rights leader, Jesse Jackson was a major candidate in the Democratic nominating race. In 1996 retired Joint Chiefs of Staff

Chairman Colin Powell, an African American and the son of immigrants, was the preferred choice of a majority of voters in many opinion polls, until he decided not to <u>seek</u> the office. And, in 2000, Senator Lieberman, an orthodox Jew, was nominated as the vice presidential candidate for the Democratic Party.   -Ceasar, p. 290

13. One may infer from the passage that

1. in the realm of politics, Walter Mondale was not gender-biased.
2. Colin Powell did not qualify to run for president.
3. Senator Lieberman did not accept the vice-presidential nomination.
4. Jesse Jackson is African-American.

14. Up to 1927 an "unwritten" standard for eligibility for President of the U.S. was that the candidate should be

1. white, Catholic male
2. natural born citizen.
3. 35 years old.
4. white, Protestant male.

GO ON TO NEXT PAGE

EXAM EIGHT, PASSAGE THREE

15. The passage states that

1. there has never been a woman chosen as a running mate.
2. resistance to the nomination of a candidate because off race, religion, or sex is weakening.
3. in 1988 an African-American won the Democratic nomination.
4. the religious barrier was challenged for the first time in 1960 with the nomination of John F. Kennedy.

16. According to the passage, one important result of Kennedy's victory was that

1. he won by a landslide.
2. Catholicism was never again viewed as a negative factor of electability.
3. religion as a barrier to electability was instituted.
4. he won even though he was not of English stock.

17. seek, as used in the last paragraph, most nearly means

1. look for.
2. search.
3. try for.
4. refuse.

18. The writer uses which pattern of organization in the last paragraph?

1. examples
2. objective data
3. description
4. comparison

GO ON TO NEXT PAGE

EXAM EIGHT, PASSAGE THREE

Human teeth have a hard resistant enamel on their exterior as well as the durable dentine underneath. This enamel is the hardest substance in the body. So tough is this enamel that if a human tooth is struck against metal, sparks are produced. The dentine is also very hard. Billiard balls and piano keys made from elephant tusks are virtually pure dentine.

Teeth have the functions of <u>shearing</u> the more solid food into smaller pieces and of grinding them into still smaller bits. It is the action of teeth in higher organisms that is responsible for most of the physical digestion that occurs. The shearing is done by the thin sharp-edged front teeth, the *incisors* and *canines*; and the crushing and grinding are accomplished by the back teeth, the premolars and molars. The word *molar* is derived from the Latin word for "millstone."

Humans have only two sets of teeth in their lifetime. The first 20 teeth are called baby teeth because they usually grow in by the time the toddler is two years old. They are also called <u>deciduous</u> teeth, because they are gradually shed, beginning about the age of six. The front teeth grow back first. By the age of about twelve, the second, or *permanent* molars are usually in place, and last of all come the third molars, the so-called wisdom teeth, completing the second set of teeth, or a permanent set of 32.

-Roohk & Karpoff, pp. 203-205

EXAM EIGHT, PASSAGE FOUR

19. The first paragraph is designed to

1. introduce the concept of dentine.
2. contrast enamel with dentine in regard to toughness.
3. define and elaborate on enamel.
4. illustrate how tough both enamel and dentine are.

20. As utilized in the passage, <u>shearing</u> is best defined as

1. the action of lopping off.
2. the action of tearing.
3. the action of crushing.
4. the action of pruning.

21. According to the passage, how many sets of permanent teeth do humans have?

1. three
2. one
3. four
4. two

22. We can deduce from the context in which <u>deciduous</u> is used in the passage that, if a tree is <u>deciduous,</u> it would most likely

1. have bark that rots.
2. change color.
3. be made of dentine.
4. shed its leaves.

GO ON TO NEXT PAGE

23. The first 20 teeth of humans are called

1. deciduous teeth.
2. permanent teeth.
3. molars.
4. wisdom teeth.

GO ON TO NEXT PAGE

EXAM EIGHT, PASSAGE FOUR

Before a European set foot in the New World, Indians had lived in the Americas long enough to make well-worn paths. By the time Europeans arrived, there were almost 200 major tribes in North America alone, each with its own set of customs and manners.

Most of the tribes occupying the Atlantic coast were relatively small. Further inland, close to Lakes Ontario and Erie, was the famous Iroquois Confederacy: the Five Nations whose system of tribal cooperation impressed Benjamin Franklin so much that he used it in planning for the thirteen colonies. Not only was each tribe obliged to come to the aid of the others in time of war, but land controlled by any member tribe was open to all.

To the south was an Indian confederation led by the Creeks. Like the Iroquois, member tribes cooperated in war and commerce. Across the Mississippi, life was changed when the Spanish introduced horses. The tribes, being mobile cultures, set up and moved tepee villages with the flow of the seasons and the buffalo. Nearly every necessity used by these Plains Indians was taken from this great shaggy animal that roamed the area in huge herds.

The Pueblo tribes of the Southwest lived in peaceful, town-oriented, apartment-like dwellings of adobe situated on cliffs. Developing irrigation methods, the Pueblos lived by farming in the arid Southwest.

EXAM EIGHT, PASSAGE FIVE

To the northwest, the Californian Indians, pursued a more primitive way of life and were still living in a Stone Age culture as late as the California Gold Rush. Finally, there were the Eskimo people in Alaska, whose placid, family-centered culture was sustained mainly by fish and whale blubber.

These first Americans are considered by historians as the "first ecologists." Most Indian groups claimed the earth was their mother, and that their home-land was a uniquely blessed place that they held in trust for future generations.
-Solberg, pp. 86-87

24. Benjamin Franklin's attitude toward native Americans of the Five Nations was

1. apathetic.
2. cynical.
3. respectful.
4. distrustful.

25. Member tribes of the Indian confederations cooperated in all of the following except

1. aiding each other in times of war.
2. sharing workloads for irrigating arid lands.
3. agreeing to reciprocal relationships in trade.
4. opening their lands to all tribes.

GO ON TO NEXT PAGE

26. The main idea of the passage is that

1. Europeans were the first to set foot on North American soil.
2. most Indians were farmers, not warriors.
3. there were many Indian tribes in North America, each with its own unique customs.
4. many of the Indian tribes pursued a primitive way of life.

27. The word arid most likely means

1. moist.
2. parched.
3. windy.
4. humid.

28. It is suggested that the overriding reason that Indians moved their tepee villages was to

1. get away from harsh winters.
2. escape their enemy.
3. move further inland.
4. facilitate trade.

29. According to the passage, the most life changing event for native Americans living near the Mississippi was the

1. existence of the buffalo.
2. development of irrigation methods.
3. introduction of the horse.
4. discovery of a new method of fishing.

GO ON TO NEXT PAGE

EXAM EIGHT, PASSAGE FIVE

Okinawa turned out to be the blood-iest fight of the Pacific War. Total American casualties were nearly 50,000, with 7,613 Americans killed. Included in that number was General Buckner, the highest ranking officer killed in the Pacific. Also included was Ernie Pyle, perhaps the best of World War II war correspondents who was fatally wounded by a Japanese sniper on the island of Le Shima.

Additionally, Japanese kamikaze attacks killed over 3,000 navy personnel. Ten major kamikaze attacks were sent against Okinawa, sinking 29 Allied ships while damaging nearly 100 others.

Japanese losses on Okinawa were approximately 110,000 killed and nearly 11,000 taken prisoner. Included in this number was General Ushyima who committed *hara kiri* on June 22, the same day the Allied forces declared Okinawa secure—83 days after it had been invaded. Also, 1,465 kamikaze fliers died in <u>forays</u> on and around Okinawa.

The terrible cost of the Okinawan campaign provoked criticism from the American press at the time and subsequently from American military analysts. General MacArthur was also critical of the operation, failing to understand why American commanders insisted on driving the Japanese off the island, particularly once we had gained our major objectives of the airfields and the harbor facilities.

His strategy would have been to isolate the Japanese on the southern part of the island and then let them <u>wither on the vine</u>, cut off from outside supplies.

–Layton, p. 146

30. War correspondent Ernie Pyle died on the island of Le Shima

1. in hand-to-hand combat.
2. in friendly fire.
3. because of illness.
4. from sniper fire.

31. In the first three paragraphs, the author gets his point across through

1. narrating the story of WWII.
2. describing the events that led up to the Okinawan campaign.
3. presenting statistics and facts of the Okinawan campaign.
4. defining Japanese terms such as *hara kiri* and *kamikaze*.

32. The word <u>forays</u> most nearly means

1. expeditions.
2. firefights.
3. ground assaults.
4. raids.

33. How many kamikaze attacks were carried out in Okinawa?

1. 3,000
2. 100
3. 29
4. 10

EXAM EIGHT, PASSAGE SIX

34. Which of the following is an opinion and not a fact?

1. Okinawa turned out to be the bloodiest fight of the Pacific War. in the Okinawan campaign.
2. General McArthur would have had better success with the Okinawan campaign than General Buckner.
3. Japanese kamikaze attacks killed over 3,000 navy personnel.
4. General Ushyima committed hara kiri on the same day the Allied forces declared Okinawa secure.

35. The phrase <u>wither on the vine</u> most nearly means

1. die slowly.
2. strengthen and re-group.
3. retreat.
4. shrink.

36. General McArthur's attitude toward the Okinawan campaign was one of

1. outrage.
2. disbelief.
3. certainty.
4. derision.

GO ON TO NEXT PAGE

EXAM EIGHT, PASSAGE SIX

Generations of Americans, when confronted with tragic events such as the sneak attack on Pearl Harbor (1941), the death of President Franklin Roosevelt (1945), and the assassination of John Kennedy (1963), asked their friends where they were at the time. The death of Elvis Presley on August 17, 1977 was so significant to millions of Americans that they raised the same question. Elvis Presley is one of the most important cultural icons in the United States in the post-World War II era. While others may have had more musical talents, Elvis seized the moment of his opportunity in 1956.

Loved by females, imitated by males, and distrusted by parents, Elvis exploded on the American music scene in 1956. Television, which reached forty million homes at the time, carried the image of Elvis Presley into the living rooms of his fans. Second generation rocker and one-time Elvis imitator, Bruce Springsteen, recently proclaimed "when I was nine, I couldn't imagine anyone not wanting to be Elvis Presley." John Lennon stated, "before Elvis there was nothing." This adulation aided the marketing of Presley. Elvis' manager, Colonel Parker, through television and the promotional skills of the William Morris Agency in New York, transformed this raw Southern boy into a veritable demigod.

As Elvis' career burned white hot in 1956, Colonel Parker seized the opportunity to tap into the Presley mania phenomenon in many creative ways. Parker negotiated a contract to market Elvis wearing apparel, jewelry, guitars,

lunch boxes, greeting cards, sodas, hound dogs and charms. Elvis received his proper cut, unlike the experience of the Beatles a few years later. Because of this unparalleled success, Elvis earned an incredible $125,000 a month from the music business by the summer. Only eighteen months earlier he had toured with the Louisiana Hayride for $18 a week!

–Sorrell & Francese

37. According to the passage, Elvis's success was

1. a long time in the works.
2. unparalled.
3. not warranted.
4. tragic like other events in history.

38. The phrase veritable demigod as used in the selection most nearly means

1. believable imitator.
2. holy father.
3. historical persona.
4. a true idol.

39. Before Elvis became a star he

1. was in the Army.
2. collaborated with Bruce Springsteen.
3. opened for the Beatles.
4. toured in Louisiana.

GO ON TO NEXT PAGE

EXAM EIGHT, PASSAGE SEVEN

40. The passage suggests that Bruce Springstein

1. held contempt for Elvis.
2. thought Elvis was foolish for being tricked by his manager, Colonel Parker.
3. admired and respected Elvis.
4. did not trust Elvis.

41. In the last paragraph, <u>cut</u> means

1. portion.
2. slash.
3. score.
4. reduction.

42. Elvis Presley became popular in the

1. early 1940s.
2. mid 1940s.
3. mid 1950s.
4. early 1960s.

43. The passage implies that Colonel Parker's attitude toward Elvis was most likely

1. complaining.
2. cynical.
3. apathetic.
4. optimistic.

GO ON TO NEXT PAGE

EXAM EIGHT, PASSAGE SEVEN

The sky changes from a dark gray to an ominous black. For a few moments the sun is still visible as a pale disk, but then it disappears as if frightened by the howling winds driving thick clouds of particles through the air. Visibility is reduced to near zero, and human and beast take shelter wherever possible. These are the common storm characteristics one could encounter in Egypt, in the Sudan, and in the United States, heralding a dust storm. The monster storms of the American southwestern regions, immortalized by the *Dust Bowl* of the 1930s, illustrate the destructive nature of such storms.

In 1930, there was no better place to be a farmer than in the Southern Plains. While the rest of the nation was struggling with the initial effects of the Great Depression, in wheat country, American farmers were reaping a record-breaking crop. But the farming practices that made the plains so productive were beginning to take a toll on the land. As the drought that started in the early 1930s persisted, the farmers kept plowing and planting with dismal results. The rain simply stopped.

It had taken a thousand years for Nature to build an inch of topsoil on the Southern Plains, but it took only minutes for one good windstorm to sweep it all away. Great black clouds of dust began to blot out the sun. In some places, the dust drifted like snow, darkening the sky for days. The dust was so thick that people scooped up bucketsful while cleaning house. Dust blocked exterior doors; to get outside, people had to climb out their windows and shovel the dust away. Farmers faced the most difficult eights years of their lives, and the 1930s *Dust Bowl* was deemed the worst drought in U.S. history.

In the fall of 1939, after nearly a decade of dirt and dust, the skies finally opened, and just as quickly as it had begun, the *Dust Bowl* was over.

-based on Ebert and ushistory.com

44. According to the passage, when a dust storm is full blown

1. the sun is still visible.
2. visibility is near zero.
3. humans are safe, but small animals must find shelter.
4. the sky first turns to red, then to gray.

45. The notorious dust storms of the 1930s occurred in the

1. American southwestern regions.
2. flatlands of Sudan.
3. deserts of Egypt.
4. northern plains of the U.S.

46. We can infer from the passage that during the decade of the dust storms

1. farmers moved East to urban areas.
2. all farmers remained—continuing the old habits of plowing and planting.
3. many farming families starved.
4. the farmers still produced plenty of wheat for distribution in the U.S.

EXAM EIGHT, PASSAGE EIGHT

47. It can be inferred from the passage that

1. dust storms are caused by Mother Nature, not mankind.
2. it was, in part, farming techniques of the times that caused the *Dust Bowl*.
3. the rest of the nation was experiencing violent dust storms as well.
4. farmers of the Southern Plains had saved enough money in the good years to tide themselves over during the drought.

48. The word <u>heralding</u> in the first paragraph most nearly means

1. signalling.
2. publishing.
3. bringing good tidings.
4. opening.

49. Of the following, which would not be a precursor to a dust storm?

1. ominous skies
2. virtually no visibility
3. a star-studded night sky
4. animals scurrying for shelter

GO ON TO NEXT PAGE

EXAM EIGHT, PASSAGE EIGHT

John of Gaunt, Duke of Lancaster, turned to Katherine and examined her. He saw that she was very young and frightened and that two enormous eyes stared up at him with passionate gratitude. He leaned down and gave her his hand. She clung to it.

The Duke was touched, alike by her instinctive bid for his protection and by her dignified recovery from sobs and disshevelment. Her beauty he had not yet clearly seen, but he felt the girl's magnetism and turned with increased anger to Hugh. "Who is this lady you've insulted?"

"She's naught but sister to one of the Queen's waiting women. I've not insulted her. She's cast a spell on me."

"I say you've most grievously insulted this poor child and—"

"Nay, my lord," interrupted Hugh. He raised his little greenish eyes and gazed at Katherine with a dumb misery. "I wish to marry her. She has neither lands nor dowry, but I would marry her."

Katherine gasped and shrank closer to the Duke, but he was staring at his knight with astonishment.

That changed matters. If this girl were indeed landless, this offer was amazing. Hugh Swynford was of good blood and possessed of considerable property. To the Duke, as to all his family, marriage was a peacetime weapon for the acquisition of new lands and the extension of power. Love of one's mate was entirely fortuitous. As lovable as his mate was, the Duke might not have felt such keen devotion for her had she not brought him vast riches.   -Seton, pp. 39-40

50. The image of Katherine in the first paragraph indicates that she is

1. a mature woman.
2. an innocent girl.
3. out of control.
4. demanding.

51. Hugh Swynford was

1. a knight in the Duke's retinue.
2. John of Gaunt's brother.
3. Katherine's fiancé.
4. brother to the Queen.

52. We can infer from the passage that John of Gaunt is

1. a cruel lord.
2. an enemy of the king.
3. a nobleman.
4. still a bachelor.

53. It is suggested in the passage that the upper classes

1. did not marry for money.
2. married in order to have children.
3. had money but lacked property.
4. rarely married for love.

GO ON TO NEXT PAGE

EXAM EIGHT, PASSAGE NINE

54. The word <u>dishevelment</u> as used in
the second paragraph most nearly means

1. filth.
2. disturbed appearance.
3. dignified state.
4. beauty.

EXAM EIGHT, PASSAGE NINE

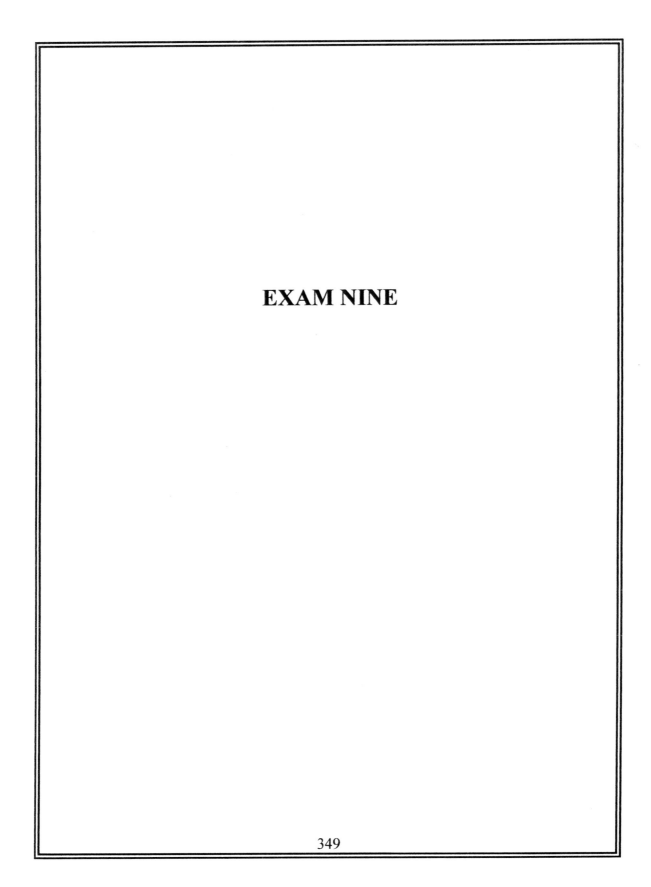

EXAM NINE

In the struggling capital of Washington, Senators were paid the munificent sum of $6 per day. And although their privileges included the use of great silver snuffboxes on the Senate floor, the aristocratic manners which had characterized the first Senates of New York and Philadelphia were strangely out of place. When the settlement of Washington became the capital city in 1800, its rugged surroundings contrasted sharply with those enjoyed at the temporary capitals in New York and Philadelphia.

Formality in Senate procedures was somewhat retained, however—although Vice President Aaron Burr, himself, was an object of some disrepute after killing Hamilton in a duel. The Vice President frequently found it necessary to call Senators to order for "eating apples and cakes in their seats" and walking between those engaged in discussion. And John Quincy Adams noted in his diary that some of his colleagues' speeches "were so wild and so bluntly expressed as to be explained only by recognizing that the member was inflamed by drink."

But certainly the Senate retained greater dignity than the House, where Members might sit with hat on head and feet on desk, watching John Randolph of Roanoke stride in wearing silver spurs, carrying a heavy riding whip, followed by a foxhound which slept beneath his desk, and calling to the doorkeeper for more liquor as he launched vicious attacks upon his opponents. Nevertheless, the House, still small enough to be a truly deliberative body, overshadowed the Senate in terms of political power during the first three decades of our government.   -Kennedy, pp. 24-25

1. The main purpose of the third paragraph is to

1. ridicule the two legislative bodies of the early U.S. government.
2. expose the fact that animals were allowed onto the House floor.
3. contrast the Senate and the House.
4. illustrate that the Senate had more political power than the House.

2. As used in this passage, the best definition for the word inflamed is

1. on fire.
2. agitated.
3. calmed.
4. confused.

3. The reader can infer that Vice President Burr

1. served prison time for killing Hamilton.
2. was not punished for killing Hamilton.
3. felt guilty about killing Hamilton.
4. was tolerated even though he killed Hamilton.

GO ON TO NEXT PAGE

EXAM NINE, PASSAGE ONE

4. In the second paragraph, the author gets his point across by

1. condemning the legislation enacted by the Senate.
2. summarizing biographical information on John Quincy Adams.
3. comparing the Senate to the House.
4. describing the chaos of the Senate sessions.

5. The passage implies that John Randolph

1. was the most powerful member of the House.
2. was not accepted by fellow legislators.
3. was inconsiderate and undignified.
4. engaged in criminal activity.

6. Which of the following was not a characteristic of the early Senate of Washington?

1. eating and drinking during sessions
2. aristocratic manners
3. a salary of $6 per day
4. using snuff which came in great silver snuff boxes

GO ON TO NEXT PAGE

EXAM NINE, PASSAGE ONE

There are numerous theories of aging, and if any theory of aging is to ultimately be proved <u>valid</u>, it will have to account for such features of aging as the increased stiffness in joints, the decreased lung capacity, as well as the different rate of aging in tissues.

One theory of aging that is supported by evidence is that the aging process is programmed into the genes of an individual from the beginning. Some evidence to support this theory is provided by the observed fact that persons who die at an early age (of natural causes) tend to have been born of parents who also died young.

Conversely, people who live into their 80s and 90s usually were born to parents who also lived well into old age. Thus, there are indications that an individual's maximum possible life span is, in part, inherited.

The obvious symptoms of aging are easily recognized—joints stiffen and muscular strength decreases. The whole body seems to become less limber and less flexible, and the skin loses some of its <u>resilience</u> and elasticity. The metabolic rate decreases, which may contribute to a general decline in energy. Lung capacity diminishes, and the pumping of blood by the heart decreases. Wounds tend to heal more slowly in the elderly, who, in general, are more prone to infections of all kinds. The aging process continues until the function of a vital tissue has become so impaired that it can no longer sustain life.

EXAM NINE, PASSAGE TWO

At one time it was thought that human cells would survive indefinitely if they were cultured like bacteria in chambers outside the body. Research has now shown, however, that after about 50 divisions, normal human cells can no longer function properly and therefore die.

Certain more advanced organisms—both plant and animal—are being studied because of their unusually long life spans. The oldest known living organisms are plants. Some bristlecone pines, for example, are over 6,000 years old.

-Roohk & Karpoff, pp.588-590

7. As used in the passage, <u>valid</u> most nearly means

1. flexible.
2. legitimate.
3. unacceptable.
4. incorrect.

8. The writer of this selection is most likely

1. a gerontologist interested in health.
2. an anatomy professor.
3. a journalist writing a piece on symptoms of aging.
4. an agist pointing out the faults of the elderly.

GO ON TO NEXT PAGE

9. Which of the following statements about the passage is not true?

1. research indicates that people who die at an early age tend to have been born of parents who died young.
2. along with aging comes decreased lung capacity.
3. symptoms of aging are easily recognized.
4. human cells can survive indefinitely.

10. Which statement below would be considered an opinion and not a fact?

1. Joints stiffen with age.
2. There are numerous theories of aging.
3. Some believe that an individual's maximum possible life span might be inherited.
4. Some bristlecone pines are over 6,000 years old.

11. According to the passage, symptoms of aging do not usually include a

1. decrease in muscular strength.
2. decrease in appetite.
3. decrease in skin elasticity.
4. decrease in the pumping of blood by the heart.

12. Which of the following statements about aging is false?

1. In general, people who live into their 90's were born to parents who exhibited longevity.
2. Theories of aging address the issue of different rates of aging in tissues.
3. With aging there comes an increase in metabolic rate.
4. The aging process continues until the function of a vital tissue can no longer sustain life.

13. resilience, as used in the passage most nearly means

1. glow.
2. rigidity.
3. flexibility.
4. toughness.

GO ON TO NEXT PAGE

EXAM NINE, PASSAGE TWO

And there it was, a thousand feet below him in the valley—Xoconosle. Sitting atop his horse, Peter stared at the dozen or so mud huts and asked himself, "Is this where The Woman really lives? Why here? Why not in some temple in Mexico City?" But he also felt an immediate rush of excitement, a thrill of discovery. He had found the place! If the rest of the world didn't know what they were missing, that was their problem, not his.

The guide took Peter to one of the mud huts at the outskirts of the village. Here lived a family that agreed to give Peter food and shelter. These arrangements made, Peter went to look for The Woman. He had imagined she would be living in a cave in the hills; but, instead, she dwelt in a hut even smaller than the one he was going to be staying in. There was no door for him to knock on, so he simply called to her, in Spanish, hoping she would come out and speak to him. A group of Tepehuan children stood a few yards away, their faces impassive, expressionless, as they watched this strangely-dressed alien standing in front of the grass-roofed dwelling.

Peter called again.

And then, from the darkness of the windowless hut, she suddenly appeared. Peter stared at The Woman for what seemed long minutes. If he had met her on the street in San Francisco, would he have looked a second time at her face? Yes, he thought, surely he would have. Like a mask carved from a branch of mahogany, that face was—rust-red, gnarled, creased, eyes like black knotholes, a bird's nest of feathery white hair perched wildly atop it all. And when she spoke, a voice like a cawing of a crow.

"You are the student," she said. "You are expected. Welcome."

-McConnell, p. 43

14. According to the passage, Peter is puzzled by all of the following except which one?

1. the Woman not residing in a cave
2. the family with whom he would live
3. the Woman's small hut
4. being in Xoconosle and not Mexico City

15. In the context of paragraph two, the word alien means

1. person from another place.
2. a Tepehuan.
3. person without legal permission for residency.
4. person from another planet.

16. The paragraph that begins with "And then, from the darkness . . ." primarily uses which pattern of organization?

1. Definition
2. Description
3. Comparison
4. Persuasion

EXAM NINE, PASSAGE THREE

17. The story best reflects the viewpoint of

1. The Woman.
2. the guide.
3. the Mexican children.
4. Peter.

18. It is implied that Peter was thrilled because

1. the elevation made him light-headed.
2. he had found the obscure, wise Woman.
3. only The Woman knew the true location of Xoconosle.
4. he had finally gotten away from San Francisco.

19. Peter called to The Woman in Spanish because

1. the guides had suggested that he address her in that manner.
2. he did not know how to speak English.
3. he wanted to impress the Mexicans.
4. he thought she might understand Spanish.

GO ON TO NEXT PAGE

EXAM NINE, PASSAGE THREE

According to Frisancho, the use of IQ as the only measure of an individual's innate intelligence is not valid. He believes there are many kinds of intelligence. There are some people with outstanding memories, some with mathematical skills, some with musical talents, some good at seeing analogies, some good at synthesizing information, and some with manual and mechanical expertise. However, these different kinds of intelligence are not <u>subsumed</u> with an IQ score.

In addition, it is evident that cultural environment is an important contributor to any measure of IQ. This inference can be illustrated by several examples. First, suppose we consider two groups of 8-year-old children: (a) one from a middle-class U.S. school and (b) one from a poor rural area from Guatemala. These children are asked the following questions: "Suppose you have 5 eggs and you drop 2, how many eggs do you have?" The U.S. children will likely answer that they have 3 eggs left, but the rural children may answer that they have 5 eggs. Based on that result, one may conclude that the Guatemalan rural children do not know how to add or subtract. However, if one takes into account the fact that the rural children have been raised in an environment associated with food shortage, just because an egg has been dropped does not mean it cannot be eaten. Hence, for the Guatemalan rural

children there are still 5 eggs. Therefore, the answer depends on the children's past <u>experience</u>.

-Frisancho, pp. 226-227

20. In the paragraph, the phrase, <u>subsumed</u> most nearly means

1. included.
2. retrieved.
3. excluded.
4. approved.

21. The reader would expect the next paragraph of the selection to be one that

1. describes a new type of intelligence test.
2. analyzes IQ scores of school children.
3. contrasts poor U.S. school children to upper class school children of Guatemala.
4. presents more examples of cultural factors influencing IQ.

22. The reader can infer that Frisancho is a(n)

1. professor who researches statistics.
2. anthropologist living in Guatemala.
3. educator interested in cultural issues.
4. mathematician.

GO ON TO NEXT PAGE

EXAM NINE, PASSAGE FOUR

23. Which of the following statements best states one of the major ideas of the passage?

1. Frisancho believes there is only one type of intelligence.
2. Cultural environment is an important contributor to any measure of IQ.
3. One result of the study is that for the Guatemalan rural children, there are still 5 eggs.
4. Guatemalan rural children do not know how to add or subtract.

24. In the current context, <u>experience</u> most nearly means

1. incident.
2. event.
3. familiarity.
4. feeling.

GO ON TO NEXT PAGE

EXAM NINE, PASSAGE FOUR

In the United States between 1959 and 1984, more than 2,500 persons were killed by lightning. About 7,000 individuals were injured during the same time period.

In many thunderstorms, individual lightning bolts are <u>obscured</u> by falling rain, mist, or by other clouds. For this reason, the number of lightning strokes is generally underestimated by the observer. However, sensitive electronic recorders, often used by power companies, and even a plain radio, reveal the almost unceasing barrage of electrical discharges generated by a thunderstorm.

It is interesting to note that more than 60 percent of all lightning takes place inside a cloud. This *intracloud discharge* is veiled by the cloud mass and may lead to what is sometimes called sheet lightning. If such lightning occurs at very high elevations, and at some distance away, the sound is refracted aloft and may not be heard from the ground. This type of lightning can be impressive, but it is harmless as far as the earth's surface is concerned.

Another form of lightning is called *intercloud lightning* because it strikes from cloud to cloud, usually at higher altitudes. These spectacular zigzag bolts can be seen quite readily as they breach considerable distances between clouds. Although of no danger to observers on the ground, these discharges may become hazardous to aircraft.

The best-known lightning, and the most feared one, is the *cloud-to-ground* type, which hurtles from the dark skies toward the earth. It may be reassuring to know that by the time we hear the crashing thunder the immediate danger has already passed. The intense heat generated by such lightning bolts, and by its return stroke, can split trees and may turn sandy surfaces into a glassy crust.   –Ebert, pp. 126-129

[According to the NOAA, 90 people are killed every year in the U.S. by lightning. New Mexico and Wyoming had the highest lightning-caused death rates.]

25. The main purpose of the passage is to

1. contrast intracloud and intercloud discharges.
2. compare cloud-to-ground lightning with intracloud lightning.
3. present examples of death-related lightning incidences.
4. classify types of lightning.

26. The phrase *intracloud discharge* most nearly means

1. within a cloud.
2. outside a cloud.
3. below cloud cover.
4. surrounding a cloud mass.

EXAM NINE, PASSAGE FIVE

27. According to the article, it is difficult to determine the number of individual lightning strikes due to all of the following except

1. other cloud masses.
2. rain.
3. radio interference.
4. mist.

28. It is stated by the author that the zigzag lightning is

1. impressive but harmless.
2. most dangerous to airplanes.
3. the same as cloud to ground lightning.
4. not found at higher altitudes.

29. The word <u>obscured</u> as used in the passage most likely means

1. unmasked.
2. disclosed.
3. clarified.
4. shrouded.

30. The reader can infer from the passage that 90 humans per year are killed by which type of lightning?

1. cloud-to-ground
2. sheet lightning
3. intercloud lightning
4. zigzag lightning

GO ON TO NEXT PAGE

EXAM NINE, PASSAGE FIVE

Police officers are at the frontline of the criminal justice system. Their job responsibilities include obtaining evidence and detaining those suspected of having committed a crime or in the process of committing a crime. The Constitution and its Amendments place restraints on how the police can discharge their duties.

The Bill of Rights is the primary source of constitutional restraints of the police. An example is the Fourth Amendment that states the police can not invade the privacy of citizens without probable cause. This allows police surveillance in public areas, but if there is a reasonable expectation of privacy, they must apply for and get a search warrant. Getting a judge to authorize a wiretap of someone's phone line is one example.

The Fourth Amendment also states that a search warrant must contain a description of the property to be searched and the persons or things to be seized. The plain view doctrine offers an exception to the provisions of a search warrant. It allows the police to seize incriminating evidence not stipulated in a search warrant if it is in plain view of officers conducting an authorized search.

The Miranda Rule is another restraint on police activities. It states that if a suspect has been taken into custody s/he must be advised of their constitutional rights. These rights include the right to remain silent, the right to an attorney, and the warning that anything said can and will be used against them.

Entrapment occurs when officers induce someone into an illegal act that they otherwise would not have committed (for the purpose of initiating prosecution against that person).

Last, there are restrictions on the use of excessive force by the police, but defining what constitutes excessive force can be hard. What about deadly force? The police are armed and can use deadly force under certain circumstances—these include the threat of deadly violence toward themselves or others.   -MacDonald, p.175-176

31. According to the passage, which of the following does not place restraints on police?

1. excessive force doctrine
2. plain view doctrine
3. the Miranda Rule
4. entrapment

32. The overall pattern of organization utilized in paragraphs four and five is

1. definition.
2. comparison.
3. cause-effect.
4. process.

GO ON TO NEXT PAGE

EXAM NINE, PASSAGE SIX

33. Overall, this passage focuses on

1. police as the frontline force of the criminal justice system.
2. how police officers can avoid the restraints placed on them.
3. The Fourth Amendment.
4. legal tenets that restrain police and exceptions to police restraints.

34. The word <u>stipulated</u> as used in the passage most nearly means

1. accomplished.
2. arranged.
3. specified.
4. omitted.

35. The author's attitude toward the subject matter is

1. admiring.
2. suspicious.
3. nostalgic.
4. objective.

GO ON TO NEXT PAGE

EXAM NINE, PASSAGE SIX

When we first saw the house, it was filled with fanciful iron beds with painted medallions of Mary, wormy chests of drawers with marble tops, mirrors, cradles, boxes and <u>lugubrious</u>, heart wrenching pictures of the Crucifixion. The owner removed everything— down to the switch plate covers and light bulbs—except a 1930s kitchen cupboard and an ugly red bed that we cannot figure out how to get down the back narrow stairs from the third floor. Finally we take the bed apart and throw it piece by piece from the window. Then we stuff the mattress through the window and my stomach flips as I watch it seem to fall in slow motion to the ground.

The Italians, out for afternoon strolls, pause in the road and look up at all the <u>mad</u> activity: the mattress flying, me screaming as a scorpion falls down my shirt when I sweep the stone walls, Ed wielding a grim-reaper scythe through the weeds. Sometimes they stop and call up, "How much did you pay for the house?"

I'm taken aback and charmed by the bluntness. "Probably too much," I answer. One person remembered that long ago an artist from Naples lived there; for most, it has stood empty as far back as they can remember.

Every day we haul and scrub. We are becoming as parched as the hills around us. We have bought cleaning supplies, a new stove and fridge. With sawhorses and two planks we set up a kitchen counter. Although we must bring hot water from the bathroom in a plastic laundry pan, we have a surprisingly manageable kitchen— I begin to get back to an elementary sense of the kitchen. Three wooden spoons, two for the salad, one for stirring. A sauté pan, bread knife, cutting knife, cheese grater, pasta pot, baking dish, and stove-top expresso pot. We brought over some old picnic silverware and bought a few glasses and plates. After long work, we eat everything in sight then tumble like field hands into bed.

–Mayes, pp. 25-26

EXAM NINE, PASSAGE SEVEN

36. As used in the first paragraph, the word <u>lugubrious</u> most nearly means

1. uplifting.
2. Christ-like.
3. somber.
4. religious.

37. The setting of the passage is

1. a future restaurant.
2. Naples.
3. Italy.
4. a nunnery.

38. <u>mad,</u> as used in the second paragraph, most nearly means

1. angry.
2. criminally insane.
3. chaotic.
4. prudent.

39. The writer believes the townspeople
to be

1. unclean and filthy.
2. lazy, always out for afternoon strolls.
3. backwards and stuck in the past.
4. frank but delightful.

40. The reader can infer that the narrator

1. is not Italian.
2. is poor.
3. is a building contractor.
4. hired a woman to help clean the
     place.

41. The passage suggests that the writer
is most heartened by the

1. garden area.
2. pulled-together kitchen.
3. accessories in the bedroom.
4. upstairs furnishings.

GO ON TO NEXT PAGE

EXAM NINE, PASSAGE SEVEN

Do the choices we make regarding fitness activities and dietary intake really impact our health and fitness? Are disease states of illnesses related to lifestyle choice? These are important questions. Below are statistical findings related to diseases or illnesses associated with poor or improper lifestyle choices.

More than half of today's health problems are lifestyle related and preventable. Nine out of the ten underlying causes of death in the United States are related to our lifestyle. What are the most prevalent health problems in our nation? Currently, the three leading causes of death are: cardiovascular disease, cancer, and stroke. All three are lifestyle related. Fortunately, 80% of the troubling aspects associated with these health problems can be prevented or delayed by living a positive, physically active, healthy life. This may seem surprising to some. Many perceive that death due to childhood disease, aging, sexually related diseases, and accidents are the primary culprits to mortality. This assumption is simply wrong.

Sadly, nearly 50% of American youth between the ages of 12-21 do not participate in regular vigorous activity. Twenty eight percent of Americans ages 18 or older have reported no physical activity in the last 30 days. And, 24% of adults lead completely sedentary lives. On average, physically active individuals outlive <u>sedentary</u> individuals. Also, physically active people lead more functionally independent, and fuller lives than inactive individuals.

- Adams, pp. 4-5

EXAM NINE, PASSAGE EIGHT

42. The writer of this selection solidifies his point through

1. examples.
2. facts and statistics.
3. persuasive argument.
4. questions.

43. According to the passage, what percent of all health problems are preventable?

1. 50
2. 90
3. 20
4. 80

44. With which of the following would the author most likely agree?

1. Aging is the number one cause of death among the elderly.
2. American youth need to exercise more often.
3. Most disease can be cured by living an active, healthy life.
4. Children are being well educated about health issues.

45. In the last paragraph, the word <u>sedentary</u> most nearly means

1. active.
2. ineffective.
3. immobile.
4. dynamic.

46. The article implies that individuals not getting enough physical activity

1. will die at an early age.
2. are susceptible to childhood disease.
3. have more accidents.
4. are at risk for cardiovascular disease, cancer, and stroke.

47. The main idea of the selection is that

1. disease states of illnesses are related to lifestyle choices.
2. nine out of the ten underlying causes of death in the United States are related to our exercise choices.
3. twenty-four percent of adults lead completely sedentary lives
4. death due to childhood disease, aging, sexually related diseases, and accidents are the primary culprits to mortality.

48. In the last thirty days, what percent of Americans 18 and over reported no physical activity?

1. 50
2. 24
3. 28
4. 0

GO ON TO NEXT PAGE

EXAM NINE, PASSAGE EIGHT

The Russian assault on Berlin, Germany was launched in April with 2.5 million men, 6250 tanks, and 7,500 aircraft. For their part, the Germans had been tardy in preparing to defend their capital city. The hastily developed plan, which focused on a series of fallback positions, encompassed most of the main government buildings.

Located within this area was a main bunker, Hitler's underground headquarters, where he spent the final months of the war. Buried six feet underground, the bunker had a roof of concrete 16 feet thick and walls six and a half feet thick. It contained 19 rooms and besides Hitler, it housed a few guards, military aides, and physicians. After mid-April, the residents of the bunker also included Eva Braun, Hitler's mistress, and Nazi Propaganda Chief Joseph Goebbels and his family.

In specially designated areas of the city, people were to be deployed at fortified strong points. Overturned trucks, streetcars, and railway cars weighted with bomb debris were to link concrete walls, trenches, and canals. These fortified positions were to slow down the Russian attack. There were about 75,000 German troops defending Berlin, so Russian troops had to advance block-by-block, and clear buildings room-by-room. As a result, the city was demolished and Berlin's civilians, mostly women and children, were caught in the crossfire.

EXAM NINE, PASSAGE NINE

On the afternoon of April 30, Hitler and Eva retired to their rooms in the bunker. Some minutes later when Hitler's valet pushed open the door, he was confronted by the sight of Eva Braun curled up on the sofa, dead of cyanide, and Hitler slumped at the other end of the sofa. To make sure that he succeeded in the suicide attempt, Hitler had put a bullet into his brain just as he bit into a cyanide capsule.

That night the surviving inhabitants of the bunker escaped. The Propaganda Chief, Goebbels, did not run. In one last act of treachery, he administered poison to his six children, then poisoned his wife and himself.

On May 2, the Berlin defense force surrendered. - Layton, pp. 90-91

49. The passage indicates that

1. the Russians were victorious because they had more air support, ground support and manpower.
2. Hitler's strategy of fallback positions was successful.
3. all Berlin's civilians were taken prisoner.
4. the fortified positions in Berlin did not slow down the Russian troops.

50. According to the passage, of the following, who was not housed in the main bunker?

1. Eva Braun
2. the Propaganda Chief
3. Hitler's valet
4. Hitler's physician

51. The circumstances of Hitler's death revealed that he

1. was assassinated.
2. was killed due to Goebbel's treachery.
3. was killed during the assault on the bunker.
4. died by his own hand.

52. The reader may conclude that the Propaganda Chief poisoned his family and then committed suicide because

1. he was ashamed of his actions during the war.
2. he was afraid to face the consequences of what he had done.
3. his wife begged him to end all of their lives.
4. he was deemed a coward by the Nazi military.

53. The passage implies that the bunker was

1. set up as a storage facility.
2. was created as a command and control center.
3. constructed to protect Hitler.
4. not well built.

54. Which of the following statements is not true?

1. One of the physicians found the bodies of Hitler and Eva Braun
2. The city of Berlin was demolished by the Russian assault.
3. During the assault, Russian troops had to advance block-by-block.
4. the Germans procrastinated in preparing to defend their capital city.

EXAM NINE, PASSAGE NINE

DIAGNOSTIC EXAM:

POST-TEST

"Who are *they*?" I asked the girl from my Spanish class, whose name I'd forgotten.

As she looked up to see who I meant (though already knowing, probably, from my tone), he suddenly looked at my neighbor, then his dark eyes flickered to mine.

He looked away quickly. I dropped my eyes at once. In that brief flash of a glance, his face held nothing of interest.

My class mate giggled in embarrassment. "Well, Bella, that's Edward and Emmett Cullen, and Rosalie and Jasper Hale. The one who left the table was Alice Cullen; they all live together with Dr. Cullen and his wife." She said this under her breath.

I glanced sideways at the beautiful boy, who was looking at his tray now,

Strange, unpopular names, I thought. The kind of names grandparents had. But maybe that was in vogue here.

"They are . . . . very nice-looking." I struggled with the conspicuous under statement.

"Yes!" she agreed with another giggle. "And, they *live* together!" Her voice held shock and condemnation.

"Which ones are the Cullens?" I asked. "They don't look related . . ."

"Oh, they're not. Dr. Cullen is really young, in his twenties or early thirties. They're all adopted. The Hales are foster children."

"They look a little old for foster children."

"They are now, Jasper and Rosalie are both eighteen, but they've been with Mrs. Cullen since they were eight. She's their aunt."

"That's really kind of nice—for them to take care of all those kids like that."

POST TEST, PASSAGE ONE

"I guess so," my class mate admitted reluctantly.

Throughout this conversation, my eyes flickered again and again to the table where the strange family sat. They continued to look at the walls and not eat. -Meyer, pp. 19-21

1. The passage suggests that Bella

1. is in love with the boy.
2. is frightened of the family sitting across the room.
3. will have some interaction with the family in the near future.
4. does not like her class mate.

2. The overall pattern of organization employed by the author is

1. contrast and comparison.
2. scholarly writing.
3. graphic description.
4. narration and storyline.

3. The reader can infer from the selection that

1. the family had been hypnotized.
2. there is something unnerving about the family.
3. Mrs. Cullen does not love her niece and nephew.
4. the teens of the family were named after their grandparents.

4. The selection suggests that Bella's class mate was shocked that

1. the Hale and Cullen teens lived together.
2. Bella did not know the family.
3. Dr. Cullen was so young.
4. Bella had forgotten her name.

5. The passage implies that Bella's class mate

1. had a crush on Jasper Hale.
2. did not think so highly of Dr. Cullen and his wife.
3. was not interested in discussing the family sitting across the room.
4. thought the names of the teens sitting across the room were odd.

6. The phrase <u>in vogue</u> in the passage most nearly means

1. modelling.
2. unfashionable.
3. trendy.
4. lawful.

7. This conversation takes place

1. at a restaurant.
2. in Spanish class.
3. in the school cafeteria.
4. at the Cullen home.

GO ON TO NEXT PAGE

POST TEST, PASSAGE ONE

"Slow" was born in 1831 in what is now South Dakota, the only son of a Sioux warrior. He earned the name because as an infant he was careful and deliberate by nature. But when he had counted his first coup on a Crow enemy, his father gave him a new name given in a vision—"Sitting Bull."

Sitting Bull rose rapidly in tribal esteem. He gained a reputation as a prophet and a man who spoke with spirits. By twenty-five he had been elected to an elite military society called the Strong Hearts. A few years later he became a chief at the same time that whites first began to move into tribal lands. Asked to sign a treaty that would have ceded some Sioux lands but kept much of their range, Sitting Bull said, "I wish all to know that I do not propose to sell any part of my country."

A new confrontation occurred. The Black Hills, sacred to the Sioux and a part of lands guaranteed them by treaty, were discovered to contain gold in 1874. Within a year, hundreds of miners were trespassing on Sioux land. The government responded by ordering the Indians out of the land and launching an expedition against those Sioux, Cheyenne, and Arapaho who stayed. Sitting Bull forged an alliance, warning that "we must stand together or they will kill us separately." As the warriors gathered, Sitting Bull went through a sacrificial Sun Dance and saw a vision of soldiers falling into the camp. He prophesied a great victory. On June 26, 1876, braves from the main camp overran and slaughtered Lt.

Colonel Custer's 264 men, the greatest Army defeat in the Indian wars.

-Solberg, p. 109

8. The phrase coup on in the first paragraph most nearly means

1. war on.
2. overthrow of.
3. truce with.
4. failure from.

9. The government broke its treaty with the Sioux nation because

1. gold was discovered on Sioux lands.
2. Sitting Bull could not get along with leaders of the Crow nation.
3. the Strong Hearts attacked miners.
4. the Sioux banded together with the Cheyenne and Arapaho.

10. Most probably Sitting Bull's warrior-father felt

1. elated about his son.
2. ashamed of his son.
3. apathetic toward his son.
4. doting toward his son.

11. The main idea of the first paragraph is that Sitting Bull

1. was deliberate and careful as a child.
2. gained a reputation as a prophet.
3. was a great warrior but not an effective chief.
4. made a major transformation from childhood to manhood.

POST TEST, PASSAGE TWO

12. The word <u>ceded</u>, as used in the passage, most nearly means

1. negotiated.
2. acquired.
3. relinquished.
4. retained.

13. The author's attitude toward Sitting Bull is

1. disdainful.
2. somber.
3. deferential.
4. impartial.

14. Sitting Bull prophesized that

1. he would become Chief.
2. there would be a victory in the battle against Lt. Colonel Custer.
3. he would offer lands to the Government.
4. gold would be discovered on Sioux lands.

15. Whites first started moving onto tribal lands

1. a few years after Sitting Bull reached his twenty-fifth birthday.
2. in 1831.
3. around 1874.
4. after Lt. Colonel Custer had defeated the Sioux.

GO ON TO NEXT PAGE

POST TEST, PASSAGE TWO

Jondalar slowly became aware that he was awake, but caution made him lie still until he could sort out what was wrong, because something most certainly was. For one thing, his head was throbbing.

He opened his eyes a crack. There was only dim light, but enough to see the cold, hard-packed dirt he was lying on. Something felt dried and caked on the side of his face, but when he attempted to reach up and find out what it was, he discovered that his hands were tied together behind his back. His feet were tied together, too.

He looked around. He was inside a small round structure, a kind of wooden frame covered with skins, which he sensed was inside a larger enclosure: there were no sounds of wind, no drafts, no billowing of the hides. Though it was cool, it wasn't freezing. He suddenly realized that he was no longer wearing his fur parka.

He became alert when he heard the sound of voices drawing near. Two women were speaking an unfamiliar language.

"Hello out there. I'm awake," he called out, in his language. "Will someone come and untie me? I'm sure there has been a misunderstanding. I mean no harm."

The entrance flap was thrown back, and through the opening he saw a figure standing, feet apart and hands on hips. She issued a sharp command. Two women entered the enclosed spaced, lifted him up, dragged him out, and propped him up.

The woman looked at him for a moment or two and then she laughed. It was harsh and <u>dissonant</u>—a jarring curse of a sound. Jondalar felt a shudder of fear. His vision blurred, and he weaved unsteadily. Then suddenly, the woman turned on her heel and stalked out. The women who were holding him up dropped him and followed her.

-Auel, pp. 429-431

16. The reader can infer from the passage that

1. the women were there to help Jondalar recover.
2. the two women who lifted Jondalar were sisters of the other woman.
3. it had been warm weather for several months.
4. Jondalar had received a blow to his head.

17. The reader can conclude that Jondalar

1. had been rescued by the women.
2. respected the leader of the women.
3. was a prisoner of the women.
4. had threatened the women.

18. When he called for help Jondalar's tone was one of

1. humility.
2. arrogant.
3. resentment.
4. anger.

POST TEST, PASSAGE THREE

19. Jondalar knew that he was in an enclosed structure within a larger structure because

1. he could see through the flap.
2. there were no sounds of wind or drafts.
3. he had been in a similar structure before.
4. the women told him.

20. The word <u>dissonant</u> in the last paragraph most nearly means

1. harmonious.
2. apathetic.
3. discordant.
4. empathetic.

21. The two women who came into the enclosure most likely

1. were guards.
2. tried to help Jondalar.
3. did not agree with the woman.
4. were prisoners, too.

22. The purpose of the last paragraph is to

1. expose the jealousy of the female leader.
2. explain how Jondalar ended up with the women.
3. confound the reader.
4. leave the reader with a sense of suspense.

POST TEST, PASSAGE THREE

GO ON TO NEXT PAGE

Have you read or heard about cases where, under the influence of hypnosis, people were able to remember occurrences of which they had previously reported no recollection? Have you read or heard about cases where in the course of therapy, individuals recover memories of abuse of which they were previously unaware? These examples are all consistent with a view of memory that many individuals hold.

According to this view, memory is like a recording device, faithfully maintaining a detailed record of situations we have experienced.

Remembering an experience, then, is a case of pushing the right playback button and <u>accessing</u> the appropriate section of the tape, so that the experience can be re-experienced just the way it originally happened. That is, memory not only faithfully records what really happened, but it also faithfully plays the experience back once it is accessed. We often, without much conscious effort, remember events in great detail, and the truthfulness of these memories seems beyond doubt. We are highly confident that the event or experience we are recounting occurred and that the details we are providing are in fact correct.

Unfortunately, some research on memory indicates that it is not like a recording device. In fact, Lynn and Payne (1997) have suggested that a more appropriate way to conceive of memory is as "the theater of the past."

According to this view, memory is not a simple recording of what actually happened, but rather a dynamic, imperfect reconstruction of the past. In this view, memory may be influenced by our present needs, beliefs, and expectancies as well as by stored information.
–Kestner, p.181

23. According to the passage, which is not true about memory?

1. It takes great effort to remember events in great detail.
2. Memory faithfully maintains a detailed record of experiences.
3. Memory can play back experiences just the way they originally happened.
4. When we recount our experiences, we believe the details we are providing are correct.

24. Lynn and Payne suggested that

1. memory is not a simple recording of what actually happened.
2. memory can be compared to a recording device.
3. a person just needs to push the right playback button to access their experiences.
4. "the theater of the past" is not a valid view of the workings of memory.

GO ON TO NEXT PAGE

POST TEST, PASSAGE FOUR

25. The purpose of the first paragraph is to

1. interest the reader by asking thought-provoking questions.
2. introduce two different views of memory.
3. define the term "recollection."
4. explain how the process of hypnosis aids memory.

26. The word, <u>accessing</u> as used in the context of the third paragraph most nearly means

1. logging on.
2. opening.
3. experiencing.
4. expunging.

27. The phrase, "the theater of the past" most nearly means

1. descriptive, dramatic scenes.
2. an accurate historic account.
3. an imperfect reconstruction of the past.
4. a dynamic stage.

GO ON TO NEXT PAGE

POST TEST, PASSAGE FOUR

In Europe when the Second World War broke out, John F. Kennedy wrote an honors thesis, "Why England Slept," discussing the dangers of unpreparedness. It was published and sold well. After graduation Kennedy toyed with the idea of careers in journalism or business, but American entry into the war intervened.

After initially being turned down because of a back injury suffered in his Harvard football days, Kennedy was accepted into the Navy. While in command of PT 109 on patrol in the Pacific in August, 1943, a Japanese destroyer came out of the fog and sliced his boat in two. Kennedy led his surviving eleven men to an island three miles away, towing one of them by a life jacket strap held in his teeth. After their rescue Kennedy got a medal for bravery ("It was involuntary," he later said dryly, "they sank my boat"). He was in the hospital for months with a ruined back. It never properly healed.

While recovering, he learned that his brother Joe had been killed during a special Air Force mission in Europe. When asked later if he made a career of politics to appease his father and replace his older brother, Kennedy said no. "But I never would have run for office if he had lived."

-Solberg, p. 208

POST TEST, PASSAGE FIVE

28. According to the passage, Kennedy's published thesis

1. was a fiasco.
2. was a success.
3. was the impetus for a career in journalism.
4. was banned for criticizing England.

29. According to the selection, during the war, Kennedy fought against

1. the Nazis.
2. Germans.
3. the English.
4. the Japanese.

30. The reader can infer that Kennedy thought that

1. he was indeed a hero.
2. he would recover fully from his back injury.
3. his brother would be the politician in the family.
4. his father forced him into politics.

31. The selections implies that Kennedy

1. wanted to be in the Air Force, not the Navy.
2. must have suffered with back pain throughout his presidency.
3. was not a particularly strong swimmer.
4. tried to avoid enlisting in the military.

32. The word <u>appease</u>, as used in the context of the last paragraph, most nearly means

1. contradict.
2. provoke.
3. placate.
4. substitute for.

33. One purpose of the second paragraph is to

1. give background on Kennedy's days at Harvard.
2. contrast Kennedy to his older brother, Joe.
3. suggest that Kennedy's back injury kept him from a career in the Air Force.
4. show that Kennedy was a humble and unpretentious man.

GO ON TO NEXT PAGE

POST TEST, PASSAGE FIVE

Tsunamis are referred to as seismic sea waves. They are encountered in ocean regions that are affected by plate movements, especially where seismic and submarine volcanic disturbances are frequent. It is not surprising, therefore, that throughout history these waves have brought death and destruction to many islands and coastal communities. This is especially so within the realms of the Pacific and the Mediterranean Sea. It is also easy to understand that such waves, often following earthquakes, are called seismic sea waves even though not all of them are caused by such disturbances.

After the energy of a disturbance is transmitted to the water, wave energy begins to travel just as in any wave system. However, it is important to realize that tsunami waves, even though they move through deep oceans, behave like shallow-water waves. The reason for this is their great length, which may exceed 100 miles. Whether an ocean wave is classified as a deep-water or shallow-water wave depends on the relationship between its length and the depth of the water through which it passes.

The tsunami is frequently visualized as a single wave, but more correctly the tsunami is a wave system that spreads out from a point of energy release. A number of waves may originate from such a source with wave periods of 10 to 20 minutes, or longer. This means that a given coast may be exposed to a series of tsunamis arriving at considerable time intervals. The first wave does not have to be the highest one. It is possible that subsequent waves are much more dangerous.   -Ebert, pp. 57-61

34. What is the author's tone toward the subject matter of the passage?

1. objective
2. subjective
3. defiant
4. frantic

35. The purpose of the first paragraph is to

1. analyze how tsunami waves move.
2. describe the term "tsunami."
3. relate that all tsunamis are caused by earthquakes.
4. alert the reader that the first wave may not be the highest one.

36. The word submarine in the first paragraph most nearly means

1. underwater.
2. on land.
3. oceanic.
4. coastal.

GO ON TO NEXT PAGE

POST TEST, PASSAGE SIX

37. The author of this selection would probably agree that

1. because earthquakes are rare, tsunamis are rare.
2. people on the coast should evacuate inland to high ground if a tsunami is imminent.
3. the traditional way of thinking that tsumanis are related to plate movements has been proven invalid.
4. tsunamis occur more often in the realm of the Atlantic Ocean.

38. The main idea of the third paragraph is that

1. tsunamis can last 20 minutes or longer.
2. the last wave is the most dangerous.
3. there is a misconception that a tsunami is a single wave, but it is a wave system.
4. shallow-water waves are as destructive as deep-water waves.

GO ON TO NEXT PAGE

POST TEST, PASSAGE SIX

In sponsoring an "ideal" society of the colony of Georgia , the English trustees had three practical motives.

First, they wished to relieve the worthy poor in Great Britain. To them, this meant removing <u>destitute</u> but deserving persons from the streets of London and other British cities, where they were a burden to society, and sending them to Georgia, where they could earn a living.

An old legend, now demolished, held that Georgia was a <u>refuge</u> for debtors from the harshness of English prisons. However, in truth, probably not more than a dozen of those unfortunates ever went to the province directly from prison. Prospective settlers leaving England aboard the *Anne* were interviewed to differentiate between the worthy poor and those not worthy; never again was a group so <u>meticulously</u> selected.

The second motive was that the trustees wished the colony to play a role in Great Britain's trade policy. It was widely believed that Georgia could produce silk and wine, which Englishmen at the time were compelled to buy at great expense. First and foremost, Georgia was to be a colony of and for small farmers. All settlers were expected to work, there being an insufficient number of white servants and no black slaves. Great plantations were to have no place, resting as they did upon massive landholding and the institution of slavery.

The third motive was military.

The new colony would be a buffer for South Carolina, which was always threatened by the Spaniards in Florida.
-Davis, pp. 8-10

39. All of the following were reasons why the colony of Georgia was established except

1. to produce tobacco.
2. as a military buffer.
3. as a settlement of small farmers.
4. to give relief to the poor in Britain.

40. The word <u>refuge</u> as underlined in the second paragraph most nearly means

1. depository.
2. state.
3. reformatory.
4. sanctuary.

41. It can be inferred from the passage that during initial settlement of the colony

1. great plantations were necessary for economic survival.
2. slavery was not part of the plans for Georgia.
3. England could not help the colony because they had great expenses of their own.
4. most of the settlers died from starvation.

POST TEST, PASSAGE SEVEN

GO ON TO NEXT PAGE

42. We can infer from the passage that

1. Spaniards were in Florida as well as in South Carolina.
2. England regarded Spain as a potential enemy.
3. Spain had a stronger military than England.
4. the Spaniards discovered Georgia soil before the English.

43. The purpose of the passage is to

1. persuade the reader that Georgia's first settlers were not criminals.
2. narrate the story of the Georgia Colony and its people.
3. explain the reasons why England founded the colony of Georgia.
4. describe Georgia's relationship with Great Britain, particularly with England.

44. As underlined in the passage, meticulously most nearly means

1. carefully.
2. randomly.
3. grandly.
4. diversely.

The rise of the middle class, a consequence of the prosperity created by the long post-war economic boom, meant that the children of the 1950's and 1960's did not have to leave school to help support their families. By the late 1960's almost 60 million Americans were in school full-time, as many as were working full-time. When educational personnel were included, 30 per cent of the entire population of the nation participated in education. This made education the biggest business in the U.S., at least in terms of number of people involved. Everyone attended through age 15, three-fourths graduated from high school, and one-half of those went on to college.

From a psychological perspective, an important result of these trends was a breakdown in authoritarian discipline. The new and great abundance of American society spelled the end of a scarcity culture, which in turn meant that discipline was no longer economically necessary. Put simply, father no longer had to decide who got what, since there was enough to go around. The unfortunate consequence was a pervasive increase in permissiveness. Each child was more likely to have his or her own room. Coupled with an increased divorce rate, which meant a loss of family cohesion, these trends produced a child-centered society where the child was more likely to be individualistic.

The psychological characteristic of this youth culture was ambivalent tensions. The youth culture refused

POST TEST, PASSAGE EIGHT

adult socialization, maintaining a sense of separation and uniqueness. This in turn produced rebellion against parental authority and a consequent generation gap. -Sorrell & Francese, p. 34

45. It can be inferred from the passage that the permissive style of parenting of the 1960's

1. brought about more respect for parents from children.
2. resulted in more criminal behavior from teenagers.
3. created a more intelligent child population.
4. caused breakdowns in relationships between parents and children.

46. As used in the passage, abundance most nearly means

1. philosophy.
2. technology.
3. quantity.
4. wealth.

47. Which statement about the content of the passage is not true?

1. After the war, one half of high school graduates went on to college.
2. America of the 1960's was a child-centered society.
3. Pre-war, education was the biggest business in the United States.
4. During the 1960's, children did not have to leave school to work.

48. The author's style of writing is

1. informal.
2. unbiased.
3. riveting.
4. argumentative.

49. Which technique is not used in the passage?

1. statistics and facts
2. cause-effect
3. academic writing
4. definition

GO ON TO NEXT PAGE

POST TEST, PASSAGE EIGHT

The service ended, and little by little the congregation dispersed. It was a relief to have Conner appear and invite him to dinner.

Dannan was not the only guest invited for Sunday dinner. The four Muldoons still in town were there, as were the Weber family and Judson Best.

"So tell us, Dannan," Conner invited during the meal, "what do you hear from the doctor you replaced, Doc MacKay?"

"Uncle Jonas? I just had a letter from him. He is enjoying being back home. The house is roomy enough for him and my father, and they each have their own bit of space. I guess they're getting along together quite nicely."

"Will your folks visit you here, Dannan?" Allison wished to know.

"My mother's health doesn't allow her to travel, and my father hates to leave her, so probably not."

"Has your mother been ill long?" the preacher asked.

"About five years. She fell while hiking with my father and injured her back. Sitting for long periods is excruciating."

Most of the heads at the table nodded. It was certainly easy to see why his mother could not travel.

"She's an amazing woman," Dannan felt a need to add, looking at the compassion on Hillary Muldoon's face. "She doesn't spend a moment pitying herself, and because we write to each other almost weekly, I never feel out of touch."

Conversation drifted to Judson, who was working part-time for Will Barland who grew a broomcorn crop. That business was expanding to the point that Judson was helping Will ship brooms across New England.

Judson's charismatic way of describing his job had everyone entranced. Indeed, they were still enjoying his anecdotes when Troy rose from the group to answer the knock on the front door.

-Wick, pp. 48-50

50. The word excruciating, most nearly means

1. exhausting.
2. agonizing.
3. monotonous.
4. exasperating.

51. Doc MacKay was Dannan's

1. father.
2. mentor.
3. mother.
4. uncle.

52. The reader can infer that the paragraph that follows the passage focuses on

1. the visitor at the door.
2. more of Judson's anecdotes.
3. Dannan's mother's back injury.
4. Dannan's adjustment to his new job.

POST TEST, PASSAGE NINE

GO ON TO NEXT PAGE

53. Dannan's relationship with his
mother is

1. strained and awkward.
2. cordial and courteous.
3. volatile and capricious.
4. devoted and steadfast.

54. As used in the passage, <u>charismatic</u>
most nearly means

1. graphic.
2. sinister.
3. captivating.
4. modest.

POST TEST, PASSAGE NINE

Unit Three

APPENDICES

A. PROGRESS CHART FOR EXAMS

B. VOCABULARY JOURNAL

C. TEST ANXIETY SCALE

D. ANSWER KEYS FOR CHAPTERS

E. ANSWER KEYS FOR EXAMS

F. GRAPHICS ANSWER KEYS

G. SOURCES

H. SCANTRONS

PROGRESS CHART FOR EXAMS

Instructions. Place a dot (•) in cell that represents your grade on each test. Then draw a line from dot-to-dot to visualize your progress.

	Pre Test	Exam 1	Exam 2	Exam 3	Exam 4	Exam 5	Exam 6	Exam 7	Exam 8	Exam 9	Post-Test
100											
90											
80											
70											
60											
50											
40											
30											
20											
10											

*REMEMBER: 61 is a passing score

391

APPENDIX B: VOCABULARY JOURNAL

CHAPTER TWO

Exercise 3 supplement: Write a sentence with each of these new words:

1. proliferation _____

2. scrupulous _____

3. ubiquitous _____

4. meticulous _____

5. parasitic _____

6. advocate _____

7. pessimistic _____

8. skeptical _____

9. culminated _____

10. mentor _____

Exercise 7 supplement: Write a sentence with each of these new words:

1. perverse

2. distorted

3. flaunt

4. prosperity

5. susceptibility

6. intricate

7. digress

8. eluding

9. forlorn

10. activists

Exercise 9 supplement Matching:

_____1. noxious	a. rebellious
_____2. profound	b. desire
_____3. defiant	c. not easily seen
_____4. suppressed	d. ancestor
_____5. inconspicuous	e. harmful
_____6. affluent	f. good-natured
_____7. aspire	g. wealthy
_____8. predecessor	h. put into practice
_____9. placid	i. thoughtful
_____10. implemented	j. censored

Exercise 11 supplement: Complete the following:

1. <u>ambivalent</u> most nearly means

2. <u>contingent</u> most nearly means

3. <u>imminent </u>most nearly means

4. <u>insidious</u> most nearly means

5. <u>genetics</u> most nearly means

6. <u>rationalized</u> most nearly means

7. <u>allegation</u> most nearly means

8. <u>redundant</u> most nearly means

9. <u>innovative</u> most nearly means

10. <u>dubious</u> most nearly means

Exercise 13 supplement: Think up as many synonyms as you can for the new vocabulary words:

1. <u>penury</u>   synonym_____

2. <u>tumultuous</u>   synonym_____

3. <u>ingest</u>   synonym_____

4. <u>autonomous</u>   synonym_____

5. <u>narcissist</u>   synonym_____

6. <u>lucrative</u>   synonym_____

7. <u>aspiration</u>   synonym_____

8. <u>phenomena</u>   synonym_____

9. <u>scrutinize</u>   synonym_____

10. <u>sporadic</u>   synonym_____

Exercise 17 supplement: Reviewing Exercise 14 through Exercise 16 in the text, write down (in the space provided) vocabulary words that you did not know beforehand. Look in your dictionary and write a definition for each word.

_____
_____
_____
_____
_____
_____
_____
_____

_____

_____

_____

_____

_____

_____

_____

_____

_____

_____

_____

Word Structure

Exercise 21 supplement: Using Charts 1 and 2 and/or a dictionary, make up ten nonsense words and write them in the space provided. Then, choose a class mate to give meanings for your newly created words.

A. Work with your classmate

1.

Classmate's meaning:

2.

Classmate's meaning:

3.

Classmate's meaning:

4.

Classmate's meaning:

5.

Classmate's meaning:

6.

Classmate's meaning:

7.

Classmate's meaning:

8.

Classmate's meaning:

9.

Classmate's meaning:

10.

Classmate's meaning:

B. Matching

1. tenacious
2. genocide
3. disinherited
4. omnipotent
5. incredulous
6. intercontinental
7. benefit
8. cognizant
9. inspector
10. circumvent

a. profit
b. stubborn
c. mass killing
d. aware
e. skeptical
f. all powerful
g. disowned
h. avoid
i. examiner
j. global

VOCABULARY WORDS FROM CHAPTER THREE
Internet Activity Vocabulary:

1.
2.
3.
4.
5.
6.
7.

8.

9.

10.

VOCABULARY WORDS FROM CHAPTER FOUR

1.

2.

3.

4.

5.

6.

7.

8.

9.

10.

VOCABULARY WORDS FROM CHAPTER FIVE
Internet Activity Vocabulary:

1.

2.

3.

4.

5.

6.

7.

8.

9.

10.

VOCABULARY WORDS FROM CHAPTER SIX
Give a definition for these words found in Chapter Six

1. acuity
2. homeland
3. obsess
4. vigilante
5. idealist

6. cohabitation
7. subside
8. debris
9. nucleus
10. unconventionally

APPENDIX C: REVISED TEST ANXIETY SCALE

The following items refer to how you feel when taking a test. Answer the following questions 1 through 20 as honestly as you can. Then go to the chart and fill it in based on your responses.

1 = almost never   *2 = sometimes*   *3 = often*   *4 = almost always*

1. Thinking about my grade in a course interferes with my work on tests.	1 2 3 4
2. I seem to defeat myself while taking important tests.	1 2 3 4
3. During tests, I find myself thinking about the consequences of failing.	1 2 3 4
4. I start feeling very uneasy just before getting a test paper back.	1 2 3 4
5. During tests I feel very tense.	1 2 3 4
6. I worry a great deal before taking an important exam.	1 2 3 4
7. During tests, I find myself thinking of things unrelated to the material being tested.	1 2 3 4
8. While taking tests, I find myself thinking how much brighter the other people are.	1 2 3 4
9. I think about current events during a test.	1 2 3 4
10. I get a headache during an important test.	1 2 3 4
11. While taking a test, I often think about how difficult it is.	1 2 3 4
12. I am anxious about tests.	1 2 3 4
13. While taking tests, I sometimes think about being somewhere else.	1 2 3 4
14. During tests, I find I am distracted by thoughts of upcoming events.	1 2 3 4
15. My mouth feels dry during a test.	1 2 3 4
16. I sometimes find myself trembling before or during tests.	1 2 3 4
17. While taking a test, my muscles are very tight.	1 2 3 4
18. I have difficulty breathing while taking a test.	1 2 3 4
19. During the test, I think about how I should have prepared for the test.	1 2 3 4
20. I worry before the test because I do not know what to expect.	1 2 3 4

Benson, J. L. and N. El-Zahhar. "Further refinement and validation of the revised test anxiety scale." *Structural equation modeling 1*, 3 (1994): 203-221.

CHARTING YOUR RESPONSES

Using the chart below, record your responses. If, for example, you circled "3" for Item 1, "Thinking about my grade in a course interferes with my work on tests," then write a "3" in the space below next to Item 1. Then add up your points for each block (going across) and write your score in the box on the far right titled Total Points. Last, add up all the boxes on the far right (going down) for Your Grand Total Points.

REVISED TEST ANXIETY SCALE

Dimension			Item Response				Total Points
Tension Max= 20 pts Min = 5 pts	Item 4	Item 5	Item 6	Item 12	Item 20		
Worry Max = 24 pts Min = 6 pts	Item 1	Item 2	Item 3	Item 8	Item 11	Item 19	
Bodily Symptoms Max = 20 pts Min = 5 pts	Item 10	Item 15	Item 16	Item 17	Item 18		
Test-Irrelevant Thinking Max = 16 pts Min = 4 pts	Item7	Item 9	Item 13	Item 14			
							TOTAL POINTS

*Estimated Test Anxious Level = 40 points and above

Unlike many tests, on this test *the lower your score the better*. According to research, students who failed the Regents' Reading Test showed an average score of 45 on this scale (Stallworth-Clark, et. al., 2000). Therefore, if you scored 45+, you will probably want to practice some strategies for coping with test anxiety.

Perhaps one of the best things you can do for yourself before taking the Regents' Reading Exam is exactly what you are doing now: that is, preparing yourself. In addition to that, there are several resources at your disposal: 1) contact the counseling center at your college; they may have handouts or counseling sessions available; 2) contact the academic success center at your college; they may give workshops on strategies for coping with test anxiety; 3) contact your Learning Support Department; teachers in this department have unequalled expertise in test taking strategies; and 4) contact student affairs at your college; they may have peer and tutoring sessions designed to address test taking.

APPENDIX D: ANSWER KEY FOR CHAPTERS

CHAPTER TWO

Exercise 1 Answers will vary.

Exercise 2

1.	proliferation	increase
2.	scrupulous	conscientious
3.	ubiquitous	ever-present
4.	meticulous	orderly
5.	parasitic	freeloading
6.	advocate	supporter
7.	pessimistic	gloomy
8.	skeptical	uncertain
9.	culminated	ended
10.	mentor	advisor

Exercise 3 Journal Work: answers will vary

Exercise 4 Answers will vary.

Exercise 5 Suggested meanings:

1. meaning of <u>perverse</u>: vicious
key words/phrases/punctuation: *heartlessly*; *dash (punctuation)*
context clue: Direct definition

2. meaning of <u>distorted</u>: out of focus
key words/phrases/punctuation: *clearly, in focus*
context clue: Contrast

3. meaning of <u>flaunt</u>: display
key words/phrases/punctuation: *like*
context clue: Example

4. meaning of <u>prosperity</u>: riches
key words/phrases/punctuation: *and*
context clue: Equating Two Things

5. meaning of <u>susceptibility:</u> weakness
key words/phrases/punctuation: *colon (punctuation)*
context clue: Direct Definition

ANSWER KEY: CHAPTER TWO

6. meaning of <u>intricate</u>: complex
key words/phrases/punctuation: *and; commas (punctuation)*
context clue: Listing

7. meaning of <u>digress</u>: go off point
key words/phrases/punctuation: 2+ sentences
context clue: Long Explanation

8. meaning of <u>eluding</u>: *avoiding, evading*
key words/phrases/punctuation: *and, commas(punctuation)*
context clue: *Listing*

9. meaning of <u>forlorn</u>: desperate
key words/phrases/punctuation: *huddled, barrel fire, alley*
context clue: Direct Definition through Description

10. meaning of <u>activists</u>: protestors
key words/phrases/punctuation: *so*
context clue: Cause-Effect

Exercise 6   Answers should resemble same as above

Exercise 7 Journal Work: answers will vary

Exercise 8

1. a
key words/phrases/punctuation: *but*

2. b
key words/phrases/punctuation: *so*

3. a
key words/phrases/punctuation: *After*

4. a
key words/phrases/punctuation: *docile, mild-mannered, calm*

5. c
key words/phrases/punctuation: *like*

6. b
key words/phrases/punctuation: *In contrast to*

ANSWER KEY: CHAPTER TWO

7. c
key words/phrases/punctuation: *scream, baby sleeping*

8. c
key words/phrases/punctuation: *on the other hand*

9. a
key words/phrases/punctuation: *home-based telephone*

10. c
key words/phrases/punctuation: *and, put into operation*

Exercise 9 Journal Work: answers will vary: Vocabulary Journal Supplement: *Matching exercise:* 1. e   2. i   3. a   4. j 5. c   6. g   7. b   8. d   9. f   10. h

Exercise 10

1. 2
2. 3
3. 1
4. 3
5. 1
6. 3
7. 3
8. 1
9. 2
10. 4

Exercise 11 Journal Work: answers will vary

Exercise 12

1. poverty: cause-effect
2. not calm, turbulent: contrast
3. take in: direct explanation
4. independent: contrast
5. egomaniacs: use of semi-colon (;) direct explanation
6. profitable: use of semi-colon (;) explanation follows semi-colon
7. ambitions: ( ) examples
8. remarkable development: example
9. carefully examine: direct explanation
10. not constant: contrast

Exercise 13 Journal Work: Answers will vary

ANSWER KEY: CHAPTER TWO

Exercise 14

1. pleasant
2. creature
3. flinch
4. skinny
5. forehead
6. extraordinary
7. souvenir
8. stepmother
9. rivals
10. overcome
11. repent
12. barefoot
13. intentions
14. tirelessly
15. debauchery

Exercise 15

1. 2	5. 3	9. 2
2. 3	6. 2	10. 2
3. 1	7. 1	
4. 3	8. 1	

Exercise 16

1. 2	3. 3	5. 3
2. 1	4. 2	

Exercise 17   Journal Work: Answers will vary

Exercise 18

1. *carry* across
2. carry away
3. *carry* into

4. *carry* out
5. able to *carry*
6. person who *carries*
7. *carry* from underneath
8. act of *carrying* (people) across (town
9. *carry* back (news)
10. *carry* vessel over land

11. *before* the sports event
12. *fore* knowledge
13. condition to meet *before* (taking a course)
14. *before* history as we know it
15. *fore*tell
16. a viewing *before* the main attraction
17. go *before*
18. planning *before* an event
19. to come *before* a specified date
20. an affix *before* the fixed root of a word

ANSWER KEY: CHAPTER TWO

Exercise 19

First set
1. i
2. c
3. b
4. g
5. j
6. h
7. e
8. a
9. d
10. f

Second set
11. i
12. j
13. a
14. f
15. b
16. d
17. h
18. c
19. g
20. e

Exercise 20

1. into
   see
   person
   person who looks into
2. around
   come
   go around the truth
3. all
   power
   all powerful
4. not
   believe
   full of
   could not believe

5. between
   between continents
6. good
   to do good for
7. know
   knew
8. not
   inherit
   did not inherit
9. people
   killing
   extermination

10. holding/hanging on
    full of
    stubborn

Exercise 21 Journal Work: answers will vary. Vocabulary Journal Supplement: B. *Matching exercise:* 1. b   2. c   3. g   4. f   5. e   6. j   7. a   8. d   9. i   10. h

ANSWER KEY: CHAPTER TWO

CHAPTER THREE

Exercise 1

1. 6 or 8
2. yellow, gray, white and brown
3. 4
4. Venus
5. Venus and the Moon
6. a flying mountain
7. 65 million years ago
8. True
9. empty space
10. Alpha Centauri
11. 8,000 times farther than Pluto
12. 1990s
13. 12
14. True
15. 1994
16. Northridge, California
17. 4:00 a.m.
18. emergency organizations
19. observatories
20. radio stations

Exercise 2 Answers will vary.

Exercise 3

1. True
2. False
3. True
4. False
5. False
6. False
7. True
8. False
9. True
10. True

Exercise 4

1. b
2. a
3. c
4. a
5. c
6. c
7. b
8. a
9. b
10. c

Exercise 5

1. *Macon Daily News*
2. tower, monitor, keyboard, mouse, printer, speakers
3. *The X-Files*

Exercise 6

1. Gerardi
2. *Sociological Inquiry*
3. Yes
4. 4
5. 2004
6. *The White Tortilla*
7. 5
8. ISBN#978-0-7575-3905-3
9. True
10. 0 (zero)

ANSWER KEY: CHAPTER THREE

Exercise 7

1. Fruitcake capital of the world
2. Cherokee
3. McCrae, Georgia
4. Wed 1:30-2:30 or by appointment
5. Statesboro, Georgia
6. Yes
7. 61 North Avenue NW
8. 706-865-2171
9. Fried Green Tomatoes
10. Forrest Gump

Exercise 8. Answers will vary.

Exercise 9

1. b
2. a
3. c
4. b
5. False
6. False
7. True
8. False
9. False
10. True

CHAPTER FOUR

Exercise 1

Answers will vary.

Exercise 2

1. b   clues: "but a radical idea in the minds of a few men "
2. c   clues: "the emblem of the Rising Sun" and [general knowledge of Pearl Harbor]
3. a   clues: "December seventh has been described by too many for me to reiterate.
4. a   clues: "None of the female civilian pilots wanted to leave."
                  "I left at once."
5. a   clues: "Delivering a trainer to Texas may be as important as delivering a bomber to Africa if you take
                the long view.
6. – 10. Answers will vary.

ANSWER KEY: CHAPTERS THREE/FOUR

Exercise 3 Answers will vary

Exercise 4

1. 1 Clue: The assumption that growing up in the same family will make people similar is a fallacy (implies that at one time in the past researchers thought it was true)
2. 2 Clue: laterborns do not use conformity as a strategy for approval; not conforming may get a sibling into more trouble
3. 2 Clue: Parents are naturally engaged with the first child; focusing more attention to it
4. 3 Clue: They may often choose pursuits in which the older sibling has not already established a dominant superiority.
5. 1 Clue: Therefore, firstborns seek to maintain close ties to the parents by conforming to parental wishes

Exercise 5

A. Step One:

-condemned man, executioner
-looked like masquerade, not real

Step Two:

-Execution, supposed to be solemn, seemed like a spectacular, fantastical event.

Step Three:

Main Idea sentence: "I" was at a beheading but felt as though the execution was a bizarre, dreamlike event.

B. Step One:

-the King and "I"'s family all looking grave
-"I" is fidgeting, in a hurry to leave
-"I" is 13-years-old
-"I" is hungry

Step Two:
-the occasion is grave, but all "I" can do is think of eating
-wants the King to hurry up

Step Three:

Main Idea sentence: "I," (thirteen years old and married nobility) is impatient to have the ordeal over with so that she can get something to eat.

ANSWER KEY: CHAPTER FOUR

C. Step One:

>   -the condemned prisoner, the Duke, was "I's" uncle
>   -Duke had royal blood; had large army; threat to King
>   -the Duke offended the King
>   -said King could not sire a son

Step Two:

>   -Duke must die because he is a threat to King

Step Three:

>   Main Idea sentence: The Duke, who is "I's" uncle, is a threat to the King and must be executed.

Exercise 6

A. Step One:

>   -China
>   -occupation + civil war = desire to be Great Power
>   -major trading nation
>   -military strategic thinking now offense

Step Two:

>   -main theme = project power

Step Three:

-Main Idea sentence: China has already become an economic power and has turned its attention to enhancing its military power.

Step Four:

>   The answer is c.

B. Step One:

>   -China foot binding – ideal three-inch lotus foot cherished
>   -excruciating procedure, many dangers
>   -why undergo such a procedure?
>   1. good marriage and
>   2. secure place in afterlife

Step Two: Chinese women with bound feet = painful and hazardous but beneficial

ANSWER KEY: CHAPTER FOUR

Step Three:

> Main Idea sentence: Traditionally, foot binding was a Chinese ritual done for obtaining good marriage—and a good marriage meant being cared for after death.

Step Four:

> The answer is c.

CHAPTER FIVE

Exercise 1

1. love
2. like
3. dislike
4. hate
5. abhor

6. syrupy
7. sweet
8. amenable
9. unpleasant
10. callous

Exercise 2. Answers will vary.

Exercise 3

1. b
2. c
3. a
4. c
5. b
6. b
7. a
8. c
9. b
10. c

ANSWER KEY: CHAPTER FIVE

Exercise 4

1. b: body paragraphs, essay, original topic, thesis
2. c: went against, paid much less, food was scarce, haunted, continual hunger, hard, noisy, dirty, restrictive
3. a: fastest growing, 800,000, across borders, slavery, forced to work, under lock and key
4. c: head hanging down, forlorn, unguarded, touched his heart
5. b: like children playing in the sun, felt happy, exciting, like a melody from the moon, whales were singing!

Exercise 5   Answers will vary.

Exercise 6

1. a
2. c
3. a
4. b

Exercise 7

1. Classification: "There are basically three types."
   Types are italicized.

2. Cause-effect:
   "failure," "was caused," "climate, hostiles, and lack of gunpowder"

3. Persuasion:
   Arguments that Barack Obama is not "too young" for the presidency
   a. John F. Kennedy was younger that 45
   b. junior execs become senior execs at 45
   b. most athletes retire at 45 years of age
4. Definition through Facts:
   Verb "to be"
   Repetition of word "hurricane"

5. Description:
   Lots of adjectives and descriptive words:
   "imposing, grey stone, embellished, grandeur, elegance, high painted ceilings, impressive"
6. Narration:
   Definite feeling a story is being told
   Want to know what role the bear will play in Amanda's life

7. Contrast:
   Two presidents being contrasted: Harding and Coolidge
   Scandal, bribes, dishonest, Unlike, Quiet Cal, cleaned up, respectable and stable

ANSWER KEY: CHAPTER FIVE

8. Example: (Although this paragraph may at first appear to be contrasting men and women, the overriding topic is Comparable Pay and the example is the pay discrepancy between men and women) Words: *example, indicators, illustrate, case in point, such as*

9. Chronology: Words: *preceded, prior, 1492, Until, sixteenth century, After, future*

CHAPTER SIX

Passage One
1. c
2. a
3. b
4. c
5. a
6. T
7. F
8. T
9. F
10. T

Passage Two
1. T
2. F
3. F
4. T
5. T
6. F
7. F
8. F
9. T
10. F

Passage Three
1. T
2. F
3. F
4. T
5. F
6. T
7. F
8. T
9. T
10. T

Passage Four
1. T
2. T
3. F
4. T
5. T
6. F
7. T
8. T
9. F
10. T

Passage Five
1. T
2. F
3. F
4. F
5. T
6. F
7. T
8. T
9. F
10. T

Passage Six
1. T
2. F
3. F
4. F
5. T
6. F
7. F
8. T
9. T
10. F

Passage Seven
1. F
2. T
3. F
4. F
5. F
6. T
7. T
8. T
9. F
10. F

ANSWER KEY: CHAPTER SIX

Passage Eight

1. T
2. F
3. F
4. F
5. T
6. T
7. F
8. T
9. F
10. F

Passage Nine

1. T
2. T
3. T
4. F
5. T
6. F
7. F
8. F
9. F
10. T

Passage Ten

1. T
2. T
3. F
4. F
5. T
6. F
7. T
8. T
9. T
10. F

ANSWER KEY: CHAPTER SIX

APPENDIX E: ANSWER KEYS FOR EXAMS

PRE-TEST

1. 2	31. 1
2. 3	32. 2
3. 1	33. 3
4. 4	34. 4
5. 1	35. 4
6. 3	36. 2
7. 1	37. 1
8. 4	38. 3
9. 1	39. 4
10. 3	40. 2
11. 4	41. 4
12. 2	42. 2
13. 3	43. 1
14. 4	44. 4
15. 3	45. 2
16. 1	46. 2
17. 2	47. 3
18. 2	48. 4
19. 4	49. 2
20. 1	50. 4
21. 3	51. 3
22. 2	52. 4
23. 4	53. 2
24. 3	54. 1
25. 4	
26. 4	
27. 3	
28. 2	
29. 1	
30. 2	

EXAM ONE

1. 2		31. 3	
2. 3		32. 3	
3. 4		33. 4	
4. 3		34. 1	
5. 2		35. 3	
6. 3		36. 4	
7. 4		37. 4	
8. 3		38. 3	
9. 2		39. 4	
10. 1		40. 1	
11. 3		41. 4	
12. 4		42. 2	
13. 3		43. 2	
14. 4		44. 3	
15. 2		45. 1	
16. 1		46. 4	
17. 3		47. 2	
18. 1		48. 3	
19. 3		49. 4	
20. 4		50. 3	
21. 2		51. 1	
22. 1		52. 2	
23. 3		53. 3	
24. 4		54. 4	
25. 1			
26. 3			
27. 2			
28. 3			
29. 1			
30. 1			

ANSWER KEY: EXAM ONE

EXAM TWO

1.	1	31.	3
2.	4	32.	3
3.	3	33.	4
4.	2	34.	2
5.	4	35.	4
6.	1	36.	1
7.	1	37.	2
8.	4	38.	1
9.	2	39.	3
10.	4	40.	2
11.	3	41.	1
12.	1	42.	3
13.	3	43.	2
14.	2	44.	4
15.	4	45.	3
16.	4	46.	1
17.	1	47.	4
18.	2	48.	2
19.	4	49.	3
20.	1	50.	1
21.	3	51.	4
22.	2	52.	4
23.	4	53.	4
24.	3	54.	1
25.	3		
26.	4		
27.	2		
28.	2		
29.	4		
30.	2		

ANSWER KEY: EXAM TWO

EXAM THREE

1. 1		31. 4	
2. 2		32. 2	
3. 4		33. 4	
4. 3		34. 3	
5. 2		35. 1	
6. 4		36. 4	
7. 3		37. 3	
8. 3		38. 3	
9. 4		39. 2	
10. 2		40. 4	
11. 1		41. 1	
12. 2		42. 3	
13. 4		43. 2	
14. 4		44. 2	
15. 3		45. 1	
16. 2		46. 3	
17. 4		47. 2	
18. 4		48. 4	
19. 1		49. 3	
20. 3		50. 3	
21. 4		51. 2	
22. 2		52. 4	
23. 1		53. 1	
24. 3		54. 4	
25. 3			
26. 4			
27. 3			
28. 3			
29. 1			
30. 2			

ANSWER KEY: EXAM THREE

EXAM FOUR

1. 4	31. 3
2. 3	32. 4
3. 1	33. 3
4. 3	34. 1
5. 4	35. 4
6. 3	36. 2
7. 1	37. 3
8. 4	38. 3
9. 2	39. 1
10. 3	40. 2
11. 4	41. 3
12. 4	42. 1
13. 4	43. 4
14. 3	44. 1
15. 4	45. 3
16. 1	46. 2
17. 2	47. 4
18. 4	48. 1
19. 1	49. 1
20. 2	50. 4
21. 4	51. 2
22. 3	52. 3
23. 4	53. 3
24. 3	54. 2
25. 2	
26. 3	
27. 1	
28. 3	
29. 2	
30. 4	

ANSWER KEY: EXAM FOUR

EXAM FIVE

1. 4		31. 4
2. 2		32. 3
3. 3		33. 1
4. 2		34. 2
5. 1		35. 3
6. 4		36. 4
7. 4		37. 4
8. 1		38. 2
9. 4		39. 3
10. 2		40. 1
11. 3		41. 4
12. 2		42. 3
13. 4		43. 2
14. 2		44. 1
15. 1		45. 4
16. 4		46. 3
17. 1		47. 4
18. 3		48. 3
19. 1		49. 2
20. 2		50. 4
21. 3		51. 1
22. 4		52. 3
23. 4		53. 1
24. 1		54. 4
25. 4		
26. 2		
27. 4		
28. 3		
29. 1		
30. 3		

ANSWER KEY: EXAM FIVE

EXAM SIX

1. 2	31. 4
2. 1	32. 3
3. 4	33. 1
4. 1	34. 2
5. 3	35. 4
6. 2	36. 3
7. 1	37. 4
8. 4	38. 3
9. 1	39. 4
10. 3	40. 2
11. 4	41. 4
12. 2	42. 2
13. 3	43. 4
14. 2	44. 3
15. 1	45. 2
16. 4	46. 1
17. 3	47. 1
18. 1	48. 4
19. 4	49. 1
20. 2	50. 3
21. 4	51. 2
22. 1	52. 4
23. 4	53. 3
24. 3	54. 2
25. 4	
26. 3	
27. 2	
28. 1	
29. 4	
30. 2	

ANSWER KEY: EXAM SIX

EXAM SEVEN

1. 4	31. 4
2. 3	32. 2
3. 2	33. 3
4. 1	34. 1
5. 3	35. 4
6. 1	36. 3
7. 4	37. 3
8. 2	38. 3
9. 4	39. 1
10. 1	40. 2
11. 2	41. 3
12. 3	42. 1
13. 3	43. 1
14. 1	44. 3
15. 4	45. 4
16. 2	46. 3
17. 4	47. 2
18. 2	48. 1
19. 2	49. 1
20. 4	50. 2
21. 1	51. 3
22. 1	52. 4
23. 2	53. 3
24. 4	54. 4
25. 3	
26. 4	
27. 2	
28. 1	
29. 2	
30. 3	

ANSWER KEY: EXAM SEVEN

EXAM EIGHT

1.	3	31.	3
2.	1	32.	4
3.	3	33.	4
4.	4	34.	2
5.	3	35.	1
6.	1	36.	2
7.	2	37.	2
8.	4	38.	4
9.	3	39.	4
10.	1	40.	3
11.	4	41.	1
12.	2	42.	3
13.	1	43.	4
14.	4	44.	2
15.	2	45.	1
16.	2	46.	3
17.	3	47.	2
18.	1	48.	1
19.	4	49.	3
20.	2	50.	2
21.	2	51.	1
22.	4	52.	3
23.	1	53.	4
24.	3	54.	2
25.	2		
26.	3		
27.	2		
28.	1		
29.	3		
30.	4		

ANSWER KEY: EXAM EIGHT

EXAM NINE

1. 3		31. 2	
2. 2		32. 1	
3. 4		33. 4	
4. 4		34. 3	
5. 3		35. 4	
6. 2		36. 3	
7. 2		37. 3	
8. 1		38. 3	
9. 4		39. 4	
10. 3		40. 1	
11. 2		41. 2	
12. 3		42. 2	
13. 3		43. 1	
14. 2		44. 2	
15. 1		45. 3	
16. 2		46. 4	
17. 4		47. 1	
18. 2		48. 3	
19. 4		49. 1	
20. 1		50. 3	
21. 4		51. 4	
22. 3		52. 2	
23. 2		53. 3	
24. 3		54. 1	
25. 4			
26. 1			
27. 3			
28. 2			
29. 4			
30. 1			

ANSWER KEY: EXAM NINE

POST TEST

1. 3	31. 2
2. 4	32. 3
3. 2	33. 4
4. 1	34. 1
5. 2	35. 2
6. 3	36. 1
7. 3	37. 2
8. 2	38. 3
9. 1	39. 1
10. 1	40. 4
11. 4	41. 2
12. 3	42. 2
13. 3	43. 3
14. 2	44. 1
15. 1	45. 4
16. 4	46. 4
17. 3	47. 3
18. 1	48. 2
19. 2	49. 4
20. 3	50. 2
21. 1	51. 4
22. 4	52. 1
23. 1	53. 4
24. 1	54. 3
25. 1	
26. 2	
27. 3	
28. 2	
29. 4	
30. 3	

ANSWER KEY: POST TEST

APPENDIX F:
GRAPHICS ANSWER KEY

In Scottish history throughout the Highlands, the bagpipes succeeded the harp as a call to arms, especially when the call to arms involved several thousand half-frozen warriors, most of them out of earshot.

The courage of pipers in battle (who were inevitably a prime target for the enemy) is legendary throughout the centuries. ① EX At the Haughs of Cromdale, there's a stone onto which a badly-wounded piper for the army climbed and continued to play until he died. The spot is still known as the "Piper's Stone." ② EX In the Battle of Philiphaugh far south in the border country of Scotland, another intrepid piper played until a bullet knocked him into the Ettrick River where he drowned.

Perhaps one of the most famous pipers of all is the clan Macdonald's piper who was sent to Duntrune Castle as a messenger during a feud during the seventeenth century. He was invited in, but then immediately overpowered and imprisoned. Luckily for the Macdonald clan, the captors neglected to confiscate their prisoner's pipes. Out over the water the sound of pipes could be heard, an unmistakable and undeniable and distinguishable note of warning.

Abruptly the piping stopped as the furious soldiers reached the dungeon and killed the piper as he played. Although no one knows the real fate of the piper, much later, under the floor of the castle hall, a skeleton was found with mutilated hands.

DIAGNOSTIC EXAM, PASSAGE ONE

1. The purpose of the last paragraph is to

   1. inform the reader.
   2. fascinate the reader.
   3. describe the piper for the reader.
   4. relate facts to the reader.

2. According to the passage, within the Scottish armies, who was the prime target of the enemy?

   1. the general.
   2. the clan leader.
   3. the piper.
   4. half-frozen warriors.

3. The word intrepid, as underlined in the passage, most nearly means

   1. fearless.
   2. cowardly.
   3. famous.
   4. eager.

4. The overall pattern of organization used in paragraph two is

   1. definition.
   2. contrast.
   3. cause-effect.
   4. examples.

5. The author of the selection would probably agree that

   1. bagpipes were an important weapon of Scottish armies.
   2. most pipers were used as messengers.
   3. the "Piper's Stone" is an ill-conceived monument.
   4. the piper of the MacDOnald clan was a coward.

6. The underlined word overpowered is best defined as

   1. killed.
   2. gagged.
   3. restrained.
   4. greeted.

In the world of classical ancient Greece and Rome the making of art was generally viewed as a manual profession. Art was taught in workshops. Greek vase painting illustrates this workshop tradition. Apprentice vase painters, some of them female, worked side-by-side with the master of the shop. Women must have been given the lesser positions within the workshop, <u>since no Greek vases signed by women are known.</u>

The Middle Ages continued to identify art as a manual profession. Artists formed <u>guilds:</u> legal organizations rather (like) trade unions. These guilds not only assured professional standards but also reinforced the distinction between the mechanical arts and the liberal arts. During the Middle Ages, liberal arts <u>encompassed</u> arithmetic, geometry, astronomy, music theory, grammar, and logic.

This traditional classification of the visual arts as mechanical was transformed during the Renaissance. <u>Both</u> artists and writers began to emphasize the scientific and intellectual aspects of art. It was argued, for example, that arithmetic was needed by the artist for the study of proportion, and that geometry figured in the proper calculation of perspective. The artist was beginning to be seen as an educated professional knowledgeable of both the <u>practice and theory of art.</u> The new attitude that the artist was a skilled and educated individual was accompanied by a new social status. Artists became the companions of intellectuals, princes, and emperors.

DIAGNOSTIC EXAM, PASSAGE TWO

7. The author concludes that female apprentice vase painters of Greece were given lesser positions because

1. no Greek vases signed by women have been found.
2. women in ancient Greece were uneducated.
3. women were not considered equal to men.
4. only women from the lower classes were apprentices.

8. The word <u>guild</u> as underlined in the passage most nearly means

clue: colon
by example: like

1. mechanical art.
2. profession.
3. artist.
4. legally organized group.

9. Overall, the main idea of the passage is that

1. visual arts were transformed into something more than a manual profession.
2. artists emphasized the scientific aspect of art.
3. artists were included in the courts of the emperors
4. guilds of the Middle Ages assured professional standards..

10. During which age was the classification of mechanical arts changed?

1. the age of the emperors.
2. ancient times of Greece.
3. the Renaissance. 1st sentence, 3rd ¶
4. era of classical Rome.

11. In this context the word <u>encompassed</u>, as underlined, most probably means

1. excluded.
2. surrounded.
3. exempted.
4. included. a listing follows the under-lined word

12. The purpose of the passage is to

1. describe.
②. educate. *factual info @ Greek and Roman art is disseminated*
3. persuade.
4. compare.

13. From the selection, the reader can assume
that princes and emperors were

1. artistic.
2. arrogant.
③. skilled and educated. *last two sentences*
4. only interested in Renaissance art.

DIAGNOSTIC EXAM, PASSAGE TWO

If we do decide that humans should travel to another planetary system, how hard would that be? If we do go to the stars, we would probably be interested <u>in visiting a system more like our own,</u> such as Gliese 777A that has one known planet with about Jupiter's mass located in about Jupiter's location. This star is about 52 light years away. A one-way trip for light takes about 52 years. How long would such a journey take for humans?

NASA successfully tested an ion engine in 1998, a design suitable for interstellar travel at 1 percent the speed of light. With time added to gently accelerate and decelerate—human beings are fragile—it would take about 10,000 years to reach Gliese 777A. Obviously, the <u>feasibility</u> of such a feat is questionable: the astronomers would not live to see their goal. Solutions such as hibernation, deep-freeze, multi-generational ships, and so on, have been proposed, but none of them is yet technically possible. <u>Boosting to speeds close to the speed of light</u> would shorten the time of the trip in the time frame of the astronauts, but <u>would require more energy than we now know how to produce at a reasonable cost.</u> The vast distances between the stars is not the last frontier, <u>but a chasm separating us from any neighboring civilizations.</u> This is one of the reasons why astronomers have difficulty accepting that aliens have already visited Earth.

14. The purpose of the passage is to

1. persuade.
2. inform.
3. criticize.
4. enlighten. *gives some unfamiliar info on*
DIAGNOSTIC EXAM, PASSAGE THREE *space travel*

15. From the information given in the passage, the reader can infer that

1. humans are afraid of planetary exploration.
2. the majority of humans do not believe there is life on other planets.
3. there is a definite interest in space *officials* exploration. *know a great deal about and*
4. the government does not support interstellar *have* travel. *made proposals travelling to other planets*

16. The planet of Gliese 777A would probably be chosen as a destination because

1. it is more like planets in our own solar system.
2. it is the closest to Earth.
3. astronomers know more about it than any other planet in the universe.
4. it is the only planet in the last frontier.

17. The word <u>feasibility</u>, as used in the passage most nearly means
sentence that
1. journey. *: colon + follows*
2. viability. *process of elimination*
3. normality.
4. financing.

18. the passage implies that boosting an engine to the speed of light

1. was achieved with the ion engine.
2. has yet to be mastered within budget.
3. lengthens the travel time in space.
4. does not require a great amount of energy.

19. Astronomers, in general, do not accept that aliens have visited Earth because

1. other intelligent life does not exist in the universe.
2. aliens do not have the technology for interstellar travel.
3. The conditions of Earth's atmosphere can not support alien life forms.
4. there are vast distances, chasms, that separate aliens from Earth.

A Type A personality, either male or female, is characterized by intense drive, aggressiveness, ambition, competitiveness, and the habit of competing with the clock. He or she may give an impression of iron control, or wear a mask of easy geniality, but the strain glints through.

By contrast, Type B's manner is more genuinely easy, open. S/he is not glancing at his watch nor preoccupied with achievement. Type B is less competitive and even speaks in a more modulated style.

Most people are mixtures of Type A and Type B, of course, and Rosenman and Friedman have sharpened their interviewing techniques to the point where they recognize four distinct subdivisions of each group, ranging from A-1, the most virulent, down to B-4, the mildest. The ways the answers are spoken are as important as the responses to the interview question. An impatient subject, who shows his impatience, is probably an A, no matter what he says. Some questions even call for a pretense of stammering on the part of the interviewer. An A intrudes into the stammer, while B waits quietly.

The extreme Type A is the person who, while waiting to see the dentist, is on the telephone making business calls. He speaks in staccato, and rushes through a sentence. He frequently sighs faintly between words which is a sign of emotional exhaustion. He rarely goes to a doctor; indeed, many Type A's die of otherwise recoverable heart attacks simply because they wait too long to call for help.

DIAGNOSTIC EXAM, PASSAGE FOUR

20. The author has written this passage primarily to
    1. contrast two types of personalities.
    2. argue the point that Type B's have a better life than Type A's.
    3. persuade the reader to aspire to Type A qualities.
    4. narrate an incident that happened because a person was Type B.

21. How can Type A personalities be described?
    1. unhappy.
    2. senseless.
    3. driven.
    4. undisturbed.

22. As used in paragraph three, virulent most nearly means
    1. kind
    2. hostile. *contrast w/ "mildest"*
    3. adaptable.
    4. impatient.

23. The last sentence in paragraph one indicates that the person is, in truth, most likely to be
    1. plain and simple.
    2. fond of practical jokes.
    3. friendly and relaxed.
    4. intensely controlled. *"but the strain glints through"*

24. According to the passage Type A's
    1. visit the doctor when they need to.
    2. think doctors are useless.
    3. wait too long to see a doctor.
    4. never visit the doctor.

25. Which of the following is not mentioned as a characteristic of a Type B personality?
    1. open
    2. patient
    3. less competitive
    4. intrusive *"B waits quietly"*

The model followed by the largest Japanese corporation draws on a long cultural tradition that emphasizes the importance of the group over the individual. When people join a major Japanese corporation, they are making a lifetime commitment which the corporation reciprocates: the corporation provides a whole range of services, including housing, recreation, health care, and continuing education. Unless the employee commits a crime, he or she will not be fired or laid off. All promotions are made from inside the organization; outsiders are not even considered. Most promotions are based on seniority, so people of the same age move more or less together through the organizational hierarchy, with little competition among them.

Workers are organized into small teams, and it is the teams—not the individual workers—whose performance is evaluated. Over the years, each individual may belong to many such teams, thereby gaining experiences throughout the corporation. Decision making is collective: rather than issue new policies, the top officials merely ratify them after they have been discussed and approved at every level of the organization (the Japanese word for this process literally means "bottom-up" decision making). Unlike Western corporations, which usually limit the relationship between organization and employee to matters that are "strictly business," Japanese corporations take considerable responsibility for their workers' welfare.

The workers, in turn, show great loyalty to the company—perhaps by wearing company uniforms, singing the company song, working exceptionally long hours, or taking part in company-organized sporting activities. In short, the activities of the corporation and the lives of its members are closely intertwined. This symbiotic relationship between organization and worker reflects a deep difference between Japanese and western cultures: to the Japanese, it indicates a bond of commitment that ensures security and solidarity.

26. The author's style of writing is

1. informal.
2. subjective.
3. argumentative.
4. matter-of-fact.

27. In the second paragraph, which of the following does the author primarily use?

1. chronology
2. narrative
3. description
4. classification.

28. As used in the passage, symbiotic means

1. estranged.
2. mutual.
3. complimentary.
4. strict.

29. It is suggested in the passage that the least attractive job applicant for a Japanese corporation is one who believes in

1. individualism
2. commitment
3. hierarchy of seniority
4. group dynamics

30. The reader can infer that someone from Japan working in the Britain might experience

1. participating in company exercises every morning.
2. the stress of having to find housing.
3. team meetings every day.
4. being asked to sing the company song.

31. What is not mentioned as a characteristic of a Japanese company?

1. "strictly business" philosophy
2. the group dynamic
3. bottom-up decision-making
4. lifetime commitment from company

DIAGNOSTIC EXAM, PASSAGE FIVE

Bulimia is the most common eating disorder in young women. It starts as a strategy to control weight, but it soon develops a life of its own. Life for bulimic young women becomes a relentless preoccupation with eating, purging, and weight watching. Pleasure is replaced by despair, frenzy and guilt. Like all addictions, bulimia is a self-destructive, compulsive, and progressive disorder. Binging and purging are the addictive behaviors; food is the narcotic.

Over time young women with bulimia are at risk for serious health problems; often they have dental problems, tears in the esophagus, gastrointestinal problems and sometimes dangerous electrolyte imbalances that can trigger heart attacks.

Young women often experience personality changes as they grow to love binging more than anything else; they become obsessed and secretive. Driven for another binge and feeling guilty about their habit, they suffer loss of control that leads to depression. Often these women are irritable and withdrawn, especially in relations with family members.

While anorexia, another eating disorder, often begins in junior high, bulimia tends to develop in later adolescence. It is called the college girl's disease because so many young women develop it in sororities and dorms.

Estimates of the incidence of bulimia run as high as one-fifth of all college-age women. Most are attractive women with good social skills. Often they are the cheerleaders and homecoming queens, the straight-A students, and the pride of their families. Bulimic young women, like their anorexic sisters are over-socialized to the feminine role. They are the ultimate people pleasers.

32. The overall pattern of organization utilized in the next to the last paragraph is

1. narration.
2. contrast.
3. cause-effect.
4. description.

33. According to the selection, women with bulimia

1. are basically very healthy.
2. can stop binging whenever they decide they want to quit.
3. are at risk for heart attack.
4. suffer physically but do not suffer emotionally.

34. As underlined in the selection, anorexia most nearly means

1. bulimia.
2. college girl's disease.
3. relations.
4. eating disorder. *,comma direct explanation*

35. The tone of the passage is

1. hopeless.
2. complaining.
3. defensive.
4. objective. *gives facts and medical info*

DIAGNOSTIC EXAM, PASSAGE SIX

36. The central focus of the passage is that

1. college girls are at risk for bulimia.
2. bulimia is a common and dangerous disorder. →
3. most female bulimics are over-socialized to the feminine role.
4. binging and purging are addictive behaviors.

Notes:
= { *bulimia = common disorder ¶1*
Over time at risk for serious health problems ¶2
Trigger heart attacks
Experience personality changes ¶3 }

37. The author would most likely agree with which of the following?

1. Bulimia very quickly overtakes a young woman's life if it is not controlled. *"as they grow to love binging more than anything else"*
2. Bulimia affects a young woman physically but not emotionally.
3. Electrolite imabalances can be easily remedied and, consequently, do not pose a threat..
4. Young women who earn straight A's are not susceptible to bulimic tendencies.

DIAGNOSTIC EXAM, PASSAGE SIX

The greatest of all the women warriors among the upper Missouri tribes lived among the Crows in the middle of the nineteenth century. Woman Chief was not a Crow Indian by birth. She was a Gros Ventre (a tribe closely tied with the Algonquin Indians) girl who, at the age of about ten, was captured by the Crows. The Crow family that adopted her soon found that she showed little interest in helping the women with their <u>domestic</u> tasks. <u>She preferred to shoot birds with a bow and arrow, to guard the family horses, and ride horseback fast and fearlessly.</u> Later she learned to shoot a gun accurately. She became the equal if not the superior of any of the young men in hunting on foot or on horseback.

She grew taller and stronger than most women. She could carry a deer home from the hunt on her back. She could kill four buffalo in a single chase, butcher them, and load them on pack horses without assistance. Yet, despite her prowess in men's activities, she always dressed like a woman. Although she was rather good-looking, <u>she did not attract the fancy of young men.</u> After her foster father died, she took charge of his lodge and family, and acted as both mother and father to his children.

She led her first war party against the Blackfeet; seventy horses were stolen. She succeeded in killing and scalping one Blackfoot and in capturing the gun of another. Her continued success as a war leader in a world dominated by men won her greater and greater honors among the Crows until she gained a place in the Council of Chiefs of the tribe, <u>ranking third in a band of 160 lodges.</u>

DIAGNOSTIC EXAM, PASSAGE SEVEN

38. <u>Domestic</u>, as used in the first paragraph, means

1. local.
2. monthly.
3. home-based. _contrast w/following sentence._
4. public.

39. In the context of this passage, Woman Chief was most unique because

1. she was not a Crow Indian by birth.
2. she was captured when very young.
3. she preferred to shoot birds than make clothes.
4. women were not usually invited to serve on the Council of Chiefs.

40. According to the passage, Woman Chief

1. was not feminine.
2. did not attract men.
3. was not good looking.
4. did not like children.

41. The reader can infer that male, Crow warriors who resided in camp with Woman Chief considered her

1. too muscular and forward.
2. overbearing and arrogant.
3. a part of their warrior circle.
4. somewhat a threat but respected her. _did not attract men but_ _received greater and greater honors_

42. The purpose of the second paragraph is to

1. entertain the reader with stories of Woman Chief.
2. describe Woman Chief's stature and character. _"taller," "stronger,"_
3. criticize the choices Woman Chief made while on the Council. _"good-looking"_
4. define a female warrior chief.

"dressed like a woman"

Pyramids did not stand alone but were part of a group of buildings which included other tombs, temples, chapels, and massive walls. The scarcity of ancient records leaves us uncertain about the uses of all the buildings in the pyramid complex or the exact burial procedures. Remnants of boats that were used for burials have been excavated—the best preserved are at Giza, Egypt. From this evidence, it is thought that the king's body was brought by boat up the Nile to the pyramid site, having already been mummified in the Valley Temple.

On the walls of Fifth and Sixth Dynasty pyramids are inscriptions known as the Pyramid Texts: an important source of information about Egyptian religion. The funeral customs and beliefs of the ancient Egyptians called for the preservation of the body and ample provisions for the afterlife. An ancient Egyptian provided for life in the next World as best as he could.

Also, on the walls the Egyptians painted idealized scenes from daily life: scenes of agricultural work such as crop harvesting, cattle tending, and fishing. They illustrated scenes of artisans at their work, including gold workers and boat-builders. Detailed and colorful scenes on the walls provide information on a wide range of topics such as dress, architecture, crafts, and food production. These scenes represented the hoped-for afterlife and were thought to ensure an ideal existence in the next world. The goods included in the tombs along with the corpses add to this invaluable information resource .

For us today, a huge amount of information about daily life in ancient Egypt can be found in the Pyramid Texts.

43. The passage indicates that pyramid complexes were primarily built for

1. religious purposes.
2. the king.
3. artisans and craftsmen.
4. daily activities.

44. According the the passage, ancient Egyptians placed "goods" in the tombs with the corpse to

1. ward off evil spirits.
2. ease some of the guilt they felt about their relationship with the person.
3. to show the gods of the afterlife the wealth of the person.
4. ensure that the person would have ample provisions for the next world.

45. We can infer from the selection that through observing paintings of daily life, we can learn how the Egyptians viewed

1. the king.
2. the afterlife.
3. pyramids.
4. the Fifth and Sixth Dynasties.

46. According to the passage, overall the Pyramid Texts give valuable information about

1. prevalent philosophies of ancient Egypt.
2. Egyptian religion and daily life. add this info
3. building pyramids. to #45 above
4. the lives of Egyptian kings.

DIAGNOSTIC EXAM, PASSAGE EIGHT

47. complex, as used in the first paragraph, is best defined as

1. difficult.
2. intricate.
(3.) group of buildings. *1st sentence*
4. phobia.

48. According to the passage, which was not mentioned as part of the daily life of an Egyptian?

1. fishing.   *process of elimination*
2. boat building.
3. gold working.
(4.) military training.

DIAGNOSTIC EXAM, PASSAGE EIGHT

The current overall estimate of the number of wild polar bears worldwide is 20,000-25,000, and about 60% of these are in Canada. Polar bears are the top predator in the arctic and evolved from brown bears. They have adapted to life in the north where temperatures do not exceed 50°F in summer and typically fall to -22°F during winter. These bears have enormous paws that function like snowshoes, distributing their weight to keep them from breaking through ice and snow. (Male bears can weigh up to 1300 lbs.) Their thick white coat is made up of water repellent hairs that conserve heat. Under their dense fur is black skin, good for absorbing the rays of the arctic sun. A layer of fat up to 4.3 inches thick keeps the bears warm, especially while swimming.

Polar bears are usually solitary animals, but they gather together on land during the ice-free season to breed. There are usually 2 cubs, each weighing only 1.3 lbs., about the size of a guinea pig. Cubs are nursed until they weigh about 22 lbs. and are large enough to venture onto the sea ice. In most areas, they stay with their mother for about 2.5 years before striking out on their own.

Threats to the survival of polar bear include global warming which is melting the sea ice. Due to the extreme distances between ice floes, polar bears are forced to swim up to 60 miles to reach their destination and are drowning from exhaustion). Unbelievably, the main threat to polar bears remains overhunting. Today, legal hunting of polar bears by non-native sport hunters is found in Canada. In addition, it has been documented that in areas such as East Greenland, both historically and currently, hunting takes place with no quota systems in place.

49. The author makes his point mostly through the use of

1. dramatic narration.
2. facts and statistics.
3. descriptive events.
4. persuasive commentary.

50. The author's attitude toward hunters killing polar bears for sport is one of

1. apathy.
2. ridicule.
3. suspicion.
4. disbelief.

51. The word solitary, as underlined, most nearly means

1. social.
2. lazy.
3. lone.
4. distinct.

52. According to the selection, where do the majority of polar bears live?

1. Alaska.
2. Greenland.
3. Iceland.
4. Canada.

DIAGNOSTIC EXAM, PASSAGE NINE

53. At this point in time, the main threat to polar bears is

1. global warming.
2. overhunting. last ¶
3. other large predators.
4. indigenous peoples of the Arctic.

54. Of the following, which keeps the polar bear warmest especially while swimming?

1. a layer of fat that is 4.3 inches thick. last sentence of 1st ¶
2. water repellent fur.
3. their enormous paws that paddle rapidly in the icy water.
4. their skin which is black.

DIAGNOSTIC EXAM, PASSAGE NINE

King James awoke to the sunlight streaming through the window of his prison cell and laid for a long time reveling in the tranquility. Distant sounds underlined the peace rather than disturbing it, and he dozed again before stretching lazily and rising slowly from his bed. Still wrapped in the half-awareness of waking he went to the window, now without its winter shutters, and leaned out, resting his arms on the ledge.

Below him was a walled and secret garden closed in with sweet scented flowering trees. He let his eye linger on the blossoms. A robin fluttered into a branch with a flurry of wings. A small movement close under the window attracted his attention. He caught his breath in the surprise of the moment, for seated on a garden bench was a girl who glowed golden in the sun, the little hat she wore on her abundant hair shining as its beads caught the light. Bright feathers curled downwards over her cheek and shadowed the half-closed eyes, but James saw the outline of the cheek and the rounded chin.

How long he watched her he could not tell, but he feasted his eyes on her beauty, lost in the delight of her being. There seemed an aura of well-being and wholesome loveliness about her. Then, she was gone.

He turned away, trembling, and sat down on his ruffled bed. Here was his golden girl; here was the woman he had searched for down the years. Panic seized him when he realized she was no child and might well be claimed already.

1. In the scenario, where is King James?

1. in his palace.
2. in jail.
3. in one of his noble's castles.
4. in garden.

2. The pattern of organization used by the author is

1. comparison.
2. example.
3. description. use of adjectives
4. persuasion.

3. As underlined in the first paragraph, reveling in, most nearly means

1. exposing.
2. shutting out.
3. denying.
4. soaking up.

4. The reader can infer that it is

1. Winter.
2. Fall.
3. Spring.
4. Christmas.

5. The tone of the last paragraph is

1. optimistic.
2. despairing.
3. apathetic.
4. objective.

6. In the last paragraph, we can infer that King James is panicked because

1. he will never get out of prison.
2. the girl may not love him back.
3. he may not have his true love.
4. the girl is too young to consider marriage.

EXAM ONE, PASSAGE ONE

The *Sultana* docked at Vicksburg in the evening of April 22, 1865. The steamer had just arrived from New Orleans. While in New Orleans the chief engineer had informed Captain Mason that one of the tube boilers was leaking. While docked at Vicksburg, the chief engineer told the captain that the boiler was not only leaking but was now "warped." With such alarming news, the captain relented and sent for a boiler repairman from Kleins Foundry who installed a patch on the boiler.

Meanwhile, the *Sultana* business agent had been busy arranging transport of Indiana soldiers who had been held prisoner in Andersonville, Georgia. All of the prisoners would be boarded on the *Sultana*—all 1,700. (The assigned limit for passengers on the *Sultana* was 376.) When they boarded, the happy, homeward-bound soldiers gladly accommodated to cramped conditions aboard the steamer. On April 24, 1865, at 3p.m, the *Sultana* backed into the Mississippi and headed upriver, bearing happy, relieved, sick Union soldiers toward home.

The *Sultana* crossed the Mississippi and established upriver headway. The boat had steamed six miles upriver when a huge explosion occurred. Perhaps 200 souls were blown immediately into the flooded river. Panic ensued, and about 800 people jumped into the flooded river. The sudden mass of men in the water took down even the competent swimmers.

Rescue brigades of citizen boaters and canoeists were in the river and along the flooded banks looking for survivors.

EXAM ONE, PASSAGE TWO

The grounded *Sultana* burned to water level and sank below the surface of the Mississippi within minutes of the removal of the last injured survivors.

The *Sultana* tragedy still remains America's worst inland marine disaster ever. More people were lost on the *Sultana* than in the sinking of the *Titanic* in 1912. #13

7. The reader can infer that the *Sultana* exploded because

1. the steamer was sabotaged by Confederate terrorists.
2. a fire started in the kitchen.
3. the chief engineer was negligent.
4. the boiler exploded.

8. At what point was the captain first informed of the faulty boiler?

1. while docked in Vicksburg.
2. when they reached Kleins Foundry.
3. while docked in New Orleans.
4. as the Union soldiers were boarding.

9. How many released prisoners got aboard the *Sultana*?

1. 800
2. 1,700
3. 200
4. 376

10. What was the main reason most of the men drowned?

1. the sudden mass of men in the water
2. the men who could not swim, clung to the others, drowning them
3. there was no debris to cling to
4. they were too weak to swim

11. The word <u>relented,</u> as used in the passage, most nearly means

1. stood firm.
2. got angry.
3. gave in. *cause-effect*
4. screamed.

12. The tone of paragraph three is

1. hopeful.
2. hostile.
3. indifferent.
4. suspenseful.

13. The *Sultana* incident is newsworthy because

1. the captain of the steamer was famous.
2. the released prisoners were being mistreated aboard the *Sultana.*
3. more people died in the *Sultana* incident than in the sinking of the *Titanic.*
4. citizens boaters and canoeists were the first responders.

EXAM ONE, PASSAGE TWO

Arthur Ashe was one of the first African-Americans to become a great tennis champion. After a heart attack ended his career, he contracted AIDS through a tainted blood transfusion. For years, while he pursued many business interests and human rights projects, he kept his illness private. Then the possibility of a newspaper report forced him to reveal his condition to the public by way of a press conference held in April, 1992.

The day after the press conference Ashe was anxious to see how people would respond. He was thinking not only about the people he knew personally but also about waiters, and taxi drivers, bartenders and doormen. He knew all the myths and fears about AIDS. He also understood that if he hadn't contracted the disease and lived with it, he would probably share some of those myths and fears. He knew that he couldn't spread the disease by coughing, breathing, or using cups in a restaurant, but he knew that in some places his cups would receive some extra soap and hot water or be smashed and thrown away.

#19

Ashe was glad that eventually he stopped concealing his condition from certain people. He had reminded himself from the outset that he had an obligation to tell anyone who might be materially or personally hurt by the news when it came out. Not one of the companies, not even HBO (for which he was a spokesperson), dropped him after he quietly revealed that he had AIDS. He waited for the phone calls and the signs that his services were no longer needed. None came.

Tennis champion Arthur Ashe died on February 6, 1993.

14. What ended Arthur Ashe's career as a tennis player?

1. marriage.
2. AIDS.
3. shoulder injury.
4. heart attack.

15. Why did Arthur Ashe reveal his condition to the public?

1. his wife begged him to disclose it
2. the possibility of a forthcoming newspaper report
3. his associates pressured him
4. his appearance was deteriorating

16. The author's tone in regard to Arthur Ashe is

1. sympathetic and complimentary. 1st sentence
2. objective and neutral. in ¶ 3, revealed
3. distrustful and critical. as an honorable
4. bitter and defensive. person

17. As used in the passage, tainted most nearly means

1. disgraced.
2. smeared.
3. contaminated.
4. unknown.

18. The fact that not one organization called Arthur Ashe after his announce-ment

1. surprised even Arthur Ashe.
2. proved that the public could not deal with people with AIDS.
3. meant that Ashe had lost respect.
4. was of no importance at all.

EXAM ONE, PASSAGE THREE

19. The purpose of the second paragraph is to

1. indicate that Ashe was being paranoid.
2. state that even the common man was concerned about Arthur Ashe.
3. illustrate the public fear associated with AIDS.
4. show that AIDS is a contagious disease.

EXAM ONE, PASSAGE THREE

Basic to the Japanese tradition of Shinto are spirits or gods, called *kami*. Spirits are located in specific places in the world: in a temple, in a crib, or in a shrine. One of the Japanese estimates is that there are eight million *kami*. This term refers both to the sense of power felt in things of the world and to particular gods. A waterfall is a powerful spirit and recognizing it communicates the sense an observer has of its immense power.

Perhaps the most important spirits are those in the house. They occupy particular places and protect the members of the household when in those places: the god of the kitchen lives in the kitchen, the bathroom god in the bathroom, and so forth. There is also a guardian *kami* of the household. This spirit is made up of many ancestors who have merged to guard the house as a corporate unit that exists over time. The village has a guardian *kami*, often a fox god or an ancestor of a founding member. Villagers may ask the village god for help in their rice harvest or for success in schooling.

People create new *kami* as needed. In a less individuated way, all equipment (from computer chips to cameras to automobile production machinery) is thought to have a spiritual side. In 1990 engineers met at Tokyo's Chomeiji shrine to thank their used-up equipment for their service. #25

20. According to some estimates, how many Japanese gods are there?

1. 8
2. 80
3. 800
4. 8,000,000

21. The pattern of organization that the author uses in paragraph two is

1. definition.
2. example.
3. contrast.
4. narration.

22. corporate, as underlined, is best defined as

1. group.
2. business.
3. company.
4. unusual.

23. One aspect of Japanese spiritualism that may seem odd to non-Japanese is that

1. Japanese are religious.
2. villages have gods who protect them.
3. people are allowed to create new gods as needed.
4. Japanese gods are powerful.

24. According to the passage, the most important spirits are those found

1. in a temple or shrine.
2. at the rice harvest.
3. in the village.
4. in the house.

EXAM ONE, PASSAGE THREE

25. What may appear strange to westerners about the 1990 engineers meeting at Chomeiji shrine is that

1. scientists met at a religious location to show reverence for inanimate objects.
2. persons of science are also religious.
3. other scientists were not invited.
4. the meeting was not held in the office.

EXAM ONE, PASSAGE FOUR

In Medieval Europe, most serfs were born, lived, and died on the same estate or manor, very traditional and limited in their outlook. Manors usually included a village, so serfs rarely needed to travel beyond the estate of their master. Serfdom represented a stage between slavery and freedom. Serfs were not sold individually; they could not be sold unless the land itself was sold. On the other hand, a serf did not rank as high as a freeman since he could not own his residence, nor marry outside the manor, nor give away his goods without the permission of his lord and master.

Serfs toiled on the land for the lord as well as for themselves. They also turned over one-tenth of their produce to the church. Each serf worked perhaps three days a week for the master and one day for the church, leaving him two days for himself and his family. It is interesting to note that if a runaway serf escaped to a town without being caught for a year and a day, he could gain his freedom.

Serfs' lives were miserable by our standards. Adults, children, and (in the winter) farm animals infested with bugs and fleas lived in a one-room, thatched hut. The hut often had a dirt floor and a hole in the roof for a chimney. In this crowded environment, accidents, disease, and malnutrition often took their toll, reducing the life expectancy of a serf to thirty or forty years. These workers had meat only a few times a year, usually at Christmas and Easter time. Their everyday fare was the perpetual cabbage soup and grain bread (and if lucky, cheese and

ale for dinner). Not aware of the germ theory of disease, medieval serfs rarely washed their utensils or their hands.

All in all, not much is known about the serfs of Medieval Europe. Written records are virtually empty of any notation of them—perhaps the nobility and clergy did not find any of them worthy of mention.

EXAM ONE, PASSAGE FOUR

26. The purpose of paragraph one is to

1. show cause and effect of the actions of a master and serf.
2. narrate the restricted life of one serf.
3. describe the status of a serf.
4. persuade the reader to be compassionate toward serfs.

27. According to the passage, life expectancy for a serf was about

1. 20-30 years.
2. 30-40 years.
3. 30-50 years.
4. 50-60 years.

28. How could a serf gain his freedom?

1. by working for the master for twelve years
2. by appealing to the village church elders
3. by escaping and not getting caught for one year and one day.
4. by marrying into the nobility

29. The main idea of paragraph three is that

1. serfs led miserable lives.
2. the types of food a serf ate were malnutritious
3. farm animals infested with bugs and fleas lived in the house with the serf's family.
4. medieval serfs rarely washed their utensils or their hands.

30. As used in paragraph three, <u>fare</u>, most probably means

1. menu. *definition by example*
2. ticket. *(cabbage soup and grain bread)*
3. habit.
4. list.

31. The author of this passage uses a style which is

1. informal but informative.
2. scientific and analytical.
3. formal and informative. *matter-of-fact descriptions*
4. argumentative and persuasive.

EXAM ONE, PASSAGE FIVE

Television images haunt us—bony, stunted bodies. This is hunger in its acute form. But hunger comes in another form. It is the day-to-day hunger that over 700 million people suffer. Every year this hunger, largely invisible, kills as many as 20 million people. So we ask ourselves, what is hunger, really? Is it the physical depletion of those suffering chronic undernutrition? Yes, but it is more.

As long as we have a conception of hunger only in physical measures, we will never truly understand it, certainly not its roots. What would it mean to think of hunger in terms of universal human emotions? Here's an idea of what we mean.

Dr. Clements writes of a family in El Salvador he tried to help whose son and daughter had died. "Both had been lost having chosen to pay their mortgage rather than keep the money to feed their children. Thus, being hungry means *anguish,* the anguish of impossible choices.

In Nicaragua four years ago, we met Amanda Espinoza who never had enough to feed her family. She had endured six stillbirths and watched five of her children die before the age of one. To Amanda, hunger means *grief.*

Walking into a home in the rural Philippines, the first words the doctor heard were an apology for the poverty of the dwelling. Being hungry also means living in *humiliation.*

In Guatemala in 1978, we learned that one of two men we had met had

been forced into hiding; the other had been killed. For the wealthy land-owners who monopolized farming in the region, the men's crime was teaching their poor neighbors better farming techniques. Guatemala's wealthy feel threatened by any change that makes the poor less dependent on jobs on their rich plantations. So, the last dimension of hunger is *fear.*

32. Underlined in the selection, the word depletion most nearly means

1. strengthening.
2. abuse.
3. weakening.
4. restoration.

33. How many emotional dimensions to hunger are there?

1. one.
2. two.
3. three.
4. four. *italicized words*

34. When reading the sentence, Here's an idea of what we mean, what would the reader expect to read in the next paragraph?

1. emotional dimensions of hunger
2. physicality of hunger
3. how Dr. Clements define physical hunger
4. statistics about hunger

35. The last four paragraphs of the selection utilize the patterns of organization of

1. description and use of adjectives.
2. narration and summation.
3. example and cause-effect.
4. comparison and contrast.

1. chose to pay mortgage
2. watched children die
3. having to apologize
4. killed, forced into hiding

EXAM ONE, PASSAGE SIX

36. The central focus of the selection is that

1. advertising uses horrific ads to persuade us to support world hunger relief organizations.
2. Guatemala's wealthy mistreat the poor farmers.
3. Dr. Clements did excellent work working with the poor.
4. hunger is not just physical; it is ¶ 2 emotional as well.

37. The scenario about Amanda Espinoza illustrated the emotional dimension of

1. fear.
2. anguish.
3. humiliation.
4. grief.

EXAM ONE, PASSAGE SIX

The (presidency) is today the paramount institution in the national government of the United States. While the Founding Fathers had no intention that it be so, (the office) has become the central energizer of government policy and the symbol at home and abroad of the American political system. (It is) the focus of the hopes (and fears) of countless individuals and groups. For better or worse, we tend to think about American history in four-or-eight-year chunks corresponding to the term in (office) of a particular president.

#42

We <u>invariably</u> turn to the president when the times are out of kilter, demanding remedial action from him and then either blaming him if improvements are not immediately forthcoming or praising him unduly if the burden of problems is eased. We depend on the president to set the agenda for Congress, to define national objectives in time of war, and to represent the United States before the world.

In these and in countless other ways, the presidency embodies the headship of the government, surely not a monarch, but just as surely more than "first among equals." I shall argue that the office has reached this position over the course of our history—not because of random events, but because of certain developments in American capitalism.

EXAM ONE, PASSAGE SEVEN

38. The writer of this excerpt is most likely

1. a history professor.
2. the editor of the *Journal of American Government* too specific
3. a political scientist. subject matter is American govt.
4. a student interning at the White House.

39. The word <u>invariably</u> as used in the second paragraph most nearly means

1. petulantly.
2. variously.
3. reluctantly. word structure
4. unfailingly. in= not (variable)

40. Which of the following is stated in the passage?

1. the American people turn to the president when times are out of kilter.
2. Americans do not commit to their president.
3. American capitalism played no part in establishing the office of the presidency.
4. the presidency today is only second to the monarchy of England.

41. The paragraph which follows this excerpt will discuss

1. how the presidency is like a monarchy.
2. the office of the presidency over the course of history.
3. presidential behavior that manifests the concept "first among equals."
4. the idea that capitalism, not random events, influenced the office of the presidency.

42. In the first paragraph, overall the author uses which pattern of organization?

1. persuasion and argument
2. definition and description repetition of topic
3. chronology and timeline
4. classification and categorization

In 1781, a slave named "Mum Bett" sued for her freedom.

Born in 1742 to African slaves in Claverack, New York, Mum Bett was purchased by her new owner, Colonel Ashley of Sheffield, Massachusetts, when she was six months old. She served as his house servant through middle age. When the master's wife, in a fit of rage, went to strike Mum Bett's sister, Mum Bett received the blow instead. Injured, she left her master's house and refused to return. When her master appealed to the court for her recovery in 1781, she sought the help of a young lawyer, Theodore Sedgwick of nearby Stockbridge.

During the years of the Revolution, Mum Bett had heard discussions about the 1780 Declaration of Rights in the Massachusetts Constitution and told the young lawyer that those rights certainly must apply to her since she was not a "dumb beast." Sedgwick argued the case for her and another of Colonel Ashley's slaves, Brom. Both slaves won their freedom, and the colonel had to pay the cost for court. Mum Bett changed her name to Elizabeth Freeman.

Although Colonel Ashley offered her wages to return, Mum Bett went to work for the Sedgwicks as their housekeeper and even protected their house from vandals during Shay's Rebellion in late 1786. After she moved in with her daughter "Little Bett," she became a respected nurse and midwife. Mum Bett lived with

#48

#47

her daughter through the War of 1812 and until her death in 1829.

43. The reader can infer from the passage that Mum Bett was a unique woman in that

1. the slave owners all respected her.
2. she, being a slave, took a slave owner to court and sued him. 1781 before Civil War
3. as a free woman, she became a midwife.
4. she forced Colonel Ashley to pay court costs.

44. A central theme of the passage is that

1. during the years of the Revolution, there were discussions about the Declaration of Rights found in the Massachusetts Constitution.
2. Colonel Ashley was the stereotypical slave owner who abused Mum Bett.
3. Mum Bett was an extremely courageous woman who fought for her civil rights.
4. most laws of Massachusetts in the late 1700s dealt with slave owner-ship.

45. We can infer from the selection that Elizabeth

1. was well liked by the Sedgwicks.
2. was given respect by the Ashleys.
3. was buried in New York.
4. loved children.

46. Why do you think Mum Bett chose the surname of Freeman?

1. that was her name at birth
2. she took Thomas Sedgwick's wife's last name
3. her daughter suggested it
4. to celebrate her freedom

EXAM ONE, PASSAGE EIGHT

47. After moving in with her daughter, Elizabeth

1. continued her duties at the Sedgwick's.
2. became a nurse and midwife.
3. served as a house servant.
4. had to retire due to illness.

48. According to the passage, why did Mum Bett leave Colonel Ashley's estate?

1. Colonel Ashley freed her.
2. She was too old to handle the physical chores.
3. His wife tried to hit Mum Bett's sister.
4. She wanted to live with her daughter.

EXAM ONE, PASSAGE EIGHT

We have found that different non-verbal signals and gestures are used in various cities. Understanding the fact that there are differences can keep one out of embarrassing situations.

Recently, while flying from Atlanta to New York, we encountered this phenomenon in a discussion with a very gracious lady who was from the South. She disliked going to New York City because of the supposed indifference that people displayed toward others. "Moreover," she said, "I especially don't enjoy not being looked at and made to feel that I don't exist. Why, in the South, we take the time to look at people and, as you know, to smile at them." Indeed, it has been observed that Peachtree St. in Atlanta is a location where one is smiled at often. We explained to our new acquaintance that individuals' nonverbal signals vary from city to city and region to region.

In densely populated areas such as New York City and Tokyo, people give the impression that they are disregarding one another. A newcomer might take their gestures to mean complete indifference. Yet studies conducted to determine how people in crowded cities react during a time of crisis—such as the 1965 New York power blackout—reveal that an overwhelming majority respond by helping others in need. These "good Samaritans" with hard-shell exteriors show their true colors at such times. In less densely populated areas where individuals depend on each other more and Southern hospitality prevails, signals

#53

#54

such as smiles, winks, and a warm "hey" are commonplace. A New Yorker, however, would probably be taken aback if greeted in this manner by a stranger.

49. The authors of this article are most probably

1. tour guides.
2. public relations agents.
3. geographers.
4. sociologists. discuss group behavior

50. The author's tone is

1. mostly nostalgic.
2. a bit ironic.
3. chatty and informal. quotations, interjections, contractions
4. somewhat persuasive.

51. The phrase, taken aback, found in the last sentence, is best defined as

1. stunned. Contrast: however
2. insulted.   w/ Southern hospitality
3. angry.
4. contented.

52. The authors of this passage would most likely agree that

1. Southerners are too friendly.
2. recognizing and understanding gestures is a valuable tool in communication.
3. people from densely populated cities are worthless during a crisis.
4. due to their hard-shell exteriors, New Yorkers are standoffish.

EXAM ONE, PASSAGE NINE

53. The woman whom the writers met on the airplane

1. was on her way to Tokyo.
2. had just spent a month in New York City.
3.)was going to New York City.
4. had just finished touring Peachtree Street area in Atlanta.

54. The phrase, <u>overwhelming majority</u>, as underlined in the passage, refers to

1. New Yorkers.
2. others in need.
3. Southerners.
4.) people in a crowded city.

EXAM ONE, PASSAGE NINE

The reforms and foreign policy of King Mongut of Thailand were carried out by his son and successor. King Rama V came to the throne as a frail youth of sixteen and died one of Thailand's most loved (and) revered kings. He had a remarkable reign of 42 years. Indeed, modern Thailand may be said to be a product of the comprehensive and progressive reforms of his reign. For these touched almost every aspect of Thai life.

King Rama V faced the Western world with a positive and eager attitude: eager to learn about Western ideas and inventions, positively working towards Western-style "progress" while at the same time resisting Western rule. He was the first Thai king to travel abroad; he did not just travel as an observer or tourist but worked hard during his trips to further Thai interests.

The King also traveled within his own country. He was passionately interested in his subjects' welfare and was intent on the monarchy assuming a more visible role in society. He wanted to see how his subjects lived and went outside his palace often, sometimes incognito—and was never recognized. His progressive outlook led him to his first official act, forbidding prostration (the requirement to lie face down) in the royal presence. He gradually abolished the institution of slavery, a momentous and positive change for Thai society.

With so many achievements to his credit and a charisma that was enhanced by his longevity, it was no wonder that the Thai people grieved long and genuinely for King Rama V when he died. October 23, the date of his death, is still a national holiday, in honor of one of Thailand's greatest and most beloved kings.

1. revered, as used in the passage, is best defined as

1. honored.
2. tolerated.
3. unpopular.
4. aged.

2. The first official act by King Rama V was

1. traveling abroad.
2. visiting his subjects around the country.
3. making his birthday a national holiday.
4. forbidding prostration.

3. The author gets his point across through the use of

1. statistical and factual documentation.
2. persuasive language.
3. respectful and admiring language.
4. impartial narrative and dialogue.

4. incognito, as used in the passage, most nearly means

1. apparent.
2. disguised.
3. unaccompanied.
4. escorted.

5. The main idea of the passage is

1. Rama V was not as good a king as his father, King Mongut.
2. the king traveled abroad as well as within his own country of Thailand.
3. a national holiday is celebrated in honor of King Rama V.
4. Rama V was one of Thailand's most loved and revered kings.

EXAM TWO, PASSAGE ONE

6. According to the passage, what was Rama V's attitude toward the West?

1. admiring but cautious.
2. bitter and distrustful.
3. apathetic and indifferent.
4. mocking and sarcastic.

EXAM TWO, PASSAGE ONE

After work one day I set out for the ballpark; I wanted to catch a Giants game. I marched out to the bleachers only to find them completely full. It was standing room only, six deep in fans. Discouraged, I turned back, hoping food would help. Passing up the hot dog kiosks, I bought a roasted squid on a stick.

The Yomiuri Giants were playing the Nippon Ham Fighters. The players bowed to each other—the game was about to begin. I glanced up at the electronic scoreboard that displayed (in Chinese characters) all the players' names and a vast array of information, including wind direction, speed, and team names. Actual team names were not taken from their geographic headquarters but rather from the companies that owned them, such as the Yomiuri news firm that owned the Giants, or the Hanshin railway company who were the owners of the Hanshin Tigers. But who in the world, I wondered, would want to be owned by the Nippon Ham Company?

The noise surged as the game began, with cheerleaders prancing atop the dugout roofs, exhorting their teams. They flailed the air with pompoms and banners in the teams' colors, and beat an ancient native drum. The noise level of the sections of "home" and "away" rooters reminded me more of American college football than baseball. Horns blared, people howled, toilet paper and confetti streamers arched through the night sky.

EXAM TWO, PASSAGE TWO

Several more differences from American baseball practices were glaring: every time a foul or a home run carried the ball into the riotous stands, it was politely returned to the #12 field. Also, no matter how obvious, the official scorers virtually refused to charge fielders with errors. Propriety prevailed, even amidst hysteria.

7. We can assume from the passage that the writer

1. had never been to a Japanese baseball game. he was stunned by all the
2. had limited experience at sports "odd" protcols events.
3. was agreeably impressed with the Japanese fans' enthusiasm.
4. thought that the Japanese protocols should be adopted by American baseball teams.

8. According to the passage, Japanese baseball teams are named after

1. their geographic headquarters.
2. famous Japanese samurai.
3. the manager's choice of names.
4. the companies that own them.

9. The purpose of the passage is to

1. describe.
2. entertain.
3. define.
4. explain.

10. According to the passage, when the writer marched out to the bleachers

1. they were empty.
2. only half of the seats were taken.
3. only fans rooting for the Nippon Ham Fighters were at the game.
4. they were crammed full.

11. When the author asks "But who in the world, I wondered, would want to be owned by the Nippon Ham Company?" he is

1. asking an academic question.
2. showing respect.
③ being sarcastic.
4. criticizing Japanese industry.

12. As used in the last sentence, propriety most likely means

① good manners.
2. indecency.
3. hysteria.
4. corruption.

EXAM TWO, PASSAGE TWO

Most school psychologists and counselors feel that the family is the most significant, single influence on the development of the child. The family is the primary structure that provides the developing human being with his or her attitudes, beliefs, values, and sense of self. Educational researchers have shown that persistence and academic performance are strongly related to family background and interactions.

The school system is probably the second most important structured environment that influences the developing human being. When a student is having difficulty adapting to the school system, the school system's intervention plans have, for the most part, tried to influence the individual student while ignoring the most significant influence in the student's life—the family.

From the family-systems perspective, many of these school intervention programs (such as punishments and individual or group counseling) are doomed to failure. This is especially true if the family's influence and value system are different from the school system's intended behavior change. For example, the school may try to stop a student from fighting at school, while the parent's message to the child is, "Don't let anyone push you around. Stand up for yourself." From the family-systems perspective, it is imperative that the family be involved if you wish to see more effective and enduring behavioral changes at school. #18

13. According to the passage, the most significant influence on the development of a child is

1. a favorite teacher.
2. the school environment.
3. the family.
4. siblings.

14. In the context of this passage, if a child does well in school, it is most likely a result of

1. cramming.
2. the family environment.
3. the school atmosphere.
4. studying with a tutor.

15. The author would probably agree that if a child is having problems with school work

1. the child should go to after school classes.
2. the child should change to a private school.
3. after-school punishment should be required.
4. school teachers should speak with the child's primary caretaker at home.

16. It can be inferred from the passage that the writer

1. believes in punishment.
2. is in favor of group counseling.
3. has been a principal.
4. is an advocate of the family-systems perspective.

17. The word structure as used in the first paragraph most nearly means

1. group framework. family is a group
2. edifice.
3. arrangement.
4. construction.

EXAM TWO, PASSAGE THREE

18. Which of the following sentences from the passage best expresses the main idea?

1. The school system is probably the second most important structured environment that influences the developing human being.
2. It is imperative that the family be involved if you wish to see more effective and enduring behavioral changes at school.
3. When a student is having difficulty adapting, the school's intervention plans have tried to influence the student while ignoring the family.
4. This is especially true if the family's value system is different from the school system's intended behavior change.

#23

Conrad Hilton, founder of Hilton hotels and father to Paris, started with only a dream—no money—just a big, big dream. But he did what most people are not willing to do. He added action, and turned his imagination into a plan. He gave the plan details, scheduled the details, and made alternate plans in case the first plan failed. Most importantly, he put his plan into action and made it come true. Hilton believed that if you don't dream big, you certainly won't achieve much. One of the basic laws that governs man is: unless you can visualize something, you cannot attain it.

Amazing as it sounds, the great majority of people in the U.S. don't spend even an hour a week, pencil in hand, planning a strategy for their financial future. Hilton once said, "Most people are so busy earning a living, they never make any money." And it's true!

As soon as the typical American has a small amount of money saved, he is tempted to spend it on depreciating assets such as cars, camping, boats, or trailers which devalue as you drive them off the lot. Most spend their entire lives saving just enough to buy something to keep up with their neighbors. They never have enough left over to make meaningful investments.

To belong to that exclusive group of millionaires, the one out of a thousand, you must begin by following the Rule of Ten Percent. Any increase in the Ten Percent Rule speeds you on the way to making your fortune. The rule is a simple one, but a difficult one for some individuals to follow:

you must save a minimum of 10% of your gross earnings. The second part of the rule is that you never, never spend that savings!

19. One of the major points of the selection is

1. most people make enough money to live "the good life."
2. most Americans spend their money on boats or trailers.
3. most Americans have a plan, but they do not execute it.
4. if you don't dream big, you certainly won't achieve much.

20. According to the selection, the reason the typical American can not save is that

1. s/he is tempted to spend it on depreciating assets.
2. relatives are always borrowing from her/him.
3. s/he gives it to neighbors.
4. her/his attitude of "I made it, so I can spend it on whatever I want."

21. depreciating assets, as underlined in the passage, most nearly means

1. reductions.
2. run down vehicles.
3. items decreasing in value. *definition by ex.*
4. valued means of transportation.

22. The style of writing employed by the author is

1. formal and staid.
2. chatty and informal. *use of contractions*
3. humorous and entertaining. *quotations*
4. somber and depressing. *exclamation points*
   use of "you"

EXAM TWO, PASSAGE FOUR

23. When Conrad Hilton initiated his first plan
of action, he

1. did not have much imagination,
   but did have a lot of capital to invest.
2. had no alternate Plan B because he
   was so sure Plan A would work.
3. was indifferent to the outcome.
4. had no money.

24. The last paragraph leaves the reader
with a sense of

1. glamor.
2. helplessness.
3. encouragement. gives reader a plan to save money
4. pride.

EXAM TWO, PASSAGE FOUR

In the nineteenth century, children lived alongside adults in Illinois' poor houses, asylums, and jails. By 1899, several issues moved social reformers to institute a juvenile court in Chicago—the nation's first separate court for children:

1) Prosecutors attempted to hold youthful offenders (between the ages of seven and 14) responsible for their crimes as adults;

2) If convicted, such juveniles would be incarcerated with an adult prison population; and

3) as in ten cases before 1900, juveniles were executed.

Consequently, in 1899 Illinois legislation gave courts jurisdiction over juveniles who were charged with crimes as well as over children who were neglected. It also provided for confidentiality in regard to the youthful offender's records. In another protective step, the act required the separation of juveniles from adults when incarcerated and barred the detention of juveniles under 12 years old in jails altogether.

On the other hand, in addition to the usual run of adult crimes, children could be charged with offenses such as truancy, habitual delinquency, and sexual delinquency. The creation of a distinct process for minors presented only a small victory for the reformers. The court relied heavily upon institutionalization rather than the family preservation initially envisioned by reformers.

In 1965 the state legislature overhauled the Illinois Juvenile Court Act, giving significant legal protections to minors, including the provision of a public defender. During the next decade, however, public opinion demanded harsher treatment. A 1982 revision to the Illinois Habitual Juvenile Offender Act decreed that any juvenile aged 15 or older (charged with murder, armed robbery, or sexual assault) face prosecution as an adult in criminal court, and if convicted be committed to the Illinois Department of Corrections.

In 1997 in Cook County alone, #29 between 1,500 and 2,000 cases were heard every day, representing 25,000 active delinquency and 50,000 active abuse and neglect cases.

25. The word incarcerated most nearly means

1. acquitted.
2. involved.
3. imprisoned.
4. executed.

26. The authors convey their point by

1. defining the word "juvenile."
2. describing the Illinois state legislature.
3. giving a testimonial.
4. presenting facts and legal information.

27. The reader can deduce from the information that the 1982 revision was a result of pressure from

1. state legislature.
2. the public.
3. federal judges.
4. reformers.

EXAM TWO, PASSAGE FIVE

28. Which of the following was not given as a
reason for changing the criminal court system in
Chicago?

1. juveniles were being jailed with the
   adult population.
2. thousands of children had been *process of elimination*
   executed.
3. children as young as seven were
   prosecuted as adults
4. there was no confidentiality for the
   youthful offenders' records.

29. The main focus of the last paragraph is

1. how difficult it is to charge parents
   with neglect.
2. how expensive it is to prosecute so
   many juvenile cases..
3. that there are not enough attorneys to
   handle all the juvenile cases.
4. that there is an overwhelming number
   of active delinquent and neglect
   cases.

30. Most probably the authors are

1. journalists.
2. criminologists.
3. state senators.
4. experts on prison systems.

EXAM TWO, PASSAGE FIVE

"Open the shutters, will you?"

The bowed head next to her bed snapped erect, and she heard the sound of rosary beads clattering to the floor.

"My lady—?"

"The shutters. Open them, please." Through the small, high window, she could see a sliver of moon glinting hard and clear; the sky was drenched silver with stars. She blinked feebly, and when she looked again, they had retreated, playful and aloof, beyond her grasp once more.

How long had she lain there? Weeks? Perhaps only days. She did not know, nor did she care enough to ask. Earlier this evening after prayers, the nun who sat by her bed had suddenly gasped and run to fetch the board and stick. She heard her race through the cloister, furiously beating the death board.

Heloise laughed to herself. She was not ready; she would not be hurried. For so long she had hungered to embrace this moment, prayed for it, ached with anticipation, and now that the time had arrived, she felt no need to hurry. Somehow she had lived through sixty-three summers, playing her tedious roles in the convent, forever smiling, never allowing the world to glimpse the real woman.

Quickly, she corrected herself. To him she had sometimes revealed her true self—sometimes. But even he could not accept her. The letters, those shameless shreds, those offerings of truth delivered up to his aghast silence; her hands clutched the coverlet in stinging memory. Ah, my very sweet

friend, she thought, you didn't understand my love. In the end you learned to love God, and even, in your own way, to love me. #36

31. The phrase, this moment, refers to the moment

1. Heloise turned sixty-three.
2. Heloise fell in love.
3. of death.
4. Heloise heard the sound of the death board.

32. We can infer from the passage that the setting is

1. day time.
2. before evening prayers.
3. night time.
4. weeks after Heloise became ill.

33. According to the passage, Heloise is

1. at a funeral home.
2. at a monastery.
3. in an infirmary.
4. in a convent.

34. The phrase death board, as under-lined in the passage, refers back to

1. prayers.
2. board and stick.
3. the nun.
4. Heloise.

35. The reader can infer from the passage that "he"

1. answered all of Heloise's letters.
2. could not read.
3. did not receive Heloise's letters.
4. never answered Heloise's letters.

EXAM TWO, PASSAGE SIX

36. The main idea of the last paragraph
is

1. the elderly nun's love for "him" was not returned in the way she had wanted.
2. due to her illness, the elderly nun was always having to correct herself.
3. every time the elderly nun remembered him, she felt a sense of peace.
4. the thought of the letters was the only thing that pulled the elderly nun through times of crisis.

There are some very real differences between fathers and mothers in terms of their involvement with a child. In general, research shows that compared to mothers, fathers spend less time with the children. In 1983 Pleck reported that employed fathers with children less than five years old spend an average of 27 minutes once per day in care giving or other activities with their children. This may not be because fathers work outside of the home. Even when both parents are home, fathers generally spend less time with children than mothers. Even when a mother works outside of the home, fathers only spend about one-third the time that mothers spend in parenting activities.

Why the disparity? One reason for the lack of involvement by fathers may be due to resistance by the mothers! Only 23 per cent of employed mothers and 31 percent of unemployed mothers stated that they wanted more help from fathers. In the study, it was concluded that the mothers were reluctant to share their role with the fathers.

In regard to punishment of children—whoever is administering it—many psychologists believe physical punishment, such as spanking or hitting should not be used at all. Physical punishment modifies the behavior of the child in the short run, but its use is also associated with many negative outcomes.

The first and most serious outcome of punishment is an increase in aggression, especially among boys. For example, parents who used punishment and threats had more aggressive sons than

those who did not use such techniques. Second, parents who use physical punishment may serve as models of aggressiveness for their children. Third, children may learn that violence is an acceptable method for resolving conflicts rather than employing other methods. Last, children who are punished frequently avoid the person who does the punishing.

37. The purpose of the first two paragraphs is to

1. compare employed mothers with unemployed mothers.
2. contrast mothers' and fathers' involvement in child-related activities.
3. persuade the reader that 27 minutes a day is enough time to spend with a child.
4. argue that fathers are better parents than mothers.

38. According to the passage, who spends the least amount of time with their children?

1. fathers.
2. mothers.
3. employed fathers.
4. employed mothers.

39. According to the passage, the reason spanking should not be used at all is because

1. it leaves physical scars and bruises.
2. it is illegal.
3. its use is associated with many negative outcomes.
4. the child will not love the father.

EXAM TWO, PASSAGE SEVEN

40. The overall purpose of the last two
paragraphs is to

1. contrast.
2. show cause-effect. *lists 4 outcomes of physical punishment*
3. illustrate.
4. describe.

41. The most serious outcome of using physical
punishment is that

1. there is an increase in aggression in
   the child.
2. there is a dramatic risk of brain
   damage.
3. the child will learn that aggression is
   an acceptable method for resolving
   problems.
4. the parent may go to prison.

42. In the Pleck study, how many minutes a day
does an employed father spend in activities
focusing on his children?

1. 23
2. 31
3. 27
4. zero

EXAM TWO, PASSAGE SEVEN

In the process of growing up, and in the process of living itself, it is all too easy for us to become isolated from (or never to form) a positive self-concept. In addition, we may never reach a joyful vision of ourselves because of the negative input from others. Further, we may never have positive self-esteem because we have defaulted on our own honesty, integrity, and/or responsibility. Our self-concepts may have been ruined because we did not stand up for what we believed was right. Last, we may have judged our own actions with inadequate understanding and compassion which resulted in a poor self-image.

Apart from problems that are biological in origin, I cannot think of a single psychological difficulty—from anxiety and depression to alcohol or drug abuse, to underachievement at school to suicide—that is not traceable to poor self-esteem. Of all the judgments we pass, none is as important as the one we pass on ourselves. Positive self-esteem is a requirement of a fulfilling life.

Let us understand what self-esteem is. It has two components, a feeling of personal competence and feeling of personal worth. In other words, self-esteem is the sum of self-confidence and self-respect. It reflects several aspects:

1. your ability to cope with the challenges of your life
2. your ability to understand your problems;

3. your right to be happy; and
4. your ability to respect and stand up for your needs

Genuine self-esteem is not expressed by self-glorification at the expense of others; it is not expressed by the quest to make oneself superior to others; and it is not expressed in order to diminish others so as to elevate oneself.

43. The pattern of organization utilized in paragraph one is

1. comparison.
2. cause-effect. *causes of low self-esteem*
3. example.
4. narration.

44. Positive self-esteem involves all of the following except

1. the sum of self-confidence and self-respect.
2. a sense of personal worth.
3. a feeling of personal competence.
4. self-glorification at the expense of others. *and process of elimination*

45. In the fourth paragraph, the phrase at the expense of most nearly means

1. paid for by.
2. by withdrawing from. *semi-colon; then,*
3. without regard for. *next sentence*
4. by sharing with.

46. The author of this piece is probably

1. a psychologist. *topic of self-esteem*
2. a nurse. *falls under the purview*
3. an educator. *of psychology*
4. a high school principal.

EXAM TWO, PASSAGE EIGHT

47. Some people never attain a positive self-concept because

1. the process of growing up is all too easy.
2. they treat themselves with compassion.
3. they ignore the opinions of others.
4. they do not stand up for what they know to be right behavior.

48. Which of the following affects an individual's self-esteem most?

1. school experiences
2. the way one sees oneself
3. the media
4. parental guidance

EXAM TWO, PASSAGE EIGHT

They were hoping for a son. It was a daughter. The future Catherine II of Russia was born at Stettin on April 21, 1729. She was given the names Sophie Augusta Fredericka Catherine. The young mother, Johanna, was distressed that she had not been able to produce a boy and spent little time watching over the cradle.

The mother was convinced that with her beauty and worldly wisdom she could have achieved a higher destiny. Instead of the brilliant rise she had once dreamed of, she had to be content with a husband of modest position. It was her family who had arranged the match, without consulting her. At fifteen, she had married Prince Christian Augustus, a man twenty-seven years her senior. Truly a person of no great importance, he was one of those obscure princes in the fragmented Germany of the eighteenth century. Her husband was a major general in the Prussian army. This worthy man, devoted to order, thrift, and religion, surrounded Johanna with affection, but that was far from enough to satisfy her. Johanna had a passion for worldly intrigue and chafed at holding so poor a place in society.

Fortunately, shortly after Catherine was born, the family was able to move into the fortified castle of Stettin. It was a small promotion. The following year, there was another piece of good news— Johanna at last gave birth to a boy. God had heard her prayers! She lavished the affection and pride she had denied her daughter upon the infant.

EXAM TWO, PASSAGE NINE

Catherine, still very young, suffered bitterly from her mother's preference for the newcomer.

49. The word, modest, as used in the selection most nearly means

1. famed.
2. worldly.
3. ordinary. *contrast w/brilliant rise*
4. shy.

50. The focus of this passage is

1. Johanna.
2. Catherine the Great.
3. the Prince.
4. Stettin.

51. Johanna's attitude toward the Prince was one of

1. adoration.
2. passion.
3. sincerity.
4. bitterness.

52. The reader can infer from the passage that Catherine's mother was

1. kind and sympathetic.
2. indifferent and impartial.
3. nostalgic and homesick.
4. self-centered and spoiled.

53. According to the passage, Johanna preferred

1. her husband to her children.
2. court life over her family.
3. her daughter to her husband.
4. her son to her daughter.

54. The phrase chafed at as underlined in the selection most likely means

1. raged at. *Cause-effect.*
2. accepted. *since she did not get what*
3. ignored. *she wanted, she raged*
4. excelled at. *at her poor position in society.*

"Who are *they*?" I asked the girl from my Spanish class, whose name I'd forgotten.

#7

As she looked up to see who I meant (though already knowing, probably, from my tone), he suddenly looked at my neighbor, then his dark eyes flickered to mine.

He looked away quickly. I dropped my eyes at once. In that brief flash of a glance, his face held nothing of interest.

My class mate giggled in embarrassment. "Well, Bella, that's Edward and Emmett Cullen, and Rosalie and Jasper Hale. The one who left the table was Alice Cullen; they all live together with Dr. Cullen and his wife." She said this under her breath.

I glanced sideways at the beautiful boy, who was looking at his tray now.

Strange, unpopular names, I thought. The kind of names grandparents had. But maybe that was in vogue here.

"They are . . . . very nice-looking." I struggled with the conspicuous understatement.

"Yes!" she agreed with another giggle. "And, they *live* together!" Her voice held shock and condemnation.

"Which ones are the Cullens?" I asked. "They don't look related . . ."

"Oh, they're not. Dr. Cullen is really young, in his twenties or early thirties. They're all adopted. The Hales are foster children."

"They look a little old for foster children."

"They are now, Jasper and Rosalie are both eighteen, but they've been with Mrs. Cullen since they were eight. She's their aunt."

"That's really kind of nice—for them to take care of all those kids like that."

#5 "I guess so," my class mate admitted reluctantly.

Throughout this conversation, my eyes flickered again and again to the table where the strange family sat. They continued to look at the walls and not eat.

1. The passage suggests that Bella

1. is in love with the boy.
2. is frightened of the family sitting across the room.
3. will have some interaction with the family in the near future.
4. does not like her class mate.

2. The overall pattern of organization employed by the author is

1. contrast and comparison.
2. scholarly writing.
3. graphic description.
4. narration and storyline. quotation marks dialogue

3. The reader can infer from the selection that

1. the family had been hypnotized.
2. there is something unnerving about the family.
3. Mrs. Cullen does not love her niece and nephew.
3. the teens of the family were named after their grandparents.

4. The selection suggests that Bella's class mate was shocked that

1. the Hale and Cullen teens lived together.
2. Bella did not know the family.
3. Dr. Cullen was so young.
4. Bella had forgotten her name.

POST TEST, PASSAGE ONE

5. The passage implies that Bella's class mate

1. had a crush on Jasper Hale.
2. (circled) did not think so highly of Dr. Cullen and his wife.
3. was not interested in discussing the family sitting across the room.
4. thought the names of the teens sitting across the room were odd.

6. The phrase <u>in vogue</u> in the passage most nearly means

1. modelling.
2. unfashionable.
3. (circled) trendy. *contrast "here" to where*
4. lawful. *Bella was from*

7. This conversation takes place

1. at a restaurant.
2. in Spanish class.
3. (circled) in the school cafeteria.
4. at the Cullen home.

POST TEST, PASSAGE ONE

"Slow" was born in 1831 in what is now South Dakota, the only son of a Sioux warrior. He earned the name because as an infant he was careful and deliberate by nature. But when he had counted his first coup on a Crow enemy, his father gave him a new name given in a vision—"Sitting Bull."

Sitting Bull rose rapidly in tribal esteem. He gained a reputation as a prophet and a man who spoke with spirits. By twenty-five he had been elected to an elite military society called the Strong Hearts. A few years later he became a chief at the same time that whites first began to move into tribal lands. Asked to sign a treaty that would have ceded some Sioux lands but kept much of their range, Sitting Bull said, "I wish all to know that I do not propose to sell any part of my country."

A new confrontation occurred. The Black Hills, sacred to the Sioux and a part of lands guaranteed them by treaty, were discovered to contain gold in 1874. Within a year, hundreds of miners were trespassing on Sioux land. The government responded by ordering the Indians out of the land and launching an expedition against those Sioux, Cheyenne, and Arapaho who stayed. Sitting Bull forged an alliance, warning that "we must stand together or they will kill us separately." As the warriors gathered, Sitting Bull went through a sacrificial Sun Dance and saw a vision of soldiers falling into the camp. He prophesied a great victory. On June 26, 1876, braves from the main camp overran and slaughtered Lt. Colonel Custer's 264 men, the greatest Army defeat in the Indian wars.

[handwritten margin notes: #13, #13, #15, #13, #14]

POST TEST, PASSAGE TWO

8. The phrase coup on in the first paragraph most nearly means

1. war on.
2. overthrow of. *new name indicates a victory*
3. truce with.
4. failure from.

9. The government broke its treaty with the Sioux nation because

1. gold was discovered on Sioux lands.
2. Sitting Bull could not get along with leaders of the Crow nation.
3. the Strong Hearts attacked miners.
4. the Sioux banded together with the Cheyenne and Arapaho.

10. Most probably Sitting Bull's warrior-father felt

1. elated about his son.
2. ashamed of his son.
3. apathetic toward his son.
4. doting toward his son.

11. The main idea of the first paragraph is that Sitting Bull

1. was deliberate and careful as a child.
2. gained a reputation as a prophet.
3. was a great warrior but not an effective chief.
4. made a major transformation from childhood to manhood. *from "Slow" to "Sitting Bull" Bull = strength*

12. The word ceded, as used in the passage, most nearly means

1. negotiated.
2. acquired.
3. relinquished. *contrast w/ "kept"*
4. retained.

13. The author's attitude toward Sitting Bull is

1. disdainful.
2. somber.
3. deferential.
4. impartial.

14. Sitting Bull prophesized that

1. he would become Chief.
2. there would be a victory in the battle against Lt. Colonel Custer.
3. he would offer lands to the Government.
4. gold would be discovered on Sioux lands.

15. Whites first started moving onto tribal lands

1. a few years after Sitting Bull reached his twenty-fifth birthday.
2. in 1831.
3. around 1874.
4. after Lt. Colonel Custer had defeated the Sioux.

POST TEST, PASSAGE TWO

Jondalar slowly became aware that he was awake, but caution made him lie still until he could sort out what was wrong, because something most certainly was. For one thing, his head was throbbing.

He opened his eyes a crack. There was only dim light, but enough to see the cold, hard-packed dirt he was lying on. Something felt dried and caked on the side of his face, but when he attempted to reach up and find out what it was, he discovered that his hands were tied together behind his back. His feet were tied together, too.

He looked around. He was inside a small round structure, a kind of wooden frame covered with skins, which he sensed was inside a larger enclosure: there were no sounds of wind, no drafts, no billowing of the hides. Though it was cool, it wasn't freezing. He suddenly realized that he was no longer wearing his fur parka.

He became alert when he heard the sound of voices drawing near. Two women were speaking an unfamiliar language.

"Hello out there. I'm awake," he called out, in his language. "Will someone come and untie me? I'm sure there has been a misunderstanding. I mean no harm."

The entrance flap was thrown back, and through the opening he saw a figure standing, feet apart and hands on hips. She issued a sharp command. Two women entered the enclosed spaced, lifted him up, dragged him out, and propped him up. #21

The woman looked at him for a

moment or two and then she laughed. #20 It was harsh and dissonant—a jarring curse of a sound. Jondalar felt a shudder of fear. His vision blurred, and he #22 weaved unsteadily. Then suddenly, the woman turned on her heel and stalked out. The women who were holding him up dropped him and followed her.

16. The reader can infer from the passage that

1. the women were there to help Jondalar recover.
2. the two women who lifted Jondalar were sisters of the other woman.
3. it had been warm weather for several months.
4. Jondalar had received a blow to his head.

17. The reader can conclude that Jondalar

1. had been rescued by the women.
2. respected the leader of the women.
3. was a prisoner of the women.
4. had threatened the women.

18. When he called for help Jondalar's tone was one of

1. humility.
2. arrogant.
3. resentment.
4. anger.

19. Jondalar knew that he was in an enclosed structure within a larger structure because

1. he could see through the flap.
2. there were no sounds of wind or : colon drafts.
3. he had been in a similar structure before
4. the women told him.

POST TEST, PASSAGE THREE

20. The word <u>dissonant</u> in the last paragraph most nearly means

1. harmonious.
2. apathetic.
3. discordant.
4. empathetic.

21. The two women who came into the enclosure most likely

1. were guards.
2. tried to help Jondalar.
3. did not agree with the woman.
4. were prisoners, too.

22. The purpose of the last paragraph is to

1. expose the jealously of the female leader.
2. explain how Jondalar ended up with the women.
3. confound the reader.
4. leave the reader with a sense of suspense.

POST TEST, PASSAGE THREE

Have you read or heard about cases where, under the influence of hypnosis, people were able to remember occurrences of which they had previously reported no recollection? Have you read or heard about cases where in the course of therapy, individuals recover memories of abuse of which they were previously unaware? These examples are all consistent with a view of memory that many individuals hold.

According to this view, memory is like a recording device, faithfully maintaining a detailed record of situations we have experienced.

Remembering an experience, then, is a case of pushing the right playback button and accessing the appropriate section of the tape, so that the experience can be re-experienced just the way it originally happened. That is, memory not only faithfully records what really happened, but it also faithfully plays the experience back once it is accessed. We often, without much conscious effort, remember events in great detail, and the truthfulness of these memories seems beyond doubt. We are highly confident that the event or experience we are recounting occurred and that the details we are providing are in fact correct.

Unfortunately, some research on memory indicates that it is not like a recording device. In fact, Lynn and Payne (1997) have suggested that a more appropriate way to conceive of memory is as "the theater of the past."

#27 According to this view, memory is not a simple recording of what actually happened, but rather a dynamic, imperfect reconstruction of the past. In this view, memory may be influenced by our present needs, beliefs, and expectancies as well as by stored information.

23. According to the passage, which is not true about memory?

1. It takes great effort to remember events in great detail.
2. Memory faithfully maintains a detailed record of experiences.
3. Memory can play back experiences just the way they originally happened.
4. When we recount our experiences, we believe the details we are providing are correct.

24. Lynn and Payne suggested that

1. memory is not a simple recording of what actually happened.
2. memory can be compared to a recording device.
3. a person just needs to push the right playback button to access their experiences.
4. "the theater of the past" is not a valid view of the workings of memory.

25. The purpose of the first paragraph is to

1. interest the reader by asking thought-provoking questions
2. introduce two different views of memory.
3. define the term "recollection."
4. explain how the process of hypnosis aids memory.

POST TEST, PASSAGE FOUR

26. The word, <u>accessing</u> as used in the context
of the third paragraph most nearly means

1. logging on.
2. opening. *CC = "and"*
3. experiencing.
4. expunging.

27. The phrase, "the theater of the past" most
nearly means

1. descriptive, dramatic scenes.
2. an accurate historic account.
3. an imperfect reconstruction of the
   past.
4. a dynamic stage.

POST TEST, PASSAGE FOUR

483

In Europe when the Second World War broke out, John F. Kennedy wrote an honors thesis, "Why England Slept," discussing the dangers of unpreparedness. It was published and sold well. After graduation Kennedy toyed with the idea of careers in journalism or business, but American entry into the war intervened.

After initially being turned down because of a back injury suffered in his Harvard football days, Kennedy was accepted into the Navy. While in command of PT 109 on patrol in the Pacific in August, 1943, a Japanese destroyer came out of the fog and sliced his boat in two. Kennedy led his surviving eleven men to an island three miles away, towing one of them by a life jacket strap held in his teeth. After their rescue Kennedy got a medal for bravery ("It was involuntary," he later said dryly, "they sank my boat"). He was in the hospital for months with a ruined back. It never properly healed.

While recovering, he learned that his brother Joe had been killed during a special Air Force mission in Europe. When asked later if he made a career of politics to appease his father and replace his older brother, Kennedy said no. "But I never would have run for office if he had lived."

28. According to the passage, Kennedy's published thesis

1. was a fiasco.
2. was a success.
3. was the impetus for a career in journalism.
4. was banned for criticizing England.

29. According to the selection, during the war, Kennedy fought against

1. the Nazis.
2. Germans.
3. the English.
4. the Japanese.

30. The reader can infer that Kennedy thought that

1. he was indeed a hero.
2. he would recover fully from his back injury.
3. his brother would be the politician in the family.
4. his father forced him into politics.

31. The selections implies that Kennedy

1. wanted to be in the Air Force, not the Navy.
2. must have suffered with back pain throughout his presidency.
3. was not a particularly strong swimmer.
4. tried to avoid enlisting in the military.

32. The word appease, as used in the context of the last paragraph, most nearly means

1. contradict.
2. provoke.
3. placate.
4. substitute for.

POST TEST, PASSAGE FIVE

33. One purpose of the second paragraph is to

1. give background on Kennedy's days
   at Harvard.
2. contrast Kennedy to his older brother,
   Joe.
3. suggest that Kennedy's back injury
   kept him from a career in the Air
   Force.
4. show that Kennedy was a humble and
   unpretentious man. *his response shows that he did not consider himself a hero*

POST TEST, PASSAGE FIVE

Tsunamis are referred to as seismic sea waves. They are encountered in ocean regions that are affected by plate movements, especially where seismic and submarine volcanic disturbances are frequent. It is not surprising, therefore, that throughout history these waves have brought death and destruction to many islands and coastal communities. This is especially so within the realms of the Pacific and the Mediterranean Sea. It is also easy to understand that such waves, often following earthquakes, are called seismic sea waves even though not all of them are caused by such disturbances.

After the energy of a disturbance is transmitted to the water, wave energy begins to travel just as in any wave system. However, it is important to realize that tsunami waves, even though they move through deep oceans, behave like shallow-water waves. The reason for this is their great length, which may exceed 100 miles. Whether an ocean wave is classified as a deep-water or shallow-water wave depends on the relationship between its length and the depth of the water through which it passes.

The tsunami is frequently visualized as a single wave, but more correctly the tsunami is a wave system that spreads out from a point of energy release. A number of waves may originate from such a source with wave periods of 10 to 20 minutes, or longer. This means that a given coast may be exposed to a series of tsunamis arriving at considerable time intervals. The first wave does not have to be the highest one. It is possible that subsequent waves are much more dangerous.

34. What is the author's tone toward the subject matter of the passage?

1. objective *matter-of-fact style*
2. subjective *no emotional words*
3. defiant *utilized*
4. frantic

35. The purpose of the first paragraph is to

1. analyze how tsunami waves move.
2. describe the term "tsunami." *repitition of topic*
3. relate that all tsunamis are caused by *w/explanation* earthquakes.
4. alert the reader that the first wave may not be the highest one.

36. The word submarine in the first paragraph most nearly means

1. underwater. *word structure*
2. on land.
3. oceanic.
4. coastal.

37. The author of this selection would agree that

1. because earthquakes are rare, tsunamis are rare.
2. people on the coast should evacuate inland to high ground if a tsunami is imminent.
3. the traditional way of thinking that tsumanis are related to plate movements has been proven invalid.
4. tsumanis occur more often in the realm of the Atlantic Ocean.

38. The main idea of the third paragraph is that

1. tsunamis can last 20 minutes or longer.
2. the last wave is the most dangerous.
3. there is a misconception that tsunami is a single wave, but it is a wave system.
4. shallow-water waves are as destructive as deep-water waves.

POST TEST, PASSAGE SIX

In sponsoring an "ideal" society of the colony of Georgia , the English trustees had three practical motives.

First, they wished to relieve the worthy poor in Great Britain. To them, this meant removing destitute but deserving persons from the streets of London and other British cities, where they were a burden to society, and sending them to Georgia, where they could earn a living.

An old legend, now demolished, held that Georgia was a refuge for debtors from the harshness of English prisons. However, in truth, probably not more than a dozen of those unfortunates ever went to the province directly from prison. Prospective settlers leaving England aboard the *Anne* were interviewed to differentiate between the worthy poor and those not worthy; never again was a group so meticulously selected.

The second motive was that the trustees wished the colony to play a role in Great Britain's trade policy. It was widely believed that Georgia could produce silk and wine, which Englishmen at the time were compelled to buy at great expense. First and foremost, Georgia was to be a colony of and for small farmers. All settlers were expected to work, there being an insufficient number of white servants and no black slaves. Great plantations were to have no place, resting as they did upon massive landholding and the institution of slavery.

The third motive was military.

The new colony would be a buffer for South Carolina, which was always threatened by the Spaniards in Florida.

39. All of the following were reasons why the colony of Georgia was established except

1. to produce tobacco.
2. as a military buffer.
3. as a settlement of small farmers.
4. to give relief to the poor in Britain.

40. The word refuge as underlined in the second paragraph most nearly means

1. depository.
2. state.
3. reformatory.
4. sanctuary.

41. It can be inferred from the passage that during initial settlement of the colony

1. great plantations were necessary for economic survival.
2. slavery was not part of the plans for Georgia.
3. England could not help the colony because they had great expenses of their own.
4. most of the settlers died from starvation.

42. We can infer from the passage that

1. Spaniards were in Florida as well as in South Carolina.
2. England regarded Spain as a potential enemy. "*threatened*"
3. Spain had a stronger military than England.
4. the Spaniards discovered Georgia soil before the English.

POST TEST, PASSAGE SEVEN

43. The purpose of the passage is to

1. persuade the reader that Georgia's first settlers were not criminals.
2. narrate the story of the Georgia Colony and its people.
3. explain the reasons why England founded the colony of Georgia. *First sentence*
4. describe Georgia's relationship with Great Britain, particularly with England.

44. As underlined in the passage, <u>meticulously</u> most nearly means

1. carefully.
2. randomly.
3. grandly.
4. diversely.

POST TEST, PASSAGE SEVEN

488

The rise of the middle class, a consequence of the prosperity created by the long post-war economic boom, meant that the children of the 1950's and 1960's did not have to leave school to help support their families. By the late 1960's almost 60 million Americans were in school full-time, as many as were working full-time. When educational personnel were included, 30 per cent of the entire population of the nation participated in education. This made education the biggest business in the U.S., at least in terms of number of people involved. Everyone attended through age 15, three-fourths graduated from high school, and one-half of those went on to college.

From a psychological perspective, an important result of these trends was a breakdown in authoritarian discipline. The new and great abundance of American society spelled the end of a scarcity culture, which in turn meant that discipline was no longer economi-cally necessary. Put simply, father no longer had to decide who got what, since there was enough to go around. The unfortunate consequence was a pervasive increase in permissive-ness. Each child was more likely to have his or her own room. Coupled with an increased divorce rate, which meant a loss of family cohesion, these trends produced a child-centered society where the child was more likely to be individualistic.

The psychological characteristic of this youth culture was ambivalent tensions. The youth culture refused

adult socialization, maintaining a sense of separation and uniqueness. This in turn produced rebellion against parental authority and a consequent generation gap.

45. It can be inferred from the passage that the permissive style of parenting of the 1960's

1. brought about more respect for parents from children.
2. resulted in more criminal behavior from teenagers.
3. created a more intelligent child population.
4. caused breakdowns in relationships between parents and children.

46. As used in the passage, abundance most nearly means

1. philosophy.
2. technology.
3. quantity.
4. wealth. *contrast to "scarcity"*

47. Which statement about the content of the passage is not true?

1. After the war, one half of high school graduates went on to college.
2. America of the 1960's was a child-centered society.
3. Pre-war, education was the biggest business in the United States. *process of elimination*
4. During the 1960's, children did not have to leave school to work.

48. The author's style of writing is

1. informal.
2. unbiased. *facts; observed psychological perspective*
3. riveting.
4. argumentative.

POST TEST, PASSAGE EIGHT

49. Which technique is not used in the passage?

1. statistics and facts   *process of elimination*
2. cause-effect
3. academic writing
4. definition

POST TEST, PASSAGE EIGHT

The service ended, and little by little the congregation dispersed. It was a relief to have Conner appear and invite him to dinner.

Dannan was not the only guest invited for Sunday dinner. The four Muldoons still in town were there, as were the Weber family and Judson Best.

"So tell us, Dannan," Conner invited during the meal, "what do you hear from the doctor you replaced, Doc MacKay?"

"Uncle Jonas? I just had a letter from him. He is enjoying being back home. The house is roomy enough for him and my father, and they each have their own bit of space. I guess they're getting along together quite nicely."

"Will your folks visit you here, Dannan?" Allison wished to know.

"My mother's health doesn't allow her to travel, and my father hates to leave her, so probably not."

"Has your mother been ill long?" the preacher asked.

"About five years. She fell while hiking with my father and injured her back. Sitting for long periods is excruciating."

Most of the heads at the table nodded. It was certainly easy to see why his mother could not travel.

"She's an amazing woman," Dannan felt a need to add, looking at the compassion on Hillary Muldoon's face. "She doesn't spend a moment pitying herself, and because we write to each other almost weekly, I never feel out of touch."

Conversation drifted to Judson, who was working part-time for Will Barland who grew a broomcorn crop. That

business was expanding to the point that Judson was helping Will ship brooms across New England.

Judson's charismatic way of describing his job had everyone entranced. Indeed, they were still enjoying his anecdotes when Troy rose from the group to answer the knock on the front door. #52

50. The word excruciating, most nearly means

1. exhausting.
2. agonizing. cause-effect
3. monotonous.
4. exasperating.

51. Doc MacKay was Dannan's

1. father.
2. mentor.
3. mother.
4. uncle.

52. The reader can infer that the paragraph that follows the passage focuses on

1. the visitor at the door.
2. more of Judson's anecdotes.
3. Dannan's mother's back injury.
4. Dannan's adjustment to his new job.

53. Dannan's relationship with his mother is

1. strained and awkward.
2. cordial and courteous.
3. volatile and capricious.
4. devoted and steadfast.

54. As used in the passage, charismatic most nearly means

1. graphic.
2. sinister.
3. captivating. direct explanation:
4. modest. "entranced"

POST TEST, PASSAGE NINE

APPENDIX G: CHAPTER SOURCES*

UNIT ONE

CHAPTER ONE: OVERVIEW

University System of Georgia, Board of Regents' Web site. Internet address: www.gsu.edu/~www.rtp/ index94.html. Retrieved: June 27, 2008.

CHAPTER TWO: VOCABULARY

Morgan, Tom. *Saints*. San Francisco: Chronicle Books, 1994.

Rowling, J. K. *Harry Potter and the Prisoner of Azkaban*. New York: Scholastic Press, 1999.

Southwick, C. H. *Global Ecology in Human Perspective*. Oxford: Oxford University Press, 1996.

Tolkien, J. R. R. *The Lord of the Rings: The Fellowship of the Rings*. New York: Ballantine Books, 1955.

Tolkien, J. R. R. *The Lord of the Rings: The Two Towers*. New York: Ballantine Books, 1955.

CHAPTER THREE: LITERAL COMPREHENSION

Berg, Aimee. "Dara Torres: Three Decades of Excellence." *USOC News*. teamusa.org/news/articles/ 2245. Retrieved: July 6, 2008.

Dickinson, Terrence. *Nightwatch: A Practical Guide to Viewing the Universe*. Ontario: Firefly Books, 2006.

Gendercide Watch. "Case Study: Honour Killings and Blood Feuds." www.gendercide.org/case_honour.html. Retrieved July 4, 2008.

Kendallhunt.com. "On-line Catalogue for Higher Education: Sociology." Retrieved: July 7, 2008.

O'Neill, Ann. "Stolen kids turned into terrifying killers." www.conn.com/2007/WORLD/africa/01/12/ childsoldiers/index.html. Retrieved: July 4, 2008.

Pickert, Kate. "Stepdaddy's Little Girl." www.nymag,.com/nymetro/news/people/features/11672. Retrieved: July 5, 2008.

Roadsideamerica.com. "Offbeat Landmarks in Georgia." www.roadsideamerica.com. Retrieved: July 5, 2008.

Willis, Dominic. "Will Smith Biography." www.tiscali.co.uk/entertainment/film/biographies/ will_smith_ biog.html. Retrieved: July 7, 2008.

---

*Some passages were adapted to facilitate reading.

CHAPTER FOUR: INFERENCE

BBC. "Chinese Foot Binding." October 22, 2003. Retrieved from: http://www.bbc.co.uk/dna/
/ h2g2/ A1155872, October 5, 2009.

Ellyson, Steve L., et al. *General Psychology*. Third edition. Dubuque: Kendall Hunt Publishing
Company, 2008.

Fort, Cornelia. "At the Twilight's Last Gleaming." *Women's Home Companion*, July, 1943.

Gregory, Phillipa. *The Other Boleyn Girl*. London: Simon & Schuster, 2001.

Gurian, Michael. *The Wonder of Boys*. New York: Penguin Putnam, 1997.

Hoffman, Matthew. *Book of Home Remedies for Dogs and Cats*. New York: Bantam Books, 1996.

Hynes, H. A. "China: the Emerging Superpower." www.fas.org/nuke/guide/china/doctrine/0046.htm.
Retrieved: July 18, 2008.

Salem, Dorothy C. The *Journey: A History of the African American Experience*. Dubuque: Kendall Hunt
Publishing, 1997.

Seton, Anya. *Katherine*. New York: Houghton Mifflin, 1954.

The Virtual Museum of the City of San Francisco. "Special Shoes For Bound-feet Women Now
a Thing Of The Past." Retrieved from: http://www.sfmuseum.net/ chin/foot.html, October 5, 2009.

Wassman, Rose and Lee Ann Rinsky. *Effective Reading in a Changing World*. Englewood Cliffs: Prentice-
Hall, Inc. 1993.

CHAPTER FIVE: ANALYSIS

Works Cited

AmeriCorps. www.americorps.org/for_individuals/choose/vista.asp. Retrieved: July 21, 2008.
Arnold, Wendy. *Historic Hotels of Scotland: A Select Guide*. San Francisco: Chronicle Books, 1988.

Easton, James. 'Rendlesham Revelations." *Fortean Times,* November 2001. www.forteantimes.com/features/
articles/257/rendlesham_revelations.html.

Ebert, Charles H. V. *Disasters*. Second edition. Dubuque: Kendall/Hunt Publishing Company,   1993.

Frisancho, A. Roberto. *Humankind Evolving: An Exploration of the Origins of Human Diversity*. Dubuque:
Kendall Hunt Publishing Company, 2006.

Gabaldan, Diana. *Outlander: A Novel*. New York: Random House, 1991.

Globalsecurity.org. "Improvised Explosive Devices (IEDs)/Booby Traps."
www.globalsecurity.or/military/intro/ied-indicators.htm. Retrieved: July 29, 2008.

Gurian, Michael. *The Wonder of Boys*. New York: Penguin Putnam, 1997.

IEEEVM. "Japanese Women and the Japanese War Effort." www.ieee-virtual-museum.org/collection/event.
php?id=3457006&1id=1. Retrieved: July 21, 2008.

Lerner, Harriet. *The Dance of Anger*. New York: Harper & Row, 1985.

MacDonald, Richard. *Thinking Sociologically: Social Scripts and Everyday Life*. Dubuque: Kendall Hunt Publishing Company, 2006.

Mobtown Blues. "Why I Plan to Vote for Barack Obama, No Matter What You Say." www.mobtownblues.typepad.com/mobtownblues/2007/02/it_was_sunny_an.html Retrieved: July 30, 2008.

Natural Resources Defense Council (NRDC). "Artic Melting Threatens Polar Bears."www.polarbearsos .org/polarmoreinfo.html. Retrieved: July 21, 2008.

Osborn, Liz. "Current Results: Key Discoveries About Our Environment." www/currentresults.com/ Weather-Extremes/US/oldest.php. Retrieved: July 25, 2008.

Plaidy, Jean. *Charles II*. London: Robert Hale, 1972.

Robbins, Tom. *Another Roadside Attraction*. New York: Bantam Books, 1971.

Seton, Anya. *Avalon*. Boston: Houghton Mifflin, 1965.

Solberg, Curtis, David Morris and Anthony Koeninger. *A People's Heritage: Patterns in U.S. History*. Second edition. Dubuque: Kendall/Hunt Publishing Company, 2000.

U.S. Department of Health and Human Services. "About Human Trafficking." Last updated, January 24, 2008. www.acf.hhs.gov/trafficking/about/index.html. Retrieved: July 21, 2008.

Zukav, Gary. Soul Stories. New York: Simon & Schuster, 2000.

References

ABC Entertainment news. "Celebs Step Up, Politics Slaps 'Em Down. http://abcnews.go.com/ Entertainment/WNT/story?id=2614629&page=1. Retrieved July 24, 2008.

CNN Political Ticker. Politicalticker.blogs.cnn.com/2007/07/16/celebs-add-star-powerp-to-08-donor-lists. Retrieved July 23, 2008.

Lichtig, Aaron. "When college athletes don't belong in college." *Yale Herald*, October 15, 1999.

New York Times. "Sports People: Football: Not a Happy Day." *New York Times*, December 18, 1992.

New York Times. "College Athletes 'Pros:' Two Michigan Men Who Played Baseball for Money Under Ban." *New York Times*, June 18, 1915.

CHAPTER SIX: READING RATE

Works Cited

Chopra, Deepak. *Quantum Healing*. London: Bantam Books, 1989.

Ebert, Charles H. V. *Disasters*. Second edition. Dubuque: Kendall/Hunt Publishing Company, 1993.

Halpern, Howard. *How to Break Your Addiction to a Person.* New York: Bantam, 1982

Knox, G. M. *New Decorating Book.* Des Moines: Meredith Corporation, 1981.

Kraus, Nicola and Emma McLaughlin. *The Nanny Diaries.* London: Penguin Books, 2002.

Mintz, Stephen. "Eye on John Brown." History Now: American History On-Line, 5, September, 2005. www. historynow.org/09_2005/historian6.html. Retrieved: July 21, 2008.

New York Times. "141 Men and Girls Die in Waist Factory Fire." *New York Times*, March 26, 1911, p. 1.

Niven, L. and B. Cooper. *Building Harlequin's Moon.* New York: Tom Doherty Assoc., 2005

Scheffel, R. L. *The ABCs of Nature.* New York: Reader's Digest, 1988.

Yeager, Selene. *The Doctors Book of Food Remedies.* Emmaus, PA: Rodale Press, 1998.

UNIT TWO*

DIAGNOSTIC EXAM

Works Cited

Dorenkamp, Angela, John F. McClymer, Mary M. Maynikan, and Arlene C. Vadum. *Images of Women in American Popular Culture.* New York: Harcourt, Brace, and Jovanivich, 1985.

McQuade, Walter and Ann Alkman. *Stress.* New York: Bantam Books, 1975.

O'Brien, Alexandra. "Death in Ancient Egypt." *Research Archives.* Chicago: The Oriental Institute, 1999. Retrieved from www.-oi.uchicago.edu/OI/DEPT/RA/ABZU/DEATH.

Pipher, Mary. *Reviving Ophelia. Saving the Selves of Adolescent Girls.* New York: Ballantine Books, 1994.

Robertson, Ian. *Sociology.* Third Edition. New York: Worth Publishers, Inc., 1987.

Shawl, Stephen, et al. *Discovering Astronomy.* Fifth edition. Dubuque: Kendall Hunt Publishing Company, 2006.

WWF (World Wildlife Fund). "Polar Bear Subpopulations around the Arctic." Retrieved August 4, 2008 from www.panda.org/about_wwf/where_we_work/europe/what_we_do/ arctic/polar_bear/about_the_bears/habitat/index.cfm.

Wallace, Ian. *Reflections on Scotland.* Norwich: Jarrold Publications, 1988.

Wilkins, David, et al. *Art Past, Art Present.* Second edition. Englewood Cliffs: Prentice Hall, 1994.

References

Sunday Times. "Polar bears drown as ice shelf melts." December 18, 2005.

EXAM ONE

Works cited

Bowen, John R. *Religions in Practice: An Approach to the Anthropology of Religion.* Boston: Allyn and Bacon, 1998.

Fawcett, Susan and Alvin Sandberg. *Evergreen with Reading.* Fourth edition. Boston: Houghton Mifflin, 1992.

Gray, Robert. "140 years later, Sultana disaster still haunts historians." Retrieved from: www.roundabout madison.com. Kentuckiana Publishing, Inc., 2008.

---

*Some passages were adapted to facilitate reading.

Greenburg, Edward S. *The American Political System.* Fifth edition. Boston: Scott Foresman and Company, 1989

Keboe, Thomas, et. al. *Exploring Western Civilization to 1648.* Dubuque: Kendall Hunt Publishing Company, 1997.

King, Betty. *The Captive James.* London: Herbert Jenkins, 1967.

Lappe, Frances Moore and Joseph Collins. *World Hunger: Twelve Myths.* New York: Grove Weidenfeld, 1986.

Nierenberg, Gerald and Henry Calero. *How to Read a Person Like a Book.* New York: Pocket Books, 1971.

Salem, Dorothy C. *The Journey.* Dubuque: Kendall Hunt Publishing Company, 1997.

References

Alchin, L. K. *"Middle Ages."* Retrieved August 7, 2008 from http://www.middle-ages.org.uk/index.htm.

EXAM TWO

Works Cited

Branden, Nathaniel. *How to Raise Your Self-Esteem.* New York: Bantam Books, 1987.

Couto, Richard, et al. *Mending Broken Promises: Justice for Children at Risk.* Dubuque: Kendall Hunt Publishing Company, 2000.

Haroldsen, Mark O. *How to Wake Up the Financial Genius Inside You.* Toronto: Bantam Books, 1984.

Katzenstein, Gary. *Funny Business.* New York: Prentice-Hall, 1989.

Kestner, Jane, et al. *General Psychology.* Dubuque: Kendall Hunt Publishing Company, 2001.

Meade, Marion. *Stealing Heaven: The Love Story of Heloise and Abelard.* New York: Soho Press Inc., 1979.

Office of the Prime Minister. *Thailand in the 90s.* Royal Thai Government, 1991.

Troyat, Henri. *Catherine the Great.* Trans by Joan Pinkham. New York: E. P. Dutton, 1980.

Valentine, Michael R. *Difficult Discipline Problems: A Family-Systems Approach.* Dubuque: Kendall Hunt Publishing Company, 1988.

References:

Dodge, L. Mara. "Juvenile Justice Reform." *Encyclopedia of Chicago*. Retrieved from: www. Encyclopedia.chicagohistory.org/pages/683.html. August 17, 2008.

EXAM THREE

Works Cited

Arthur, L. Based on "Stonehenge, England," by Martin Gray. Retrieved from: www. sacredsites.com/europe/england/stonehenge.html. August 17, 2008; and "The Georgia Guidestones: Nuberg, Georgia." Retrieved from: www. msnbc.msn. com /id/12739940/. August 17, 2008.

Downhower, Jerry F. and Dana L. Wrensch. *Knowing Ourselves: Human Biology and Evolution*. Dubuque: Kendall Hunt Publishing Company, 1992.

Ebert, Charles, H. V. *Disasters*. Second edition. Dubuque: Kendall Hunt Publishing Company,

Fraser, Antonia. *The Lives of the Kings and Queens of England*. New York: Alfred A. Knopf, 1975.

Goldberg, Herb. *The Hazards of Being Male*. New York: Signet Books, 1977.

Hunt, Lynn et. al. *The Challenge of the West*, Volume Two. Toronto: D. C. Heath and Company.

Martin, James, et al. *America and Its Peoples*. New York: Addison Wesley Longman, Inc., 1997.

Norton, Mary Beth et al., *A People and a Nation, Vol. II: Since 1865*. Third edition. Copyright by Houghton Mifflin Company. Used with permission.

Smith, Catherine. "Mies Van der Rohe: Architect as Visionary." Paper completed for Department of Art, University of Georgia, 2001

References

"Maryhill, Washington." Retrieved from hometown.aol.com/Gibson0817/maryhill.htm. August10, 2008.

"Stonehenge, England." Retrieved from: www.sacredsites.com/europe/england/stonehenge.html. August 10, 2008.

EXAM FOUR

Amling, Frederick. *Investments: An Introduction to Analysis and Management*. Englewood Cliffs: Prentice Hall, Inc., 1965.

Downhower, Jerry F. and Dana L. Wrensch. *Knowing Ourselves: Human Biology and Evolution*. Dubuque: Kendall Hunt Publishing Company, 1992.

Layton, Donald. *World War II: A Global Perspective.* Dubuque: Kendall Hunt
      Publishing Company, 1998.

McCarter, L. Gilbert. *Living with Art.* Second edition. New York: Alfred A Knopf, Inc., 1988.

Runyan, Milton A. and Violma F. Bergane (eds.). *Around the USA in 1,000 Pictures.* Garden
      City: Nelson Doubleday, Inc., 1955.

Schiamberg, Lawrence B. *Child and Adolescent Development* by. New York: MacMillan
      Publishing Company, 1988.

Solberg, Curtis, David Morris and Anthony Koeninger. *A People's Heritage: Patterns in U.S.
      History.* Second edition. Dubuque: Kendall/Hunt Publishing Company, 2000.

Wallace, Ann and Gabrielle Taylor. *Royal Mothers.* London: Judy Piatkus Publishers Limited,
      1987.

White, E. B. *Charlotte's Web.* New York: Harper and Row, Publishers, 1952.

EXAM FIVE

Allen, Lee M. and Richard T. Saeger. *Georgia State Politics: The Constitutional Foundation*
      Second edition. Dubuque: Kendall/Hunt Publishing Company, 1994.

Beliefnet. "Top 15 Inspirational Olympic Moments." Retrieved from: www.beliefnet.com/
      gallery/inspirationalolympicmoments.html. September 5, 2008. Reprinted with permission.

Brown, Dan. *Deception Point.* New York: Simon & Schuster, Inc., 2001.

Ferrier, Neil (ed.). *Churchill—Man of the Century.* New York: Doubleday and Company, 1965.

Francis, Grant R. *Scotland's Royal Line, The Tragic House of Stuart.* London: J. Murray, 1928.

Keller, David. "Shanghaied!" *American Heritage Magazine.* Vol. 46, 5, September 1995.

MacDonald, Richard. *Thinking Sociologically: Social Scripts and Everyday Life.* Dubuque:
      Kendall Hunt Publishing Company, 2006.

Solberg, Curtis, David Morris and Anthony Koeninger. *A People's Heritage: Patterns in U.S.*

      History. Second edition. Dubuque: Kendall/Hunt Publishing Company, 2000.

EXAM SIX

Artistwd. "Bringing Them Home: The 'Stolen Generation' Report. Part 2, Tracing the History.
      Retrieved from: www.artistwd.com/joyzine/australia/stolen_gen/index.php, September,
      2008.

Auel, Jean. *The Mammoth Hunters*. New York: Crown Publishers, Inc., 1985.

BBC News. "The Agony of Australia's Stolen Generation." Retrieved from: http://news.bbc.co.uk/go/pr/fr/-/2/hi/asia-pacific/6937222.stm. August 9, 2007.

Coelho, Paulo. *The Alchemist*. New York: Harper Collins, 1993.

Council for Ethics in International Policy. "The Stolen Generation: Aborginal Children in Australia," by Danielle Celermajer. Human Rights Dialogue: "Cultural Rights," Series 2, 12 (Spring 2005).

Frisancho, A. Roberto. Humankind *Evolving: An Exploration of the Origins of Human Diversity*. Dubuque: Kendall Hunt Publishing Company, 2006.

Friedman, Dina, et al. *Inside Business Writing*. Dubuque: Kendall Hunt Publishing Company, 2006.

Levi, Primo. *Survival in Auschwitz: The Nazi Assault on Humanity*. New York: Simon & Schuster, 1996.

MacDonald, Richard. *Thinking Sociologically: Social Scripts and Everyday Life*. Dubuque: Kendall Hunt Publishing Company, 2006.

NASA. "Description and Purpose of the International Space Station." Retrieved from: www.boeing.com/defense-space/space/spacestation/index.html. September 26, 2008.

EXAM SEVEN

Berendt, John. *Midnight in the Garden of Good and Evil: A Savannah Story*. New York: Random House, 1994.

Ebert, Charles, H. V. *Disasters*. Second edition. Dubuque: Kendall Hunt Publishing Company, 1993.

Ellyson, Steve L., et al. *General Psychology*. Third edition. Dubuque: Kendall Hunt Publishing Company, 2008.

Kestner, Jane, et al. *General Psychology*. Dubuque: Kendall Hunt Publishing Company, 2001.

Layton, Donald. *World War II: A Global Perspective*. Dubuque: Kendall Hunt Publishing Company, 1998.

Lockwood, Max. "Women deserve equal partnership in work," *The Claxton Enterprise*. Claxton, Georgia, March 4, 1999.

Shawl, Stephen, et al. *Discovering Astronomy*. Fifth edition. Dubuque: Kendall Hunt Publishing Company, 2006.

van Blerkom, Dianna. *College Study Skills: Becoming a Strategic Learner*. Belmont: Wadsworth Publishing Company, 1994.

Wall, Steve and Harvey Arden. *Wisdomkeepers: Meetings with Native American Spiritual Elders.* Hillsboro, Oregon; Beyond Words Publishing, 1990.

EXAM EIGHT

Ceaser, James W. *American Government: Origins, Institutions, and Public Policy.* Seventh edition. Dubuque: Kendall Hunt Publishing Company, 2002.

Ebert, Charles H. V. *Disasters.* Second edition. Dubuque: Kendall/Hunt Publishing Company, 1993

Kestner, Jane, et al. *General Psychology.* Dubuque: Kendall Hunt Publishing Company, 2001.

Layton, Donald. *World War II: A Global Perspective.* Dubuque: Kendall Hunt Publishing Company, 1998.

Levey, Judith S. and Agnes Greenhall, eds. *The Concise Columbia Encyclopedia.* New York: Columbia University Press, 1983.

Roohk, Bonita and Arnold J. Karpoff. *Introducing Biology.* Dubuque: Kendall Hunt Publishing Company 1990.

Seton, Anya. *Katherine.* Boston: Houghton Mifflin Company, 1954.

Solberg, Curtis, David Morris and Anthony Koeninger. *A People's Heritage: Patterns in U.S. History.* Second edition. Dubuque: Kendall/Hunt Publishing Company, 2000.

Sorrell, R. and Carl Francese. *From Tupelo to Woodstock: Youth, Race and Rock & Roll in America, 1954-1969.* Dubuque: Kendall Hunt Publishing Company.

ushistory.com "Disasters, The 1930s." Retrieved from: http://www.u-s-history.com/pages/h1583.html. June 24, 2009.

EXAM NINE

Adams, Thomas M. *Concepts of Health-Related Fitness.* Dubuque: Kendall/Hunt Publishing Company, 2002.

Ebert, Charles, H. V. *Disasters.* Second edition. Dubuque: Kendall Hunt Publishing Company, 1993.

Frisancho, A. Roberto. *Humankind Evolving: An Exploration of the Origins of Human Diversity.* Dubuque: Kendall Hunt Publishing Company, 2006.

Kennedy, J. F. *Profiles in Courage.* New York: Harper & Row Publishers, 1956.

Layton, Donald. *World War II: A Global Perspective.* Dubuque: Kendall Hunt Publishing Company, 1998.

MacDonald, Richard. *Thinking Sociologically: Social Scripts and Everyday Life*. Dubuque: Kendall Hunt Publishing Company, 2006.

Mayes, Frances. *Under the Tuscan Sun*. New York: Broadway Books, 1997.

McConnell, James V. "Nirvana" in *Understanding Human Behavior*. New York: Holt, Rinehart and Winston, Inc., 1974.

Roohk, Bonita and Arnold J. Karpoff. *Introducing Biology*. Dubuque: Kendall Hunt Publishing Company 1990.

POST TEST

Auel, Jean. *The Plains of Passage*. New York: Crown Publishers, Inc., 1990.

Davis, Harold E. *The Fledgling Province: Social and Cultural Life in Colonial Georgia, 1733-1766*. Chapel Hill: The University of North Carolina Press, 1976.

Ebert, Charles, H. V. *Disasters*. Second edition. Dubuque: Kendall Hunt Publishing Company, 1993.

Kestner, Jane, et al. *General Psychology*. Dubuque: Kendall Hunt Publishing Company, 2001.

Meyer, Stephenie. *Twilight*. Boston: Little, Brown and Company. 2005.

Solberg, Curtis, David Morris and Anthony Koeninger. *A People's Heritage: Patterns in U.S. History*. Second edition. Dubuque: Kendall/Hunt Publishing Company, 2000.

Sorrell, R. and Carl Francese. *From Tupelo to Woodstock: Youth, Race and Rock &Roll in America, 1954-1969*. Dubuque: Kendall Hunt Publishing Company.

Wick, Lori. *Leave a Candle Burning*. New York: Thomson Gale, 2006.

APPENDIX H: SCANTRONS

PRE-TEST: DIAGNOSTIC EXAM

LAST NAME	FIRST NAME	MI

Name grid bubbles: A–Z for each letter position (Last Name, First Name, MI)

1 ① ② ③ ④ 11 ① ② ③ ④ 21 ① ② ③ ④ 31 ① ② ③ ④ 41 ① ② ③ ④ 51 ① ② ③ ④

2 ① ② ③ ④ 12 ① ② ③ ④ 22 ① ② ③ ④ 32 ① ② ③ ④ 42 ① ② ③ ④ 52 ① ② ③ ④

3 ① ② ③ ④ 13 ① ② ③ ④ 23 ① ② ③ ④ 33 ① ② ③ ④ 43 ① ② ③ ④ 53 ① ② ③ ④

4 ① ② ③ ④ 14 ① ② ③ ④ 24 ① ② ③ ④ 34 ① ② ③ ④ 44 ① ② ③ ④ 54 ① ② ③ ④

5 ① ② ③ ④ 15 ① ② ③ ④ 25 ① ② ③ ④ 35 ① ② ③ ④ 45 ① ② ③ ④

6 ① ② ③ ④ 16 ① ② ③ ④ 26 ① ② ③ ④ 36 ① ② ③ ④ 46 ① ② ③ ④

7 ① ② ③ ④ 17 ① ② ③ ④ 27 ① ② ③ ④ 37 ① ② ③ ④ 47 ① ② ③ ④

8 ① ② ③ ④ 18 ① ② ③ ④ 28 ① ② ③ ④ 38 ① ② ③ ④ 48 ① ② ③ ④

9 ① ② ③ ④ 19 ① ② ③ ④ 29 ① ② ③ ④ 39 ① ② ③ ④ 49 ① ② ③ ④

10 ① ② ③ ④ 20 ① ② ③ ④ 30 ① ② ③ ④ 40 ① ② ③ ④ 50 ① ② ③ ④

SKILLS ANALYSIS

Vocabulary	Literal Comprehension	Inference	Analysis
3, 6, 8, 11, 17, 21, 22, 28, 34, 38, 47, 51	2, 7, 10, 24, 25, 31, 33, 40, 44, 46, 48, 50, 52, 53, 54	5, 13, 15, 16, 18, 19, 23, 29, 30, 37, 39, 41, 43, 45	1, 4, 12, 14, 20, 26, 27, 32, 35, 42, 49
	Main Idea	**Main Idea** 9, 36	

EXAM ONE

1 ① ② ③ ④   11 ① ② ③ ④   21 ① ② ③ ④   31 ① ② ③ ④   41 ① ② ③ ④   51 ① ② ③ ④

2 ① ② ③ ④   12 ① ② ③ ④   22 ① ② ③ ④   32 ① ② ③ ④   42 ① ② ③ ④   52 ① ② ③ ④

3 ① ② ③ ④   13 ① ② ③ ④   23 ① ② ③ ④   33 ① ② ③ ④   43 ① ② ③ ④   53 ① ② ③ ④

4 ① ② ③ ④   14 ① ② ③ ④   24 ① ② ③ ④   34 ① ② ③ ④   44 ① ② ③ ④   54 ① ② ③ ④

5 ① ② ③ ④   15 ① ② ③ ④   25 ① ② ③ ④   35 ① ② ③ ④   45 ① ② ③ ④

6 ① ② ③ ④   16 ① ② ③ ④   26 ① ② ③ ④   36 ① ② ③ ④   46 ① ② ③ ④

7 ① ② ③ ④   17 ① ② ③ ④   27 ① ② ③ ④   37 ① ② ③ ④   47 ① ② ③ ④

8 ① ② ③ ④   18 ① ② ③ ④   28 ① ② ③ ④   38 ① ② ③ ④   48 ① ② ③ ④

9 ① ② ③ ④   19 ① ② ③ ④   29 ① ② ③ ④   39 ① ② ③ ④   49 ① ② ③ ④

10 ① ② ③ ④   20 ① ② ③ ④   30 ① ② ③ ④   40 ① ② ③ ④   50 ① ② ③ ④

SKILLS ANALYSIS

Vocabulary	Literal Comprehension	Inference	Analysis
3, 11, 17, 22, 30, 32, 39, 51	1, 8, 9, 10, 14, 15, 20, 24, 27, 28, 33, 37, 40, 47, 48, 53, 54	4, 6, 7, 13, 18, 23, 25, 34, 41, 43, 44, 45, 46, 49, 52	2, 5, 12, 16, 19, 21, 26, 31, 35, 38, 42, 50
	Main Idea 29	Main Idea 36	

EXAM TWO

LAST NAME | FIRST NAME | MI

(Name grid bubbles: blank, A–Z for each column)

1 ① ② ③ ④   11 ① ② ③ ④   21 ① ② ③ ④   31 ① ② ③ ④   41 ① ② ③ ④   51 ① ② ③ ④

2 ① ② ③ ④   12 ① ② ③ ④   22 ① ② ③ ④   32 ① ② ③ ④   42 ① ② ③ ④   52 ① ② ③ ④

3 ① ② ③ ④   13 ① ② ③ ④   23 ① ② ③ ④   33 ① ② ③ ④   43 ① ② ③ ④   53 ① ② ③ ④

4 ① ② ③ ④   14 ① ② ③ ④   24 ① ② ③ ④   34 ① ② ③ ④   44 ① ② ③ ④   54 ① ② ③ ④

5 ① ② ③ ④   15 ① ② ③ ④   25 ① ② ③ ④   35 ① ② ③ ④   45 ① ② ③ ④

6 ① ② ③ ④   16 ① ② ③ ④   26 ① ② ③ ④   36 ① ② ③ ④   46 ① ② ③ ④

7 ① ② ③ ④   17 ① ② ③ ④   27 ① ② ③ ④   37 ① ② ③ ④   47 ① ② ③ ④

8 ① ② ③ ④   18 ① ② ③ ④   28 ① ② ③ ④   38 ① ② ③ ④   48 ① ② ③ ④

9 ① ② ③ ④   19 ① ② ③ ④   29 ① ② ③ ④   39 ① ② ③ ④   49 ① ② ③ ④

10 ① ② ③ ④   20 ① ② ③ ④   30 ① ② ③ ④   40 ① ② ③ ④   50 ① ② ③ ④

SKILLS ANALYSIS

Vocabulary	Literal Comprehension	Inference	Analysis
1, 4, 12, 17, 21, 25, 45, 49, 54	2, 8, 10, 13, 20, 23, 28, 31, 33, 34, 38, 39, 41, 42, 44, 47, 53	5, 6, 7, 11, 14, 15, 16, 19, 24, 27, 30, 32, 35, 46, 48, 51, 52	3, 9, 22, 26, 37, 40, 43
	Main Idea 18	Main Idea 29, 36, 50	

EXAM THREE

1 ① ② ③ ④   11 ① ② ③ ④   21 ① ② ③ ④   31 ① ② ③ ④   41 ① ② ③ ④   51 ① ② ③ ④

2 ① ② ③ ④   12 ① ② ③ ④   22 ① ② ③ ④   32 ① ② ③ ④   42 ① ② ③ ④   52 ① ② ③ ④

3 ① ② ③ ④   13 ① ② ③ ④   23 ① ② ③ ④   33 ① ② ③ ④   43 ① ② ③ ④   53 ① ② ③ ④

4 ① ② ③ ④   14 ① ② ③ ④   24 ① ② ③ ④   34 ① ② ③ ④   44 ① ② ③ ④   54 ① ② ③ ④

5 ① ② ③ ④   15 ① ② ③ ④   25 ① ② ③ ④   35 ① ② ③ ④   45 ① ② ③ ④

6 ① ② ③ ④   16 ① ② ③ ④   26 ① ② ③ ④   36 ① ② ③ ④   46 ① ② ③ ④

7 ① ② ③ ④   17 ① ② ③ ④   27 ① ② ③ ④   37 ① ② ③ ④   47 ① ② ③ ④

8 ① ② ③ ④   18 ① ② ③ ④   28 ① ② ③ ④   38 ① ② ③ ④   48 ① ② ③ ④

9 ① ② ③ ④   19 ① ② ③ ④   29 ① ② ③ ④   39 ① ② ③ ④   49 ① ② ③ ④

10 ① ② ③ ④   20 ① ② ③ ④   30 ① ② ③ ④   40 ① ② ③ ④   50 ① ② ③ ④

SKILLS ANALYSIS			
Vocabulary	Literal Comprehension	Inference	Analysis
5, 8, 19, 25, 40	2, 4, 6, 9, 11, 12, 13, 14, 15, 17, 22, 23, 26, 28, 29, 31, 32, 34, 39, 41, 45, 46, 51, 52, 54	3, 10, 16, 18, 20, 21, 30, 38, 42, 47, 48, 49, 53	1, 7, 24, 33, 37, 43, 50
	Main Idea 35	Main Idea 27, 36, 44	

EXAM FOUR

1 ① ② ③ ④   11 ① ② ③ ④   21 ① ② ③ ④   31 ① ② ③ ④   41 ① ② ③ ④   51 ① ② ③ ④

2 ① ② ③ ④   12 ① ② ③ ④   22 ① ② ③ ④   32 ① ② ③ ④   42 ① ② ③ ④   52 ① ② ③ ④

3 ① ② ③ ④   13 ① ② ③ ④   23 ① ② ③ ④   33 ① ② ③ ④   43 ① ② ③ ④   53 ① ② ③ ④

4 ① ② ③ ④   14 ① ② ③ ④   24 ① ② ③ ④   34 ① ② ③ ④   44 ① ② ③ ④   54 ① ② ③ ④

5 ① ② ③ ④   15 ① ② ③ ④   25 ① ② ③ ④   35 ① ② ③ ④   45 ① ② ③ ④

6 ① ② ③ ④   16 ① ② ③ ④   26 ① ② ③ ④   36 ① ② ③ ④   46 ① ② ③ ④

7 ① ② ③ ④   17 ① ② ③ ④   27 ① ② ③ ④   37 ① ② ③ ④   47 ① ② ③ ④

8 ① ② ③ ④   18 ① ② ③ ④   28 ① ② ③ ④   38 ① ② ③ ④   48 ① ② ③ ④

9 ① ② ③ ④   19 ① ② ③ ④   29 ① ② ③ ④   39 ① ② ③ ④   49 ① ② ③ ④

10 ① ② ③ ④   20 ① ② ③ ④   30 ① ② ③ ④   40 ① ② ③ ④   50 ① ② ③ ④

SKILLS ANALYSIS

Vocabulary	Literal Comprehension	Inference	Analysis
2, 7, 9, 15, 21, 29, 33, 39, 44, 45, 52	4, 6, 11, 13, 14, 17, 18, 19, 30, 31, 35, 36, 43, 47, 51, 54	3, 10, 20, 22, 25, 26, 34, 40, 42, 46, 48, 49, 50, 53	1, 5, 8, 12, 16, 23, 24, 27, 28, 32, 37, 38, 41
	Main Idea	Main Idea	

EXAM FIVE

1 ① ② ③ ④   11 ① ② ③ ④   21 ① ② ③ ④   31 ① ② ③ ④   41 ① ② ③ ④   51 ① ② ③ ④

2 ① ② ③ ④   12 ① ② ③ ④   22 ① ② ③ ④   32 ① ② ③ ④   42 ① ② ③ ④   52 ① ② ③ ④

3 ① ② ③ ④   13 ① ② ③ ④   23 ① ② ③ ④   33 ① ② ③ ④   43 ① ② ③ ④   53 ① ② ③ ④

4 ① ② ③ ④   14 ① ② ③ ④   24 ① ② ③ ④   34 ① ② ③ ④   44 ① ② ③ ④   54 ① ② ③ ④

5 ① ② ③ ④   15 ① ② ③ ④   25 ① ② ③ ④   35 ① ② ③ ④   45 ① ② ③ ④

6 ① ② ③ ④   16 ① ② ③ ④   26 ① ② ③ ④   36 ① ② ③ ④   46 ① ② ③ ④

7 ① ② ③ ④   17 ① ② ③ ④   27 ① ② ③ ④   37 ① ② ③ ④   47 ① ② ③ ④

8 ① ② ③ ④   18 ① ② ③ ④   28 ① ② ③ ④   38 ① ② ③ ④   48 ① ② ③ ④

9 ① ② ③ ④   19 ① ② ③ ④   29 ① ② ③ ④   39 ① ② ③ ④   49 ① ② ③ ④

10 ① ② ③ ④   20 ① ② ③ ④   30 ① ② ③ ④   40 ① ② ③ ④   50 ① ② ③ ④

SKILLS ANALYSIS

Vocabulary	Literal Comprehension	Inference	Analysis
11, 14, 15, 18, 20, 23, 27, 33, 42, 44, 48, 53	1, 2, 13, 19, 26, 29, 31, 37, 38, 40, 45, 47, 49	4, 5, 6, 9, 16, 17, 34, 36, 39, 41, 46, 51, 52, 54	3, 7, 8, 10, 21, 22, 24, 25, 28, 30, 35, 43, 50
	Main Idea	Main Idea 12, 32	

EXAM SIX

1 ① ② ③ ④   11 ① ② ③ ④   21 ① ② ③ ④   31 ① ② ③ ④   41 ① ② ③ ④   51 ① ② ③ ④

2 ① ② ③ ④   12 ① ② ③ ④   22 ① ② ③ ④   32 ① ② ③ ④   42 ① ② ③ ④   52 ① ② ③ ④

3 ① ② ③ ④   13 ① ② ③ ④   23 ① ② ③ ④   33 ① ② ③ ④   43 ① ② ③ ④   53 ① ② ③ ④

4 ① ② ③ ④   14 ① ② ③ ④   24 ① ② ③ ④   34 ① ② ③ ④   44 ① ② ③ ④   54 ① ② ③ ④

5 ① ② ③ ④   15 ① ② ③ ④   25 ① ② ③ ④   35 ① ② ③ ④   45 ① ② ③ ④

6 ① ② ③ ④   16 ① ② ③ ④   26 ① ② ③ ④   36 ① ② ③ ④   46 ① ② ③ ④

7 ① ② ③ ④   17 ① ② ③ ④   27 ① ② ③ ④   37 ① ② ③ ④   47 ① ② ③ ④

8 ① ② ③ ④   18 ① ② ③ ④   28 ① ② ③ ④   38 ① ② ③ ④   48 ① ② ③ ④

9 ① ② ③ ④   19 ① ② ③ ④   29 ① ② ③ ④   39 ① ② ③ ④   49 ① ② ③ ④

10 ① ② ③ ④   20 ① ② ③ ④   30 ① ② ③ ④   40 ① ② ③ ④   50 ① ② ③ ④

SKILLS ANALYSIS			
Vocabulary	**Literal Comprehension**	**Inference**	**Analysis**
4, 5, 22, 25, 35, 42, 44, 51, 52	2, 6, 10, 13, 15, 17, 20, 23, 28, 30, 31, 34, 38, 39, 40, 48, 49, 50, 53, 54	3, 7, 11, 12, 16, 19, 21, 24, 27, 29, 45, 46, 47	1, 8, 9, 14, 26, 32, 33, 37, 41, 43
	Main Idea 18, 36	**Main Idea**	

EXAM SEVEN

1 ① ② ③ ④ 11 ① ② ③ ④ 21 ① ② ③ ④ 31 ① ② ③ ④ 41 ① ② ③ ④ 51 ① ② ③ ④

2 ① ② ③ ④ 12 ① ② ③ ④ 22 ① ② ③ ④ 32 ① ② ③ ④ 42 ① ② ③ ④ 52 ① ② ③ ④

3 ① ② ③ ④ 13 ① ② ③ ④ 23 ① ② ③ ④ 33 ① ② ③ ④ 43 ① ② ③ ④ 53 ① ② ③ ④

4 ① ② ③ ④ 14 ① ② ③ ④ 24 ① ② ③ ④ 34 ① ② ③ ④ 44 ① ② ③ ④ 54 ① ② ③ ④

5 ① ② ③ ④ 15 ① ② ③ ④ 25 ① ② ③ ④ 35 ① ② ③ ④ 45 ① ② ③ ④

6 ① ② ③ ④ 16 ① ② ③ ④ 26 ① ② ③ ④ 36 ① ② ③ ④ 46 ① ② ③ ④

7 ① ② ③ ④ 17 ① ② ③ ④ 27 ① ② ③ ④ 37 ① ② ③ ④ 47 ① ② ③ ④

8 ① ② ③ ④ 18 ① ② ③ ④ 28 ① ② ③ ④ 38 ① ② ③ ④ 48 ① ② ③ ④

9 ① ② ③ ④ 19 ① ② ③ ④ 29 ① ② ③ ④ 39 ① ② ③ ④ 49 ① ② ③ ④

10 ① ② ③ ④ 20 ① ② ③ ④ 30 ① ② ③ ④ 40 ① ② ③ ④ 50 ① ② ③ ④

SKILLS ANALYSIS			
Vocabulary	Literal Comprehension	Inference	Analysis
10, 16, 24, 26, 30, 43, 51	3, 4, 9, 11, 14, 15, 17, 20, 22, 27, 28, 32, 33, 42, 47, 53	2, 6, 12, 13, 21, 29, 31, 34, 35, 38, 39, 41, 44, 50, 52, 54	1, 5, 8, 18, 23, 36, 37, 45, 46, 48, 49
	Main Idea 25	Main Idea 7, 19, 40	

EXAM EIGHT

1 ① ② ③ ④   **11** ① ② ③ ④   **21** ① ② ③ ④   **31** ① ② ③ ④   **41** ① ② ③ ④   **51** ① ② ③ ④

2 ① ② ③ ④   **12** ① ② ③ ④   **22** ① ② ③ ④   **32** ① ② ③ ④   **42** ① ② ③ ④   **52** ① ② ③ ④

3 ① ② ③ ④   **13** ① ② ③ ④   **23** ① ② ③ ④   **33** ① ② ③ ④   **43** ① ② ③ ④   **53** ① ② ③ ④

4 ① ② ③ ④   **14** ① ② ③ ④   **24** ① ② ③ ④   **34** ① ② ③ ④   **44** ① ② ③ ④   **54** ① ② ③ ④

5 ① ② ③ ④   **15** ① ② ③ ④   **25** ① ② ③ ④   **35** ① ② ③ ④   **45** ① ② ③ ④

6 ① ② ③ ④   **16** ① ② ③ ④   **26** ① ② ③ ④   **36** ① ② ③ ④   **46** ① ② ③ ④

7 ① ② ③ ④   **17** ① ② ③ ④   **27** ① ② ③ ④   **37** ① ② ③ ④   **47** ① ② ③ ④

8 ① ② ③ ④   **18** ① ② ③ ④   **28** ① ② ③ ④   **38** ① ② ③ ④   **48** ① ② ③ ④

9 ① ② ③ ④   **19** ① ② ③ ④   **29** ① ② ③ ④   **39** ① ② ③ ④   **49** ① ② ③ ④

10 ① ② ③ ④   **20** ① ② ③ ④   **30** ① ② ③ ④   **40** ① ② ③ ④   **50** ① ② ③ ④

SKILLS ANALYSIS

Vocabulary	Literal Comprehension	Inference	Analysis
2, 10, 17, 20, 22, 27, 32, 35, 38, 41, 48, 54	4, 14, 15, 16, 21, 23, 25, 29, 30, 33, 37, 39, 42, 44, 45, 49, 51	1, 5, 8, 9, 12, 13, 24, 28, 34, 36, 40, 43, 46, 47, 50, 52, 53	3, 7, 11, 18, 19, 31
	Main Idea	Main Idea 6, 26	

EXAM NINE

1 ① ② ③ ④   11 ① ② ③ ④   21 ① ② ③ ④   31 ① ② ③ ④   41 ① ② ③ ④   51 ① ② ③ ④

2 ① ② ③ ④   12 ① ② ③ ④   22 ① ② ③ ④   32 ① ② ③ ④   42 ① ② ③ ④   52 ① ② ③ ④

3 ① ② ③ ④   13 ① ② ③ ④   23 ① ② ③ ④   33 ① ② ③ ④   43 ① ② ③ ④   53 ① ② ③ ④

4 ① ② ③ ④   14 ① ② ③ ④   24 ① ② ③ ④   34 ① ② ③ ④   44 ① ② ③ ④   54 ① ② ③ ④

5 ① ② ③ ④   15 ① ② ③ ④   25 ① ② ③ ④   35 ① ② ③ ④   45 ① ② ③ ④

6 ① ② ③ ④   16 ① ② ③ ④   26 ① ② ③ ④   36 ① ② ③ ④   46 ① ② ③ ④

7 ① ② ③ ④   17 ① ② ③ ④   27 ① ② ③ ④   37 ① ② ③ ④   47 ① ② ③ ④

8 ① ② ③ ④   18 ① ② ③ ④   28 ① ② ③ ④   38 ① ② ③ ④   48 ① ② ③ ④

9 ① ② ③ ④   19 ① ② ③ ④   29 ① ② ③ ④   39 ① ② ③ ④   49 ① ② ③ ④

10 ① ② ③ ④   20 ① ② ③ ④   30 ① ② ③ ④   40 ① ② ③ ④   50 ① ② ③ ④

SKILLS ANALYSIS

Vocabulary	Literal Comprehension	Inference	Analysis
2, 7, 13, 15, 20, 24, 26, 29, 34, 36, 38, 45	6, 9, 10, 11, 12, 23, 27, 28, 37, 43, 48, 50, 51, 54	3, 5, 14, 18, 19, 22, 30, 31, 39, 40, 41, 44, 46, 49, 52, 53	1, 4, 8, 16, 17, 21, 25, 32, 35, 42
	Main Idea	Main Idea 33, 47	

POST-TEST

1 ① ② ③ ④   11 ① ② ③ ④   21 ① ② ③ ④   31 ① ② ③ ④   41 ① ② ③ ④   51 ① ② ③ ④

2 ① ② ③ ④   12 ① ② ③ ④   22 ① ② ③ ④   32 ① ② ③ ④   42 ① ② ③ ④   52 ① ② ③ ④

3 ① ② ③ ④   13 ① ② ③ ④   23 ① ② ③ ④   33 ① ② ③ ④   43 ① ② ③ ④   53 ① ② ③ ④

4 ① ② ③ ④   14 ① ② ③ ④   24 ① ② ③ ④   34 ① ② ③ ④   44 ① ② ③ ④   54 ① ② ③ ④

5 ① ② ③ ④   15 ① ② ③ ④   25 ① ② ③ ④   35 ① ② ③ ④   45 ① ② ③ ④

6 ① ② ③ ④   16 ① ② ③ ④   26 ① ② ③ ④   36 ① ② ③ ④   46 ① ② ③ ④

7 ① ② ③ ④   17 ① ② ③ ④   27 ① ② ③ ④   37 ① ② ③ ④   47 ① ② ③ ④

8 ① ② ③ ④   18 ① ② ③ ④   28 ① ② ③ ④   38 ① ② ③ ④   48 ① ② ③ ④

9 ① ② ③ ④   19 ① ② ③ ④   29 ① ② ③ ④   39 ① ② ③ ④   49 ① ② ③ ④

10 ① ② ③ ④   20 ① ② ③ ④   30 ① ② ③ ④   40 ① ② ③ ④   50 ① ② ③ ④

SKILLS ANALYSIS			
Vocabulary	Literal Comprehension	Inference	Analysis
6, 8, 12, 20, 26, 27, 32, 36, 40, 44, 46, 50, 54	9, 14, 15, 19, 23, 28, 29, 39, 47, 51	1, 3, 4, 5, 7, 10, 16, 17, 18, 21, 24, 30, 31, 37, 41, 42, 45, 52, 53	2, 13, 22, 25, 33, 34, 35, 43, 48, 49
	Main Idea 11, 38	Main Idea